2024
Tax Preparation Course

Quick Start Guide

CONGRATULATIONS on choosing the most advanced tax preparation learning system anywhere, built on the powerful Prendo365 platform by the California tax experts, Latino Tax Professionals! Our system is user-friendly and easy to learn. And there's an optional textbook available to support the online content.

This instructor guide will help you get started quickly and ensure you make the most of Prendo365. Begin your journey by following the steps below to create and/or log in to your Prendo365 account.

First-Time User Purchased Online or Through Sales Rep

Step 1   As a registered purchaser, you'll receive an email from adressmailer@workato.com with the subject line **Welcome to Prendo365 – DO NOT REPLY** – the email contains a password and username to access your account. Check your spam/junk folder if you do not see it.

Step 2   Open the email and click on the Prendo365 link. This will direct your browser to the Prendo365 login page.

Step 3   To register and log in, you MUST complete and save the required fields marked with a red asterisk to continue.

Step 4   Scroll down to 'Courses' on the left side of your dashboard and click on your course icon to begin!

First-Time User Obtained Through an Instructor or Office Manager

Step 1   Type prendo365.com into the address bar of your browser then press the 'enter' key. (We recommend Google Chrome or Firefox for the best user experience.)

Step 2   Click on the 'Register' button on the top right.

Step 3   Your username is your email address*. (Remember which email address and password you use). Complete all required fields.

Step 4   If you have an instructor, click on the drop-down menu, '*do you have an instructor*' and select your instructor. Otherwise, click 'I Accept the terms of the privacy policy' and click 'Next.'

Step 5   Enter your PTIN and State information for Continuing Education Credits, if applicable. If you do not have a PTIN, type 'NA.' Complete all required fields.

Step 6   Open the email you received from adressmailer@workato.com — it contains your temporary password. Click the link to confirm your registration and use the temporary password provided to sign in.

Step 7   Enter the temporary password and then create a new password that you will remember. Click 'Save Changes.'

Step 8   Scroll down to 'Courses' on the list to the left side of your dashboard and click on your course icon to begin!

*If you receive a message that your email is already in the system, an account has been created by a staff member, instructor, or an online purchase. If you've forgotten your password, click on 'Forgot your password?' to reset it, or you can chat with support at prendo365.com.

Returning User

Step 1 Type prendo365.com into the address bar of your browser then press the 'enter' key. (We recommend Google Chrome or Firefox for the best user experience.)

Step 2 Click the 'Sign In' button.

Step 3 Enter your username and password. Forgot your password? Click 'Forgot your Password?' and follow the onscreen instructions.

Step 4 Haven't started your course yet? Find your course on the dashboard. On the left side under 'Courses' open your course by clicking the thumbnail. Then click 'Start Learning Now.'

Step 5 Started your course already? Find your course once again on the dashboard under 'Courses' and click the thumbnail to open it. Then choose 'Resume Where You Left Off' to go to the last section completed.

Still have questions? Chat at prendo365.com, email questions to edsupport@latinotaxpro.com or call 866.936.2587.

LTP Commitment

Every effort has been made to ensure this publication provides accurate, current, authoritative information to the aspiring tax professional. It is presented with the understanding that Latino Tax Professionals is not engaged in rendering legal or accounting services or other professional advice and assumes no liability in connection with its use. Consistent with the principles laid out in Circular 230, and in keeping with LTP's commitment to professionalism and ethical practices, this text has been prepared with thorough attention to due diligence. However, the possibility of mechanical or human error does exist. The text is not intended to address every situation that may arise. Consult additional sources of information, as needed, to determine the solution of tax questions.

Tax laws are constantly changing and are subject to differing interpretations. In addition, the facts and circumstances of a particular situation may not be the same as those presented here. Therefore, the student should do additional research to understand fully the information contained in this publication and the complexities and risks of providing professional advice to clients and applying this information in any specific situation.

LTP Mission

LTP promotes entrepreneurship, education, diversity, and knowledge among tax preparation businesses across the nation — a number that is growing every year. Not only do we provide education, we also support tax professionals who have decided to open their own tax preparation businesses or for current business owners who are committed to expanding their businesses and preparing for a successful future.

➢ Our **GOAL** is to help you grow your practice and increase your profits.
➢ Our **VISION** is to give you the best education, leadership, and business-skill training available.
➢ Our **MISSION** is to give tax professionals a unified, powerful voice on a national level.

LTP believes the best way to begin tax preparation is by understanding Form 1040 and its role as the foundation for tax preparation. The chapters in this textbook are designed to give the student basic instructions on every aspect of Form 1040, and how they can guide taxpayers through the process of preparing their return efficiently, correctly, and in compliance with tax regulations. When the chapter is completed, the student will go online and complete multiple-choice review questions with feedback for review.

Our Editorial and Production Team

Authors	Kristeena S. Lopez, MA Ed, EA	
	Carlos C. Lopez, MDE, EA	
Editor	Joel Postman, BA	
Contributing Staff	Andres Santos, EA	Niki Young, BS, EA
	Josue Rojas, EA	Javier Aldama, BS
	Roberto Pons, EA	Roberto Cerda, BS
	Ricardo Rivas, EA	
	Pascual Garcia, EA	
Graphic Designers	Susan Espinoza, BS	
	Adrian Ortiz, BS	
	David Lopez	

ISBN: 9798327876354   **Made in California, USA**

Published Date: May 9, 2024

Tax Preparation Prerequisite

This course is designed for individuals who have minimal or no prior experience in tax preparation. It is designed to equip aspiring tax preparers with the foundational knowledge required for this profession. The course will also emphasize compliance with IRS due diligence requirement. Mastering tax industry-specific terminology is essential. A comprehensive understanding of the terminology used by the Internal Revenue Service (IRS) is critical for success as a professional tax preparer and will be a central focus of this course. By dedicating the necessary time and effort to this learning experience, you will gain the skills needed to embark on a career as a tax preparer. This course will provide you with the tools to prepare for a rewarding profession in the tax preparation industry, provided you approach it with diligence and a commitment to learning.

Course Description

We designed our **Tax Preparation** course for individuals who want to learn tax law in order to prepare taxes for others. This course provides the student with a basic, foundational understanding of federal tax law. Increasing one's knowledge of tax law and practice will help you grow your business, increase profits, comply with the latest tax laws, and provide excellent service to clients!

In this beginner course, you will learn:

➢ How to prepare a federal individual tax return
➢ How to prepare Schedule A, Schedule C, Schedule E, and Schedule F
➢ The requirements for each filing status, dependents, and standard and itemized deductions
➢ Which forms to use and how its information flows to Form 1040
➢ Credits the taxpayer qualifies for and how to properly complete each form to claim them

➤ How and when to submit an amended return and an extension to file a tax return

Our proprietary Professional Training System, Prendo365.com, combines traditional textbook-based courses with online interactive media, such as chapter eBooks, chapter videos, chapter review questions and exam and chapter Practice Tax Return (PTR) exercises.

In our textbooks and chapter eBooks, you will find detailed explanations of each specific line or section of Form 1040, and review questions to test your knowledge of the material you have learned to that point. After finishing each chapter, you have the opportunity to take a chapter exam and complete a Practice Tax Return (PTR) exercise. Each chapter in the course is the foundation for the next.

Practice Tax Returns are in PDF format and include links to the necessary tax forms. LTP encourages the student to complete the PTR by hand. Each Practice Tax Return has its own set of review questions.

Review questions and PTRs may be taken as many times as necessary to achieve the required score. If you have obtained the required score of 70% or better, but choose to obtain a higher score, be aware that Prendo365 records the most recent score, even if it is less than your prior score.

Included in this course:

- ➤ **eBook** The online course includes an eBook for every chapter
- ➤ **Online Questions** "To Test Your Knowledge"
- ➤ **Online Practice Tax Returns** (PTR) There is a quiz at the end of each chapter
- ➤ **Online Finals** You will have one final exam at the end of the course
- ➤ **Printed Textbook** (Optional. Must be purchased separately)

This course has been copyrighted and published by Latino Tax Professionals Association, LLC.

Chapter Exams

To pass the course, students must take and pass the exams for each chapter. The chapter review questions, which are not scored, are designed to help the student recall subject matter from the chapter and prepare for the chapter exams.

Final Exams

There are 3 required final exams that must be passed with a score of 70% or better. The first one is right after the Ethics and Preparer Penalties, this final exam consists of 10 questions.

The federal law exam will be at the end of the textbook and will consist of 215 questions and must pass with a 70% or better. The California final is required and will consist of 75 questions. The California Practice Tax Return (PTR) is not required, but LTP encourages students to complete the return with a 70% or better. If you want to try and improve your score you must remember that if you scored an 75% or better and your score will be erased to the most current

In compliance with IRS regulations, this course does include the final federal and state tax law exam. It does include chapter exams, chapter practice tax return quizzes and a Practice Tax Return Final Exam which **you must pass with a score of 70% or better to complete the course and receive your certificate.**

Practice Tax Returns

LTP has created practice tax returns (PTR) to assist the student in understanding tax preparation. Each PTR is based on a scenario encompassing the course content that has been included up to that point. For example, if a lesson covers income, the tax calculations will not reflect any credits that have not yet been discussed in the course, even if the taxpayer in the scenario would have qualified for them. Ideally, the student would prepare the PTR by hand and then answer the PTR review questions online. LTP does not discourage the use of software for tax preparation.

In the field, when preparing a Schedule A, the preparer and the taxpayer have two choices for reporting the taxes paid during the tax year: State Tax Withheld or Sales Tax. You can use Sales Tax with either one if you purchased a vehicle or your city, county sales tax is more than the State sales tax. The PTR instructions in the course will use a fixed Sales Tax when students prepare the practice tax return. Be aware that rates and the amount of tax withheld could vary by individual state, county and city.

Note: The IRS and the states update their tax forms and tax law at the end of the current year, so you will be using tax year 2023 forms and schedules to learn tax law and complete the course.

Textbook Updates

The digital version of the textbook is updated throughout the year to always contain the most recent information. When course content is updated, users of Prendo365 will receive a notification indicated by an icon of a bell in the upper right corner of the screen. The physical copy of the textbook is also updated periodically.

Table of Contents

Chapter 1 Ethics and Preparer Penalties

Introduction

The Internal Revenue Service has published guidelines, known as Circular 230, outlining requirements that ensure the tax preparer follows ethical practices and performs "due diligence" in the preparation of the taxpayer's return. This chapter will give a brief description of the rules and regulations outlined in Circular 230 that govern the responsibilities of the tax preparer.

The dictionary defines due diligence as "the care that a reasonable person exercises to avoid harm to other persons or to their property." In business, due diligence refers to practicing prudence by carefully assessing associated costs and risks prior to completing a transaction. In tax preparation, due diligence refers to actions that an individual will perform to satisfy a legal requirement. Due diligence should always be a part of our daily decision-making process.

Form 8867, the Paid Preparer's Due Diligence Checklist, was introduced in 2006. The form was originally created to allow the paid preparer to report Earned Income Credit (EIC). In 2006, the paid preparer penalty for failure to comply with the diligence requirements was $100. In 2011 the penalty was raised to $500. The penalty amount is for each failure to comply with the diligence requirements. For 2023, the penalty was $560 for each failure to comply. The 2024 Form 8867 penalty amount is $600 per failure report. A tax preparer could be fined a total of $2,400 per Form 8867 for not completing the required due diligence.

When the taxpayer wants to claim certain credits and filing statuses, the tax preparer needs to complete and attach an accurate Form 8867 to the taxpayer's return. The preparer must ask questions to determine if the taxpayer qualifies for the following credits and filing statuses:

1. Earned Income Credit (EIC)
2. Child Tax Credit (CTC)
3. Additional Child Tax Credit (ACTC)
4. Other Dependent Credit (ODC)
5. American Opportunity Tax Credit (AOTC)
6. Head of Household Status

Objectives

At the end of this lesson, the student will:

➢ Identify the due diligence requirements of the tax preparer when completing a tax return with refundable credits
➢ Clarify what documentation the IRS requires to be maintained when preparing specific credits used on tax returns
➢ Understand what documents the tax preparer should maintain for their records.
➢ Recognize what credits are on Form 8867
➢ Know who is the paid preparer

Resources

Form 886	Instructions Form 8867
Form 8867	Publication 596
Circular 230	

Part 1 Ethics and Office of Professional Responsibility (OPR)

"Ethics" is defined as the discipline of dealing with what is good and bad and acting with moral duty and obligation. It is a system of principles or moral values. It is also the rules and standards governing the conduct of a person or the members of a profession (e.g., tax practice ethics).

The rules and standards governing the ethical conduct of tax professionals are contained in Circular 230. These rules and standards are the ethics of tax practice. "Ethical behavior" is defined as "of ethics or relating to ethics." In addition, it is being in accordance with or conforming to the accepted principles of right and wrong that govern the conduct of a profession (i.e., professional standards of conduct).

Most people would define ethics as "doing the right thing," which leads one to believe that individuals will, as a matter of common sense and conscience, instinctively react in an ethical manner in all situations. As evidenced by financial scandals such as those involving Bernie Madoff and Lehman Brothers, this is not always true. "Doing the right thing" was not the basis for the decisions made by the leaders of the organizations involved in these stories. As a result, many have become generally disillusioned and untrusting of the business community.

The U.S. Treasury Department requires enrolled agents, and enrolled actuaries to have a certain amount of continuing tax education hours. Attorneys and certified public accounts are regulated by their individual state. California, Oregon, Maryland, New York, and Connecticut are the only states that require unenrolled tax preparers to have annually continuing tax education hours. The U.S. Treasury Department encourages registered tax return preparers to annually complete the Annual Filing Season Program (AFSP), which includes two hours of ethics.

OPRs Mission

The mission of the Office of Professional Responsibility (OPR) is to ensure that all tax practitioners, tax preparers, and third parties in the tax system adhere to professional standards and follow the law. OPR is the governing body responsible for interpreting and applying Circular 230 to all who prepare tax returns, whether they are signing or non-signing tax practitioners. OPR has exclusive responsibility for practitioner conduct and discipline.

OPR has oversight of practitioner conduct as well as exclusive responsibility with respect to practitioner discipline, including disciplinary proceedings and sanctions. If the OPR has received a report or has reason to believe that a practitioner may not have followed the procedures outlined in Circular 230, they may execute the following disciplinary proceedings:

➤ Disqualify a practitioner from further submissions in connection with tax matters
➤ Propose a monetary penalty on any practitioner who engages in conduct subject to sanction. The monetary penalty may be proposed against the individual or a firm or both and can be done in addition to another form of discipline.
➤ Negotiate an appropriate level of discipline with a practitioner or initiate an administrative proceeding to Censure, Suspend, or Disbar the practitioner
  o Censure: A public reprimand in which an offender is included on a quarterly list issued by the IRS that states the offender's city and state, name, professional designation, and the effective date(s) of the censure. If censured, offenders can still prepare taxes, but they are more closely monitored, and their discredited names and reputations can negatively impact their businesses. This is the lightest form of punishment.

- o Suspend: If a tax preparer is suspended, it means they cannot prepare any returns for one to fifty-nine months; how long a tax preparer is suspended is determined by the OPR on a case-by-case basis.
- o Disbar: If a tax preparer is disbarred, they cannot prepare any returns whatsoever for at least five years

These penalties and punishments are connected to the activities that the tax preparer has been associated with on behalf of the employer, for it is the employer's legal responsibility to know what their employees are doing as the employer may be liable for the actions of their employee.

Example: Omar Tax Service (OTS), as an entity subject to the Circular 230 guidelines, needs to have a person in charge of ensuring all OTS and IRS procedures are followed and handled correctly. If employee Travis is caught preparing returns in some way that is non-compliant with these guidelines, there are two potential scenarios:

1. If Omar Tax Service did not have someone to ensure the procedures of both the IRS and OTS were being followed correctly, then OTS is liable for their employee's actions.
2. If OTS did have somebody in place to ensure all procedures were followed properly, and did so in full compliance with Circular 230, then Travis is considered a rogue employee, and OTS may not be liable for his actions because OTS correctly followed all the required procedures.

OPR's Authority

OPR oversees the conduct of tax practice. The oversight extends to all individuals who make a presentation to the IRS relating to a taxpayer's rights, privileges, or liabilities under the laws or regulations administered by the IRS. This authority generally extends to any individual who interacts with federal tax administration in person, orally, in writing, or by the preparation and submission of documents.

OPR oversees a practitioner's conduct and discipline, including disciplinary proceedings and sanctions. After serving a practitioner a notice and granting them an opportunity for a conference, OPR could negotiate an appropriate level of discipline with the practitioner or could, in fact, initiate an administrative proceeding to censure (a public reprimand), suspend (one to fifty-nine months), or disbar (five years) the practitioner.

Information Provided to the IRS and OPR

If an authorized officer or employee of the IRS or OPR requests information or records regarding or in reference to a taxpayer, the tax preparer is required by law to comply with the request promptly unless they believe in good faith or on reasonable grounds that such records or information is privileged or that the request for, or effort to obtain such record or information is of doubtful legality.

If the requested information is not in the possession of the tax professional or his or her client, the tax professional must promptly notify the requesting IRS or OPR personnel of that fact. In the case of requests from the IRS, the practitioner must make reasonable inquiries of the client regarding the identity of any person who has the records. The tax professional is not required to actually speak with anyone other than their client, but they must ask their client about the identity of any person who may have the records or information that was requested and then provide that information to the IRS.

A practitioner may not interfere, or attempt to interfere, with any proper and lawful effort by the IRS and its officers or employees or with the director of the Office of Professional Responsibility and his or her employees to obtain any record(s) or information unless the practitioner believes in good faith and on reasonable grounds that the record(s) or information is privileged.

As stated in §10.34(b) in regard to the submission of any documents that may be requested by the IRS or OPR, the tax professional cannot advise a client to submit any document to the IRS that falls under one or both of the following two categories:

➢ Frivolous
➢ Contains or omits information in a manner demonstrating an intentional disregard of a rule or regulation unless the tax professional also advises the client to submit a document that evidences a good faith challenge to the rule or regulation

Example: The IRS requests information about John Henry. Andres prepared Mr. Henry's return for the past two years; however, the year in question is prior to Mr. Henry becoming Andres' client. Andres has copies of Mr. Henry's tax return for the year in question, which contains the name, address, and identification number of the individual who prepared the return. Andres is required to provide the IRS with the information about the preparer listed on the return, but not the return itself. Andres needs to inform the client of the IRS request.
(Treasury Circular 230, §10.20, §10.34(b)).

Individual Representation Rights

The following is a summary of the individuals who can practice before the IRS and their representation rights.

a. ***Attorney***: Any attorney who is not currently under suspension or disbarment from practice before the Internal Revenue Service may do so by filing a written declaration stating that the individual is currently qualified as an attorney and is authorized to represent the party or parties

b. ***Certified public accountant*** (CPA): Any certified public accountant who is not currently under suspension or disbarment from practice before the Internal Revenue Service may do so by filing a written declaration that the individual is qualified as a certified public accountant and is authorized to represent the party or parties

c. ***Enrolled agents***: Any individual enrolled as an agent pursuant to this part who is not currently under suspension or disbarment from practice before the Internal Revenue Service may practice before the Internal Revenue Service. (Enrolled agents take a three-part test and must pass each part)

d. ***Enrolled actuaries***: Any individual who is enrolled as an actuary by the Joint Board for the Enrollment of Actuaries pursuant to 29 U.S.C. 1242 who is not currently under suspension or disbarment from practice may do so by filing a written declaration stating that the individual is currently qualified as an enrolled actuary and is authorized to represent the party or parties on their behalf

e. ***Enrolled retirement plan agents***: An individual enrolled as a retirement plan agent pursuant to this part who is not currently under suspension or disbarment from practice before the Internal Revenue Service may practice before the IRS

f. ***Annual Filing Season Program Participants (AFSP)***: This voluntary program recognizes the efforts of return preparers who are not attorneys, certified public accountants, or enrolled agents. The IRS issues an Annual Filing Season Program Record of Completion to return preparers who obtain a certain number of continuing education hours in preparation for a specific tax year. As an AFSP Record Holder, your representation is limited.

The AFSP Record holder can represent clients whose returns one prepared and signed, but only before examination with the customer service representatives, and the Taxpayer Advocate Service (TAS).

Practice Before the IRS

"Practice before the IRS" constitutes all matters connected with a presentation to the IRS, or any of its officers or employees, related to a taxpayer's rights, privileges, or liabilities under the laws or regulations administered by the IRS. Such presentations include, but are not limited to, preparing documents, filing documents, and corresponding and communicating with the IRS. It also includes rendering oral and written advice with respect to any entity, transaction, plan, arrangement, or any matter that has a potential for tax avoidance or evasion; and representing a client at conferences, hearings, and meetings.

Tax Professionals Standards of Competence

A practitioner must possess the appropriate level of knowledge, skill, thoroughness, and preparation necessary for competent engagement in practice before the Internal Revenue Service. A practitioner may become competent for the matter for which the practitioner has been engaged through various methods, such as consulting with experts in the relevant area or studying the relevant law.

If the tax professional is not competent in a subject matter, they may consult another individual who the tax professional knows or believes has established competence in the field of study. When the tax professional does consult with another individual, they must consider the requirements of Internal Revenue Code §7216.

Taxpayer Information Retention

The tax professional is required to furnish the taxpayer with a complete copy of the tax return. This copy can be provided in any acceptable standard, including electronic formats, as agreed upon by both parties. Importantly, the copy is not mandated to include the client's Social Security number.

A thorough copy of the taxpayer's return incorporates Form 8453 and other documents the tax professional cannot transmit electronically when applicable, in addition to the electronic segment of the return.

The electronic portion can be presented on a replica of an official form or on an unofficial form. However, when using an unofficial form, the tax professional must cross-reference data entries to the numbers or descriptions on an official form. In cases where a taxpayer submits a completed paper return for electronic filing, and the electronic portion mirrors the provided information, the tax professional is exempt from supplying a printout of the electronic segment to the taxpayer.

It is advisable for the tax professional to counsel the taxpayer to retain a comprehensive copy of their return and any accompanying materials. Additionally, clients should be informed that, if necessary, they must submit an amended return as a paper return and mail it to the submission processing center handling paper returns for the taxpayer.

Compliance Procedures

Any practitioner who has or shares principal authority and responsibility for overseeing a firm's practice of providing advice concerning federal tax issues must take reasonable steps to ensure that the firm has adequate procedures to raise awareness and to promote compliance with Circular 230 by the firm's members, associates, and employees, and that all such employees are complying with the regulations governing practice before the IRS. These compliance procedures are stated in full in Circular 230 subparts A, B, and C, which can be found on the IRS website.

Any individual or individuals who share principal authority will be subject to discipline for failing in the following ways through willfulness, recklessness, or gross incompetence:

> ➤ The individual does not take reasonable steps to ensure the procedures of the firm are adequate
> ➤ The individual does not take reasonable steps to ensure the firm's procedures are properly followed
> ➤ The individual fails to take prompt action to correct any noncompliance despite knowing (or being in a situation where it was the individual's duty to know) that one or more individuals who are associated with or employed by the individual are engaged in a pattern or practice that does not comply with the firm's position

Taxpayers should receive and be advised to keep copies of the following:

> ➤ Form 8879 (PIN program)
> ➤ Any Form W-2, Form 1099, etc., and any other backup material for their return
> ➤ A copy of the return that was electronically filed, in a form they can understand
> ➤ A copy of Form 9325, *General Information for Taxpayers Who File Electronically*, which tells taxpayers the procedure to follow if they do not receive their refund
> ➤ For those who request a bank product, a copy of the signed bank application and the disclosure statement

Part 1 Review

To obtain the maximum benefit from each part go online now and watch the video.

Part 2 Responsibilities of the Tax Preparer

The paid tax preparer must understand the ethical responsibility to prepare accurate tax returns based on tax law and the information provided by the taxpayer.

OPR will propose censure, suspension, or disbarment of any practitioner from practice before the IRS if the individual shows themself to be incompetent or disreputable and/or fails to comply with any regulations found in Circular 230. OPR may impose a monetary penalty for an individual or their employer subject to Circular 230. The monetary penalty relates to activities the tax preparer associates with on behalf of the employer. The employer should have known what the employee was doing.

You can find the following explanations of tax professionals' responsibilities under Treasury Circular 230. This summary does not address all provisions of the regulations. The tax professional should read Circular 230 for a complete understanding of the duties and obligations of someone practicing before the IRS. Preparing a tax return is also considered practicing before the IRS.

Tax Return Preparer

LTP believes that taxpayers should choose a tax return preparer who will be available for them in case the IRS examines their tax return. Most tax return preparers are professional, honest, and provide excellent customer service to their clients. However, dishonest, and unscrupulous tax return preparers do exist. The taxpayer should always check their return for errors to avoid penalties, along with financial and legal problems.

Taxpayers should be aware of the qualifications and responsibilities of the tax return preparer they intend to work with. First, anybody who is paid to prepare tax returns should have a complete understanding of tax matters and is required to have a Preparer Tax Identification Number (PTIN).
A paid tax return preparer is primarily responsible for the overall accuracy of the taxpayer's return. By law, the paid tax preparer is required to sign the return and include their PTIN. Although the tax return preparer signs the return, the taxpayer is ultimately responsible for the accuracy of every item reported on the return. The paid tax preparer is subject to §6694 penalties if there are inaccuracy and if the tax preparer is responsible individual.

The Internal Revenue Service has also established ethical guidelines and practices for tax preparers. These guidelines, laws, and standards, in part, protect the *Taxpayer Bill of Rights* and are detailed in Circular 230, the consistent, definitive standard of tax professional responsibility that protects not only the taxpayer but the tax professional as well.

Everything the tax practitioner does, every choice they make as a tax professional, affects not only him or herself but the professional's clients, coworkers, and firm as well. Decisions and judgments made in tax preparation are not always black and white. The paid tax preparer's first responsibility is to his or her clients, but one must still make decisions within the boundaries of the law. Issues are often not clearly defined and leave room for interpretation, and when making decisions or judgments as a professional tax preparer in such situations, you should take the following steps:

➢ Determine the nature of the issue in question
➢ Obtain as much information and documentation from the client as possible
➢ Research the issue thoroughly, documenting all findings, facts, and positions
➢ Consider relevant case studies
➢ Examine all possible solutions to the questions
➢ Weigh the consequences of each solution and how each solution may affect all parties involved (the taxpayer, the preparer, and the firm)
➢ Inform the client of your position and explain the consequences of the available answers
➢ Choose a solution that is legal, ethical, and actionable for all parties involved and comfortable for both you and your client

Señor 1040 Says: Privilege does not apply in a criminal matter unless the practitioner is an attorney.

Best Practice Guidelines

In addition to careful compliance with IRS due diligence regulations, tax professionals should also follow professional best practices when providing advice and preparing tax returns for submission to the IRS to ensure they are providing their clients with the highest possible quality of representation in federal tax matters.

Tax professional best practices include the following:

➢ Communicate clearly with clients regarding the terms of the engagement. This means determining what the client is seeking and what they expect from the practitioner. In turn, make sure the client understands the scope and type of services that will be rendered.

➢ Establish the facts. Determine which facts are relevant to the matter at hand and evaluate the reasonableness of any assumptions or representations.

➢ Relate the applicable law to the relevant facts and arrive at a conclusion based on this support

➢ Advise the client based on the meaning and implications of any findings. Inform him or her of any tax repercussions as a result of any actions or lack thereof (e.g., accuracy-related penalties, interest, etc.).

➢ Act fairly and with integrity in practice before the IRS

A practitioner must inform a client of any penalties that are likely to apply to the client with respect to a position taken on a tax return in the following scenarios:

➢ If the practitioner advised the client with respect to the position

➢ If the practitioner prepared or signed the tax return or any document, affidavit, or other paper submitted to the Internal Revenue Service

➢ The practitioner must also inform the client, if relevant, of the requirements for adequate disclosure and of any opportunity to avoid any such penalties by disclosure

A practitioner, when advising a client to take a position on a tax return, document, affidavit, or other paperwork submitted to the IRS or when preparing or signing a tax return as a preparer, may generally rely in good faith, without verification, upon information furnished by the client.

The practitioner may not, however, ignore the implications of information furnished to or actually known by the practitioner and must make reasonable inquiries if the information as furnished appears to be incorrect, incomplete, or inconsistent with an important fact or other factual assumption.

Tax advisors responsible for overseeing a firm's practice of providing advice on federal tax issues and preparing or assisting in the preparation of submissions to the IRS should take reasonable steps to ensure that the firm's procedures for all members, associates, and employees are consistent with these best practices.

Personal Tax Compliance Responsibilities

The tax professional is responsible for ensuring the timely filing and payment of personal income tax returns and the tax returns for any entity over which the tax professional has, or shares, control. Failing to file 4 of the last 5 years' income tax returns, or 5 of the previous 7 quarters of employment/excise tax returns, is per se disreputable and incompetent conduct that can lead to sudden, indefinite suspension of the practitioner. The willful evasion of the assessment or payment of tax also violates Circular 230 regulations (Treasury Circular 230, §10.51(a)(6)).

Conflict of Interest

A conflict of interest exists when representing a client who is directly averse to another client of the paid tax professional. A conflict of interest also exists if there is a significant risk that representing a client will be materially limited by the tax professional's responsibilities to another client, a former client, a third person, or their interests. When a conflict of interest exists, the tax professional may not represent a client in an IRS matter unless:

1. The tax professional reasonably believes that they can provide competent and diligent representation to all affected clients.
2. The law does not prohibit the tax professional's representation.
3. All affected clients give informed, written consent to the tax professional's representation. The tax professional must retain these consents for 36 months following the termination of the engagement and make them available to the IRS/OPR upon request (Treasury Circular 230, §10.29).

Documenting

Documents are files or notes that were created at the time of the interview with the taxpayer. Documentation is an important part of due diligence. The tax professional needs to be diligent in keeping records of how the tax return was prepared. Documents proving the taxpayer's income, expenses, credits claimed on the tax return and how the tax return was prepared should be kept. Documentation could save the preparer from incurring a due diligence penalty. Good intention in saving the taxpayer's documentation while failing to keep records of how the return was prepared is only good intention and will not save the tax preparer from a due diligence penalty. There are three words that could save a preparer from penalties: DOCUMENT, DOCUMENT, & DOCUMENT.

Documentation should be completed during the interview of the client no matter how the interview takes place, such as in person, via phone, or virtually. When determining HOH filing status, make sure that the individual has paid more than half of the cost of keeping up a home with a qualifying dependent. (Discussed in more detail in the Filing Status chapter).

Reasonable inquiries include asking pertinent questions, which should result in obtaining the information needed to complete Form 8867. Certain questions should determine the age of the taxpayer and/or dependents to help determine filing status and which credit(s) the taxpayer may qualify for.

The following questions are samples to determine taxpayer's filing status:

➢ Were you single on December 31?
➢ Were you married on December 31?
➢ Did you live apart from your spouse the entire year?
➢ Do you have qualifying children?
➢ Did the qualifying children live with you the entire year?
➢ How many months did the qualifying children live with you?
➢ Does anyone else live in your house?
➢ Do you live with another taxpayer? If so, what is that individual's relationship to you? Parent, in-laws, cousin, grandchild, etc.?

Document Guidelines and Procedures

A practitioner may not willfully, recklessly, or through gross incompetence sign a tax return or claim for refund that the tax practitioner knows or reasonably should know contains any of the following:

➢ An unreasonable basis
➢ An unreasonable position as described in §6694(a)(2) of the IRC Code
➢ A willful attempt by the practitioner to understate the tax liability or to intentionally disregard the rules and regulations as described in §6694(b)(2)

A paid tax preparer who guarantees a specific refund amount is an example of the kind of action that would trigger this penalty. Another example is if the preparer attempts to reduce the taxpayer's liability by intentionally disregarding information provided by the taxpayer; in this case, the preparer is guilty of a willful attempt to understate tax liability. This does not mean that the preparer may not rely in good faith on the information furnished by the taxpayer. However, the tax preparer must make reasonable inquiries if the information furnished by the taxpayer appears to be incorrect or incomplete.

If the tax professional receives a request for documents, records, or information concerning one of their clients from the IRS or the OPR, they must comply with the request unless the tax professional reasonably believes that the information is privileged. If the requested information is not in the tax professional or the tax professional client's possession, the tax professional must promptly inform the requesting IRS or OPR personnel of that fact.

A practitioner may not advise a client to take a position on a document, affidavit, or any other paper(s) submitted to the Internal Revenue Service unless the position is not frivolous. A position is frivolous if it purposefully contains or omits information that demonstrates an intentional disregard of a rule or regulation. If challenged, it is the taxpayer's responsibility to prove to the IRS that a position is not frivolous, and it is then up to the IRS to make the final decision thereof.

A practitioner may not advise a client to submit any document, affidavit, or other paper to the IRS under the following circumstances:

➢ If the purpose of the submission is to delay or impede the administration of the federal tax laws
➢ The information is frivolous
➢ The content omits information or demonstrates an intentional disregard of a rule or regulation unless the practitioner also advises the taxpayer to submit a document that shows evidence of a good faith challenge to the rule or regulations

A practitioner must inform the client of any penalties that are reasonably likely to apply to the client with a position that was taken on the tax return. The tax preparer also needs to inform the client on how to avoid penalties.

The tax practitioner may generally rely in good faith upon any information provided by the taxpayer without having to verify the information the client has given. However, the tax practitioner cannot ignore any potential implications of the documentation that was given to him or any actual knowledge he may have of any errors thereof. A reasonable inquiry about the information furnished is necessary if the taxpayer's provided information seems to be inconsistent or incomplete.

Who Prepared the Return?

A tax return preparer is any person who prepares for compensation or employs one or more individuals to prepare all, or a substantial portion of the tax return or any claim for refund of tax. A signing tax return preparer is an individual tax return preparer responsible for the overall substantive accuracy of preparing such return or claim for refund.

A tax return preparer is any and all of the following:

➢ Any person who prepares all or a substantial portion of any tax return or claims for refund in exchange for compensation or employs one or more persons to prepare for payment
➢ Any individual paid to prepare or assist with tax preparation of all or substantially all of a tax return or claim for refund must have a PTIN number and is subject to the duties and restrictions

relating to practice in subpart B of Circular 230. Subpart B is §10.20 through §10.53. Anyone who prepares a return for compensation must have a PTIN.

➢ Any individual preparing or assisting others in preparing tax returns or claiming for refunds who may appear as a witness for the taxpayer before the IRS or furnish information at the request of the IRS or any of the IRS officers or employees

➢ Any individual preparing or assisting others to prepare all or a substantial portion of a document about any taxpayer's tax liability for compensation is subject to the duties and restrictions relating to practice in §10.20 through §10.53 (subpart B as well as subpart C) and §10.60 through §10.82

A signing tax return preparer is the individual tax return preparer primarily responsible for the overall substantive accuracy of the preparation of such return or claim for refund. Even if someone else provides all the information and materials needed for the tax return, effectively "preparing" most of the return's material, the individual that inputs and arranges the material for the actual submission of the return or claim for refund is the person who must sign the return and thus claim responsibility for its accuracy. The person who needs to sign the return and claim responsibility for its accuracy is whoever prepares the majority of the tax return.

A non-signing tax return preparer is any person who prepares all or a substantial portion of a return or claims for a refund but does not possess the primary responsibility for its accuracy. The individual was not the individual who inputted the information into the tax return or chose the tax return positions.

Whether or not an individual should be considered a non-signing or signing tax return preparer also depends on how much time the preparer spends advising the taxpayer. To be eligible to be a non-signing preparer, events that have occurred should represent less than 5% of the accumulated time incurred by the non-signing tax return preparer. The preparer calculates the percentage of time spent on the advice they give, whether written or oral, when given to the taxpayer and the signing tax preparer. §301.7701-15

Example: Kristie is Maria's administrative assistant. Kristie collects information from Julie, Maria's client, to help Maria prepare the tax return. Maria signs the return. Kristie is not the paid preparer of Julie's tax return.

Factors to consider in determining what makes a substantial portion include:

1. The size and complexity of the item relative to the taxpayer's gross income
2. The size of the understatement attributable to the item compared to the taxpayer's reported tax liability

Example 1: Timothy prepares Form 8886, "*Reportable Transaction Disclosure Statement.*" He does not prepare the tax return or advise the taxpayer regarding the tax return position for the transaction to which Form 8886 relates. The preparation of Form 8886 is not directly relevant to the determination of the existence, characterization, or amount of an entry on a tax return or claim for a refund. Timothy is preparing Form 8886 to disclose a reportable transaction and not to prepare a substantial portion of the tax return and is not considered a tax return preparer under §6694.

Example 2: Vicente prepares a schedule for Jose's Form 1040, reporting $4,000 in dividend income, and gives Jose oral or written advice about his Schedule A, which results in a medical expense deduction totaling $5,000, but does not sign the return. Vicente is a non-signing tax return preparer because the aggregate total amount of the deduction is less than $10,000.

A tax refund claim includes a credit claim against any tax. A claim for refund also includes a claim for payment under §6420, 6421, or 6427.

Example 1: Jose received employment tax information from Maria, who prepares her recordkeeping. Jose did not render any tax advice to Maria or exercise any discretion or independent judgment on Maria's tax positions. Jose just processed the information that Maria gave to him. Jose signed the return as authorized by the client according to Form 8655, *Reporting Agent Authorization,* and filed Maria's return using the information supplied by Maria. Jose is a tax return preparer.

Example 2: Matthew rendered tax advice to Sharon on determining whether her workers are employees or independent contractors for federal tax purposes. Matthew received compensation for his advice and is the tax return preparer.

The following individuals are not tax return preparers:

1. An official or employee of the Internal Revenue Service (IRS) performing official duties
2. Any individual who provides tax assistance under the Volunteer Income Tax Assistance (VITA) program established by the IRS, but the individual can only prepare returns for VITA
3. Any organization sponsoring or administering a VITA program established by the IRS, but only concerning the sponsorship or administration
4. An individual who provides tax counseling for the elderly under a program established under §163 of the Revenue Act of 1978, but only concerning those returns prepared as part of that program.
5. An organization sponsoring or administering a program to provide tax counseling for the elderly established under §163 of the Revenue Act of 1978, but only concerning that sponsorship or administration
6. An individual who provides tax assistance as part of a qualified Low-Income Taxpayer Clinic (LITC) as defined by §7526, subject to the requirements, but only for the LITC tax returns.
7. Any organization that is a qualified LITC
8. An individual providing just typing, reproduction, or other mechanical assistance in the preparation of a return or claim for a refund
9. An individual preparing a return or claim for refund of a taxpayer, or an officer, a general partner, member, shareholder, or employee of a taxpayer, by whom the individual is regularly and continuously employed, compensated or in which the individual is a general partner
10. An individual preparing a return or claim for a refund for a trust, estate, or other entity, of which the individual either is a fiduciary or is an officer, general partner, or employee of the fiduciary
11. An individual preparing a claim for a refund for a taxpayer in response to:
    a. A notice of deficiency issued to the taxpayer
    b. A waiver of restriction on assessment after initiating an audit of the taxpayer or another taxpayer if the audit determines the other taxpayer affects, directly or indirectly, the taxpayer's liability
12. A person who prepares a return or claim for a refund for a taxpayer with no explicit or implicit agreement for compensation, even if the person receives an insubstantial gift, return service, or favor

Written Tax Advice

In providing written advice concerning any federal tax matter, the tax professional must:

1. Base advice on reasonable assumptions
2. Reasonably consider all relevant facts that a tax professional knows or should know
3. Use reasonable efforts to identify and ascertain the relevant facts

The tax professional cannot rely upon representations, statements, findings, or agreements that are unreasonable or known to be incorrect, inconsistent, or incomplete.

The tax professional must always consider the possibility of an IRS audit to a tax return or that a matter could raise an audit. When providing written advice, the tax professional may rely in good faith on the advice of another practitioner only if that advice is reasonable, considering all facts and circumstances. The tax professional cannot rely on the advice of a person they know, or should have known, is not competent to provide the advice, or has an unresolved conflict of interest as defined in §10.29 (Treasury Circular 230, §10.37).

Errors and Omissions

If the tax professional knows that a client has not complied with the U.S. revenue laws or has made an error in, or omission from, any return, affidavit, or other documents which the client submitted or executed under U.S. revenue laws, the tax professional must promptly inform the client of the noncompliance, error, or omission and advise the client regarding the consequences under the Code and regulations of the noncompliance, error, or omission. Depending on the facts and circumstances, the consequences of an error or omission could include (among other things) additional tax liability, civil penalties, interest, criminal penalties, and an extension of the statute of limitations (Treasury Circular 230, §10.21).

Due Diligence

Tax professionals must exercise due diligence in preparing and filing tax returns and the correctness of their representation to their clients or the IRS. The tax professional can rely on another person's work if they are carefully engaged, supervised, trained, and evaluated, considering the nature of the relationship between the tax professional and that person. The tax professional generally may rely in good faith and without verification on information furnished by the client, but the tax professional cannot ignore other information furnished to them or which they know. The tax professional must make reasonable inquiries if any information furnished to them appears to be incorrect, incomplete, or inconsistent with other facts or assumptions (Treasury Circular 230, §10.22, §10.34(d)).

The tax professional could rely on the work product of another person if the individual used reasonable care in engaging, supervising, training, and evaluating that person, taking proper account of the nature of the relationship between the tax professional and the taxpayer.

The tax professional may also generally rely in good faith and without verification upon information furnished by their client, but the tax professional cannot ignore other information furnished to them or known by them. The tax professional must make reasonable inquiries if any information furnished to them appears to be incorrect, incomplete, or inconsistent with other facts or assumptions.

Purpose of Form 8867

The paid preparer is required to perform due diligence when preparing tax returns with or without refundable credit. Treasury regulations §6695(g) requires the paid tax preparer to meet certain requirements when interviewing the client. Questions must be asked that will give the preparer enough information to complete Form 8867. IRS provides guidelines on how to interview.

Under guidelines set forth by the IRS, the preparer is required to:

1. Meet the knowledge requirement by interviewing the taxpayer, asking adequate questions, contemporaneously documenting the questions and the taxpayer's responses on the return or in their notes, reviewing adequate information to determine if the taxpayer is eligible to claim the credits(s) and/or head of household (HOH) filing status, and to figure the amount(s) of the credit(s) claimed
2. Complete Form 8867 truthfully and accurately and complete actions described on Form 8867 for any applicable credit(s) claimed and HOH filing status, if claimed
3. Submit Form 8867 in the manner required
4. Keep all five of the following records for 3 years from the latest date when the tax return was sent to the IRS:
   a. A copy of Form 8867
   b. The applicable worksheet(s) or if tax preparer created their own for any credits claimed
   c. Copies of any documents provided by the taxpayer on which the preparer relied to determine the taxpayer's eligibility for the credit(s) and/or HOH filing status and to figure amount(s) of the credits
   d. A record of how, when, and from whom the information used was obtained to prepare Form 8867 and the applicable worksheet(s)
   e. A record of any additional information tax preparer relied upon, including questions asked and the taxpayer's responses, to determine taxpayer's eligibility for the credit(s) and/or HOH filing status and to figure the amount(s) of the credits(s)

Creating Form 8867 Truthfully and Accurately

When completing Form 8867, each year is considered individually. Questions that were asked in the past only relate to the past, and not to the current tax year. It may seem like the same questions are being asked over and over with the same results, but providing this information completely and accurately is essential. People's lives change, and the tax professional must ask the taxpayer about any changes. Asking the same questions multiple times to understand the taxpayer's situation is critical to preparing an accurate and truthful return. Records furnished by the taxpayer must also support the credits, income, and expenses claimed on the tax return.

Submitting Form 8867 Truthfully and Accurately

A tax preparer needs to complete Form 8867 by answering the questions that pertain to the taxpayer. Completing Form 8867 is not a cookie-cutter procedure. Every taxpayer is unique and so are the questions asked to determine due diligence that must be done by the taxpayer and the tax preparer.

Refundable Credits Due Diligence

Tax preparers must take additional steps to safeguard their compliance with the refundable credits due diligence. Ignoring or failing to follow tax law could result in penalties and other consequences for the paid tax preparer and their clients. A paid tax preparer who prepares returns with *Earned Income Tax Credit* (EITC), *Child Tax Credit* (CTC), *Other Dependent Credit* (ODC), or the *American opportunity tax credit* (AOTC) must meet due diligence requirements. These requirements focus on accurately determining the client's eligibility and the amount of each credit. The four requirements are:

1. Complete and submit Form 8867 (Treasury Reg. §1.6695-2(b)(1))
2. Compute the credits (Treasury Reg. §1.6695-2(b)(2))
3. Knowledge of who and what is required for credits (Treasury Reg. §1.6695-2(b)(3))
4. Keep records for three years (Treasury Reg. §1.6695-2(b)(4))

Most due diligence penalties are a result of failure to comply with the knowledge requirement. To meet the knowledge requirement, one should:

➢ Ask questions regarding the information provided by the client to determine if the client truly can claim the credits or filing status
➢ Assess if the information given is complete. Collect additional information if facts seem to be missing
➢ Determine if the information is consistent; recognize contradictory statements, and statements you know are true
➢ Conduct a thorough, in-depth interview with each client, every year. Don't rely on the statement "everything is the same as last year"
➢ Ask enough questions to be sure the prepared tax return is correct and complete
➢ Document, at the time of the interview, any questions asked and the clients' answers

Documents must be kept for three years from the latest of:

➢ The due date of the return (not including extensions)
➢ The date the tax return was electronically filed
➢ For a paper return, the date the return was presented to the client for signature

Señor 1040 Says: The paid tax preparer cannot solely rely on software for their refundable credit due diligence. Professional software may not comply with Treasury Regulation 1.6695(b)(3). It is the paid tax preparer's due diligence responsibility to make sure that they have complied with Treasury Regulation 1.6695.

Most Common EIC Errors

1. Claiming EIC for a child who does not meet the qualifying child requirements
2. Filing as single or head of household when married
3. Incorrectly reporting income or expenses

Consequences of Filing EIC Returns Incorrectly

Tax professionals should know that clients come to them to prepare an accurate tax return. The client trusts a tax professional to know and understand the guidelines for preparing correct tax returns. If a tax preparer incorrectly files EIC returns, it will affect their client, themselves, and, if an employee, their employer.

The following are some basic consequences that can occur when a paid tax preparer files an incorrect EIC tax return for their client.

➢ The client must pay back the amount in error as well as interest on the amount
➢ The client may have to file Form 8862 for up to 10 years
➢ The client may be banned from claiming EIC for the next 2 years if the error is because of reckless or intentional disregard of the rules
➢ The client may be banned from claiming EIC for the next 10 years if the error is because of fraud

If the IRS examines a refundable tax credit return for a preparer, and the IRS finds that the preparer did not meet the four due diligence requirements (IRC §6694), they may be given a penalty:

> ➤ A $600 penalty for returns completed in 2024 for each failure to comply with due diligence requirements. For 2023 the penalty was $545
> ➤ The penalty is $1,000 or 50% of the income derived by tax preparer with the respect to the return or claim for refund

Remember the four due diligence requirements are:

1. Complete and submit Form 8867 (Treasury Reg. §1.6695-2(b)(1))
2. Compute the credits (Treasury Reg. §1.6695-2(b)(2))
3. Knowledge of who and what is required for credits (Treasury Reg. §1.6695-2(b)(3))
4. Keep records for three years (Treasury Reg. §1.6695-2(b)(4))

Example: Anet prepared a tax return for Lewis. Lewis qualified for refundable credits. Anet was audited and had no documentation and was assessed a penalty for not completing her due diligence on Form 8867. Her penalty for failure to meet the due diligence requirements containing EIC, CTC/ACTC/ODC, or AOTC filed in 2021 is $545 per credit per return. The amount Anet will be assessed for Lewis' return is $545.00 x 4 = $2,180.00.

If the tax preparer receives a return-related penalty, they can also face:

1. Loss of their tax preparer designation
2. Suspension or expulsion from IRS e-file program
3. Other disciplinary action by the IRS Office of Professional Responsibility (OPR)
4. Injunctions barring the preparer from preparing tax returns or imposing conditions on the tax returns they have prepared

The IRS can also penalize the employer if an employee fails to comply with the EIC due diligence requirements.

Self-employed Taxpayer's Due Diligence

Refundable credits due diligence regarding Schedule C require the paid preparer to take additional steps to ensure that the taxpayer filing a Schedule C with refundable credits complies with tax law. Per Internal Revenue Code (IRC) §6695(g), paid tax preparers are required to make additional inquiries of taxpayers who appear to be making inconsistent, incorrect, or incomplete claims for the credit.

Paid tax return preparers can generally rely on the taxpayer's representations until EIC due diligence requirements are involved. The paid tax preparer must take additional steps to determine the net self-employment income used to calculate refundable credits eligibility is correct and complete. The additional inquiries made to comply with due diligence and the client's response must be documented. The statute requires the return preparer to be reasonable, well-informed, and knowledgeable in tax law.

It is very important that the information is documented, and the paid tax preparer can prove that they have asked these questions or similar ones that will arrive at the same goal. The IRS is auditing these types of returns. A good tax professional does not want to receive paid preparer penalties or sanctions. The paid tax preparer should ask sufficient questions to taxpayers claiming self-employment income.

Some questions that need to be asked include:

1. Does the client have and conduct a business?
2. Does the client have records to support the records of the income and expenses claimed on the return?
3. Can the client reconstruct their income and expenses, if necessary?
4. Has the client included all income and related expenses reported on Schedule C?

Client Records

At the client's request, the tax professional must promptly return any client records necessary for the client to comply with their federal tax obligations, even if there is a dispute over fees. The tax professional may keep copies of these records. Suppose state law allows the tax professional to retain a client's records in the case of a fee dispute. In that case, the tax professional can only return the records attached to the client's return. Still, the tax professional must provide the client with reasonable access to review and copy any additional client records retained by the tax professional necessary for the client to comply with their federal tax obligations. The term "client records" includes all written or electronic materials provided by the client or a third party to the tax professional.

"Client records" also include any tax return or other document that the tax professional prepared and previously delivered to the client if that return or document is necessary for the client to comply with their current federal tax obligations. The tax professional is not required to provide a client with a copy of their work product. That is, any return, refund claim, or other documents that the tax professional prepared but has not yet delivered to the client if:

1. The tax professional is withholding the document pending the client's payment of fees related to the document
2. The tax professional contract with the client requires the payment of those fees before delivery (Treasury Circular 230 §10.28)

Part 2 Review

To obtain the maximum benefit from each part go online now and watch the video.

Part 3 Preparer Conduct and Penalties

Preparer's Incompetence and Disreputable Conduct

The following is a summary of what is considered incompetence and disreputable conduct for which a practitioner may be sanctioned. The following was extracted from Circular 230 §10.51.

1. Conviction of any criminal offense under federal tax laws
2. Conviction of any criminal offense involving dishonesty or breach of trust
3. Conviction of any felony under federal or state law for which the conduct involved renders the practitioner unfit to practice before the IRS
4. Giving false or misleading information or participating in any way in the giving of false or misleading information to the Department of the Treasury or any officer or employee
5. Solicitation of employment as prohibited under §10.30, the use of false or misleading representations with intent to deceive a client or prospective client to gain employment or

insinuate that the practitioner can obtain special consideration with the IRS, or any officer or employee

6. Misappropriation of, or failure to remit properly or promptly, funds received from a client for the payment of taxes or other obligations due the United States
7. Directly or indirectly attempting to influence or offer or agree to attempt to influence the official action of any officer or employee of the IRS using threats, false accusations, duress, or coercion, or any special inducement or promise of an advantage or by bestowing of any gift, favor, or item of value
8. Knowingly aiding and abetting another person to practice before the IRS during a suspension, disbarment, or ineligibility of such other individual
9. Contemptuous conduct in connection with practice before the IRS, including the use of abusive language, making false accusations or statements, knowing them to be false, or circulating or publishing malicious or libelous matter
10. Willfully representing a taxpayer before an officer or employee of the IRS unless the practitioner is authorized to do so

The penalty assessed depends on which of the above incompetence and disreputable conduct rules the preparer has violated. For example, if the preparer understated based on unreasonable position the penalty could be the greater of $250 or 50% of income obtained.

The IRS has the authority to penalize the tax preparer for not being compliant with their due diligence in preparing a tax return with the following:

1. Earned Income Credit (EIC)
2. Child Tax Credit (CTC)
3. Additional Child Tax Credit (ACTC)
4. Other Dependent Credit (ODC)
5. American Opportunity Tax Credit (AOTC)
6. Head of Household Status

Although the ODC is not refundable it is still a credit for which the preparer needs to ask questions regarding the dependent.

When completing Form 8867 the preparer should not just mark the question "yes" or "no" without asking the taxpayer for this information. Don't assume that the answers to the questions are the same from year to year. Form 8867 is the form that determines if the tax preparer completed their due diligence in asking the appropriate questions. Compiling Taxpayers' Information will guide you in identifying questions to help you determine if the taxpayer truly qualifies for the credits and filing status. As a beginner preparer, you will soon find out that some taxpayers have learned to "work the system." Your job is to ask and document the taxpayers' answers to your questions.

Failure to Furnish Tax Return Copy to Taxpayer

The penalty for the paid tax preparer is $60 for each failure to comply with IRC §6107 regarding furnishing a copy of a return or claim to a taxpayer. The maximum penalty imposed on any tax return preparer shall not exceed $30,000 in a calendar. See IRC, §6695(a).

Failure to Sign Return

The penalty for each failure to sign a return or claim for refund as required by regulations is $55 for the paid tax preparer. The maximum penalty imposed on any tax return preparer shall not exceed $28,000 (tax year 2023) in a calendar year. For returns filed in 2024 the penalty is $60 for each failure and maximum penalty is $30,000. See IRC, §6695(b).

A tax return is not considered to be valid unless the return has been signed. If the filing status is MFJ, both the taxpayer and spouse must sign the return. If the taxpayer and spouse have a representative sign the return for them, Form 2848 must be attached. If the taxpayer is filing a joint return, and he/she is the surviving spouse, the taxpayer must sign the return stating he/she is filing as the surviving spouse. The taxpayer and spouse (if filing jointly) must make sure to date the return and enter their occupation(s) and a daytime phone number. See Publication 501 and IRC §6695(b).

If the taxpayer received an identity protection PIN (IP PIN), he/she is responsible for entering it in the boxes on the tax return. The tax professional does not enter it for the taxpayer. If the taxpayer has misplaced their IP PIN, the taxpayer should notify the IRS by telephone at 1-800-908-4490. The IP PIN is a 6-digit number.

When filing the return electronically, the return must still be signed using a personal identification number (PIN)—this is not the same number as the IP PIN. There are two ways to enter the PIN: self-select or practitioner PIN. The self-select PIN method allows the taxpayer and spouse (if filing jointly) to create their own PIN and enter it as their electronic signature. The practitioner PIN method allows the taxpayer to authorize the tax practitioner to generate or enter the PIN for the taxpayer(s). A PIN is a five-digit combination that can be any number except all zeros.

Señor 1040 Says: There is a difference between the electronically-filed PIN and the IP PIN. Do not mix up these numbers.

Failure to Furnish Identifying Number

The penalty for each failure to comply with IRC §6109(a)(4) regarding furnishing an identifying number on a return or claim is $55. The maximum penalty imposed on any tax return preparer shall not exceed $28,000 (tax year 2023) in a calendar year. For returns filed in 2024 the penalty is $60 for each failure and maximum penalty is $30,000. See IRC §6695(c).

Preparer's Failure to Retain a Copy or List of Tax Return

The penalty is $55 for each failure to comply with IRC §6107(b) regarding retaining a copy or list of a return or claim. The maximum penalty imposed on any tax return preparer shall not exceed $28,000 for tax year 2023. For returns filed in 2024 the penalty is $60 for each failure and maximum penalty is $30,000. See IRC §6695(d). This list is what tax returns you completed for the current tax year. The preparer must maintain records for 4 years.

Preparer's Filing Information Returns Incorrectly

If the tax professional is negligent or intentionally files incorrect information returns, the penalty is $55 per return or item on the return, with a maximum penalty of $28,000 (2023). For returns filed in 2024 the penalty is $60 for each failure and maximum penalty is $30,000. See IRC §6695(e).

Preparer's Fraud and False Statements

A tax preparer who has been convicted of a felony for fraud and making false statements could be assessed a fine of not more than $100,000 ($500,000 in the case of a corporation), subject to imprisonment of not more than three years, and required to pay for the cost of the IRS prosecution. See IRC §7206.

Preparer's Understatement Due to Unreasonable Positions

If the preparer takes an unreasonable position for the tax return or claim for a refund, the penalty is $1,000 or 50% (whichever is greater). See IRC §6694(a).

Preparer's Understatement Due to Willful or Reckless Conduct

The penalty is the greater of $5,000 or 75% of the income derived by the tax return preparer with respect to the return or claim for refund. See IRC §6694(b).

Action to Enjoin Tax Return Preparers

A federal district court may enjoin a tax return preparer from engaging in certain proscribed conduct, or in extreme cases, from continuing to act as a tax return preparer altogether. See IRC §7408.

Promoting Abusive Tax Shelters

This penalty applies to tax preparers who organize or sell abusive tax shelters. If the statements are false, the penalty is 50% of the gross income the individual made of the activity. The penalty is $1,000 or 100% whichever is the least amount of the gross income the individual made for the activity. See IRC §6700.

Part 3 Review

To obtain the maximum benefit from each part go online now and watch the video.

Takeaways

Tax preparers must understand the ethical guidelines and practices established by the Internal Revenue Service provided in Circular 230. The Office of Professional Responsibility oversees these ethical guidelines and practices, and it also regulates practitioners' conduct and discipline. Additionally, OPR oversees the correct level of discipline to practitioners or imposes administrative proceedings to censure, suspend, or disbar practitioners from practicing before the IRS.

Tax preparers must recognize their rights, responsibilities, and representation limitations. We at LTP believe that everything a tax practitioner does—every choice one makes as a tax professional—affects not only themselves, but coworkers, the firm, and ultimately the taxpayer. We also believe that a paid tax preparer's first responsibility is to their client when making decisions and/or judgments about tax preparation. Preparer conduct also reflects on the profession and its reputation, which requires trust and confidence from taxpayers.

TEST YOUR KNOWLEDGE!
Go online to take a practice quiz.

Chapter 2 Compiling Taxpayer's Information

Introduction

This chapter explains the importance of interviewing the taxpayer. Each chapter segment will cover a section of Form 1040 with sample interview questions needed for completing the section discussed. The tax professional must understand the importance of asking knowledgeable questions to establish the information necessary for completing the taxpayer's return, and to determine whether the taxpayer can claim certain credits. Interview questions and taxpayer responses should be documented. Tax preparation, knowledge, and understanding are essential to an accurate tax return.

The tax preparer cannot expect to generate an accurate return simply by entering information into tax software. The saying "garbage in, garbage out" applies here. The tax preparer could obtain a higher refund for the taxpayer by entering incorrect information, but this is the wrong approach for the tax practitioner and the client.

This chapter provides a brief overview of current year forms and sample questions to determine the best and most accurate tax position for the taxpayer. Asking the taxpayer knowledgeable questions from the beginning gives the tax preparer truthful answers to complete the tax return while avoiding issues with the Internal Revenue Service and the Franchise Tax Board.

This chapter will familiarize you with the most used forms. As you continue through the book, you'll find additional information on the topics introduced in this chapter. Our goal is to give you a solid foundation for how to prepare a tax return, and then build on that foundation as you progress through the course. At the end of this course, you should be able to prepare a tax return containing Schedule 1, 2, & 3, and Schedule A.

Objectives

By the end of this chapter, you will:

➢ Know the various parts of Form 1040
➢ Recognize items from each section
➢ Understand the importance of asking questions to determine the best tax situation for the client
➢ Remember questions from each section to create their own interviewing approach

Resources

Form 1040 Schedule 1 Schedule 2 Schedule 3	Publication 17 Tax Topic 301, 303, 352	Instructions Form 1040 Eight Facts about Filing Status

Part 1 Form 1040

Form 1040 changed in 2017 as a result of the Tax Cuts and Jobs Act. The form changed again in 2020. Most of the content on Form 1040 was divided into six (6) schedules for the 2018 tax year; for the 2023 tax year filing, there are three (3) schedules.

Portion of Form 1040

The Following Sections are Found on the 2023 Form 1040:

> Filing Status
> General Information such as:
>> o Name
>> o Address
>> o Taxpayer Identification Number
> Standard Deduction Dependents
> Income
> Refund
> Amount You Owe
> Third Party Designee
> Sign Here
> Paid Preparer Use Only

Filing Status

Portion of Form 1040

There are five filing status options for the federal return:

> Single (S)
> Married filing jointly (MFJ)
> Married filing separately (MFS)
> Head of household (HOH)
> Qualifying Surviving Spouse (QSS)

Filing status is determined on the last day of the tax year. A detailed explanation of filing status will be discussed in a later chapter. All individuals on the taxpayer's return must have a taxpayer identification number (TIN), typically a Social Security Number (SSN) or an Individual Taxpayer Identification Number (ITIN).

Interview Pointers

Below are sample questions to determine a taxpayer's correct filing status:

➢ Are you single?
➢ Are you legally married?
➢ Do you have children?
➢ Did the children live with you the entire year? If not, how long did the children live with you?
➢ How many months did the children live with you?
➢ What documentation do you have to prove the children lived with you? (Tax preparer needs to see the documentation.)
➢ Does anyone else live in your house?
➢ Do you live with another taxpayer?

The tax professional must determine the correct filing status by asking pertinent questions such as these.

General Information: Name, Address, and Taxpayer Identification Number

Gathering information from the taxpayer is vital for the preparation of an accurate tax return. Information collected by the tax preparer verifies the identity of the taxpayer, and that of the taxpayer's spouse, if filing jointly. The taxpayer will be glad you asked relevant questions to complete the tax return correctly. By gathering the taxpayer's information through straight forward interview process, you'll make tax return preparation easier. A well-organized interview also prevents misunderstandings between the tax preparer and taxpayer.

The following personal information is needed from the client:

➢ A current government-issued photo identification for the taxpayer and his or her spouse, if filing jointly
➢ The taxpayer or spouse's SSN, ITIN, ATIN, or TIN. You should review the physical card and add a copy to the taxpayer's electronic folder
➢ The following information for everyone on the tax return:
    o SSN, ITIN, ATIN, or TIN
    o Date of birth
    o Date of death if the taxpayer or spouse died during the tax year
    o Current address
    o Income
➢ The taxpayer's current address
➢ The amount of total income earned for the year

The names of the taxpayer and spouse (if applicable) must match the names on their Social Security cards, Adoption Tax Identification Numbers (ATIN), or Individual Tax Identification Numbers (ITIN). If the couple has recently married and has not filed the name change with the Social Security Administration, the current name on the Social Security card must be used. If not, the return could be rejected when filing electronically. Taxpayers who do not have a Social Security Number (SSN) should apply for an SSN or an ITIN.

When filing a federal return, Social Security Administration records are used to match all names, Social Security numbers, and dates of birth, for everyone on the tax return. The exception to this is when a taxpayer is filing his or her tax return with an ITIN, in which case the SSN on the W-2 will not match. (ITINs will be covered in detail later.) The tax preparer should make sure the Social Security Numbers on all W-2 forms match the taxpayer and spouse's Social Security numbers as displayed on their Social Security cards. If not, the taxpayer must have their employer correct the tax document(s). Tax professionals need to ensure these documents are accurate before filing the return.

Interview Pointers

Here are questions to ask regarding the taxpayer's personal information, which will help determine changes from the prior year return and the current year filing status.

➢ Did you bring your Social Security card(s)?
➢ Did any personal changes occur (new dependents)?
➢ Did your name change?
➢ Did you get married?
➢ Did you get divorced?
➢ Was there a death in the family? (Tax return related.)
➢ Did you have a job change?
➢ Did you have any births during the year? (Tax return related.)
➢ Do you want to contribute $3 to the Presidential Election Campaign Fund?

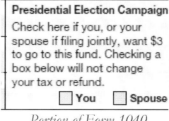

Presidential Election Campaign
Check here if you, or your spouse if filing jointly, want $3 to go to this fund. Checking a box below will not change your tax or refund.
☐ **You**   ☐ **Spouse**

Portion of Form 1040

The Presidential Election Campaign Fund is intended to reduce a candidate's dependence on large contributions from individuals and groups. This aims to place candidates on an equal financial footing for the general election. The fund also helps pay for pediatric medical research. If the taxpayer wants $3 to go to the fund, check the box. If the taxpayer is filing a joint return, both taxpayers can have $3 each go to the fund. Checking the box does not affect the refund amount or the amount owed.

Standard Deduction

The standard deduction is based on the taxpayer's filing status. Each filing status matches a deduction of a predetermined amount. That amount is subtracted from the taxpayer's total income resulting in the taxpayer's adjusted gross income. Itemized Deductions are amounts reported on Schedule A, and will be described later in the course. The itemized deduction amount is generally used when the taxpayer's deduction exceeds their standard deduction.

The following factors determine an additional standard deduction allowable to certain taxpayers.

➢ Is the taxpayer age 65 or older?
➢ Is the taxpayer blind?
➢ Is the taxpayer claimed as a dependent on another individual's tax return?

Blind taxpayers and taxpayers age 65 or older each have an additional exemption that can be claimed when filing status is determined.

Standard deduction amounts apply to most people and are for the current year's filing status.*

Filing Status and Standard Deduction	Tax Year 2022	Tax Year 2023	Tax Year 2024
Single	$12,950	$13,850	$14,600
Married Filing Jointly and Qualifying Surviving Spouse	$25,900	$27,700	$29,200
Married Filing Separately	$12,950	$13,850	$14,600
Head of Household	$19,400	$20,800	$20,800

*Do not use this chart if:

➢ The taxpayer was born before January 2, 1959
➢ The taxpayer is blind
➢ Someone else can claim the taxpayer or taxpayer's spouse as a dependent if filing status is MFJ

Dependents

Basic information to collect is:

➢ Dependent(s) name (as it appears on the SSN, ATIN, or ITIN)
➢ DOB of the dependent(s)
➢ Relationship to taxpayer

Note: If you prepare the tax return by hand, there is no place to enter the DOB (just remember that the dependent's age is important to calculate certain credits).

On the paper Form 1040, you will see only four lines for dependents. To add additional dependents, mark the box on the left and follow the instructions. When the return is prepared using tax software, the worksheet should be automatically generated. When filing a paper form, make sure the worksheet is attached to the tax return.

Dependents (see instructions):		(2) Social security number	(3) Relationship to you	(4) Check the box if qualifies for (see instructions):	
If more than four dependents, see instructions and check here . ☐	(1) First name Last name			Child tax credit	Credit for other dependents
				☐	☐
				☐	☐
				☐	☐
				☐	☐

Portion of Form 1040

Interview Pointers

Here are questions to ask to determine if the taxpayer has qualifying dependents:

➢ Do you have any dependents?
➢ Did the dependents live with you?
➢ Did the dependents live with you the entire year?
➢ What are the dependents' dates of birth?
➢ Do you have proof that the dependents live with you?
  ○ Lease agreement
  ○ School records
  ○ Medical records
➢ Do you have the dependents' SSN, ATIN, or ITIN documentation with you? If not, can you bring them in later so I can keep a copy for our records?
➢ Can somebody else claim them as dependents?

Dependents will be studied in detail in a later chapter.

Income Form 1040, Lines 1 – 15

Income	1a	Total amount from Form(s) W-2, box 1 (see instructions)	1a	
Attach Form(s) W-2 here. Also attach Forms W-2G and 1099-R if tax was withheld.	b	Household employee wages not reported on Form(s) W-2	1b	
	c	Tip income not reported on line 1a (see instructions)	1c	
	d	Medicaid waiver payments not reported on Form(s) W-2 (see instructions)	1d	
	e	Taxable dependent care benefits from Form 2441, line 26	1e	
	f	Employer-provided adoption benefits from Form 8839, line 29	1f	
If you did not get a Form W-2, see instructions.	g	Wages from Form 8919, line 6	1g	
	h	Other earned income (see instructions)	1h	
	i	Nontaxable combat pay election (see instructions)	1i	
	z	Add lines 1a through 1h	1z	
Attach Sch. B if required.	2a	Tax-exempt interest . . .	2a		b	Taxable interest	2b	
	3a	Qualified dividends . . .	3a		b	Ordinary dividends	3b	
	4a	IRA distributions	4a		b	Taxable amount	4b	
Standard Deduction for—	5a	Pensions and annuities . .	5a		b	Taxable amount	5b	
• Single or Married filing separately, $13,850	6a	Social security benefits . .	6a		b	Taxable amount	6b	
	c	If you elect to use the lump-sum election method, check here (see instructions) . . . . . ☐		
• Married filing jointly or Qualifying surviving spouse, $27,700	7	Capital gain or (loss). Attach Schedule D if required. If not required, check here . . . . . ☐	7	
	8	Additional income from Schedule 1, line 10	8	
	9	Add lines 1z, 2b, 3b, 4b, 5b, 6b, 7, and 8. This is your **total income**	9	
• Head of household, $20,800	10	Adjustments to income from Schedule 1, line 26	10	
	11	Subtract line 10 from line 9. This is your **adjusted gross income** . . .	11	
• If you checked any box under Standard Deduction, see instructions.	12	**Standard deduction or itemized deductions** (from Schedule A)	12	
	13	Qualified business income deduction from Form 8995 or Form 8995-A . . .	13	
	14	Add lines 12 and 13	14	
	15	Subtract line 14 from line 11. If zero or less, enter -0-. This is your **taxable income**	15	

For Disclosure, Privacy Act, and Paperwork Reduction Act Notice, see separate instructions.   Cat. No. 11320B   Form **1040** (2023)

Portion of Form 1040

The tax information needed to complete this section includes all income for both the taxpayer, and the spouse if Married Filing Jointly. Sources of income include:

- ➢ Form W-2 series
- ➢ Form 1099 series (G, DIV, INT, NEC, MISC., R, etc.)
- ➢ Social Security Benefits

Wage income is reported on Form 1040, line 1a. Other income is reported on Form 1040, lines 1b - h. Interest is reported on Form 1040, lines 2a and 2b. Qualified dividends are reported on Form 1040, lines 3a and 3b. IRAs, pensions, and annuities are reported on Form 1040, lines 4a - 5b. Social Security benefits are reported on Form 1040, line 6.

Income Recordkeeping

Both taxpayer and tax professional must keep with the client's tax return copies of all Forms W-2, 1099 series, and other income documents. If parents elect to claim their children's investment income, those forms should also be kept with the parents' tax return.

Interest earned as a beneficiary of an estate or trust is generally taxable income. Taxpayers should receive a Schedule K-1 for their portion of the interest. A copy of the Schedule K-1 should be kept with the tax return.

If the taxpayer is a U.S. citizen or resident alien, they must report income from sources outside the United States unless the income is exempt under U.S. law. All sources and amounts must be reported for all earned and unearned income. See Publication 54.

Interview Pointers

Here are questions to determine the type of income the taxpayer received, and which tax form or schedule will be used to report the income:

- ➢ Did you receive a W-2 or W-2G?
- ➢ How many jobs did you have last year?
- ➢ Did you receive any income not reported on a W-2?
- ➢ Did you earn any interest or dividends?
  - ○ Checking account
  - ○ Savings account
- ➢ Did you have an investment broker?
  - ○ Savings bonds and CDs
- ➢ Did you receive Social Security benefits or railroad retirement benefits?
- ➢ Did you receive a pension or annuity?
- ➢ Did you take a distribution from an IRA?
  - ○ Roth or Traditional?
- ➢ Did you receive alimony income or separate maintenance payments? (Reported on Schedule 1, line 2a)
- ➢ Did you receive disability income?
- ➢ Did you receive rental income? File Schedule E, and report net income on Schedule 1, line 5.
- ➢ Do you own a business? (When a taxpayer has a business, you must perform an extensive and thorough interview. This ensures the taxpayer reports all income, including cash payments received for work or services performed, as well as all expenses. As a preparer, you must make sure you have the necessary knowledge of Schedule C, and all the required information from the taxpayer, to prepare the tax return correctly. Do your due diligence!)
- ➢ Did you receive Form 1099-NEC or Form 1099-MISC?

➢ Did you receive Form 1099-K?
➢ Did you receive an education scholarship? (Reported on Schedule 1, line 8r)
➢ Did you receive a refund from state taxes last year? (Reported on Schedule 1, line 1)
➢ Did you receive income from other sources such as prizes, jury duty pay, Schedule K-1, royalties, foreign income, etc.? (Reported on Schedule 1, line 8)
➢ Did you receive unemployment or paid family leave? (Reported on Schedule 1, line 7)
➢ Did you receive any other form of income whatsoever? (Reported on Schedule 1, line 8z)

More information on Schedule 1 will be found later in this chapter.

Form 1040, page 2, lines 16 - 33

This section is used to report information from other forms and schedules. Line 16 is the tax the individual will need to pay. This includes income tax and any additional tax owed. Line 33 reports the total payments made by the individual through withholding, estimated payments, and from credits.

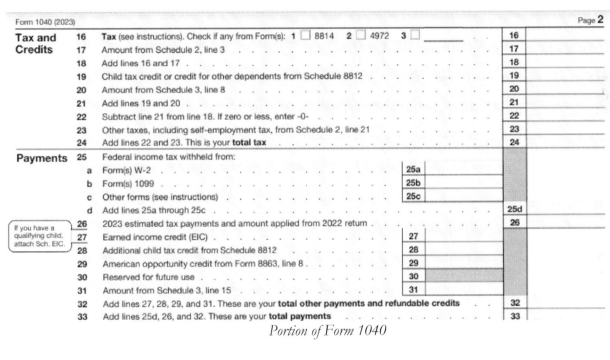

Portion of Form 1040

Refund

Portion of Form 1040

On Form 1040, page 2, if the amount on line 33 is more than the amount on line 24, the taxpayer may receive a refund, reported on line 34. If the taxpayer is receiving a refund and would like to have the refund deposited directly into a checking or savings account, enter the taxpayer's routing and account numbers on lines 35b and 35d. The account type (savings or checking) must be marked on line 35c. A taxpayer must file Form 8888 if the refund check is to be a paper check or to have it deposited into up to three different accounts. Make sure to check the box at the end of line 35a to show that the form is attached. Not all software companies support this form; taxpayers wanting to file Form 8888 may need to file a paper return via mail.

Line 36 is used if the taxpayer wants the refund to be applied to their estimated payments for the following tax year.

Interview Pointers

These questions determine how the taxpayer will receive their refund:

> ➢ Do you want the refund to be directly deposited into your checking or savings account? (Make sure to see a physical check and not a deposit slip.)
> ➢ Do you want a paper check from the IRS?
>   > o If so, is the address on the tax return current?
> ➢ Would you like to have your refund applied to next year's estimated payments? (Normally, you would ask this question to self-employed taxpayers who are receiving a refund; this could lower the estimated payments.)

Amount Owed

Form 1040, page 2, line 37: Amount a taxpayer owes.

| Amount You Owe | 37 | Subtract line 33 from line 24. This is the **amount you owe**. For details on how to pay, go to *www.irs.gov/Payments* or see instructions . . . . | 37 | |
| | 38 | Estimated tax penalty (see instructions) . . . . | 38 | |

Portion of Form 1040

Form 1040, page 2, line 38: The amount of the penalty, if any, for not paying enough tax during the year.

This is reported using Form 2210, which should be attached to the return after completion.

Interview Pointers

These questions determine how the taxpayer will pay their balance due.

> ➢ Do you want to mail your balance due to the IRS?
> ➢ Do you want to pay your balance due electronically?
> ➢ Do you want to pay your balance due with a credit card?

Third Party Designee

On Form 1040, page 2, the taxpayer would designate someone who could discuss the tax return with the IRS.

| Third Party Designee | Do you want to allow another person to discuss this return with the IRS? See instructions . . . . ☐ **Yes.** Complete below. ☐ **No** | | |
| | Designee's name | Phone no. | Personal identification number (PIN) ☐☐☐☐☐ |

Portion of Form 1040

Checking the Yes box allows a third-party to talk on behalf of the taxpayer to provide certain information to the IRS. The authorization will automatically end no later than the filing due date for the current-year tax return (without extensions). For example, if the paid preparer is filing the 2023 tax return, and the return is due on April 15, 2024, the authorization automatically expires on April 15, 2025. A PIN (personal identification number) must be entered. PINs are not given or provided by any agency but are instead created by the third-party designee. However, whatever PIN is created must be kept and documented; this is what the IRS will ask for to verify they are talking to the authorized third-party designee.

If the taxpayer marks the box No, then no one will be the taxpayer's designee.

The IRS may call the designee to answer any questions that arise during the processing of the return. The designee may perform the following actions:

➢ Give information that is missing from the return to the IRS
➢ Call the IRS for information that is missing from the tax return
➢ Upon request, receive copies of notices or transcripts related to the return
➢ Respond to certain IRS notices about math errors and the preparation of the return

When checking the box, authorization is limited to matters concerning the processing of the tax return.

Interview Pointers

The following questions determine if the taxpayer wants to authorize a third-party designee. Make sure you thoroughly understand what a third-party designee's responsibilities are.

➢ Would you like the tax preparer to be able to talk to the IRS regarding this return?
➢ Would you like to have another individual talk to the IRS about your current year tax return?

Signing Form 1040

The taxpayer (and spouse if filing jointly) must sign the return in the section shown below, found on the second page of Form 1040.

Portion of Form 1040

If either the taxpayer or spouse received an Identity Protection (IP) PIN from the IRS due to identity theft, the taxpayer must enter the number in the box provided. If both the taxpayer and spouse suffered from identity theft, only the taxpayer would enter the IP PIN. Make sure to enter the IP PIN on the correct line if the spouse, taxpayer or both had identity theft.

Portion of Form 1040

Paid Preparer Use Only

Paid preparers must enter their PTIN, business name, business address, employer identification number (EIN), and business phone number. If the paid preparer is self-employed, he or she must check the box. The paid preparer must sign the return in the appropriate box; otherwise, the paid preparer could be charged a $50 penalty per return. This is a paid preparer penalty not a company penalty.

Paid Preparer Use Only	Preparer's name	Preparer's signature	Date	PTIN	Check if: ☐ Self-employed
	Firm's name			Phone no.	
	Firm's address			Firm's EIN	

Go to *www.irs.gov/Form1040* for instructions and the latest information.   Form **1040** (2023)

Portion of Form 1040

Form 1040-SR, for Seniors

The added benefit of Form 1040-SR is that it automatically calculates the higher standard deduction for seniors. Form 1040-SR is four pages instead of two for the regular Form 1040. The additional pages are due to the font size on the form.

Señor 1040 Says: Remember, the additional exemption amount is only for taxpayer and spouse and is automatically added to the standard deduction when using Form 1040-SR.

When a taxpayer files Married filing separately and one spouse itemizes deductions, the other taxpayer must itemize their deductions even if the standard deduction gives the taxpayer a better tax break.

Form 1040-SR Department of the Treasury—Internal Revenue Service

U.S. Tax Return for Seniors 2023 OMB No. 1545-0074 IRS Use Only—Do not write or staple in this space.

For the year Jan. 1–Dec. 31, 2023, or other tax year beginning _____, 2023, ending _____, 20 _____ See separate instructions.

Your first name and middle initial	Last name	Your social security number

If joint return, spouse's first name and middle initial	Last name	Spouse's social security number

Home address (number and street). If you have a P.O. box, see instructions. | Apt. no.

City, town, or post office. If you have a foreign address, also complete spaces below. | State | ZIP code

Foreign country name | Foreign province/state/county | Foreign postal code

Presidential Election Campaign
Check here if you, or your spouse if filing jointly, want $3 to go to this fund. Checking a box below will not change your tax or refund.
☐ You ☐ Spouse

Filing Status
Check only one box.
☐ Single ☐ Married filing jointly (even if only one had income) ☐ Married filing separately (MFS)
☐ Head of household (HOH) ☐ Qualifying surviving spouse (QSS)
If you checked the MFS box, enter the name of your spouse. If you checked the HOH or QSS box, enter the child's name if the qualifying person is a child but not your dependent:

Digital Assets
At any time during 2023, did you: (a) receive (as a reward, award, or payment for property or services); or (b) sell, exchange, or otherwise dispose of a digital asset (or a financial interest in a digital asset)? (See instructions.) . . . . ☐ Yes ☐ No

Standard Deduction
Someone can claim: ☐ You as a dependent ☐ Your spouse as a dependent
☐ Spouse itemizes on a separate return or you were a dual-status alien

Age/Blindness { You: ☐ Were born before January 2, 1959 ☐ Are blind
Spouse: ☐ Was born before January 2, 1959 ☐ Is blind

Dependents (see instructions):

(1) First name Last name	(2) Social security number	(3) Relationship to you	(4) Check the box if qualifies for (see instructions):	
			Child tax credit	Credit for other dependents
If more than four dependents, see instructions and check here ☐			☐	☐
			☐	☐
			☐	☐
			☐	☐

Portion of Form 1040-SR

Interview Pointers

These questions determine if the taxpayer should use the standard or itemized deduction. For questions relating to home ownership deductions, be aware that a taxpayer may have owned their home prior to the beginning of the current tax year, and it could be paid off. The other option is that the taxpayer purchased the home during the current tax year. (Itemized deductions will be covered in detail in a later chapter.)

➢ Do you pay rent or own a home?
  o If the taxpayer owns a home:
    ▪ Did you pay mortgage interest?
    ▪ Did you pay real estate taxes (property taxes)?
  o If the taxpayer purchased a home during the current tax year:
    ▪ Ask for the buyer's final closing statement
➢ Did you have medical expenses?
➢ Do you have medical insurance? (Out-of-pocket payments made by the taxpayer may be deductible on Schedule A.)
➢ Did you have debt from a mortgage or credit card canceled or forgiven by a commercial lender?
➢ Did you live in an area that was affected by a presidentially-declared natural disaster?
  o If yes, where and when?
➢ Did you receive the First-Time Homebuyer Credit in 2008?
➢ Did you make any charitable contributions last year?

- o Were they cash or noncash?
- o Do you have receipts? Can you bring them, so I can have a copy with your tax papers?
- ➢ Did you receive Form 1095-A? (If so, the taxpayers' insurance premiums cannot be deducted on Schedule A.)
- ➢ Do you have an exemption granted by the Marketplace? (If so, you need that number to complete the tax return.)
- ➢ Did you take any higher education classes?
- ➢ Did you pay someone to care for your children? (Only ask this if there are dependents on the return).

Part 1 Review

To obtain the maximum benefit from each part go online now and watch the video.

Part 2 Schedule 1, 2, & 3

Form 1040, Schedule 1, Part I

Schedule 1 reports additional income and adjustments to income. Each schedule's form, if used, is attached to Form 1040; however, a taxpayer might not use every schedule. A change to Schedule 1 for 2023 is that other income now includes line 1 a - u.

SCHEDULE 1 (Form 1040) Department of the Treasury Internal Revenue Service	**Additional Income and Adjustments to Income** Attach to Form 1040, 1040-SR, or 1040-NR. Go to *www.irs.gov/Form1040* for instructions and the latest information.	OMB No. 1545-0074 2023 Attachment Sequence No. 01
Name(s) shown on Form 1040, 1040-SR, or 1040-NR		Your social security number
Part I Additional Income		

Portion of Schedule 1

Additional income consists of the following items:

- ➢ Taxable refunds
- ➢ Alimony received
- ➢ Schedule C income or loss
- ➢ Form 4797 other gains or losses
- ➢ Schedule E income
- ➢ Schedule F income or loss
- ➢ Unemployment and paid family leave
- ➢ Sale of stocks or assets (if the taxpayer had a loss and not a gain on the sale report on line 4)
- ➢ Other income such as:
  - o Net Operating loss
  - o Gambling winnings
  - o Cancelation of debt
  - o Alaska Permanent Fund dividends
  - o Jury duty pay
  - o Hobby income
  - o Wages earned while incarcerated
  - o Etc.

Total income is the combination of all lines from Form 1040, Schedule 1, Part I. Some income reported on Schedule 1, lines 3, 4, 5, and 6 could result in a negative number that is subtracted from the total income.

Form 1040, Schedule 1, Part II

Schedule 1 (Form 1040) 2023   Page **2**

| **Part II** | **Adjustments to Income** |

Portion of Schedule 1

Adjustments to income are not the same as itemized deductions filed on Schedule A; adjustments lower the taxpayer's gross income so they pay the least amount of tax. Adjustments to income are:

> ➢ Educator expense, line 11
> ➢ Deductible part of self-employment tax, line 15
> ➢ Alimony paid (if the agreement was signed prior to December 31, 2018), line 19a
> ➢ Contributing to an IRA, SEP, SIMPLE, and other qualified plans, line 20
> ➢ Student loan interest deduction, line 21

Interview Pointers

To determine a taxpayer's adjusted gross income (AGI) on line 26, the tax preparer must ask the following questions:

> ➢ Did you pay alimony or separate maintenance payments? (Only applicable if the agreement was signed prior to December 31, 2018)
> ➢ Were there any changes in your tax status from last year to this year?
> ➢ Do you have an IRA?
> ➢ What life changes did you have this year?
> ➢ If the W-2 is from a school district: "I see that you have a W-2 from a school district. What is your job title?"
>   ○ The answer will determine if the taxpayer(s) qualify for the educator expense
> ➢ If the individual has more than one W-2: "I see that you have two different W-2s. Did you change jobs this year? If so, did you move? If so, how far is it from your old workplace to your new workplace?" (Due to the Tax Cuts and Jobs Act, adjustments on this line are limited to certain taxpayers until 2026. This topic will be covered in more detail later). Not all states conform to this rule. You need to know if your state conforms or not.
> ➢ If the W-2 is from the armed forces: "I see that you have a W-2 from the armed forces. Are you full-time or in the reserves? Were you in a combat zone?"

Adjustments and Deductions

Adjustments and deductions are often confused as they appear to function very similarly. The differences between the two will be explained in full throughout the course; but for now, it's important to understand that adjustments are used to lower one's AGI *before* credit deductions are considered. This is important because credit deduction amounts will be calculated based on the taxpayer's AGI.

The taxpayer can choose to itemize deductions or use standard deductions to reduce their taxable income. Standard deductions are annually preset amounts based on the taxpayer's filing status. Itemized deductions are generally used when the taxpayer's deduction exceeds their standard deduction. Itemized deductions are reported on Schedule A, which will be covered in a later chapter. Taxpayers are typically free to either itemize their deductions or take the standard deduction amounts, and they are encouraged to calculate both and then choose which option is better for their situation. Subtracting applicable deductions from the taxpayer's total income becomes the taxpayer's adjusted gross income.

The government allows deductions for certain costs of everyday life when they determine how much tax the taxpayer owes. Instead of taxing all the money the taxpayer earned, they consider money spent on things like health care, education, and saving for retirement. This helps make sure taxes are based on what the taxpayer actually got to keep after covering living expenses, rather than the total amount they were paid.

Schedule 2 Additional Taxes

SCHEDULE 2 (Form 1040)	Additional Taxes	OMB No. 1545-0074
Department of the Treasury Internal Revenue Service	Attach to Form 1040, 1040-SR, or 1040-NR. Go to *www.irs.gov/Form1040* for instructions and the latest information.	2023 Attachment Sequence No. 02
Name(s) shown on Form 1040, 1040-SR, or 1040-NR		Your social security number

Part I   Tax

1	Alternative minimum tax. Attach Form 6251	1	
2	Excess advance premium tax credit repayment. Attach Form 8962	2	
3	Add lines 1 and 2. Enter here and on Form 1040, 1040-SR, or 1040-NR, line 17 . .	3	

Portion of Schedule 2

Schedule 2, Part 1 – Tax

The tax to be paid is determined by the taxpayer's taxable income. Tax tables are also based on taxable income. The current year's tax tables can be found in the Form 1040 Instruction on the IRS website. Schedule 2, page 1 is used to report any additional tax that must be declared. Other taxes are covered in detail in a later chapter. Additional taxes are reported as follows:

Line 1: Alternative minimum tax (AMT). Attach Form 6251.

Line 2: Excess advanced premium tax credit repayment. Attach Form 8962.

Line 3: Add lines 1 and 2.

Schedule 2 Part II – Other Taxes

Line 4: Self-employment tax. Schedule SE should be attached.

Line 5: Unreported tip income, attach Form 4137.
Line 6: Uncollected Social Security and Medicare tax on wages, attach Form 8919.

Line 7: Total additional Social Security and Medicare tax from lines 5 and 6.

Line 8: Additional tax on IRAs and other qualified retirement plans are reported attach Form 5329.

Line 9: Household employment tax is reported, attach Schedule H.

Part II	**Other Taxes**			
4	Self-employment tax. Attach Schedule SE		**4**	
5	Social security and Medicare tax on unreported tip income. Attach Form 4137	**5**		
6	Uncollected social security and Medicare tax on wages. Attach Form 8919	**6**		
7	Total additional social security and Medicare tax. Add lines 5 and 6		**7**	
8	Additional tax on IRAs or other tax-favored accounts. Attach Form 5329 if required. If not required, check here . . . . ☐		**8**	
9	Household employment taxes. Attach Schedule H		**9**	
10	Repayment of first-time homebuyer credit. Attach Form 5405 if required		**10**	
11	Additional Medicare Tax. Attach Form 8959		**11**	
12	Net investment income tax. Attach Form 8960		**12**	
13	Uncollected social security and Medicare or RRTA tax on tips or group-term life insurance from Form W-2, box 12		**13**	
14	Interest on tax due on installment income from the sale of certain residential lots and timeshares		**14**	
15	Interest on the deferred tax on gain from certain installment sales with a sales price over $150,000		**15**	
16	Recapture of low-income housing credit. Attach Form 8611		**16**	

(continued on page 2)

For Paperwork Reduction Act Notice, see your tax return instructions.   Cat. No. 71478U   Schedule 2 (Form 1040) 2023

Portion of Schedule 2

Line 10: First-time homebuyer credit repayment; Form 5405 is used to report this and should be attached.

Line 11: Additional Medicare Tax, attach Form 8959.

Line 12: Net investment income tax (NIIT), attach Form 8960.

Line 13: Uncollected social security and Medicare or RRTA tax on tips or group-term life insurance from box 12, Form W-2.

Line 14: Interest on tax due on installment income from the sale of certain residential lots and timeshares.

Line 15: Interest on the deferred tax on gain from certain installment sales with a sales price over $150,000.

Line 16: Recapture of low-income housing credit, attach Form 8611.

Interview Pointers

Ask these questions to determine if the taxpayer will be paying other taxes:

➢ Did you have a childcare provider come to your home or did you go to their home? (If the provider came to the taxpayer's home, the taxpayer may need to file Schedule H.)
➢ Did you withdraw money from your IRA or 401(k)? (Depending upon the taxpayer's age and what the money was used for, it could result in an additional tax.)

      o   How much did you withdraw?
      o   What did you use it for?
- Did you have healthcare coverage for the entire year?
- Did you or your spouse receive Form 1095-A? (Did you purchase health insurance through an exchange?)
- Are you self-employed? (Ask this question if the taxpayer is filing a Schedule C.)
  - Did you receive Form 1099-MISC or NEC?
  - Did you receive Form 1099-K?
- Did you or your spouse receive a first-time home buyer loan and are paying it back?
- Did you report all your tips (direct and indirect) to your employer? (Ask this question if the taxpayer has income in box 7 of the W-2.)
- Do you have other additional taxes?
  - Tax on a Health Savings Account (HSA)?
  - Additional tax on HSA distributions?
  - Recapture of a charitable contribution?

Schedule 3 Additional Credits and Payments

Schedule 3 is used to report nonrefundable credits, other payments, and refundable credits. Refundable credits are payments toward the taxpayer's tax liability; if the result is more than the tax, the excess is a refund to the taxpayer.

Form 1040, line 25 reports the amount of federal withholding from all income sources, such as W-2, Form 1099-R, unemployment compensation, etc. Earned income tax credit (EITC), the additional child tax credit, and the refundable portion of the American opportunity credit are reported on Form 1040, lines 27-29.

Schedule 3 Part I: Nonrefundable Credits

A nonrefundable credit is used to reduce the taxpayer's tax liability to zero. If the individual has more credits, they are not able to use them to lower the tax liability. The taxpayer forfeits the remaining credit. A nonrefundable credit can reduce the taxable income dollar for dollar. Nonrefundable credits will be covered in a later chapter. Some common nonrefundable credits are:

- Education credits
- Foreign tax credit
- Credit for child and dependent care expenses
- Certain residential energy credits
- Retirement savings contributions credit

SCHEDULE 3 (Form 1040)	Additional Credits and Payments	OMB No. 1545-0074
Department of the Treasury Internal Revenue Service	Attach to Form 1040, 1040-SR, or 1040-NR. Go to *www.irs.gov/Form1040* for instructions and the latest information.	2023 Attachment Sequence No. 03
Name(s) shown on Form 1040, 1040-SR, or 1040-NR		Your social security number

Part I   **Nonrefundable Credits**

Portion of Schedule 3

Schedule 3 Part II: Other Payments and Refundable Credits

A refundable credit can generate a larger refund than the amount of tax paid through withholdings or estimated tax payments throughout the year. This means the taxpayer could get a refund from refundable credits that he or she qualifies for. Refundable credits will be covered in a later chapter.

Schedule 3 (Form 1040) 2023   Page **2**

Part II	**Other Payments and Refundable Credits**

Portion of Schedule 3

Line 9: Net premium tax credit, attach Form 8962. The premium tax credit (PTC) is a tax credit for certain taxpayers who enroll in a qualified health plan. A qualified health plan is a health insurance plan or policy that is purchased through the Marketplace or a state program.

Line 10: Amount paid with extension request. If the taxpayer got an automatic extension of time to file their current year tax Form 4868, enter the amount of the payment or any amount that was paid. If you made a payment without using Form 4868, do not include the amount on line 10.

Line 11: Report excess social security and tier I railroad retirement benefits (SSA-1099). If the taxpayer had more than one employer and earned more than $160,200, taxpayer may have an excess of Social Security or tier one railroad retirement tax.

Line 12: Used to report credit for federal tax on fuels used for a nontaxable purpose (for example, off-highway business use). Form 4136 is used to report nontaxable federal tax on fuels. The form must be attached to the tax return.

Line 14: Add lines 13a - z. Total amount of payments or refundable credits.

Line 15: Add lines 9 - 12 and 14.

Other payments and refundable credits will be reviewed in a later chapter.

Interview Pointers

These questions will determine the taxpayer's total tax payments:

➢ Did you make estimated payments during the tax year?
➢ Did you have last year's refund applied to the current tax year estimated payments?
➢ Did you take any higher education classes?
➢ Did you pay any money along with the request to file an extension? (Only ask if the taxpayer filed an extension.)

Señor 1040 Says: Make sure to do your due diligence for **all** tax returns with refundable credits.

Part 2 Review

To obtain the maximum benefit from each part go online now and watch the video.

Part 3 Filing the Federal Tax Return

Once the tax professional has gathered the required information and ensured its accuracy, it is time to file the return.

If a United States taxpayer has worldwide income (income earned anywhere in the world), they need to file a tax return. Immigrants who are unauthorized to be or work in the United States need to file their taxes; the IRS makes it very clear that the information provided for returns and filing are used for tax purposes only. The IRS does not share taxpayer information with any government immigration agency.

The Filing Process

To begin, gather information and materials from the taxpayer to complete an accurate return. The tax professional will need the following:

- ➢ Income reported on forms such as Form W-2 or 1099 Series.
- ➢ Receipts, checks, or invoices for payments and expenses.
- ➢ Other statements that show other income received by the taxpayer (such as a statement reporting gambling winnings from a casino or interest from a bank).
- ➢ Current driver's license or other form of government-issued picture identification.
- ➢ Social Security card with SSN number or some other form of taxpayer ID.
- ➢ Full name, date of birth, and SSN or other equivalent, for spouse and any dependent(s.)

This is the bare minimum needed to begin the tax preparation process. There will most likely be additional documents and information needed to complete the return depending on the taxpayer's specific situation. Some of the concepts behind this have already been discussed, and others will be introduced throughout this course as you learn more about tax preparation and tax law.

How to Assemble a Federal Tax Return

When assembling the return to be mailed to the IRS, make sure the attachment sequence order shown in the upper right-hand corner is in numerical order starting with Form 1040. If the taxpayer must attach supporting statements, the preparer must arrange them in the same order as the schedules and attach them at the end of the return. When mailing the return, attach a copy of all income forms such as Form(s) W-2, W-2G, and/or 1099-R to page 1 of Form 1040.

Portion of Schedule 1

Where to File a Paper Return

Based on where the taxpayer lives, the type of tax return and whether there is a refund or balance due determines where the taxpayer would send a paper return. Electronic filing has several advantages over filing a paper return. There are often separate mailing addresses for returns with enclosed payments and for returns without. Electronic filing eliminates the need to mail in a physical paper return. This option is discussed further in the e-filing chapter. Filing electronically is quicker and more secure than snail mail.

When to File a Return

The IRS states that, for tax returns and payments, the tax return must meet the "timely mailing/timely paying" rule. If the taxpayer owes taxes, they must be paid by April 15 or the next business day if April 15 falls on a weekend or legal holiday, even if the taxpayer has successfully filed for an extension of time.

How to File a Return

The following methods can be used to file a tax return:

➢ Electronic filing (e-file)
➢ Private delivery service: FedEx, UPS, etc.
➢ United States Postal Service

If a tax professional prepares 11 or more returns, they must e-file all returns. Electronically filed returns are postmarked with the date and time of the return's electronic transmission.

Filing Deadlines

Individual Tax Returns: Forms 1040 and 1040NR (Non-Resident)

➢ The first deadline was April 15, 2024
➢ The extended deadline is October 15, 2024

Partnership Returns: Form 1065

➢ The first deadline was March 15, 2024
➢ The extended deadline is September 16, 2024

Trust and Estate Income Tax Returns: Form 1041

➢ The first deadline was April 15, 2024
➢ The extended deadline is October 2, 2024

Note the change: extensions for fiduciary returns now last five-and-a-half months instead of only five months.

C-corporation Returns: Form 1120

➢ The first deadline for corporations is the 15th day of the 4th month after the close of their tax year, and the extended deadline is 10th month after the close of the tax year.

EXCEPTION: for corporations with a fiscal year from July 1 to June 30, the first deadline will remain September 15 (which is the fifteenth day of the third month following the end of the fiscal year) and the extended deadline will remain February 15 (five months after the first deadline) through the fiscal year ending on June 30, 2026.

S-corporation Returns: Form 1120-S

 ➤ The first deadline is March 15, 2024, for corporations.
 ➤ The extended deadline is September 16, 2024.

Foreign Bank Account Reports: FinCEN Form 114

 ➤ The first deadline is April 15, 2024; note the change of deadline.
 ➤ The extended deadline is October 15, 2024.

See IRS section 6072.

Part 3 Review

To obtain the maximum benefit from each part go online now and watch the video.

Part 4 What is an ITIN (Individual Tax Identification Number)?

An ITIN is a tax processing number, issued by the IRS, for certain resident and nonresident aliens, their spouses, and their dependents. It is a nine-digit number beginning with the number 9. The IRS started issuing ITINs in 1996 and requires foreign individuals to use an ITIN as their unique identification number on federal tax returns. With ITINs, taxpayers can be effectively identified, and their tax returns processed efficiently.

Only individuals who have a valid filing requirement, a withholding requirement, or are filing a U.S. federal income tax return to claim a refund of over-withheld tax are eligible to receive an ITIN. The ITIN does not provide Social Security benefits, is not valid for identification outside of the tax system, and does not change immigration status. The ITIN holder enters their ITIN in the space provided for the SSN when completing and filing their federal income tax return.

Who needs an ITIN?

All tax returns (Form 1040), statements, and other related tax documents used to file a tax report require a taxpayer identification number (TIN). If an individual does not qualify for a Social Security number, then the individual must apply for an ITIN.

Individuals who may need an ITIN include:

 ➤ A nonresident alien eligible to obtain the benefits of a reduced rate of withholding under an income tax treaty
 ➤ A nonresident alien not eligible for an SSN required to file a U.S. tax return or filing a U.S. tax return only to claim a refund
 ➤ A nonresident alien not eligible for an SSN electing to file a joint tax return with a spouse who is a U.S. citizen or resident alien
 ➤ A U.S. resident alien who files a U.S. tax return but is not eligible for an SSN
 ➤ An alien individual, claimed as a spouse for an exemption on a U.S. tax return, who is not eligible for an SSN
 ➤ An alien individual, who is not eligible for an SSN, claimed as a dependent on another person's U.S. tax return

> ➤ A nonresident alien student, professor, or researcher who is not eligible for an SSN and is filing a U.S. tax return or claiming an exception to the tax return filing requirement

Reason to Apply for an ITIN

Form W-7
(Rev. August 2019)
Department of the Treasury
Internal Revenue Service

Application for IRS Individual Taxpayer Identification Number
► For use by individuals who are not U.S. citizens or permanent residents.
► See separate instructions.

OMB No. 1545-0074

An IRS individual taxpayer identification number (ITIN) is for U.S. federal tax purposes only.
Before you begin:
• *Don't submit this form if you have, or are eligible to get, a U.S. social security number (SSN).*

Application type (check one box):
☐ Apply for a new ITIN
☐ Renew an existing ITIN

Reason you're submitting Form W-7. Read the instructions for the box you check. **Caution:** If you check box **b, c, d, e, f,** or **g,** you must file a U.S. federal tax return with Form W-7 unless you meet one of the exceptions (see instructions).

a ☐ Nonresident alien required to get an ITIN to claim tax treaty benefit
b ☐ Nonresident alien filing a U.S. federal tax return
c ☐ U.S. resident alien **(based on days present in the United States)** filing a U.S. federal tax return
d ☐ Dependent of U.S. citizen/resident alien — If **d**, enter relationship to U.S. citizen/resident alien (see instructions) ► ....
e ☐ Spouse of U.S. citizen/resident alien — If **d** or **e**, enter name and SSN/ITIN of U.S. citizen/resident alien (see instructions) ► ....
f ☐ Nonresident alien student, professor, or researcher filing a U.S. federal tax return or claiming an exception
g ☐ Dependent/spouse of a nonresident alien holding a U.S. visa
h ☐ Other (see instructions) ► ....
Additional information for **a** and **f**: Enter treaty country ► .... and treaty article number ► _____

Portion of W-7

A nonresident alien must apply for an ITIN to report earned income and claim the tax treaty benefits they qualify for:

Box a. Check this box for certain nonresident aliens who must get an ITIN to claim certain tax treaty benefits whether they file a tax return or not. If box a is checked, then check box h as well. Enter on the dotted line next to box h the exceptions that relate to the taxpayer's situation. See Publication 901.

Box b. Nonresident alien filing a U.S. tax return.

This category includes:

1. A nonresident alien who must file a U.S. tax return to report income directly or indirectly engaged in a trade or business in the United States
2. A nonresident alien who is filing a U.S. tax return only to get a refund

See Publication 519.

Box c. U.S. resident alien (based on the number of days present in the United States) filing a U.S. tax return.

Check Box c for a foreign individual living in the United States who does not have permission to work from the USCIS and is ineligible for an SSN but may still have a filing requirement. See Publication 519.

Box d. Dependent of a U.S. citizen/resident alien.

Check box d for an individual who can be claimed as a dependent on a U.S. tax return and is not eligible to get an SSN. Dependents of U.S. military personnel are exempt from the requirements of submitting original documents or certified copies of identifying documents, but a standard copy is required. A copy of the U.S. military ID is required, or the applicant must be applying from an overseas APO/FPO address. See Publications 501 and 519.

Box e. Spouse of a U.S. citizen/resident alien.

This category includes:

1. A resident or nonresident alien spouse who is not filing a U.S. tax return (including a joint return) and who is not eligible to get an SSN, but who, as a spouse, is claimed as an exemption
2. A resident or nonresident alien electing to file a U.S. tax return jointly with a spouse who is a U.S. citizen or resident alien

A spouse or a person in the U.S. military is exempt from submitting original documents or certified copies of identifying documents, but a standard copy will be required. A copy of the U.S. military ID is required, or the applicant must be applying from an overseas APO/FPO address. See Publications 501 and 519.

Box f. Nonresident alien student, professor, or researcher filing a U.S. tax return or *claiming an exception.*

Check box f if the individual applicant has not abandoned their residence in a foreign country and who is a bona fide student, professor, or researcher coming temporarily to the United States solely to attend classes at a recognized institution of education, to teach, or to perform research.

If this box is checked, complete lines 6c and 6g and provide an actual passport with a valid U.S. visa. If the applicant is present in the U.S. on a work-related visa (F-1, J-1, or M-1), but will not be employed (applicant's presence in the U.S. is study-related), attach a letter from the DSO (Designated School Official) or RO (Responsible Officer) instead of applying with the Social Security Administration (SSA) for an SSN. The letter must state clearly that the applicant will not be securing employment while in the U.S. and their presence here is solely study related. This letter can be submitted with the applicant's Form W-7 in lieu of the denial letter from the SSA. See Publications 519.

Box g. Dependent/spouse of a nonresident alien holding a U.S. visa.

Check box g when the individual can be claimed as a dependent or a spouse on a U.S. tax return, is unable or not eligible to get an SSN, and has entered the U.S. with a nonresident alien who holds a U.S. visa. If this box is checked, be sure to include a copy of the visa with the W-7 application.

Box h. Other.

If box h is checked, it is because boxes a-g do not apply to the applicant. Be sure to describe in detail the reason for requesting an ITIN and attach all supporting documents.

Common Errors on Form W-7

Always make sure that you input the correct information; double check each document and Form W-7 for errors.

Supporting Identification Documentation is Unacceptable

Identification documentation must be one of the 13 acceptable documents.

COA Form W-7 not Attached

A valid COA must be attached to the W-7

Supporting Identification Documentation is Not Original or Certified

All identification documentation sent to the IRS must be original documents unless the Certifying Acceptance Agent (CAA) is completing the W-7. CAAs are the only ones who are able to send certified copies. Make sure that the required original identification documents or certified copies (if applicable) are submitted with Form W-7. See Publication 519

Many ITIN holders use a different name with a Social Security number. When submitting a W-7 application with a tax return, the names on the W-2s should match the names on the application. The IRS must ensure that the W-2 income is associated with the correct individual. Remember, the purpose of the ITIN is to allow foreign individuals to report their income. Ensuring that the name on the W-2 matches the legal name can be tricky. Taxpayers who need an ITIN may not want to ask their employer to change their records for fear of being dismissed for submitting inaccurate information.

Not Submitting Required Documents

Make sure that the required original identification documents or certified copies (if applicable) are submitted with Form W-7.

Name and/or Taxpayer Identification Number of the U.S. Person is Missing

If reason "d" or "e" is selected on Form W-7, then the full named and TIN (SSN or ITIN) of the U.S. citizen or resident alien must be entered in the space to the right. Do not abbreviate country names.

A previously issued ITIN and name must be entered in the spaces provided. If the applicant's legal name changed since the TIN was issued, documents such as a marriage certificate or other documents must be attached to Form W-7 to support the name change.

Date of Entry

Another common mistake occurs when the date of entry line on the passport is empty. In this situation the IRS will no longer allow the passport to be a stand-alone identification document.
Without this information, the IRS cannot match the taxpayer's date of entry with their beginning work history. In this situation, the applicant should submit documents that establish when they began working and the type of work they have been doing.

For certain dependents, a passport without a date of entry is not accepted as a stand-alone document. See Publication 1915.

Passport Rejection

The most common reason the IRS rejects passports is because they are not signed. The IRS will not accept an original passport that is not signed. Everyone entering the U.S. with a passport must sign it. Some countries, such as India, do not allow children to sign passports.

Expiration of ITINs

An expired ITIN only needs to be renewed if it is needed on a U.S. federal tax return. An ITIN is expired if it has not been used on a tax return for the past three consecutive years.

The IRS uniform policy applies to any ITIN, regardless of when it was issued. Only about a quarter of the 21 million ITINs issued since the program began in 1996 are being used on tax returns. The expiration policy ensures that anyone who legitimately uses an ITIN for tax purposes can continue to do so, while at the same time expiring millions of unused ITINs.

ITIN Tax Related Exceptions

There are certain exceptions under which taxpayers are not required to include a form W-7 with their tax return. These exceptions generally require submission of supporting documentation, sometimes referred to by the IRS as "information returns."

Exception 1: Third Party Withholding on Passive Income

This exception may apply if the taxpayer is the recipient of partnership income, interest income, annuity income, rental income, or other passive income that is subject to third party withholding or covered by tax treaty benefits.

To claim this exception, the taxpayer must include additional supporting documentation with Form W-7, such as a letter or signed statement from the bank, financial institution, or withholding agent proving that the asset that generates income and belongs to the taxpayer is subject to IRS reporting requirements that take place in the current tax year.

Exception 2: Other Income

This exception may apply if:

1. The taxpayer is claiming the benefits of a U.S. income tax treaty with a foreign country and the taxpayer received any of the following:
   a. Wages, salary, compensation, and honoraria payments
   b. Scholarships, fellowships, and grants
   c. Gambling winnings
2. The taxpayer is receiving a taxable scholarship, fellowship, or grant income, but not claiming the benefits of an income tax treaty

Exception 3: Third Party Reporting of Mortgage Interest

If the ITIN applicant has a home mortgage loan on real property that they own in the United States, that is subject to third party reporting of mortgage interest they may be eligible to claim this exception. Information returns are applicable to exception 3. may include Form 1098, *Mortgage Interest Statement.*

An information return is a form that is filed with the IRS or that the taxpayer uses to report information to the IRS. It differs from a tax return as it does not report a tax due. One that could be used regularly is Form 1099-NEC, distributed to independent contractors. The form does not compute the contractor's tax due, but simply provides the amount the payor is paying the payee.

If the applicant is eligible to claim exception 3, the applicant must submit documentation showing evidence of a home mortgage loan. Evidence would include a copy of the sales contract or similar documentation.

Exception 4: Third Party Withholding Dispositions by a Foreign Person of United States Real Property

This exception may apply if the individual is a party to a disposition of a U.S. real property interest by a foreign person, which is generally subject to withholding by the transferee or buyer (withholding agent). If the applicant uses this exception with their information return, one of the following may be included:

➤ Form 8288, *U.S. Withholding Tax Return Dispositions by Foreign Persons of U.S. Real Property Interests*
➤ Form 8288-A, *Statement of Withholding on Dispositions by Foreign Persons of U.S. Real Property Interests*
➤ Form 8288-B and a copy of the contract of the sale, *Application for Withholding Certificate for Dispositions by Foreign Persons of U.S. Real Property Interests*

For the seller of the property, copies of Forms 8288 and 8288-A submitted by the buyer should be attached to Form W-7.

Exception 5: Reporting Obligations under Treasury Decision 9363(T. D. 9363)

This exception may apply if the taxpayer has an IRS reporting requirement under TD-9363 and is submitting Form W-7 with Form 13350.

If the applicant is eligible for this exception, Form 13350 should be submitted with the W-7 application, along with a letter from their employer on corporate letterhead stating they have been designated as the person responsible for ensuring compliance with IRS information reporting requirements.

Aliens

Determining if a taxpayer is a resident, nonresident, or dual-status alien dictates whether and how the taxpayer must file a return.

Resident Alien

The taxpayer is a resident alien of the United States for tax purposes if he/she meets either the "green card test" or the "substantial presence test" for the current calendar tax year. If the taxpayer has been a resident for the entire year, they must file a tax return following the same rules that apply to a U.S. citizen. See Publication 519.

Nonresident Alien

A nonresident alien is a person who has not passed the green card test or the substantial presence test. Tax forms are different for the nonresident alien. For example, there are only three options for filing status on Form 1040NR: Single, Married Filing Separately, and Surviving spouse.

Dual-status Alien

An alien who makes a change from nonresident alien to resident alien or from resident alien to nonresident alien is considered a dual-status alien. Different rules apply for each part of the year the taxpayer is a nonresident or a resident alien.

Publication 519 will help in determining the taxpayer's alien status. This topic is not covered in depth in this textbook.

Tax Return Compliance

The IRS is enhancing compliance activities relating to certain credits, including the child tax credit. The changes will improve the ability of the IRS to review returns claiming this credit, including those returns utilizing ITINs for dependents. For example, additional residency information will be required on Schedule 8812, Child Tax Credit, to ensure eligibility criteria for the credit is met.

Information derived from the ITIN process will be better utilized in the refund verification process. New pre-refund screening filters were put in place to flag returns for audits that claim questionable refundable credits. Increased compliance resources will also be deployed to address questionable returns in this area. As part of these overall efforts, ITIN holders may be asked to revalidate their ITIN status as part of certain audits to help ensure the numbers are used appropriately.

Part 4 Review

To obtain the maximum benefit from each part go online now and watch the video.

Takeaways

Knowing tax law and gathering the necessary information to satisfy the due diligence knowledge requirement is just the beginning of becoming a great tax preparer. What truly marks a successful career in tax preparation is applying this knowledge correctly to a tax return; this is the paramount responsibility of a tax professional.

Knowing the tax law and how to apply each law to each individual situation is the puzzle that the tax professional must solve throughout their career. Every situation is different, and the tax professional must learn how to put the pieces of the puzzle together to prepare an accurate tax return.

TEST YOUR KNOWLEDGE!
Go online to take a practice quiz.

Chapter 3 Filing Status, Dependents, and Deductions

Introduction

In the realm of tax law understanding the difficulties of filing status, dependents, and deductions is vital. These fundamental elements not only shape an individual's tax liability but also influence various financial decisions throughout the year. Filing status determines how an individual or household reports their income to the Internal Revenue Service (IRS), while dependents and deductions play crucial roles in reducing taxable income and maximizing potential refunds.

The significance of these aspects cannot be overstated, as they directly impact taxpayers' financial well-being and compliance with tax regulations. However, navigating the maze of tax laws and regulations surrounding filing status, dependents, and deductions can be daunting, even for the most seasoned individuals.

This chapter examines the complexities of filing status, dependents, and deductions, providing a comprehensive analysis of their roles, regulations, and implications. By studying relevant tax laws, IRS guidelines, and case studies, we aim to shed light on the complexities of these crucial components of the tax system.

Objectives

At the end of this chapter, the student will be able to:

➤ Recognize how to determine the standard deduction
➤ Understand who qualifies for the higher standard deduction
➤ Explain the qualifying child test requirements
➤ Identify the difference between a qualifying child and a qualifying relative
➤ Describe the difference between custodial and noncustodial parents
➤ List the five filing statuses
➤ Clarify the requirements for each filing status
➤ Identify types of income to determine support
➤ Recognize the requirements to claim a qualifying dependent

Resources

Form 1040	Publication 17	Instructions Form 1040
Form 2120	Publication 501	Instructions Form 2120
Form 8332	Publication 555	Instructions Form 8332
	Tax Topic 352, 851, 857, 858	

Part 1 Filing Status

At first glance filing status appears to be simple to determine; however, tax professionals must know, understand, and apply the requirements for each filing status. Choosing the correct filing status determines the filing requirements, deductions, correct tax, and taxpayer eligibility for certain credits and deductions. See Publication 17 and Publication 501.

The five federal filing statuses are:
1. Single (S)
2. Married filing jointly (MFJ)
3. Married Filing Separately (MFS)
4. Head of household (HOH)
5. Qualifying surviving spouse (QSS) with a dependent child.

State law governs whether a taxpayer is married or legally separated under a divorce or separate maintenance decree and how this affects the taxpayer's filing status. A taxpayer is generally considered unmarried for the whole year if, on the last day of the current tax year, the taxpayer is unmarried or legally separated from their spouse under a divorce or separate maintenance decree.

Under the Revenue Ruling 2013-17, same-sex couples will be treated as married for all federal tax purposes, including income, gifts, and estate taxes. The ruling applies to all federal tax provisions where marriage is a factor, including filing status, claiming a person and dependency exemptions, taking the standard deduction, employee benefits, contributing to an IRA, and claiming the earned income tax credit or child tax credit.

Single (S)

A taxpayer is classified as filing as Single if, as of the last day of the current tax year, they are either unmarried or legally separated from their spouse through a divorce or separate maintenance decree. In cases of divorce, taxpayers are considered unmarried for the entire tax year if the divorce is finalized on, by, or before the last day of the filing year. If a divorce is solely for tax purposes and the taxpayers remarry the subsequent year, they must file a joint return for both tax years. The determination of marital status, including legal separation, is governed by state law, and tax professionals need to be aware of the specific laws in the state where they operate.

In instances when a marriage is annulled, the parties are considered unmarried, regardless of whether they filed a joint tax return. If the IRS notifies the couple that their filing status is incorrect, they will need to amend their returns to reflect Single or Head of Household status for all incorrectly filed years. An annulment legally invalidates the marriage, rendering it as if it never existed in the eyes of the law.

A widow(er) may file as Single if they were widowed before January 1 of the current tax year and did not remarry before the end of the same tax year. However, it's important to note that the taxpayer might qualify for a different filing status that could potentially further reduce their tax liability.

Married Filing Jointly (MFJ)

The taxpayer must file Married Filing Jointly (MFJ) if they meet any of the following criteria on December 31 of the current tax year being filed:

➢ Taxpayers are married and filing a joint return even if one had no income or deductions
➢ Taxpayers are living together in a common-law marriage that is recognized in the state where the taxpayers now live, or in the state where the common-law marriage began
➢ Taxpayers are married and living apart but are not legally separated under a decree of divorce or separate maintenance
➢ A spouse died during the tax year, and the taxpayer did not remarry before the end of the tax year.

➢ If a spouse died during the current tax year, and the taxpayer remarried before the end of the tax year, the taxpayer and his or her new spouse may file MFJ. A tax return must still be filed for the deceased spouse, and, in this instance, the decedents' filing status would be MFS for the tax year.

See Revenue Ruling 2013-17 regarding the content above.

Community Property and Income

Community property states operate under the principle that property acquired by a husband and wife after marriage is jointly owned by them "in community." This means that if a wife purchases property under her name before marriage, it is considered her sole property. However, if she acquires property after marriage, it is deemed as belonging to both spouses, even if only her name is on the title.

Community property states, including Arizona, California, Idaho, Louisiana, Nevada, New Mexico, Texas, Washington, and Wisconsin, do not handle community property tax liability in the same way. Tax professionals preparing state taxes for individuals in these states must conduct thorough research to understand the nuances for each state before filing tax returns.

Alaska, while not a community property state, provides couples with the option to choose community property rules through a community property agreement or community trust, even though it is considered an equitable property state. On the other hand, Wisconsin's divorce laws presume an equal division of all marital property between spouses.

Exceptions to community property rules exist, and tax preparers must be aware of them. For instance, property acquired before marriage or inherited during the marriage is typically considered separate property of the spouse who owns it. In Arizona, California, Nevada, New Mexico, Washington, and Wisconsin, income generated from separate properties is also regarded as separate income for the owning spouse. Consequently, if spouses file separately, this income is reported solely on the owner's return, a principle known as the "California Rule."

Conversely, in Idaho, Louisiana, and Texas, income from separate properties is treated as community income. Therefore, if spouses file separately, this income is shared on their individual tax returns, following the "Texas Rule." Understanding these exceptions is essential for accurate tax preparation in community property states.

According to §66 of the Internal Revenue Code (IRC), when spouses are living apart, the spouse who earned the income will retain it separately. Living apart entails the following:

➢ They are married to each other
➢ They lived apart for an entire tax year
➢ They did not file a joint return
➢ One or both have earned income, none of which is transferred between them

Individuals who meet all the above requirements must follow the rules below to cover the reporting of income on their separate returns:

➢ Earned income (other than trade, business, or partnership income) is treated as income of the spouse who rendered the personal services
➢ Trade or business income is treated as the taxpayer's income unless the spouse substantially exercises control and management of the entire business

➢ Community income derived from the separate property owned by one spouse is treated as the income of the owner

All other community income is taxed in accordance with the applicable community property laws. See Code §897(a).

Innocent Spouse

Married taxpayers often choose to file a joint tax return due to the benefits of the filing status. However, both taxpayers are jointly and individually responsible for any tax, interest, or penalty due on a joint tax return. Even after a couple is separated or divorced, a former spouse could be held responsible for amounts due on previously filed joint returns.

In this instance, the taxpayer might be able to claim they are an "innocent spouse," an individual who was not aware of a position claimed by the other person on a joint tax return that resulted in liability for understatement of income. In this situation, the innocent spouse can file for relief using Form 8857 to try to prove that they were not aware of the position on the return. The IRS will review the request for relief, come to a decision, and respond with their ruling. The taxpayer may appeal the decision if they find the ruling unacceptable.

To be eligible for the relief, the taxpayer must meet the following criteria:

➢ Must have filed a joint return with an erroneous understatement of tax responsibility relating directly to their spouse
➢ Must have no knowledge of the error
➢ The IRS identified the error and must agree that it is fair to relieve the taxpayer of the tax penalties
➢ The taxpayer must apply for relief within two years of the IRS initial collections notice

Example: Lincoln and Amelia were married and filed joint tax returns for 2022 and 2023. Amelia always let her husband handle the finances and tax preparation. She simply signed the tax return when Lincoln told her to, never questioning the man she thought she could implicitly trust. However, after finalizing their divorce on May 15, 2023, Amelia received a letter demanding penalties and interest from the IRS. Alarmed, Amelia found a tax preparer who helped her discover that her ex-husband Lincoln had illegally claimed business expenses on their personal 2022 and 2023 tax returns, causing significant penalties and interest to accrue for filing a fraudulent return. Based on her lack of knowledge, the tax preparer correctly advised her to file Form 8857 to apply for relief on the 2022 and 2023 tax returns.

Spousal Abandonment

Spousal abandonment occurs when the abandoning spouse has left their family with no intention of returning or having responsibility for their family. In a legal context, failing to provide for a dependent, ailing spouse, or a minor child could be considered criminal spousal abandonment. Separation with no intent of reconciling is not spousal abandonment. Spousal abandonment often requires the abandoned spouse to file a separate return and receive all the unfavorable tax consequences that come with it. For example, the taxpayer must use the Tax Rate Schedule for married taxpayers filing separately. To mitigate such harsh treatment, Congress enacted provisions commonly referred to as the "abandoned spouse rules" which allow married taxpayers to file as Head of Household to bypass the tax consequences of married filing separately.

Married Filing Separately (MFS)

Married taxpayers, whether living together or apart, may choose to file Married Filing Separately (MFS) in the following circumstances:

> ➢ They want to be responsible for their own tax liability
> ➢ If the MFS filing status results in the taxpayers paying less tax than filing jointly

Taxpayers need to be advised that MFS filing status has limitations in deductions, adjustments, and credits.

Taxpayers who elect to file MFS must enter their spouse's full name and Social Security number or ITIN in the spaces provided. They are also generally subject to the following special rules:

> ➢ They are generally subject to higher tax rates
> ➢ They must live apart for the entire year to claim the credit for the elderly or disabled
> ➢ They are unable to claim certain credits
> ➢ Their capital loss deduction is limited to $1,500
> ➢ They must itemize deductions if their spouse does so
> ➢ Their Individual Retirement Account (IRA) contributions are limited by their income amount
> ➢ They cannot exclude interest from qualified U.S. savings bonds used for higher education expenses
> ➢ Their alternative minimum tax is half of that allowed for MFJ

See Publication 501.

If the taxpayers live in a community property state and file a separate return, the laws of the state in which the taxpayers reside govern whether they have community property income or separate property income for federal tax purposes. See Publication 555.

Head of Household (HOH)

The taxpayer must file Head of Household (HOH) if they meet any of the following criteria on December 31 of the tax year being filed:

> ➢ The taxpayer would be considered unmarried on the last day of the year
> ➢ A qualifying child or relative lived in the home for more than half the year (there are exceptions for temporary absences). Children of divorced or separated parents, or parents who lived apart, can be claimed based on the residency test in most cases.
> ➢ The taxpayer paid for more than half the cost of keeping up the home for the tax year

A married taxpayer could be considered as head of household if they maintain separate homes for more than the last six months of the year and a qualifying child lived with them. The filing status to choose on the tax return is Head of Household.

Keeping Up a Home

To qualify for the HOH filing status, a taxpayer must pay more than half of the cost for maintaining a household. Expenses can include rent, mortgage interest payments, repairs, real estate taxes, insurance, utilities, and food eaten in the house. Costs do not include clothing, education, medical treatment, vacations, life insurance, and the rental value of the home the taxpayer owns. Keeping up a house and monetary support will be discussed later in this chapter.

Suppose the taxpayer receives payments from Temporary Assistance for Needy Families (TANF) or other public assistance programs to pay rent or upkeep on the home. In that case, those payments cannot be included as money the taxpayer paid. However, they must be included in the total cost of keeping up the home to figure whether the taxpayer paid over half of the cost.

> *Señor 1040 Says:* Remember, assistance given by TANF to pay for rent must be included in the total cost of keeping up a home.

Differences Between Filing Head of Household and Single

The distinction between filing as Single (S) and filing as Head of Household (HOH) hinges on whether the unmarried taxpayer maintains a home for a Qualifying Person. In order to qualify for the Head of Household status, there must first exist a household of individuals who live together and have qualifying relationships to form a family unit. If the taxpayer's living situation doesn't meet these criteria, they must file as Single.

A taxpayer would file as Single instead of Head of Household in the following scenarios:

➢ If the taxpayer resides alone, they are technically the only person in their home, and as there is no household to lead, they must file as Single
➢ If the taxpayer lives within a household but doesn't meet the qualifications to be its head, whether due to inadequate support contribution or other reasons, despite being a member of the household, they aren't its head and thus would file as Single
➢ In cases where a taxpayer has a qualifying dependent but doesn't meet the requirements to qualify as the Head of Household, they would file as Single with a Dependent instead of Head of Household

Example 1: Tyler lives alone in a suburban house, and no one else lives with him. He files Single because even though he is the "head" of his house, there is not a household or group of individuals of qualifying relationships living together to be considered a family unit.

Example 2: Joseph and four of his friends live in a house they rent together and split all the living costs evenly amongst themselves. Assuming none of them are married or in a registered domestic partnership, they will all file Single since none provide more than 50% of support for the house to qualify as a Head of Household. The group does not possess sufficient qualifying relationships to be considered a family unit and cannot be considered a household; therefore, there is neither a head of household nor a household.

Example 3: Barry resides with his parents, Henry and Nora, and his son Don. Henry and Nora collectively earn $350,000 annually. Barry's income as a part-time educational aide amounts to $27,840 per year. While Barry does not contribute more than 50% towards the household expenses, he does provide over 50% of the support for his son, Don. Consequently, Barry is required to file taxes as "Single with a Dependent" due to several factors. First, he cannot file as Head of Household since he does not contribute the majority of the household's financial support. Second, Barry is unmarried and not engaged in a registered domestic partnership, making the "Single" filing status appropriate. Third, Don qualifies as Barry's dependent as he is Barry's child and receives over half of his support from Barry. Therefore, the most suitable tax filing status for Barry is "Single with a Dependent."

Qualifying Surviving Spouse with Dependent Child

The taxpayer can file as a Qualifying Surviving Spouse (QSS) with dependent child if they meet all of the following criteria on December 31 of the tax year being filed:

> ➢ The taxpayer was entitled to file a joint return with their spouse for the tax year in which the spouse died (whether the taxpayer filed a joint return or not)
> ➢ The taxpayer did not remarry before the end of the tax year
> ➢ The taxpayer has a dependent child who qualifies as their dependent for the tax year
> ➢ The taxpayer paid more than half the cost of keeping up a home that was the main home for the taxpayer and the dependent child for the entire year

For the tax year in which the spouse died, the taxpayer can file MFJ or QSS. If the taxpayer continues to meet the requirements, the taxpayer will file as QSS with a dependent child for the next two years. If the taxpayer has not remarried and still has a qualifying dependent child living with them after the two years, the taxpayer's filing status would change to HOH.

Example: John's wife died in 2022, and John has not remarried and has continued to keep up a home with his qualifying children, Riley and Galvan. For tax year 2022, John filed MFJ. In 2023 and 2024, he would qualify to file as Qualifying Surviving Spouse if Riley and Galvan are still qualifying dependents. Starting in tax year 2025, however, if John still has qualifying children and has not remarried, he would not be able to file as a QSS with dependent children and would instead qualify to file as HOH.

Exemptions and Suspensions

Exemptions are dollar amounts that can be deducted from an individual's total income, thereby reducing their taxable income. A suspension is the temporary removal or reduction of exemptions, deductions and certain other tax provisions that may affect a taxpayer's tax liability.

Similar to a deduction, a personal exemption reduces the amount of income used to compute tax liability. Unlike tax deductions, an exemption is simply a set amount of reduction given on the return.

The Tax Cuts and Jobs Act in 2017 suspended the personal exemption for tax years **2018 to 2025**. Though there may not be a filing requirement for the federal portion of a return currently, a taxpayer might still have a filing requirement for the state and, in the future, potentially for the federal return as well.

The taxpayer can generally claim an exemption for himself, his or her spouse, and any qualifying dependents. The total amount of reduction provided from any personal exemptions before the tax year 2017 goes on Form 1040, line 42, and Form 1040A, line 26. Form 1040EZ, line 5, is the sum of the total standard deduction amount added to the personal exemption amount.

Rules for Dependent Exemptions

> ➢ The taxpayer cannot claim any dependents if they file a joint return or if they could be claimed as a dependent by another taxpayer

➢ The taxpayer cannot claim a married person who files a joint return as a dependent unless the joint return is only a claim for a refund

➢ The taxpayer cannot claim a person as a dependent unless the individual is a U.S. citizen, a U.S. resident, a U.S. national, or a resident of Canada or Mexico for some part of the year; there are exceptions to this rule, but they are beyond the scope of this course

➢ A taxpayer cannot claim a person as a dependent unless that person is their qualifying child or qualifying relative

The taxpayer is allowed one exemption for each person claimed on the tax return. The taxpayer can claim an exemption for a dependent even if they file a tax return.

Part 1 Review

To obtain the maximum benefit from each part go online now and watch the video.

Part 2 Dependent Filing Requirements

Dependent Exemptions

A taxpayer can claim a qualifying child or a qualifying relative as a dependent if the following three tests are met:

➢ Dependent taxpayer test
➢ Joint return test
➢ Citizen or resident test

Dependent Taxpayer Test

If a taxpayer is claimed as a dependent by another person, that individual cannot claim any dependents on their return. If the taxpayer is filing a joint return and the spouse was a dependent for someone else, they cannot claim any dependents on their joint return. They can only file to receive their refund.

If gross income is $4,700 (for tax year 2023) and for 2024 the amount is $5,050. Generally, the taxpayer cannot be claimed as a dependent unless the taxpayer is under age 19 or a full-time student under the age of 24.

Qualifying Child

To be considered the qualifying dependent of the taxpayer, a child must meet all five tests:

1. **Relationship**: The child must be the taxpayer's child, stepchild, foster child, sibling, stepsibling, or a descendant of any of these individuals (e.g., grandchild)
2. **Age**: The child must be under a certain age or meet other criteria (such as being a full-time student) to qualify as a dependent. Generally, the child must be under 19 years old at the end of the tax year, or under 24 years old if they are a full-time student.
3. **Residency**: The child must have lived with the taxpayer for more than half of the tax year. Temporary absences for purposes such as school, vacation, medical care, military service, or detention in a juvenile facility are generally not considered interruptions in residency.

4. **Support**: The child must not have provided more than half of their own support during the tax year. Support includes food, shelter, clothing, education, medical and dental care, recreation, and transportation.
5. **Joint Return**: If the child is married, they must not have filed a joint return with their spouse unless it was only to claim a refund and there would be no tax liability for either spouse if they had filed separately

These tests determine whether a child qualifies as a dependent for the taxpayer, separate from the qualifications for claiming dependent exemptions.

Children of Parents Who Live Apart, Divorce, or Separate

In most cases, a child will be treated as the dependent of the custodial parent. A child will be treated as the qualifying child of their noncustodial parent if all the following apply:

1. The parents were any of the following:
    a. Divorced or legally separated under a decree of divorce or separate maintenance,
    b. Separated under a written separation agreement,
    c. Living apart for the last six months of the year, whether married or not;
2. The child received over half of their support for the year from the parents;
3. The child is in the custody of one or both parents for more than half of the year;
4. If either of the following is true:
    a. The custodial parent signed a written declaration stating that the custodial parent will not claim the child as a dependent for the current year, and the noncustodial parent attaches the written declaration to his or her return
    b. A pre-1985 decree of divorce, separate maintenance, or written separation agreement, which applies to 2023, states that the noncustodial parent can claim the child as a dependent and will provide at least $600 for the support of the child during the year

If all four of the above statements are true, the noncustodial parent can only do the following:

➢ Claim the child as a dependent
➢ Claim the child as a qualifying child for the child tax credit or the credit for other dependents

See Sec 152(e).

Custodial vs. Noncustodial Parent

If the parents divorced or separated during the year and if the child lived with both parents before the separation, the "custodial parent" is the parent with whom the child lived for the greater part of the year.

A child is treated as living with a parent for a night if the child sleeps as follows:

➢ At the parent's home, whether the parent is present or not
➢ In the company of the parent when the child does not sleep at a parent's house (for example, going on vacation)

The rule for divorced or separated parents also applies to parents who never married and lived apart for the last six months of the year.

If the child lived with each parent for an equal number of nights, the parent with the higher adjusted gross income (AGI) is the custodial parent. If the child is emancipated under state law, the child is treated as having not lived with either parent.

Tie-Breaker Rules

The following rules apply to determine which parent will claim the qualifying child:

> ➤ If both claimants are the parents and file a joint return, they can claim the child as a qualifying child. Even if there are other qualified claimants, the child cannot be the qualifying child of another person.
> ➤ If only one claimant is the child's parent, the child will be the parent's qualifying child
> ➤ If both claimants are parents and do not file a joint return, the IRS will treat the child as a qualifying child of the parent with whom the child lived the longest during the year
> ➤ If one of the above does not resolve the dispute, then the IRS will treat the child as the qualifying child of the claimant with the highest AGI for the year. Also, use this rule as a tiebreaker in the following instances:
>> ○ If the child lived with each of his two parents for the same amount of time
>> ○ If no parent can claim the child as a qualifying child
>> ○ If a parent can claim the child as a qualifying child, but no parent claims the child

Child in Canada or Mexico

A child living in a foreign country cannot be claimed as a dependent unless the child is a U.S. citizen, U.S. resident alien, or U.S. national. However, a taxpayer may claim their child as a dependent if the child lives in Canada or Mexico, even if the child is not a U.S. citizen, resident alien, or national.

Written Declaration Form 8332

The custodial parent can use Form 8332 to make a written declaration to release the exemption to the noncustodial parent. If the custodial parent has multiple dependents, a separate form should be used for each child. The release of the exemption can have various conditions:

> ➤ It can be released for one year.
> ➤ It can be designated for specified years (e.g., alternate years).
> ➤ It can be designated for all future years, as specified in the declaration.
> ➤ The custodial parent can revoke the release from the noncustodial parent.

If the custodial parent releases their claim to the exemption for the child for any future year, Form 8332 must be attached to each year that the taxpayer can claim the exemption. If the return is filed electronically, Form 8332 should be filed with the tax return. Tax professionals should retain copies of Form 8332 for their records.

Señor 1040 Says: The household of the divorced or separated parent, whom a court order has given legal and physical custody, is the child's principal place of residency. Ask the taxpayer questions about adding a qualifying dependent who is not a newborn baby.

Qualifying Relative

There are four tests that must be met for a person to be a qualifying relative:

1. Not a qualifying child test
2. Member of household or relationship test
3. Gross income test
4. Support test

Unlike a qualifying child, a qualifying relative can be any age, and there is no age test for a qualifying relative. A child is not the taxpayer's qualifying relative if the child is the taxpayer's qualifying child or the qualifying child of anyone else.

Not a Qualifying Child Test

A child who is not the qualifying child of another taxpayer could qualify as the taxpayer's qualifying relative if:

1. The child's parent is not required to file an income tax return, or
2. The child's parent only files a return to get a refund

Relationship Test

The relationship of the child to the taxpayer must be one of the following:

➢ Son or daughter
➢ Stepchild
➢ Eligible foster child
➢ Brother or sister
➢ Half-brother or half-sister
➢ Stepbrother or stepsister
➢ A descendant of any of these (for example, the taxpayer's grandchild)

An adopted child is always the taxpayer's child. The term "adopted child" includes one lawfully placed with the taxpayer for legal adoption.

A foster child is an individual who is placed with the taxpayer by an authorized placement agency or by judgment, decree, or other order of any court of competent jurisdiction.

The Adopted Child Exception

The Adopted Child Exception applies when the taxpayer is a U.S. citizen who has legally adopted a child who is not a U.S. citizen or U.S. national.

The child will meet the citizen test if they lived with the taxpayer, as a member of the household, all year. Children lawfully placed with the taxpayer for legal adoption also meet the requirement.

Exceptions for Stillborn Children and Children Born Alive

A child who was born or who died during the year is considered to have lived with the taxpayer the entire year if they were alive for any part of the year. Similarly, if the child lived with the taxpayer all year except for any required hospital stay following birth, they are considered to have lived with the taxpayer the entire year.

However, the taxpayer cannot claim a stillborn child as a dependent. Nevertheless, they may claim an exemption for a child born alive during the year but died shortly after, even if the child only lived for a moment. This is contingent upon state or local law treating the child as having been born alive.

Proof of a live birth must be provided through an official document such as a birth certificate. Additionally, to be claimed as a dependent, the child must qualify as a qualifying child or relative and meet all other applicable tests.

Kidnapped Children

A kidnapped child can meet the residency test if the following statements are factual:

➢ Law enforcement authorities presumed someone who is not a member of the taxpayer's family or the child's family kidnapped the child
➢ The child lived with the taxpayer more than half of the time before the date of the kidnapping
➢ On the child's return, the child lived with the taxpayer more than half of the portion of the year following the date of the child's return home

This treatment applies until the child returns; however, the last year you can treat the child as such is the earlier of:

➢ The year there is a determination that the child is dead
➢ The year the child would have reached age 18

Age Test

To meet this test, a child must be one of the following:

➢ Under the age of 19 at the end of the year
➢ A student under the age of 24 at the end of the year
➢ Younger than the taxpayer or spouse if filing a joint return
➢ Permanently and totally disabled at any time during the year, regardless of age

Example 1: Mr. and Mrs. Swift have Jonathon, Mr. Swift's brother, living with them. Jonathon, age 23, is a full-time student. Mr. and Mrs. Swift are both 21-years-old. Even though he is a student, Jonathon cannot be their dependent since he is older than both.

Example 2: Mr. and Mrs. Swift have Jonathon, Mr. Swift's brother, living with them. Jonathon, age 23, is a full-time student. Mr. and Mrs. Swift are both 25-years-old. If Jonathon meets all the other tests, he can be their dependent since he is younger than both.

Additional Qualifying Child Rules

A dependent must also meet the following conditions to qualify as a child of a taxpayer:

➢ The child must have lived with the taxpayer for more than half of the year, though some exceptions may apply
➢ The child must not have provided more than half of their support for the year
➢ If the child meets the rules to be a qualifying child of more than one person, the taxpayer must be the person most entitled to claim the child as a qualifying child. This information is explained in full in "Special Rules for a Qualifying Child of More Than One Person" below.

Special Rules for a Qualifying Child of More Than One Person

Sometimes, a child meets the relationship, age, residency, and support tests to be a qualifying child for more than one person. Even if an individual is a qualifying child of several people, only one claimant (a person attempting to claim something) can claim the child as their qualifying child.

If a taxpayer and one or more others have the same qualifying child, it is up to everyone involved to decide who will claim the child as a qualifying child. That individual can claim the following tax benefits based on the qualifying child (provided the taxpayer is eligible for each one):

➢ Child tax credit
➢ HOH filing status (if applicable)
➢ Child and dependent care expenses
➢ Earned income credit

When one parent claims the child, other taxpayers cannot share the tax benefits. If two or more taxpayers attempt to claim the child, the IRS will determine who will be able to claim the child based on the Tie-breaker Rules. (Tie-breaker Rules are discussed later in this chapter).

Qualifying Relative

Meet the following conditions to be considered a qualifying relative:

➢ The person cannot be the taxpayer's qualifying child or anyone else's qualifying child.
➢ The person must be only one of these things:
  o Be related to the taxpayer in one of the ways listed under "Relatives Who Do Not Need to live with the taxpayer"
  o Live with the taxpayer all year as a member of their household. This relationship must not violate local law.
➢ The person's gross income for the year must be less than $4,700. Exceptions apply.
➢ The taxpayer must provide more than half of the person's total support for the year. Exceptions apply.

Citizen and Residency Tests

The taxpayer's child must have lived with the taxpayer for more than half of the year to meet these tests. Additionally, the taxpayer cannot claim a person as a dependent unless the person is a U.S. citizen, U.S. resident, U.S. national, or a resident of Canada or Mexico. However, there are exceptions to these requirements for a group of adopted children, temporary absences, children born or died during the year, kidnapped children, and children of divorced or separated parents.

A Child's Citizenship and Place of Residence

In determining a child's citizenship and residency, you generally look to the citizenship and residence of their parents. If the taxpayer was a U.S. citizen when their child was born, the child might also be a U.S. citizen, even if the other parent was a nonresident alien and the child was born in a foreign country. In such cases, the child meets the citizen test.

A U.S. national is an individual who owes their allegiance to the United States. This category includes American Samoans and Northern Mariana Islanders who became U.S. nationals instead of U.S. citizens.

However, students brought to the United States under a qualified international education exchange program and placed in American homes temporarily are typically not considered U.S. residents and will not meet the residency test. As a result, the taxpayer cannot claim them as dependents. More information on this topic can be found in Publication 526.

For the residency test, the taxpayer's home can be any location where they regularly live, and a traditional home is not necessary. For instance, if a child lived with the taxpayer for more than half of the year in one or more homeless shelters, the child still meets the residency test.

Full-Time Student

Taxpayers may be eligible for additional deductions for qualifying costs related to dependents who are full-time students. A full-time student is defined as a student who enrolls for the number of hours or courses considered full-time attendance by the school.

To qualify as a student for tax purposes, the taxpayer's dependent must meet one of the following criteria during some part of each of any five calendar months of the year (the months do not need to be consecutive):

➢ Enrolled as a full-time student at a school with regular teaching staff, a prescribed course of study, and a regularly enrolled student body
➢ Engaged in full-time, on-farm training courses provided by a qualifying school or by a state, county, or local government agency

A qualifying "school" can include elementary schools, junior or senior high schools, colleges, universities, or technical, trade, or mechanical schools for the purpose of the full-time student deduction. However, on-the-job training courses, correspondence schools, or online schools do not qualify.

Additionally, vocational high school students who participate in "co-op" jobs in private industry as part of their classroom study course and practical training are considered full-time students for the deduction.

Temporary Absence Exceptions

The taxpayer's child lived with them during periods of time when one or both are temporarily absent due to any of the following:

➢ Business
➢ Detention in a juvenile facility

- Education
- Illness
- Vacation
- Military service

One must assume that the child will return home after the temporary absence.

Joint Return Test to be a Qualifying Child

The child cannot file a joint return for the year to meet this test. The exception to this rule is if the taxpayer's child and the spouse are not required to file a tax return but decide to file a joint return solely to claim a refund.

For example:

1. April, aged 17, is married to Joe, aged 18, and they reside with April's parents. Although both April and Joe have some earned income, they are not required to file a return. They file a joint return solely to receive a refund on the taxes withheld. If they meet all other dependency tests, April's parents may be eligible to claim them as dependents.
2. Aaron, aged 18, lived with his parents while his wife, Mackenzie, served in the military. Aaron's parents supported him financially. Mackenzie earned $25,000 during the year, and she and Aaron will file a joint return. Despite being supported by his parents, Aaron cannot be claimed as a dependent on their return because he and Mackenzie filed jointly, and Mackenzie's income exceeds the threshold for dependent eligibility.

Permanently and Totally Disabled

The taxpayer's child is permanently and totally disabled if both apply:

- The child cannot engage in any substantial gainful activity due to a physical or mental condition
- The condition is determined by a physician that the child's disability will last or can be expected to last continuously for at least a year or could lead to death

Support Tests to be a Qualifying Child

Determine the total amount of support that a taxpayer provides for a proposed dependent before the taxpayer can claim a qualifying child or qualifying relative. Full support includes amounts spent to provide food, lodging, clothing, education, medical and dental care, recreation, transportation, and similar necessities. Generally, the amount of an item of support is the amount of the expense incurred by providing the item.

To meet the support test successfully, the child cannot have provided more than half of his or her support for the year. This test is different from the support test to be a qualifying relative. "Keeping Up a Home" will be discussed in the next section. If a child receives a scholarship, and the student is full-time, the scholarship does not count toward determining the child's support.

Foster Care Payments and Expenses

Payments received from a placement agency for the child's support are considered support provided by the agency. If the agency is state- or county-based, provided payments are considered support from the state or county for the child.

Part 2 Review

To obtain the maximum benefit from each part go online now and watch the video.

Part 3 Member of Household or Relationship Test

To meet this test, either of the following must be true:

➢ The person lived with the taxpayer all year as a member of the taxpayer's household
➢ If the person did not live with the taxpayer all year, then they must be related to the taxpayer in one of the ways listed in the next section of the chapter

If the person was the taxpayer's spouse at any time during the year, that person cannot be the taxpayer's qualifying relative.

Relatives Who Do Not Need to Live with the Taxpayer to be Considered a Member of Their Household or Meet the Relationship Test

A person related to the taxpayer in any of the following ways does not have to live with the taxpayer all year as a member of the taxpayer's household to meet this test:

➢ The taxpayer's child, stepchild, eligible foster child, or any descendant thereof (e.g., a grandchild)
➢ The taxpayer's brother, sister, half-brother, half-sister, stepbrother, or stepsister
➢ The taxpayer's father, mother, grandparent, any other direct ancestor, or stepfather or stepmother, but **not** a foster parent
➢ A son or daughter of the taxpayer's brother, sister, half-brother, or half-sister
➢ A brother or sister of the taxpayer's father or mother
➢ The taxpayer's son-in-law, daughter-in-law, father-in-law, mother-in-law, brother-in-law, or sister-in-law

Relationships that are established by marriage do not end by death or divorce.

Adopted Child

An adopted child is always treated as the taxpayer's own child. The term "adopted child" includes a child who was lawfully placed with the taxpayer for legal adoption.

Joint Return

If the taxpayer files a joint return, the qualifying relative does not have to be related to the spouse who provides support. For example, Sal and Julie are married, and Julie's uncle received more than half of his support from Sal. Julie's uncle could be Sal's qualifying relative, even though he does not live with Sal. However, if Sal and Julie file separate tax returns, Julie's uncle is a qualifying relative only if he lives with Sal all year as a member of Sal and Julie's household.

Temporary Absence

A qualifying relative is considered to have lived with the taxpayer as a member of the taxpayer's household during periods of time when either the taxpayer or spouse is absent due to specific circumstances such as:

➢ Business
➢ Education
➢ Illness
➢ Military service
➢ Vacation

Even if the person has been placed in a nursing home to receive medical care for an indefinite period, the absence can be considered temporary.

Death or Birth

A person who died during the year would meet the test if they lived with the taxpayer as a household member until their death. The same is true if a child was born and lived with the taxpayer during the year.

Local Law Violated

A person does not meet the member of the household test if the relationship between the taxpayer and that person violates local law at any time during the year.

Example: Noah's girlfriend Mia lived with him as a member of his household all year. However, Noah's relationship with Mia violates the state's laws where he lives. Therefore, Mia does not meet the household member or the relationship test, and Noah cannot claim her as a dependent.

Cousin

A cousin is a descendant of a brother or a sister of the taxpayer's mother or father. If the cousin lives with the taxpayer all year as a member of the taxpayer's household, the cousin could qualify as a qualifying relative.

Gross Income Test

To meet this test, a person's gross income must be less than $4,700 for 2023 and $5,050 for 2024. "Gross income" is any and all non-tax-exempt revenue that comes in the form of money, property, or services, including gross receipts (sales) from rental property, specific scholarships and fellowship grants, all taxable unemployment compensation, and a partner's share of the gross (not net) income from a partnership. Certain Social Security benefits that are tax-exempt income are not considered gross income. See Publication 501.

Qualifying Relative Support Test

The taxpayer determines whether they have provided more than half of a relative's total support by comparing the taxpayer's contribution to the relative's support with the entire amount of support the relative received from all sources. These amounts include any support the relative provided from their own funds. Additionally, a taxpayer's funds are not considered a means of support unless used exclusively for this purpose. See Worksheet 1 in Publication 501.

Example: Robin is retired and lives with her adult son, Ryan. Ryan provides 100% of the food consumed at home. Robin received $2,400 in Social Security benefits and $300 in interest. Robin paid Ryan $2,000 for lodging and $400 for recreation and has $3,000 in her savings account. Even though Robin received a total of $2,700, she only spent $2,400 for her support. Ryan spent more than $2,400 for his mother's support and received no other help, so Ryan has provided more than half of Robin's support.

The individual total support includes tax-exempt income, savings, and borrowed amounts. These are examples of tax-exempt income: certain Social Security benefits, welfare benefits, nontaxable life insurance proceeds, armed forces family allotments, nontaxable pensions, and tax-exempt interest.

Calculated yearly support when paid.

The taxpayer cannot use support paid in 2022 for 2023, and a taxpayer's support is still calculated on a calendar year even if they use a fiscal-year accounting method.

Disabled Dependent Working at a Sheltered Workshop

For the gross income test, income received for services provided at a sheltered workshop by an individual who is permanently and totally disabled at any time during the year is not considered part of gross income. However, certain conditions must be met: the individual's presence at the workshop must primarily be for the availability of medical care, and the income must solely come from activities at the workshop that are incidental to medical care. A "sheltered workshop" refers to a facility that meets specific criteria: it provides special instruction or training aimed at alleviating the individual's disability, and it is operated by specific tax-exempt organizations or by a governmental entity such as a state, U.S. possession, political subdivision, or the District of Columbia.

Armed Forces Dependency Allotments

If government agencies contributed support to the taxpayer, and the taxpayer has a portion of their income taken out of their wages to support their dependent, they could qualify as a dependent for the taxpayer, as long as they provide more than half of that person's support. If the taxpayer uses part of the income to support individuals the taxpayer has not previously claimed, those individuals may qualify as dependents. See Publication 501.

Example: Doug is in the Armed Forces. He authorizes an allotment to his widowed mother, Sophia, and she uses it to support herself and her brother, Doug's uncle. If the portion that Doug gives her is more than half of their support, Doug can claim Sophia and his uncle as dependents.

Military housing allowances that are tax-exempt are treated as dependency allotments when figuring the support test.

Tax-Exempt Income

Calculating a person's total support includes tax-exempt income, savings, and borrowed amounts used to support the qualifying relative. Though tax-exempt income consists of all the following, we are only emphasizing the first two, which are the most common:

➢ Certain Social Security benefits
➢ Welfare benefits
➢ Nontaxable life insurance proceeds
➢ Armed forces family allotments
➢ Nontaxable pensions
➢ Tax-exempt interest

Example: Olivia is Jose's niece, and she lives with Jose. Olivia has taken out a student loan of $2,500 to pay her college tuition, and Jose has provided $2,000 for Olivia's support. Jose cannot claim an exemption for Olivia because, due to her student loan, he has not provided more than half of her support.

Social Security Benefits for Determining Support

If a husband and wife collectively receive benefits via a single check issued to both spouses, the total amount is typically divided equally between them unless they can demonstrate an alternative arrangement. In such cases, each spouse is considered to have provided support for themselves with an equal share of the benefit. Additionally, if a child receives Social Security benefits and utilizes them for their own support, the support is considered to have been provided by the child.

Support Provided by the State (Welfare, Food Stamps, Housing, and others)

There are numerous benefits provided by the government and certain agencies to individuals that are not considered support provided by the taxpayer. Benefits provided by the state to a disadvantaged person are considered amounts provided by the state, and not as amounts provided by the taxpayer.

Payments received for the support of a foster child from a child placement agency are considered support provided by the agency, not the foster parents. In the same way, payments received for the support of a foster child from a state or county agency are considered support provided by the state or county, not the foster parents.

The taxpayer must pay more than half of the cost of an individual's support to claim them as a qualifying relative. Expenses can include rent, mortgage interest payments, repairs, real estate taxes, utilities, insurance, and food eaten in the home. Costs do not include clothing, education, medical treatment, vacations, life insurance, or the rental value of the house the taxpayer owns.

Suppose the taxpayer receives payments from Temporary Assistance for Needy Families (TANF) or any other public assistance programs to help them pay rent or pay for upkeep on their home. In that case, those payments are money the taxpayer paid. However, the taxpayer must include the payments in the total cost of keeping up the home when determining who paid over half of the cost-of-living expenses.

Example: Tammy spent $700 of her own money and $300 of her TANF support to pay for the upkeep of the home she and her dependents live in for the entire year. The $300 she received from TANF counts as support from Tammy to any of her dependents, and counts toward the total upkeep amount ($1,000) used to determine the head of household filing status and claimant strength.

Use the blank worksheet below to determine if the dependent is a qualifying relative of the taxpayer's household for the following two examples. When interviewing clients and asking support questions, LTP has found that most clients give a monthly amount, so when preparing a return, the tax preparer would need to confirm whether the numbers given were monthly or annually. In the scenarios below, the calculated numbers are annual amounts.

Example 1: Scenario

Mary Vega (age 37) and her daughter, Sierra (age 9), lived with Mary's aunt all year. Using the following information, determine if Mary paid more than half of their support. If the total amount paid by Mary is less than the amount paid by her aunt, Mary and her daughter could be qualifying relatives of her aunt.

Expenses paid by Mary

Electric	$2149
Water	$480
Repairs	$1500
Food eaten in the house	$2600
Telephone	$576

Expenses paid by Mary's aunt

Mortgage interest	$3202
Property taxes	$798
Food eaten in the house	$600
Property insurance	$280

Cost of Keeping a Household

	Amount paid by taxpayer	Total costs
Property taxes	$	$
Mortgage interest expense	$	$
Rent	$	$
Utility charges	$	$
Repairs/maintenance	$	$
Property insurance	$	$
Food consumed on the premises	$	$
Other household expenses	$	$
TOTALS	$	$
Subtract total amount taxpayer paid		$
Amount others paid		$

Example 1: Answers

Cost of Keeping a Household

	Amount paid by taxpayer (Mary)	Total costs
Property taxes	$	$798
Mortgage interest expense	$	$3,202
Rent	$	$
Utility charges	$3,205	$3,205
Repairs/maintenance	$1,500	$1,500
Property insurance	$	$280
Food consumed on the premises	$2,600	$3,200
Other household expenses	$	$
TOTALS	**$7,305**	**$12,185**
Subtract total amount taxpayer paid		**($7,305)**
Amount others paid		**$4,880**

If the total amount paid by Mary is more than the amount paid by her aunt, Mary meets the requirement of paying more than half the cost of keeping up the home.

Mary paid more than 50% of her support; therefore, she would not be claimed as a qualifying relative on her aunt's tax return.

Example 2: Scenario

Steven Renwick (age 27) and his cousin, Sasha Sweet (age 21), lived together all year. Use the following information to determine if Steven can claim Sasha as a dependent. Sasha receives $550 per month from TANF to pay rent.

Expenses paid by Steven (taxpayer)

Electric	$1,200
Food eaten in the home	$6,100
Telephone	$800
Water	$325
Renter's insurance	$1,200

Expenses paid by Sasha

Rent	$6,600
Repairs	$661
Food eaten in the home	$965

Cost of Keeping a Household

	Amount paid by taxpayer	Total costs
Property taxes	$	$
Mortgage interest expense	$	$
Rent	$	$
Utility charges	$	$
Repairs/maintenance	$	$
Property insurance	$	$
Food consumed on the premises	$	$
Other household expenses	$	$
TOTALS	$	$
Subtract total amount taxpayer paid		$
Amount others paid		$

Example 2: Answers

Cost of Keeping a Household

	Amount paid by taxpayer (Steven)	Total costs
Property taxes	$	$
Mortgage interest expense	$	$
Rent	$	$6,600
Utility charges	$2,325	$2,325
Repairs/maintenance	$	$661
Property insurance	$	$
Food consumed on the premises	$6,100	$7,065
Other household expenses	$1,200	$
TOTALS	**$9,625**	**$10,551**
Subtract total amount taxpayer paid		**($9,625)**
Amount others paid		**$926**

Steven did not pay more than 50% of Sasha's support; he cannot claim Sasha as a qualifying relative.

Total Support

When determining the total support for a qualifying relative, certain items are excluded from the calculation. These exclusions include federal, state, and local income taxes paid by the individual from their personal income, Social Security and Medicare taxes paid individually, life insurance premiums, funeral expenses, scholarships received by the student's relative or child, and Survivors' and Dependents' Educational Assistance payments used for the support of the child.

However, total support does encompass essential expenses such as food, lodging, clothing, education, medical and dental care, recreation, transportation, and other daily provisions.

Deceased Taxpayers

The general filing requirements that apply to other taxpayers also apply when preparing a tax return for a decedent. The word "Deceased," followed by the decedent's name and the date of death, should be written at the top of the return. Only income that the decedent actually or constructively received before their death should be reported, along with expenses paid by the decedent before their death. If the decedent was the taxpayer's dependent prior to death, the total exemption amount should be claimed.

If a personal representative (such as an executor, administrator, or other individual overseeing the decedent's property) is appointed, that person should sign the return. If the surviving spouse acts as the personal representative, "filed as surviving spouse" should be written in the signature location. If someone other than the spouse claims a refund for the decedent, the representative should file Form 1310, Statement of Person Claiming Refund Due to a Deceased Taxpayer, along with the return. In any case, a final return for the decedent must be filed. Sec. 7703(b)(1) & (b)(2)

Allowances for a Surviving Spouse

If the taxpayer's spouse died during the current tax year and the taxpayer does not remarry in the year of death, the surviving spouse may file a joint return.

Inherited Property

Property the taxpayer received as a gift, bequest, or inheritance is not included as income and is not taxable. However, if the inherited property produces income such as interest or rent, that income is taxable. Sec 1014.

Income in Respect of the Decedent

Income in respect of the decedent includes all gross income that the decedent had a right to receive and was not includable in the decedent's final return. If the estate acquires the right to receive revenue from the decedent, the income is reported in the decedent's estate's return (Form 1041) by tax year received rather than in the decedent's final return. If payment is not reported on Form 1041, this becomes the responsibility of the person to whom the estate properly distributes the income. However, if someone acquires the direct right to the income without going through the estate, then that person will be required to report the income.

Deductions in Respect of the Decedent

Decedent deductions can include items such as business expenses, interest, taxes, or income-producing expenses for which the decedent was liable but that were not deductible on the decedent's final tax return. The decedent's estate can pay and deduct these items in the same year. If the estate is not liable for the expenses, the individual who acquired the decedent's property due to death is subject to tax liability. Life insurance received is generally not a taxable event.

Part 3 Review

To obtain the maximum benefit from each part go online now and watch the video.

Part 4 Deductions

There are two types of deductions available to taxpayers: standard deductions and itemized deductions. These deductions are subtracted from the taxpayer's adjusted gross income to reduce their tax liability. Taxpayers must choose the deduction method that results in the lowest taxable liability for them.

Itemized deductions encompass a variety of personal expenses clearly designated as deductions to help taxpayers lower their tax liability. These may include expenses such as medical bills, charitable contributions, and certain deductible taxes. Itemizing deductions requires taxpayers to keep records of their actual personal expenses throughout the tax year.

On the other hand, the standard deduction is a predetermined dollar amount based on the taxpayer's filing status. Unlike itemized deductions, the standard deduction does not require taxpayers to retain receipts for actual personal expenses.

However, the standard deduction may not be an option for every taxpayer. In cases where the standard deduction amount is zero or if specific circumstances apply, taxpayers may be required to itemize deductions. Such circumstances include:

➢ Being married and filing a separate return while the spouse itemizes deductions.
➢ Filing a tax return for a short tax year due to a change in the annual accounting period.
➢ Being a nonresident or dual-status alien during the tax year. A dual-status alien is both a nonresident and a resident alien during the year, and if the nonresident alien is married to a U.S. citizen or resident alien at the end of the year, they can choose to be treated as a U.S. resident.

Further details on itemized deductions are available in Publication 519.

Standard Deductions

The Standard deduction amount varies depending on the taxpayer's filing status. The Standard deduction is a set dollar amount that reduces taxable income. Other factors used to determine the amount of the allowable standard deduction are:

➢ Taxpayer is age 65 or older
➢ Taxpayer is blind

Standard Deduction for Most People

These deduction amounts apply to most people and are for the current year's filing status.*

Filing Status and Standard Deduction	Tax Year 2022	Tax Year 2023	Tax Year 2024
Single	$12,950	$13,850	$14,600
Married Filing Jointly and Qualifying Surviving Spouse	$25,900	$27,700	$29,200
Married Filing Separately	$12,950	$13,850	$14,600
Head of Household	$19,400	$20,800	$21,900

*Do not use this chart if:

> ➢ The taxpayer was born before January 2, 1959
> ➢ The taxpayer is blind
> ➢ Someone else can claim the taxpayer or taxpayer's spouse as a dependent if filing status is MFJ

Example 1: Lilly is filing for tax year 2023. She is 26 years old, never married, and does not have children or other dependents. Lilly's filing status will be Single. As shown in the above chart, her standard deduction will be $13,850.

Example 2: Using example 1 with these changes: Lilly is married and filing a joint return. Lilly and her spouse will use the standard deduction of $27,700.

Example 3: Using example 2 with these changes: Lilly and her husband had a son born during the tax year. Lilly and her husband have decided to file separate tax returns. Since they are still married and living together, they must use the MFS filing status. As per the chart, Lilly's standard deduction will be $13,850.

Example 4: Using example 2 with these changes: Lilly and her husband divorced during the tax year. Lilly has sole custody of her son and will file using the Head of Household filing status. Her standard deduction is $20,800.

Standard Deduction for Age 65 and Older or Blind

A higher standard deduction is allowed for taxpayers aged 65 or older by the end of the tax year. A taxpayer is age 65 on their 65th birthday and the date immediately beforehand.

Example: Frank turned 65 on January 1, 2024, so he is considered 65 December 31, 2023, the day before his birthday. Frank is considered 65 for the entire tax year. Frank qualifies for the standard deduction amount for the 65 or older taxpayer.

A higher standard deduction is also allowed for taxpayers who are considered blind on the last day of the year. If the taxpayer is partially blind, they must get an official statement from a licensed eye physician (either an optometrist or an ophthalmologist). The note should state that the taxpayer's field of vision is not more than twenty degrees or that the taxpayer cannot see better than 20/200 in their best eye, even with glasses or contact lenses.

If the examining physician determines that the eye condition will never improve beyond its limits, the physician must include this fact in their statement. This would apply if the taxpayer could correct their vision beyond these limits solely using contact lenses that can only be worn briefly, due to pain, infection, or ulcers. In that case, the taxpayer can still take the higher standard deduction for which they otherwise qualify. Keep the doctor's statement with the rest of the taxpayer's records.

The higher standard deduction is also allowed for the spouse of a taxpayer who is age 65 or older or blind under the following circumstances:

➢ The taxpayer and their spouse file a joint tax return
➢ The taxpayer filed a separate return, the spouse had no gross income, and another taxpayer could not claim an exemption for the spouse

If the taxpayer is a dependent on another tax return and was born before January 2, 1958, or is blind, multiply the amount of the additional standard deduction by $1,700 if that taxpayer is Single. If taxpayers are married, multiply the amount of the other standard deduction by $1,350.

2023 Standard Deduction Worksheet for People Born Before January 2, 1959, or Blind

Check the correct number of boxes below, then proceed to the chart.

1. Taxpayer — Born before January 2, 1959 ☐ Blind ☐
2. Spouse, if claiming exemption — Born before January 2, 1959 ☐ Blind ☐

Total number of boxes checked _____

If filing status is:	And at the end of 2023 you were….	Standard Deduction is:
Single	1	$15,700
	2	$17,550
Married Filing Jointly	1	$29,200
	2	$30,700
	3	$32,200
	4	$33,700
Married Filing Separately	1	$14,350
	2	$15,750
	3	$17,150
	4	$18,550
Qualifying Surviving Spouse	1	$29,200
	2	$30,700
Head of Household	1	$22,650
	2	$24,500

Señor 1040 Says: If the taxpayer is MFS and their spouse itemizes or is a dual-status alien, the taxpayer **cannot** take the standard deduction. The taxpayer *must* itemize their deductions.

Standard Deduction for Dependents

The standard deduction amount is limited if the taxpayer is a dependent on another return. The dependent's standard deduction amount will either be a) $1,250; or b) the taxpayer's earned income amount for the year, plus $400 if it does not exceed the regular standard deduction, whichever is greater. If the taxpayer is 65 or older or blind, they may still be eligible for a higher standard deduction even if claimed as a dependent.

Earned income consists of salaries, wages, tips, professional fees, and all other monetary amounts received for any work the taxpayer performed. Include scholarships or fellowship grants in the gross income to calculate the standard deduction correctly. For more information on what qualifies as a scholarship or fellowship grant. See Publication 970.

2023 Standard Deduction Worksheet for Dependents

This worksheet is used only if someone else can claim the taxpayer or spouse as a dependent if filing MFJ.

1. Enter the taxpayer's earned income (defined below). If none, enter a zero.	1. $
2. Additional amount	2. $400
3. Add lines 1 and 2	3. $
4. Minimum standard deduction	4. $1,250
5. Enter the larger of line 3 or line 4	5. $

6. Enter the amount shown below for taxpayer's filing status.
    Single or MFS: $12,950
    MFJ: $25,900
    Head of Household: $19,400
	6. $

7. Standard deduction a. Enter the smaller of line 5 or line 6. If born after January 1, 1959, and not blind, stop here. This is the standard deduction. Otherwise, go to line 7b.	7a. $
b. If born before January 2, 1958, or blind, multiply $1,750 ($1,400 if married) by the number in.	7b. $
c. Add lines 7a and 7b. Enter the total here and on Form 1040 or Form 1040-SR, line 12a.	7c. $

Determining the Correct Federal Filing Status

The following scenarios are based on the information you have been studying so far. Determine the best answer for each question.

1. James, age 19, works full time, and his W-2 shows $17,000 in box 1. He claims that his 14-year-old sister lived with him all year long. He tells you that his mother and brother have lived in the same

household all year long. His mother's income is $32,000. James wants to claim his sister as his dependent. Which scenario best describes James' filing status based on the information provided?

    a.   James will file Single and claim his sister as a dependent
    b.   James will file Single with no dependents
    c.   James will file Head of Household and claim his sister as a dependent
    d.   James does not have to file a tax return because his mother will claim him as a dependent

Feedback: James cannot claim his sister since his mother lives in the same home, and she has the higher income. James is not a dependent on his mother's return since his income is $17,000. James will file Single with no dependents.

2. Linda, age 56, works full-time and her W-2 shows $27,000 in box 1. Linda tells you that her 22-year-old daughter, Julie, was a full-time student until she graduated in June. Julie lived with her until November when Julie married Todd. Linda wants to claim Julie as her dependent. Linda tells you that Julie and Todd filed a joint return to receive their federal withholding, and their total income was less than $6,000. Which scenario best describes Linda's filing status based on the information provided?

    a.   Linda will file Head of Household without Julie as her dependent
    b.   Linda will file Head of Household and claim Julie as her dependent
    c.   Linda will file Single with no dependents
    d.   Linda will file Single with Julie as her dependent

Feedback: Linda can claim Julie as her dependent since Julie meets the residency requirements, the relationship requirements, and the joint return test. Therefore, Linda's filing status would be Head of Household, and Linda will claim Julie as her dependent.

3. Javier, age 45, and Janice, age 42, support Javier's uncle, Chris, who does not live with them. Javier gives Chris $500 per month for support. Which of the following questions must you ask Javier to determine if Chris is their dependent?

    1.   How much and what kind of income did Chris receive?
    2.   Can any other taxpayer claim Chris as a dependent?
    3.   Do you have documentation that shows your support?
    4.   Does Chris have any dependents?

    a.   All the questions must be asked
    b.   3 and 4
    c.   1 and 2
    d.   1, 2, and 3

Feedback: To make sure the taxpayer can claim a relative as a dependent, the tax professional must ask specific questions to determine if the relative is a Qualifying Relative. All the questions must be asked. The following Qualifying Relative Checklist can help you determine who meets the member of the household test:

➢ A child, stepchild, foster child, or a descendant of any of them (for example, your grandchild) (A legally adopted child is considered your child)
➢ A brother, sister, half-brother, half-sister, stepbrother, or stepsister
➢ A father, mother, grandparent, or other direct ancestors, but not foster parent
➢ A stepfather or stepmother

➢ A son or daughter of your brother or sister
➢ A son or daughter of your half-brother or half-sister
➢ A brother or sister of your father or mother
➢ A son-in-law, daughter-in-law, father-in-law, mother-in-law, brother-in-law, or sister-in-law

Any of these relationships that were established by marriage aren't ended by death or divorce.

4. Jonathan, age 37, wants to claim his mother as a dependent on his tax return. His mother receives Social Security benefits of $22,000. Jonathan's W-2 box 1 shows $22,000. Based on the information provided, which scenario best describes Jonathan's filing status?

 a. Jonathan will file Single and claim his mother as a dependent
 b. Jonathan will file Single with no dependents
 c. Jonathan will file Head of Household and claim his mother as a dependent
 d. Jonathan does not have to file a tax return because his mother will claim him as a dependent

Feedback: Jonathan cannot claim his mother since he did not provide more than 50% of her support due to his mother's Social Security benefits. Jonathan will file Single with no dependents.

5. Mia, age 28, has a son Bobby, age 6. Mia and Bobby lived the entire year with Mia's mother. Mia has a full-time job and is a full-time student. Box 1 of her W-2 shows $19,000. Mia's mother, Billie, wants to claim Bobby as her dependent. Billie's W-2 has $12,000 in box 1. Mia provides all the support for Bobby. Which scenario best describes Mia's filing status based on the information provided?

 a. Mia will file Single with no dependent
 b. Billie will file Head of Household and claim Bobby
 c. Mia will file Head of Household and claim Bobby as her dependent
 d. Billie will file Head of Household and claim Mia and Bobby as her dependents, since they live with her

Feedback: Billie is unable to claim either Mia or Bobby since Mia makes more than Billie does. Mia can file Head of Household since she provides 100% of Bobby's support. Billie is not able to claim Mia or Bobby since she made less income than Mia. Mia will file Head of Household and claim Bobby as her dependent.

6. Esperanza, age 19, is a full-time student and has a part-time job. Esperanza and her daughter Elissa, age 3, live with Esperanza's parents. Her W-2 box 1 shows $4,000 in income. Esperanza's parents' combined income is $75,000. Both Esperanza and Elissa are on her parents' medical insurance. Which scenario best describes Esperanza's filing status based on the information provided?
 a. Esperanza will file Single with no dependent
 b. Esperanza will file Single, as a dependent, on another return, with no dependent
 c. Esperanza will file Head of Household and claim Elissa as a dependent
 d. Esperanza will file Single and claim Elissa as a dependent

Feedback: Esperanza and Elissa are both dependents on Esperanza's parents' tax return because her parents provided the majority of support for both Esperanza and her daughter. Because Esperanza only earned $4,000 on her W-2, which is below the dependent exemption threshold, she's filing a tax return to receive her federal tax withholding back (if applicable). Esperanza will file Single, as a dependent on another return, with no dependent.

7. Colton and Brittney are legally married. They have a separation agreement and have been living apart since November 2022. They filed a joint return for 2022. Brittney's earned income is $46,000 and her

daughter Mika lives with her 100% of the time. Colton's earned income is $31,000. Colton wants to claim Mika as his dependent for the tax year 2023. Based on the information provided, which scenario best describes what must happen for Colton to be able to claim Mika?

    a. Colton can file Head of Household and claim Mika since she is his daughter
    b. Brittney must sign Form 8332 to allow Colton to claim Mika
    c. Mika can choose which parent she wants to claim her
    d. Brittney will file Head of Household and claim Mika since her income is higher than Colton's, and Mika has lived with her 100% of the time

Feedback: Colton will not be able to claim Mika unless Brittney signs Form 8332. Mika has lived with Brittney 100% of the time, and Brittney's earned income is more than Colton's. Tie-breaker rules could also help determine filing status and who can claim Mika. Colton must have Brittney sign Form 8332 to be able to claim Mika. Apply the following rules to determine which person can claim the child as a qualifying child:

➢ If the parents file jointly, both will claim the child as a qualifying child
➢ If only one taxpayer is the child's parent, the child is the qualifying child of the parent
➢ If the parents do not file a joint return, the IRS will treat the child as a qualifying child of the parent whom the child lived with for the longest time during the year. Children who live with each parent an equal amount of time are qualifying children for both parents. The IRS then treats them as qualifying children of the parent with the highest AGI for the year.
➢ If no parent can claim the child as a qualifying child, the child is the qualifying child of the person with the highest AGI for the year
➢ If a parent can claim the child as a qualifying child and no parent claims the child, the child is the qualifying child of the person with the highest AGI for the year

8. Pedro and Celeste are legally married and have two children. Celeste does not want to pay Pedro's back taxes and self-employment tax. Pedro has his own business. Celeste owned the house before their marriage (they do not live in a community property state). Celeste's W-2 box 1 shows $150,000. Pedro's gross income from his Schedule C is $15,000. Which scenario best describes Pedro and Celeste's filing status based on the information provided?

    a. Pedro should file as Head of Household with the two children, and Celeste should file Single
    b. Celeste should file as Head of Household with the two children, and Pedro should file Single
    c. Pedro and Celeste should file Married Filing Separately and then decide who claims the children and the deductions
    d. Pedro and Celeste don't have to file a tax return since they can't decide how to file

Feedback: A married taxpayer may choose MFS if any of the following applies:

➢ If they are married, living together, or apart
➢ If they want to be responsible for their tax liability
➢ If it results in less tax than they would owe on a joint return; however, let taxpayers know that MFS filing status has severe limitations in deductions, adjustments, and credits

Pedro and Celeste should file Married Filing Separately and then decide who claims the children and the deductions.

9. Peter, age 21, and his son Paul lived with Peter's parents the entire year. Peter's W-2 box 1 shows $4,050. Peter is a full-time student. Peter would like to file on his own and claim his son, Paul. Peter and his son are both on his parents' medical insurance. His parents, Mateo and Melissa, have a combined income of $175,000. Which scenario best describes Peter's filing status based on the information provided?

    a. Peter will file Single and be a dependent on his parents' return
    b. Peter will file Single and be a dependent on another return and claim Paul as a dependent
    c. Mateo and Melissa will file Married Filing Jointly and claim Peter and Paul as dependents
    d. Peter will file Single on his return and declare he is a dependent on another return, and Mateo and Melissa will file Married Filing Joint and claim Peter and Paul as their dependents

Feedback: The taxpayer should pay more than half of the cost of keeping up a home for the year, but Peter has not provided more than 50% for his or Paul's support, which means he cannot claim Paul as his dependent. Peter will file Single on his return and declare he is a dependent on another return, and Mateo and Melissa will file Married Filing Jointly and claim Peter and Paul as their dependents.

10. Benjamin and Charlotte are legally married (Charlotte has an ITIN), and they have three children with SSNs. Charlotte is a stay-at-home mom, and Benjamin's W-2 box 1 shows $29,000. Benjamin and his family live with his brother Charles. Which scenario best describes Benjamin and Charlotte's filing status based on the information provided?

    a. Benjamin and Charlotte will file Married Filing Jointly and claim all three children as dependents
    b. Benjamin will file as Head of Household and claim Charlotte and his three children as dependents
    c. Benjamin will file single and let Charles claim the others as dependent
    d. Charles will claim Benjamin and his family as dependents since they all live with him

Feedback: Even though Charlotte has an ITIN, this does not eliminate the need to include her on the tax return. Benjamin and Charlotte are legally married, and Benjamin and Charlotte are not dependents on Charles' tax return just because the family lives there. Similarly, since neither Benjamin and Charlotte nor Charles provide more than 50% of support for each other, neither would claim the other as a dependent. Benjamin and Charlotte will file Married Filing Jointly and claim all their children as dependents.

Part 4 Review

To obtain the maximum benefit from each part go online now and watch the video.

Takeaways

The tax professional must understand the available filing statuses and ask the taxpayer questions to determine the correct filing status for their situation. Some clients might have preconceived ideas about the status they should use, or they might tell the tax professional their filing status is Head of Household because a friend told them so. However, the tax preparer's responsibility is to perform a thorough interview and complete the paid tax preparer's Due Diligence Form 8867. A taxpayer's filing status determines the taxpayer's tax liability and many tax credits, so make sure to claim the correct filing status.

Tax Topic 303 has a checklist of the most common errors on a tax return. "What is My Filing Status?" is on the list. The IRS has created an interactive tax assistant (ITA) to help answer questions that will help identify the appropriate filing status for the taxpayer. For example, "What was your marital status on the last day of the year?" is the first question in the ITA. The paid preparer is obligated to be aware of the consequences of preparing tax returns incorrectly. Make sure you do your due diligence and get it right.

It is important to understand how to determine a qualifying child or a qualifying relative to prepare an accurate tax return. Knowledge of tax law is imperative; the tax professional cannot rely on software alone to prepare an accurate tax return. Ensure the individual the taxpayer wants to claim qualifies as the taxpayer's dependent by understanding the rules for a qualifying child and a qualifying relative. Knowledge of the taxpayer's situation is crucial in preparing correct tax returns. If the IRS audits a tax preparer, your excuse better not be that you did not ask the taxpayer enough questions.

TEST YOUR KNOWLEDGE!
Go online to take a practice quiz.

Chapter 4: Income

Introduction

In this chapter, you'll learn about income and how it's reported on Form 1040, focusing on lines 1 through 7, along with Part I of Schedule 1, which covers Additional Income and Adjustments to Income. It also sheds light on various types of taxable and nontaxable income. A tax professional must discern between the many categories of taxable income, tax-exempt income, and other earnings listed on Schedule 1, line 10, and understand how to calculate the taxable income percentage for Social Security benefits.

The IRS has the authority to tax all income from any source, encompassing compensation for services, profits from property sales, interest and dividends, rental and royalty income, pensions and annuities, gambling winnings, and even income from illegal activities. Collectively, an individual's earnings are termed "worldwide income." However, not all monetary gains or property acquisitions are subject to taxation.

Typically, interest and dividends become taxable income when the interest is credited to the taxpayer's account, and they have the ability to withdraw the funds. This chapter also studies exceptions to the taxation of interest and dividends, including instances where they are not considered taxable income.

Objectives

At the end of this chapter, the student will know how to:

➢ Explain "worldwide income"
➢ Understand how and where to report wages and other compensation
➢ Differentiate earned vs. unearned income
➢ Identify where income is reported
➢ Identify the different types of interest income
➢ Recognize which tax forms report interest income
➢ Understand the different types of savings bonds
➢ Explain where to report dividend income
➢ Understand when Schedule B is required to be filed with the tax return
➢ Indicate how to report interest and dividend income on the tax return

Resources

Form W-2 and Instructions	Schedule B and Instructions
Form W-4 and Instructions	Schedule D and Instructions
Form 1040 and Instructions	Publication 550
Form 1099-B and Instructions	Publication 554
Form 1099-DIV and Instructions	Publication 575
Form 1099-INT and Instructions	Publication 590 A & B
Form 1099-G and Instructions	Publication 915
Form 1099-OID and Instructions	Tax Topics 401, 403, 404, 410, 417, 418, 420,
Form 1099-R and Instructions	423, 553, 557, 558, 856, 903
Form SSA-1099 and Instructions	

Part 1 Form W-4 and Form W-2

The tax professional needs to understand the importance of Form W-4, *Employee's Withholding Certificate*. Form W-4 is the IRS document that an employee completes for their employer to determine how much should be withheld from the employee's paycheck for federal income taxes and sent to the IRS. Accurately completing the W-4 will avoid overpaying taxes or having a balance due come tax time. Many taxpayers do not understand the form and want to have as much income as possible on their paycheck. Improperly calculating the information on the W-4 can result in problems for the taxpayer.

The IRS has an online tax withholding estimator to help taxpayers determine whether they are having enough income withheld. The IRS wants the taxpayer to "pay as you go," paying tax over time rather than paying a large amount at the end of the year. This is to ensure the taxpayer pays enough withholding and is not left with a large liability when they file their taxes. To prepare to use the estimator online, gather the following documents.

1. Most recent paycheck(s), from both the taxpayer and spouse if filing jointly.
2. Income from other sources, if applicable.
3. The taxpayer's most recent tax return.

The estimator is only as accurate as the information that is entered. Below is the link to the estimator. https://www.irs.gov/individuals/tax-withholding-estimator.

Tax Withholding

When an employee starts a new job, they typically fill out a Form W-4. This form provides information to the employer about the employee's tax filing status, number of dependents, and any additional withholding allowances they may be eligible for. Based on this information, the employer calculates the amount of federal, state, and local income tax to withhold from the employee's paycheck.

The withheld taxes are then sent by the employer to the appropriate tax authorities on a regular basis, typically either monthly or quarterly.

Tax withholding helps ensure that individuals pay their taxes in a timely manner and reduces the risk of underpayment penalties. It also simplifies the tax filing process for employees, as they may only need to reconcile any differences between the taxes withheld and their actual tax liability when they file their tax returns at the end of the year.

Withholding Exemption

Exemption from withholding refers to the situation where a taxpayer is not subject to having income tax deducted from their paycheck by their employer. This can occur if the taxpayer had no tax liability in the previous year and expects to have none in the current year. To claim exemption from withholding, the taxpayer can write "Exempt" on Form W-4 in the space provided below Step 4(c), then complete Steps 1(a), 1(b), and 5. No other steps need to be taken.

However, it's important to note that exemption from withholding only applies to income tax and not to Social Security or Medicare tax. If a taxpayer meets certain criteria, they may be eligible to claim exemption for the current tax year:

➤ The taxpayer had the right to a refund of all federal income tax withheld because they had no tax liability the previous year.

> ➤ The taxpayer expects a refund of all federal income tax withheld because they expect to have no tax liability for the current year.

The employee needs to inform their employer of changes in circumstances that may affect withholding status. If a taxpayer initially claims exemption but later finds they must pay income tax, they must file a new Form W-4. If the taxpayer claims exemption in one year but expects to owe income tax the following year, they should file a new Form W-4 as soon as possible.

If a taxpayer wishes to change their W-4 during the year, the employer must put the new Form W-4 into effect no later than the start of the first payroll period ending on or after the 30th day after the taxpayer submits the new form. However, if the change is for the next year, it will not take effect until then.

Señor 1040 Says: Students are not automatically exempt from tax withholding.

Household Workers Withholding

If a taxpayer paid an employee $2,700 or more in cash wages for 2024, the taxpayer must report and pay Social Security and Medicare taxes on all the wages. A household worker is an employee who performs household work in a private home, local college club, or local fraternity or sorority chapter. Tax is withheld only if the taxpayer has asked the employer to do so. If the taxpayer does not have enough tax withheld, the individual must make estimated payments. To be able to file the appropriate forms to have the taxes withheld, the employer of the household worker must obtain an employer identification number by submitting an SS-4 EIN Application to the IRS. The taxpayer must employ an individual that can legally work in the United States. The employee needs to complete Form I-9, and the employer needs to verify the information and give the employee a W-2.

A taxpayer who is an employee should receive a Form W-2 from their employer(s) that shows the wages the taxpayer earned in exchange for services performed. A W-2 is the tax form generated by employers that details the employees' earnings and government withholdings for a given tax year. A tax year's W-2 should be distributed to the employees by the end of the first month after the tax year ends; for example, W-2s for tax year 2023 should have been delivered by January 31, 2024. A taxpayer will receive a W-2 from each employer they are employed by and should give each W-2 they have received to the individual preparing the tax return. Most taxpayers will only receive one W-2, although it is possible to receive more than one if a taxpayer has worked multiple jobs during a given tax year. If employees notice an error on their Form W-2, they should notify their employer and request a corrected Form W-2 before filing their taxes.

Tax professionals use the information provided on a W-2 to determine the client's earned income for the year. The total amount of wages is reported on Form 1040, line 1. Wages include salaries, vacation allowances, bonuses, commissions, and fringe benefits. Compensation includes everything received in payment for personal services.

How to Read the W-2

Below is the W-2 that an employee receives from their employer. It is important for the tax professional to know what is reported on each line of the W-2 so that they will know how to use the information provided in the form when preparing the employee's tax return.

22222	a Employee's social security number			
	OMB No. 1545-0008			
b Employer identification number (EIN)		1 Wages, tips, other compensation	2 Federal income tax withheld	
c Employer's name, address, and ZIP code		3 Social security wages	4 Social security tax withheld	
		5 Medicare wages and tips	6 Medicare tax withheld	
		7 Social security tips	8 Allocated tips	
d Control number		9	10 Dependent care benefits	
e Employee's first name and initial Last name Suff.		11 Nonqualified plans	12a	
		13 Statutory employee Retirement plan Third-party sick pay	12b	
		14 Other	12c	
			12d	
f Employee's address and ZIP code				
15 State Employer's state ID number	16 State wages, tips, etc.	17 State income tax	18 Local wages, tips, etc.	19 Local income tax	20 Locality name

Form **W-2** Wage and Tax Statement **2023** Department of the Treasury—Internal Revenue Service
Copy 1—For State, City, or Local Tax Department

Copy of Form W-2

The Lettered Boxes of Form W-2

Box a: Employee's Social Security Number

The Social Security number on the W-2 should match the number shown on the employee's Social Security card. If the Social Security number is incorrect, the employee should notify the employer and request a corrected Form W-2.

> Note: ITINs are not replacements for Social Security numbers. ITINs are only available to resident and nonresident aliens ineligible for U.S. employment that need identification for tax purposes. Under normal circumstances, ITIN holders cannot receive a W-2 because they lack an SSN, but it is possible for an ITIN holder to receive a W-2 using an unlawful SSN. When entering the W-2 information into software for these clients, make sure that the SSN does not auto-populate into box a, because this is where the ITIN number needs to go.

Box b: Employer Identification Number (EIN)

This box shows the employer identification number (EIN) assigned to the employer by the IRS. EINs consist of two digits and a dash followed by seven more digits, as seen in this example: 00-0000000.

Box c: Employer's Name, Address, and ZIP Code

This entry should be the same as the information shown on the employer's Form 941, 941-SS, 943, 944, CT-1 or Form 1040, Schedule H.

Box d: Control Number

Though it is often left blank, this box can be used by employers to distinguish between individual W-2s whenever needed. For example, if an employer has multiple employees with the same first and last names, they can distinguish between them using control numbers.

Boxes e and f: Employee's Name and Address

The taxpayer's name should match the name shown on the Social Security card (first, middle, and last). The taxpayer's name may be different if the taxpayer has recently married, divorced, or had a name change of any kind. The taxpayer's address should include the number, street, apartment and suite number, or a P.O. Box number if mail is not delivered to a physical address.

The Numbered Boxes of Form W-2

Box 1: Wages, Tips, and Other Compensation

Shows the total taxable wages, tips, and other compensation paid to the employee during the year before any payroll deductions or tax withholdings were subtracted.
The following items are included in the total amount provided in box 1:

- ➢ Total wages and bonuses (including signing bonuses, prizes, and awards) paid to employees during the year
- ➢ Total noncash payments, including certain fringe benefits
- ➢ Total tips reported by the employee to the employer; allocated tips are not reported in this box
- ➢ Certain employee business expense reimbursements
- ➢ An S corporation's cost of accident and health insurance premiums for a shareholder with 2% or more of the company
- ➢ Certain taxable benefits from a section 125 cafeteria plan, if the employee chooses cash
- ➢ Employee contributions to an Archer MSA
- ➢ Contributions to an Archer MSA from an employer if included in the employee's income
- ➢ Employer contributions for qualified long-term care services to the extent that such coverage is provided through flexible spending plans or similar arrangements
- ➢ The taxable portion of the cost of group-term insurance of more than $50,000
- ➢ Unless excludable under an education assistance program, payments for non-job-related education expenses or for payments under a nonaccountable plan
- ➢ The amount included as wages because the employer paid the employee's share of Social Security and Medicare taxes
- ➢ Designated Roth contributions made under a section 401(k) plan, a section 403(b) salary reduction agreement, or a governmental section 457(b) plan
- ➢ Distributions to an employee or former employee from a nonqualified deferred compensation plan (NQDC) or a nongovernmental section 457(b) plan
- ➢ Amounts included as income under an NQDC (nonqualified deferred compensation) plan because of section 409A
- ➢ Amounts includable in income under section 457(f) because the amounts are no longer subject to a substantial risk of forfeiture
- ➢ Payments to statutory employees who are subject to Social Security and Medicare taxes
- ➢ Cost of current insurance protection under a compensatory split-dollar life insurance arrangement
- ➢ Employee contributions to a health savings account (HSA)

- Employer's contributions to an HSA if included in the employee's income
- Nonqualified moving expenses and expense reimbursement
- Payments made to former employees while on active duty in the armed forces or other uniformed services
- All other compensation, including certain scholarships and fellowship grants; other compensation includes taxable amounts paid to the employee from which federal income tax was not withheld

An employer may use an additional Form W-2 to show an employee's compensation apart from their earned wages based on their bookkeeping practices.

Box 2 through Box 11

Box 2: Federal Income Tax Withheld

Shows the total federal income tax withheld from the employee's wages for the year. Parachute payments include compensation for certain covered employees, and are taxed at 20%, including the 20% excise tax withheld on excess parachute payments.

If the taxpayer claims itemized deductions, and/or extra withholding deducted from each pay period, this could influence the withholding amount.

Box 3: Social Security Wages

Shows the total amount of non-tip wages used to figure out the taxpayer's Social Security pay-in and pay-out amounts. The total of boxes 3 and 7 cannot exceed the Social Security yearly pay-in limit of $168,600.00.

Box 4: Social Security Tax Withheld

Shows the total employee Social Security tax withholding, which is 6.2% of total compensation to the Social Security wage limit of $160,200.00 for 2023. The Social Security Administration sets the Social Security wage limit every year and can also change the taxed percentage, though they rarely do. For 2024, the Social Security wage limit of $167,700.00.

Box 5: Medicare Wages and Tips

The wages and tips subject to Medicare tax are determined using the same method as the Social Security tax in boxes 3 and 7 except that there is no wage base limit for Medicare tax.

Box 6: Medicare Tax Withheld

This box shows the total employee Medicare tax withheld. The tax withholding percentage is 1.45%. Medicare tax withholdings are determined from the employee's total income amount in box 1.

Box 7: Social Security Tips

This box shows the tips the employee reported to the employer, which are not included in box 3. The combined amount of boxes 3 and 7 is used to figure Social Security tax and should not exceed the maximum yearly Social Security wage base limit.

Box 8: Allocated Tips

Shows allocated tips paid to the employee. Allocated tips will be discussed later in this chapter. The amount in box 8 is not included in the amounts in boxes 1, 3, 5, or 7.

Box 10: Dependent Care Benefits

Shows the total amount of dependent-care benefits paid by the employer to the employee under a dependent-care assistance program (Section 129). This amount could also include the fair market value (FMV) of employer-provided or employer-sponsored day-care facilities and the amounts paid or incurred in a section 125 cafeteria plan. All dependent care benefit amounts paid or earned are reported in this box, regardless of employee forfeitures, including those exceeding the $5,000 exclusion.

Box 11: Nonqualified Plans

The purpose of box 11 is for the SSA to determine if any part of the amount reported in boxes 1, 3, or 5 was earned in a prior year. The SSA uses this information to verify that it has properly applied the Social Security earnings test and paid the correct amount of benefits. Box 11 shows a distribution to an employee from a nonqualified plan or a nongovernmental section 457 plan, and this amount is also reported in box 1.

Box 12: Codes

Box 12 consists of "sub-boxes" 12a, 12b, 12c, and 12d

Though sometimes left completely blank, these boxes are used as needed when certain, infrequent items are reported to the taxpayer by their employer for tax purposes. Each "sub-box" consists of a small space followed by a line and a larger space. If used, the employer will place a letter in the small place that designates one of the codes explained below, with the code's corresponding amount placed in the larger space. The selection of which "sub-box" a code is placed in and what order the codes are shown are arbitrary. No more than four codes can be entered in box 12. Box 12 has 4 sub-boxes that are used to report the income listed below. If the employer only needs to report one item, enter it in box a. Only four items are reported on one W-2; if more than four items are reported, then an additional W-2 must be used. The following are the codes that must be reported in box 12.

> **Code A***:* Uncollected Social Security or RRTA tax on tips. The employee's Social Security or Railroad Retirement Tax Act (RRTA) tax on all the employee's tips that the employer could not collect because the employee did not have enough funds to deduct the tax. This amount is not included in box 4.

> **Code B**: Uncollected Medicare tax on tips (but not Additional Medicare Tax). Shows the employee's Medicare tax or RRTA Medicare tax on tips that the employer could not

collect because the employee did not have enough funds from which to deduct the tax. This amount is not included in the total shown in box 6.

Code C: Taxable cost of group-term life insurance over $50,000. Shows the taxable cost of group-term life insurance coverage over $50,000 provided to the employee (including a former employee). This amount is included in boxes 1 and 3 up to the Social Security wage limit.

Code D: Elective deferrals to a section 401(k) cash or deferred arrangement. Shows deferrals under a SIMPLE retirement account part of section 401(k) arrangement.

Code E: Elective deferrals under section 403(b) salary reduction agreement.

Code F: Elective deferrals under section 408(k)(6) salary reduction SEP.

Code G: Elective deferrals and employer contributions (including non-elective deferrals) to any governmental or nongovernmental section 457(b) deferred compensation plan.

Code H: Elective deferrals to a section 501(c)(18)(D) tax-exempt organization plan.

Code J: Nontaxable sick pay (information only, not included in boxes 1, 3, or 5).

Code K: 20% excise tax on excess golden parachute payments.

Code L: Business expense reimbursements under an accountable plan that are excluded from the employee's gross income.

Code M: Uncollected Social Security or RRTA tax on the cost of group-term life insurance over $50,000 (former employees only).

Code N: Uncollected Medicare tax on the taxable cost of group-term life insurance over $50,000 (former employees only).

Code P: Excludable moving expense reimbursements paid directly to a member of the U.S. Armed Forces employee. The amount for moving expense reimbursement is not included in boxes 1, 3, or 5. For tax years 2018 through 2025, these reimbursements have been suspended for all other moving taxpayers.

Code Q: Nontaxable combat pay.

Code R: Employer contributions to an Archer MSA. The tax professional must use Form 8853 to report the amount and attach the form to the return.

Code S: Employee salary reduction contributions under section 408(p) SIMPLE (not included in box 1).

Code T: Adoption benefits (not included in box 1). If Code T is used, complete Form 8839 to determine which benefits are taxable and nontaxable.

Code V: Income from the exercise of nonstatutory stock options(s) are included in boxes 1 and 3 (up to the Social Security wage base).

Code W: Employer contributions to a health savings account (HSA) including amounts contributed using section 125 cafeteria plan. Form 8889 reports the amount and is attached to the client's return.

Code Y: Deferrals under section 409A nonqualified deferred compensation plan.

Code Z: Income under section 409A on a nonqualified deferred compensation plan that fails to satisfy section 409A is shown here. This amount is included in box 1.

Code AA: Designated Roth contributions under a section 401(k) plan.

Code BB: Designated Roth contributions under a section 403(b) plan.

Code DD: Cost of employer-sponsored health coverage. The amount reported with this code is nontaxable.

Code EE: Designated Roth contribution under a governmental section 457(b) plan. This amount does not apply to contributions under a tax-exempt organization 457(b) plan.

Code FF: Permitted benefits under a Qualified Small Employer Health Reimbursement Arrangement (QSEHRA).

Code GG: Income from qualified equity grants under section 83(i).

Code HH: Aggregate deferrals under section 83(i) elections as of the close of the calendar year.

Box 13: Statutory Employee, Retirement Plan, and Third-Party Sick Pay

If the retirement plan box is checked, special limits may apply to the amount of traditional IRA contributions that can be deducted. See Publication 590.

Statutory Employee

This checkbox is intended for statutory employees whose earnings are subject to Social Security and Medicare taxes but are not subject to federal income tax withholding. It should not be checked for common-law employees. Some workers, despite being classified as independent contractors under common-law rules, are treated as employees by statute. The following categories are considered statutory employees:

➤ Drivers who operate as agents or are compensated on commission and engage in the distribution of beverages (excluding milk), meat, vegetables, fruit, bakery products, or provide pickup and delivery services for laundry or dry cleaning.
➤ Full-time life insurance sales agents whose primary business activity involves selling life insurance, annuity contracts, or both, primarily for one life insurance company.
➤ Individuals who work from home on materials or goods provided by their employer which must be returned to the employer or to an employer's representative if specific instructions on how to complete the work are provided by the employer.

> ➤ Full-time traveling or city salespersons who represent their employer and submit orders to the employer from wholesalers, retailers, contractors, and operators of hotels, restaurants, or similar establishments. The goods sold must be merchandise for resale or supplies for use in the buyers' business operations. Sales must be the primary business activity for the employer.

See Publication 15-A, section 1.

Retirement Plan

This box is checked if the employee was an "active participant" (for any part of the year) in any of the following:

> ➤ A qualified pension, profit-sharing, or stock bonus plan described in section 401(a), including a 401(k) plan.
> ➤ An annuity plan described in section 403(a).
> ➤ An annuity contract or custodial account described in section 403(b).
> ➤ A simplified employee pension (SEP) plan described in section 408(k).
> ➤ A SIMPLE retirement account described in section 408(p).
> ➤ A trust described in section 501(c)(18).
> ➤ A plan for federal, state, or local government employees or by an agency or instrumentality thereof, other than a section 457(b) plan.

An employee is an active participant if covered by:

> ➤ A defined benefit plan for any tax year in which one is eligible to participate.
> ➤ A defined contribution plan for any tax year that employer or employee contributions (or forfeitures) are added to their individual account.

Third-Party Sick Pay

This box will be checked only if a third-party sick-pay provider's program covers the individual. Sick pay can include short- and long-term benefits. See Publication 15-A.

Box 14: Other.

Employers use this box to report other information such as state disability insurance taxes withheld, union dues, uniform payments, health insurance, retirement plan and other additional items that may need to be reported.

Box 15 through Box 20

State and local income tax information. You will need to research the exact nature of these taxes, which vary by state. (if applicable).

If the employee has an error on their Form W-2, they should notify the employer and request a corrected Form W-2. As a tax professional you should not prepare the return until the Form W-2 is corrected.

Part 1 Review

To obtain the maximum benefit from each part go online now and watch the video.

Part 2 Income

There are two major types of income: *earned* and *unearned income*. Earned income is revenue the taxpayer received for working and includes the following types of income:

➢ Wages, salaries, tips, and other types of taxable employee pay
➢ Net earnings from self-employment
➢ Gross income received as a statutory employee
➢ Union strike benefits
➢ Long-term disability benefits received prior to reaching the minimum retirement age

Unearned income is any amount received indirectly and not as a direct repayment of any services rendered or work provided. Unearned income includes:

➢ Interest and dividends
➢ Pensions and annuities
➢ Social Security and railroad retirement benefits (including disability benefits)
➢ Alimony and child support
➢ Welfare benefits
➢ Workers' compensation benefits
➢ Unemployment compensation
➢ Income while an inmate
➢ Workfare payments (review Publication 596 for a definition)

Form 1040, lines 1a - z

The following picture shows which form is used to report income. All income is reported based on the tax form the taxpayer receives and the form used to report it.

Income	1a	Total amount from Form(s) W-2, box 1 (see instructions)	1a	W-2
Attach Form(s) W-2 here. Also attach Forms W-2G and 1099-R if tax was withheld.	b	Household employee wages not reported on Form(s) W-2	1b	Not on W-2
	c	Tip income not reported on line 1a (see instructions)	1c	Not on line 1a
	d	Medicaid waiver payments not reported on Form(s) W-2 (see instructions)	1d	Not on W-2
	e	Taxable dependent care benefits from Form 2441, line 26	1e	Form 2441, line 26
	f	Employer-provided adoption benefits from Form 8839, line 29	1f	Form 8839, line 29
If you did not get a Form W-2, see instructions.	g	Wages from Form 8919, line 6	1g	Form 8919, line 6
	h	Other earned income (see instructions)	1h	Excessive deferrals
	i	Nontaxable combat pay election (see instructions) 1i		
	z	Add lines 1a through 1h	1z	

Portion of Form 1040

Line 1a: Total Amount from Form(s) W-2, box 1.

If the taxpayer is an employee, the taxpayer would receive Form W-2 showing wages earned in exchange for services performed. A W-2 is a tax form created by employers to detail earnings and government withholdings for a given tax year. The W-2 should be distributed to employees by January 31, 2024, for the 2023 tax year. The tax professional uses the W-2 to determine the client's earned income for the year. A taxpayer may receive multiple W-2s if they worked more than one job during the year.

Line 1a of Form 1040 reports the total amount of wages earned. Wages include salaries, vacation allowances, bonuses, commissions, and fringe benefits. Compensation includes everything received in payment for personal services.

Line 1b: Household employee wages not reported on Form(s) W-2.

Reports wages that are not reported on Form W-2 for household employees. See Tax Topics 756.

Line 1c: Tip Income not reported on line 1a.

Reports allocated tip income that was not included on Form 1040, line 1a.

Line 1d: Medicaid Waiver Payments not reported on Form(s) W-2.

Reports Medicaid waiver payments that were received and were included in earned income to claim refundable credits.

Line 1e: Taxable Dependent Care Benefits from Form 2441, line 26.

Reports the taxable dependent care benefits reported on Form 2441, line 26. Make sure to complete Form 2441 first.

Line 1f: Employer-provided adoption benefits from Form 8839, line 26.

Reports the total amount of adoption benefits that were paid by the employer. Employer-provided benefits should be in box 12 on the W-2, with code T.

Line 1g: Wages from Form 8919, line 6.

Reports wages that are reported on Form 8919, line 6.

Line 1h: Other Earned Income.

Reports the following income types:

1. Excess elective deferrals over $22,500, excluding catch-up amounts. The SIMPLE plan limit is $15,500. If the plan is a 403(b) the maximum is $25,500. See Publication 571.
2. Disability pensions shown on Form 1099-R.
3. Corrective distributions from a retirement plan shown on Form 1099-R of excess elective deferrals and contributions, plus earnings.

Line 1i: Nontaxable Combat Pay election.

Reports the nontaxable combat pay that was used to calculate the Earned Income Tax Credit (EITC).

Line 1z: Add lines 1a through 1h.

Add all the lines together.

Attach Sch. B if required.	**2a**	Tax-exempt interest . . .	**2a**	Form 1099-INT	**b**	Taxable interest	**2b**	Form 1099-INT
	3a	Qualified dividends . . .	**3a**	Form 1099-DIV	**b**	Ordinary dividends	**3b**	Form 1099-DIV
	4a	IRA distributions	**4a**	Form 1099-R	**b**	Taxable amount	**4b**	Form 1099-R
Standard Deduction for – • Single or	**5a**	Pensions and annuities . .	**5a**	Form 1099-R	**b**	Taxable amount	**5b**	Form 1099-R
	6a	Social security benefits . .	**6a**	SSA-1099	**b**	Taxable amount	**6b**	SSA 1099

Portion of Form 1040

Form 1099-INT

Banks and investment companies use Form 1099-INT to inform taxpayers of interest they've earned. Interest is generally reported on Form 1099-INT or a substitute statement. Form 1099-INT shows the interest earned for the year. It is not attached to the tax return when filing. Certain interest is not reported on Form 1099-INT, but must still be reported on the tax return. For example, Samantha received a Schedule K-1 reporting interest from a partnership of which she is a member. A substitute statement can come from an individual payer and not a large institution and must contain all the information found on Form 1099-INT.

☐ VOID ☐ CORRECTED

PAYER'S name, street address, city or town, state or province, country, ZIP or foreign postal code, and telephone no.	Payer's RTN (optional)	OMB No. 1545-0112	**Interest Income**
	1 Interest income $	Form **1099-INT** (Rev. January 2022) For calendar year 20 ___	
PAYER'S TIN / RECIPIENT'S TIN	**2** Early withdrawal penalty $		Copy 1
	3 Interest on U.S. Savings Bonds and Treasury obligations $		**For State Tax Department**
RECIPIENT'S name	**4** Federal income tax withheld $	**5** Investment expenses $	
Street address (including apt. no.)	**6** Foreign tax paid $	**7** Foreign country or U.S. possession	
	8 Tax-exempt interest $	**9** Specified private activity bond interest $	
City or town, state or province, country, and ZIP or foreign postal code	**10** Market discount $	**11** Bond premium $	
FATCA filing requirement ☐	**12** Bond premium on Treasury obligations $	**13** Bond premium on tax-exempt bond $	
Account number (see instructions)	**14** Tax-exempt and tax credit bond CUSIP no.	**15** State **16** State identification no.	**17** State tax withheld $ $

Form **1099-INT** (Rev. 1-2022)   www.irs.gov/Form1099INT   Department of the Treasury - Internal Revenue Service

Form 1099-INT

As with any form including the taxpayer's name, address, and taxpayer identification number (TIN), make sure the information is correct.

Box 1: Reports interest income paid to the recipient not included in box 3. Form 1099-INT is issued for interest earned of $10 or more.

Box 2: Reports interest or principal that was forfeited because of an early withdrawal penalty. Do not reduce the amount in box 1 by the forfeited amount. Form 1040, Schedule 1, line 18 reports Box 2 will adjust the taxpayer's tax liability.

Box 3: Reports interest from U.S. Savings Bonds and Treasury obligations (another word used for bonds). For taxable covered securities and acquired at a premium, see Box 12. The amount in this box may or may not be taxable. Review Publication 550.

Box 4: Reports federal income tax withheld. If the taxpayer does not receive a TIN (taxpayer identification number), the payer is required to withhold tax at a 24% rate on the amount in box 1.

Box 5: Investment expenses for a single-class real estate mortgage investment conduit (REMIC) only. Also, include the amount in box 1.

Box 6: Reports foreign taxes paid.

Box 7: Shows foreign country or U.S. possession taxes paid.

Box 8: Shows tax-exempt interest paid to the person's account during the calendar year. This amount may be subject to backup withholding.

Box 9: This box shows Specified Private Activity bond interest. Specified Private Activity Bonds are defined in section 141 and were issued after Aug 7, 1986.

Box 10: This box shows the value of a taxable or tax-exempt covered security acquired with a market discount, but only if the taxpayer made an election under section 1278(b) to include the market discount in income as it accrues. The taxpayer must notify the payer of the election in writing [certain restrictions apply, see Regulations section 1.6045-1(n)(5)].

Box 11: Bond premium. A taxable covered security other than a U.S. Treasury obligation acquired at a premium.

Box 12: For a U.S. Treasury obligation that is a covered security. This box shows the amount of premium amortization allocable to the interest payment(s).

Box 13: Bond Premiums on Tax-Exempt Bonds. If you report a tax-exempt covered security acquired at a premium, the amount entered is the bond premium amortization that is allocable to the interest paid during the year.

Box 14: Tax-Exempt and Tax Credit Bond CUSIP Number. The CUSIP is entered for single bonds or accounts containing a single bond.

Box 15-17: State information. These boxes indicate where the taxpayer lives as well as any state in which the taxpayer may have earned their income.

> *Señor 1040 Says*: Make sure Form 1099-INT is the year that you are preparing the tax return for. It is important to verify the year on all income reporting documents the taxpayer received.

When to Report Interest Income

Interest income is reported based on the accounting method the taxpayer is using to report their income. The two most common accounting methods are cash and accrual. With the accrual method, the taxpayer reports income in the tax year during which they earned it, regardless of when they received the payment.

If taxpayers use the cash method, they generally report their interest income in the year in which it was actually or constructively received. Use the special rules to report the discount on certain debt instruments such as U.S. savings bonds and original issue discount (OID).

The taxpayer does not need IRS approval to use any permitted accounting method and chooses their preferred method when they file their first tax return. If they change their mind and wish to change their accounting method on a later return, they must file Form 3115 to obtain IRS approval.

Taxpayers should always keep a list showing their sources of income. For example, all Forms 1099-INT and Forms 1099-DIV should be kept with the taxpayer's yearly tax return. If parents choose to claim their child's investment income, the related forms should also be kept with their tax returns. Interest earned as a beneficiary of an estate or trust is generally taxable income. In this situation, taxpayers should receive a Schedule K-1 for their portion of the interest. A copy of the Schedule K-1 should be kept with the tax return as well.

When is Payment Received?

Interest is received when it is credited to the taxpayer's account or made available to the taxpayer; the taxpayer does not need to have physical possession of the money. The taxpayer is considered to have received interest, dividends, or other earnings from any deposit, bank accounts, savings, loans, similar financial institution, or life insurance policy when the income has been credited to the taxpayer's account and is able to be withdrawn.

The accrual method reports income earned, whether it was received or not. Interest is earned over the life term of the debt instrument. With coupon bonds, interest is taxable the year the coupon becomes due and payable; it does not matter when the coupon payment is mailed. See Publication 550.

Backup Withholding

Interest income is generally not subject to regular withholding, but it may be subject to the backup withholding rate of 24% in the following situations:

➢ The taxpayer fails to provide the TIN (taxpayer identification number) in the required manner
➢ The IRS notifies the income provider that the TIN is incorrect
➢ The taxpayer is required to certify that the TIN provided is correct
➢ The IRS notifies the income provider to start withholding because the taxpayer is subject to backup withholding

There are civil and criminal penalties for giving false information to avoid backup withholding. If the taxpayer willfully falsified information, they may be subject to criminal penalties including fines and/or imprisonment. If backup withholding is deducted from interest income, the income provider, (or payer), must give the taxpayer Form 1099-INT to indicate the amount that was withheld.

Accounts and Payee-Identifying Numbers

Banks and other financial institutions pay interest and other income on accounts and other investments. When opening an account, an individual is required by federal law to provide their SSN to any financial institution or individual who needs the information to make a return, statement, or any other form of document. The primary SSN must be provided, for instance, when opening a joint account.

Example: Gina and her son, Trenton, opened a joint account with Trenton's birthday money. Gina and Trenton must provide Trenton's SSN to the bank, and his name would appear on the account first. If they do not provide the primary SSN to the payer, the account holder (Trenton) would have to pay a penalty.

Truncating

A payer identification number is any government issued number used by the IRS for the purpose of identification, including Social Security numbers (SSN), individual tax identification numbers (ITIN), employer identification numbers (EIN), taxpayer identification numbers (TIN), and adoption identification numbers (ATIN). Anyone issuing documents containing taxpayer identification information may truncate payee-identifying numbers by replacing the first 5 numbers of payer identification numbers with an X or * (XXX-XX-0000 or ***-**-1111, for example). This can be done on payee statements such as Forms 1097, 1098, 1099, 3921, 9322, and 5498, but it may not be done on Form W-2G.

Number and Certification

For new accounts paying interest or dividends, the payer will give the taxpayer Form W-9: Request for Taxpayer Identification. The taxpayer must certify under penalty of perjury that the TIN is correct, and they are not subject to backup withholding.

If the taxpayer neglects to make this certification, backup withholding will begin on the taxpayer's new account or investment. If the taxpayer has been notified that backup withholding will be deducted from their income due to not providing a TIN, the taxpayer can stop the withholding by providing the information to the payer. A payer is the one who administers the account, such as the bank.

Line 2a Tax-Exempt Interest

Certain types of interest income are tax-exempt and are reported on Form 1040, line 2a. Interest paid by state and local governments is exempt from federal taxation but may be taxable at the state level. The fact that this interest is tax-exempt does not mean that it is not reported; tax-exempt interest must be reported. Tax-exempt interest is included when determining how much Social Security could be taxable to the taxpayer and spouse.

Taxpayers are required to use Schedule B if any of the following are true:

> ➢ The taxpayer received over $1,500 of taxable interest or ordinary dividends

> The taxpayer received interest from a seller-financed mortgage and the buyer used the property as a personal residence
> The taxpayer received interest or ordinary dividends
> The taxpayer had a financial interest in, or signature authority over, a financial account in a foreign trust
> The taxpayer accrued interest from a bond
> The taxpayer is reducing the interest income on a bond by the amortizable bond premium
> The taxpayer is reporting original issue discount (OID) in an amount less than the amount on Form 1099-OID
> The taxpayer is claiming the exclusion of interest from U.S. savings bonds series EE, or I issued after 1989

Government Bonds

A government bond is a debt security issued by the government to support government spending. This section will give an overview of the most common federal government bonds. If the taxpayer purchases a government bond for a discount when interest has been defaulted or when interest has accrued and has not been paid, the transaction is considered as "trading a bond flat." The defaulted or unpaid interest is not income and is not taxable to the taxpayer. When an interest payment is received, it reduces the capital of the remaining cost of the bond. Interest that accrues after the date of purchase is taxable interest for the year received or accrued.

Interest for a bond can be reported in one of two ways. First, the taxpayer can elect to pay the interest as it is accrued. In this case, the taxpayer would pay taxes on the interest each year. Taxpayers who use the accrual basis must report interest as it accrues. They cannot postpone reporting interest until they receive it or until the bonds mature. The second option is the cash method in which taxes on the savings bonds are paid when they are redeemed or when the bond has matured. If this option is selected, the taxpayer would report all the interest in the year the bond is redeemed.

Series EE and Series E Bonds

Series EE and series E bonds are issued at a discount and sold for less than the face value of the bond. The buyer makes money by holding them until the bond's maturity date, at which point the face value is paid to the taxpayer. Series EE bonds were first offered in January 1980 and have a 30-year maturity period. Before July 1980, series E bonds were issued. The original 10-year maturity period of series E has been extended to 40 years for bonds issued before December 1965 and to 30 years for bonds issued after November 1965. Both paper series EE and E bonds were issued at a discount. Electronic bonds are issued at face value. Paper savings bonds are no longer sold at financial institutions. Owners of paper series EE bonds can convert them to electronic bonds. These converted electronic bonds do not retain the denomination listed on the paper certificate but are posted at their purchase price with accrued interest.

Series H and HH Bonds

Series H and HH bonds are issued at face value. Interest is paid twice a year and must be reported when received. Series H bonds have a maturity period of 30 years. Series HH bonds were first offered in 1980 and were last offered in August 2004. Series H bonds are treated the same way as series HH. Series HH bonds mature at 20 years. The last series H bonds matured in 2009, and the last series HH bonds will mature in 2024.

Series I Bonds

Series I bonds were first offered in 1998. These are inflation-indexed bonds issued at face value with a maturity period of 30 years. The face value plus all accrued interest is payable at maturity.

If the taxpayer uses the cash method of reporting income, they can report the interest on their series EE, series E, and series I bonds using one of the following two methods:

➢ Method 1: Postpone reporting the interest earned until either the year in which the bonds were cashed or disposed of, or the year the bonds mature, whichever is earliest.
➢ Method 2: Choose to report the increase in redemption value as interest earned each year.

The taxpayer must use the same method for all Series EE, Series E, and Series I bonds they own. If method 2 is not used, method 1 must be used. If the taxpayer wants to change from method 1 to method 2, the taxpayer does not need permission from the IRS. However, if the taxpayer wants to change from method 2 to method 1, permission must be requested by attaching a statement with the following information to the tax return for the year of the change:

➢ "131" printed or typed at the top of the statement
➢ The taxpayer's name and Social Security number written beneath "131"
➢ The year the change was requested (beginning and ending dates)
➢ Identification and information from the savings bonds for which the change is being requested
➢ The statement must include:
  ○ All interest received on any bonds acquired during or after the year of change when it is realized upon disposition, redemption, or final maturity, whichever is earliest.
  ○ All interest on the bonds acquired before the year of the change when the interest is realized upon disposition, redemption, or final maturity; whichever is earliest, with the exception of interest already reported in prior years.

Taxpayers may file an automatic extension on their tax returns to give them more time to file the statement. On the statement, the following should be typed: "Filed pursuant to section 301.9100-2." To qualify for the extension, the original tax return should have been filed by the required due date (normally April 15) based on the type of tax return being filed. See Publication 550.

> *Señor 1040 Says:* Interest on U.S. savings bonds is exempt from state and local taxes. Form 1099-INT will indicate the amount of interest that is earned for U.S. savings bonds in box 3.

Municipal Bonds

State and local governments issue municipal bonds to provide funding for capital improvement projects. Municipal bonds are not taxable by the federal government. Not all states or localities tax municipal bond interest income. Some states and localities tax all municipal bond interest, while others tax municipal bond interest income from other states or localities only.

A mortgage revenue bond (MRB) is issued by a local housing authority to finance mortgages for qualifying taxpayers. Those who qualify are normally low-income first-time homebuyers. Investors often prefer these bonds since they are tax-free and are secured by monthly mortgage payments. Every state has MRBs, and they are limited by the minimum state issuance. The purchase price of the home cannot exceed a certain percentage of the area's average purchase price.

State or Local Government Obligations

Interest received on a state or local government obligation is generally not taxable. The issuer should tell the receiver whether the interest is taxable, and then give the receiver a periodic statement showing the tax treatment of the obligation. If the obligation was invested through a trust, a fund, or other organization, that issuer should provide that information.

Even if the interest may not be subject to income tax, the receiver may have to report capital gains or losses when the obligation is sold.

Line 2b Taxable Interest

Interest is a cost created by those who lend money (lenders) that is charged to the people they lend money to (borrowers). A taxpayer will pay interest whenever they borrow money and will earn money whenever they lend or deposit money, such as into an interest-earning bank account.

Certain interest is taxable income if it is credited to the taxpayer's account and can be withdrawn. Interest is typically not calculated based on the original amount of borrowed money (called the principal) but is instead usually determined by multiplying a predetermined percentage point by the total amount of money currently owed to the lender by the borrower. For example, John borrowed $5,000 at a 5% interest rate. Although his principal was $5,000, after making several payments, he now owes $4,365, making his interest payment for the month 5% of $4,365, or $218.25.

Taxable Interest

Taxable interest is reported using Schedule B and includes interest received from bank accounts, loans made to others, and interest from other sources. The taxpayer could be the payer or the recipient of the interest. Examples of sources of interest are:

➢ Banks
➢ Credit unions
➢ Government entities (federal and state)
➢ Certificates of deposit (CDs)
➢ Life insurance
➢ Installment sales

U.S. Obligations

Interest on U.S. obligations (U.S. Treasury bills, notes, or bonds) is taxable at the federal level, but exempt from taxation in most states. Make sure to verify whether your state taxes this interest.

Interest and Community Property States

If a taxpayer lives in a community property state and receives an interest or dividend distribution, one-half of the distribution is considered to be received by each spouse. If the taxpayer and spouse file MFS, each must report one-half of the distribution on their separate returns. If the distribution is not considered community property under state law, each taxpayer must report their separate distributions.

Example: Johanna and Jacob are filing MFS, and they have a joint money market account. Under certain state's laws, half the income belongs to Johanna and the other half belongs to Jacob. Each would report half of the income.

Foreign Accounts and Trust Requirements

In a global economy, many people in the United States have foreign financial accounts. The law requires owners of foreign financial accounts to report their accounts to the U.S. Treasury Department, even if the accounts don't generate any taxable income. Account owners need to report accounts by the April due date following the calendar year that they own a foreign financial account.

The U.S. government requires individuals to report foreign financial accounts because foreign financial institutions may not be subject to the same reporting requirements as domestic ones.

Reporting Requirements

The Bank Secrecy Act requires a U.S. person who owns a foreign bank account, brokerage account, mutual fund, unit trust, or other financial account to file a *Report of Foreign Bank and Financial Accounts (FBAR)* if the taxpayer has any of the following:

1. Financial interest in, signature authority, or other authority over one or more accounts in a foreign country, and
2. The aggregate value of all foreign financial accounts exceeds $10,000 at any time during the calendar year.

A U.S. person is a citizen or resident of the United States or any domestic legal entity such as a partnership, corporation, limited liability company, estate, or trust. A foreign country includes any area outside the United States or outside the following U.S. territories and possessions:

➢ Northern Mariana Islands
➢ District of Columbia
➢ American Samoa
➢ Guam
➢ Puerto Rico
➢ United States Virgin Islands
➢ Trust Territories of the Pacific Islands
➢ Indian lands, as defined in the Indian Gaming Regulatory Act

How to Report

Taxpayers required to report their foreign accounts should file the FBAR electronically using the BSA E-Filing System. The FBAR is due April 15. If April 15 falls on a Saturday, Sunday, or legal holiday, the FBAR is due the next business day. Taxpayers don't file the FBAR with individual, business, trust, or estate tax returns.

If two people jointly own a foreign financial account or if several people each own a partial interest in an account, then each person has a financial interest in that account. Each person must report the entire value of the account on FBAR.
Spouses do not need to file a separate FBAR if they complete and sign Form 114, Record of

Authorization to Electronically File FBARs, and:

> ➤ All reportable financial accounts are jointly owned with the filing spouse, and
> ➤ All the accounts are jointly owned.
>   ○ The taxpayer must complete and sign FinCen Form 114a authorizing the spouse to file for themselves and timely file the FBAR reporting all the joint accounts.

Part 2 Review

To obtain the maximum benefit from each part go online now and watch the video.

Part 3 Dividends

Dividends are a share of the profits generated by a company that can be paid in money, stock, stock rights, other property, or services; they can also be paid by a corporation, mutual fund, partnership, estate, trust, or association that is taxed as a corporation. Distributions are benefits from a closely held entity such as an S-corporation, partnership, Limited Liability Company, and trusts.

Dividends can be paid in the form of additional stock, which is sometimes referred to as a reinvested dividend. These are fully taxable to the recipient and must be reported, although some amounts reported as dividends may be taxed at different rates.

Form 1099-DIV: Reporting Dividend Income

☐ VOID ☐ CORRECTED		

PAYER'S name, street address, city or town, state or province, country, ZIP or foreign postal code, and telephone no.	**1a** Total ordinary dividends $	OMB No. 1545-0110 Form **1099-DIV** (Rev. January 2022)	**Dividends and Distributions**
	1b Qualified dividends $	For calendar year 20 ___	
	2a Total capital gain distr. $	**2b** Unrecap. Sec. 1250 gain $	Copy 1 **For State Tax Department**
PAYER'S TIN RECIPIENT'S TIN	**2c** Section 1202 gain $	**2d** Collectibles (28%) gain $	
	2e Section 897 ordinary dividends $	**2f** Section 897 capital gain $	
RECIPIENT'S name	**3** Nondividend distributions $	**4** Federal income tax withheld $	
Street address (including apt. no.)	**5** Section 199A dividends $	**6** Investment expenses $	
	7 Foreign tax paid $	**8** Foreign country or U.S. possession	
City or town, state or province, country, and ZIP or foreign postal code	**9** Cash liquidation distributions $	**10** Noncash liquidation distributions $	
	11 FATCA filing requirement ☐	**12** Exempt-interest dividends $	**13** Specified private activity bond interest dividends $
Account number (see instructions)	**14** State **15** State identification no.	**16** State tax withheld $ $	

Form **1099-DIV** (Rev. 1-2022)   www.irs.gov/Form1099DIV   Department of the Treasury - Internal Revenue Service

Form 1099-DIV

As with all forms, make sure the taxpayer's name, address, and TIN are correct. The following is provided for informational purposes and describes what is reported in each box of Form 1099-DIV. The most common entries on Form 1099-DIV are: Box 1a, 1b, 2a, 3, 5, 7, and 11.

Box 1a, Total ordinary dividends: Included are money market funds, net short-term capital gains from mutual funds, and other distributions of stock. Reinvested dividends and section 404(k) dividends paid directly from the corporation are taxable. Report this amount on Form 1040, page 1, line 3b.

Box 1b, Qualified dividends: The portion that meets the IRS criteria for a lower capital gains tax rate is shown in box 1a. Report this amount on Form 1040, page 1, line 3a.

Box 2a, Total (long-term) capital gain distributions: Shows total capital gain distributions from a regulated investment company or real estate investment trust. Amount shown in box 2a is reported on Schedule D, line 13.

Box 2b, Unrecaptured Section 1250 gain: From certain depreciable real property. This box shows the amount in box 2a that is unrecaptured Section 1250 gain from depreciable property.
Box 2c, Section 1202 gain: Shows any amount in box 2a that is a Section 1202 gain from certain small business stocks.

Box 2d, Collectibles (28%) gain: Shows any amount included in box 2a that has a 28% rate gain from sales or exchanges of collectibles. Apart from this fact, this concept is beyond the scope of this course.

Box 3, Nondividend distributions: Nondividend distributions are shown here, if determinable.

Box 4, Federal income tax withheld: This box shows the amount of federal income tax withheld. Federal taxes are usually withheld when backup withholding is required.

Box 5, Section 199A Dividends: Shows Section 199A dividends paid to the taxpayer. This amount is included in box 1a.

Box 6, Investment Expenses: Shows the taxpayer's reported pro rata share of certain amounts deductible by a non-public offering from a regulated investment company (RIC) in computing the taxable income. Do not include any investment expense in box 1b.

Box 7, Foreign tax paid: Shows foreign tax paid on dividends and other distributions on stock. Report this amount in U.S. dollars.

Box 8, Foreign country or U.S. Possession: Enter the name of the foreign country or U.S. Possession to which the foreign taxes were reported and paid in box 7.

Box 9, Cash Liquidation Distributions: Shows cash distributed as part of a liquidation.

Box 10, Noncash Liquidation Distributions: Shows noncash distributions made as part of a liquidation. Place the fair market value as of the date of distribution.

Box 11, Foreign Account Tax Compliance Act (FATCA) Filing Requirement: Taxpayer is reporting distributions in boxes 1 through 3 and 9, 10, 12, and 13 on Form 1099-DIV.

Box 12, Exempt-Interest Dividends: This box shows exempt-interest dividends paid by a RIC or from a mutual fund. Include also specified private activity bond interest dividends.

Box 13, Specified Private Activity Bond Interest Dividends: This box reports exempt-interest dividends paid by a RIC minus an allocable share of the expenses.

Box 14-16, State Boxes: Shows state information depending upon the state the taxpayer lives in.

Dividends and other distributions that earn $10 or more are reported to the taxpayer on Form 1099-DIV by the payee. If the taxpayer's ordinary dividends are more than $1,500, the taxpayer would complete Schedule B, Part III, in addition to receiving Form 1099-DIV.

Form 1040, line 3a, Qualified Dividends

Qualified dividends are taxed at the taxpayer's capital gains rate. Qualified dividends are included with ordinary dividends on Form 1040, page 1, line 3a. Qualified dividends are shown in box 1b of Form 1099-DIV.

Form 1040, line 3b, Ordinary Dividends

Ordinary dividends are the most common type of dividend distributions and are taxed as ordinary income (as are mutual fund dividends) at the same tax rate as wages and other ordinary income of the taxpayer. All dividends are considered ordinary unless they are specifically classified as qualified dividends. Dividends received from common or preferred stock are considered ordinary dividends and are reported in box 1a of Form 1099-DIV. Ordinary dividends received on common or preferred stock can be reinvested and taxed as ordinary income.

Dividends That Are Really Interest

Certain distributions that are often reported as "dividends" are actually interest income. The taxpayer will report as interest any received dividends from deposits, or shared accounts, from the following sources:

- ➢ Credit unions
- ➢ Cooperative banks
- ➢ Domestic building and loan associations
- ➢ Federal savings and loan associations
- ➢ Mutual savings banks

These dividends will be reported as interest in box 1 of Form 1099-INT. Generally, amounts received from money market funds are dividends and should not be reported as interest.

Capital Gains Distributions

Capital gains distributions are paid to the taxpayer by brokerage firms, mutual funds, and investment trusts. The capital gains distributions from mutual funds are long-term capital gains regardless of how long the taxpayer owned the stock. Distributions of net-realized short-term capital gains are reported on Form 1099-DIV as ordinary dividends.

Nontaxable Dividends

Nontaxable dividends are a return of a shareholder's original investment. These distributions are not treated the same as ordinary dividends or capital gain distributions. Nondividend distributions reduce the taxpayer's basis in the stock. Return of capital distributions are not taxable until the taxpayer's remaining basis (investment) is reduced to zero. The basis of the stock has been reduced to zero when the taxpayer receives a distribution, and then it is reported as a capital gain. The holding period determines the reporting of short-term or long-term capital gain.

Form 1040, line 4: IRA Distributions

Any money received from a traditional IRA is a distribution and must be reported as income in the year it was received. Report the nontaxable distribution on Form 1040, line 4 and report the taxable distributions on line 4b. Distributions from a traditional IRA are taxed as ordinary income. Not all distributions will be taxable if the taxpayer made nondeductible contributions. Complete Form 8606 to report the taxable and nontaxable portions of the IRA distribution.

The following distributions are not subject to the early withdrawal penalty:

➢ A rollover from one IRA to another
➢ Tax-free withdrawals of contributions
➢ The return of nondeductible contributions

These funds will be reported as received, but the taxable portion will be reduced or eliminated.

Normal IRA distributions are usually fully taxable because contributions to the IRA account were fully tax-deferred when they were originally made. Form 5329, *Additional Taxes on Qualified Plans*, is not required if the early withdrawal penalty is the only reason for using the form. This penalty is in addition to any tax due on the distributions, though some exceptions to it exist.

Form 1040, line 5a and line 5b, Pensions and Annuities

A distribution is a payment received by taxpayers from their pension or annuity. If taxpayers contributed "after-tax" dollars to their pension or annuity plan, they could exclude part of each annuity payment from income as a recovery of their cost. The tax-free part of the payment is figured when the annuity starts and remains the same each year, even if the amount of the payment changes. A pension is a contract for a fixed sum to be paid regularly following retirement from service. If the taxpayer wants to have taxes withheld from their pensions or annuities, they will use W-4P. The tax-free portion of the payment is calculated using one of the following methods:

General Rule

When receiving annuity payments from a nonqualified retirement plan, the general rule applies. According to this rule, taxable and tax-free portions of annuity payments are determined by life expectancy tables provided by the IRS.

Simplified Method

The Simplified Method for annuities is a method used to determine the taxable portion of annuity payments received from a nonqualified retirement plan. It simplifies the calculation by spreading the tax liability evenly over the expected duration of the annuity payments. Here's how it works:

1. Determine the Total Expected Return: Start by calculating the total amount you expect to receive in annuity payments over your lifetime. This is often referred to as the "total expected return."
2. Determine the Exclusion Ratio: Next, calculate the exclusion ratio, which is the ratio of your investment in the contract (usually the amount you paid into the annuity) to the total expected

return. This ratio represents the portion of each annuity payment that is considered a return of your original investment and therefore not subject to taxation.

3. Apply the Exclusion Ratio: Multiply each annuity payment by the exclusion ratio to determine the taxable portion of the payment. The remaining portion is considered tax-free return of your investment.

4. Report Taxable Portion: Report the taxable portion of the annuity payments as income on your tax return.

See Sec 72(d)(1)Tax Topic 411

Guaranteed Payments

The annuity contract provides guaranteed payments based on the investment amount and may be payable even if the taxpayer and the survivor annuitants do not live to receive the minimum payment.

Form 1040, line 6a: Social Security Benefits

The Social Security system was designed to provide supplemental monthly benefits to taxpayers who contributed to the system. It is indexed for inflation, provides Medicare benefits, disability, and certain death insurance, and is reported on Form SSA-1099 based on the amount listed in Box 5 of the W-2. Taxpayers also have the option to have federal taxes withheld from Social Security. See IRC Sec 86 and Publication 915.

When a taxpayer has Social Security or its equivalent from other countries, such as Canada, that income could be taxable in the United States. Remember the IRS rule "gross income means all income from whatever source derived". However, if this income was not taxed in Canada, it may not be taxable in the United States. See IRC Sec 61(a).

Social Security benefits are not taxable if income does not exceed these base amounts:

➢ $25,000: If Single, Head of Household, Qualifying Surviving Spouse.
➢ $25,000: If Married Filing Separately and lived apart from spouse the entire year.
➢ $32,000: If Married Filing Jointly.
➢ $0: If Married Filing Separately and lived with spouse at some time during the year.

Form 1040, line 6b: Taxable Amount

50% taxable: If the income plus half of the Social Security benefits exceeds the above base amounts, up to half of the benefits must be included as taxable income. The following are base amounts for the applicable filing statuses:

➢ $34,000: Single, Head of Household, Qualifying Surviving Spouse and Married Filing Separately and lived apart from spouse
➢ $44,000: Married Filing Jointly

85% taxable: For taxpayers who file MFS and lived with their spouse, they would skip lines 8 -15 on the Social Security benefit worksheet. Most taxpayers assume they will not be taxed if their income falls below the base amount, but they fail to include tax-exempt interest or half of their Social Security income when determining the amount.

Example: Napoleon and Ilene file a joint return. Both are over the age of 65 and have received Social Security benefits during the current tax year. In January, Napoleon's Form SSA-1099 showed benefits of

$7,500 in box 5. Ilene's Form SSA-1099 showed a net benefit of $3,500 in box 5. Napoleon received a taxable pension of $20,800 and interest income of $500, which was tax exempt. Their benefits are not taxable for the current year because their income is not more than the base amount of $32,000.

Any benefit repayments made during the current year would be subtracted from the gross benefits received. It does not matter whether the repayment was for a benefit received in the current year or in an earlier year; it only matters what year the repayment was received.

Social Security and Equivalent Railroad Retirement Benefits (Tier 1)

The taxpayer should receive Form SSA-1099 from the SSA, which reports the total amount of Social Security benefits paid in box 3. Box 4 of the form shows the amount of any benefits that were repaid from a prior year. Railroad retirement benefits that should be treated as Social Security benefits are reported on Form RRB-1099.

Railroad Retirement Benefits

Railroad Retirement Benefits (RRB) is a benefits program that began before Social Security; its recipients are not covered under Social Security because they receive more money than they would have under the SSA. Tier 1 benefits are reported to the taxpayer on Form RRB 1099, are equivalent to Social Security benefits, and are treated as such. Tier 1 benefits are reported to the IRS on Form 1040, Line 6b.

Tier 2 benefits are above the Social Security equivalent and are treated like pensions, allowing retirees to receive both tier 1 and tier 2 benefits. As with other pensions, the "cost" they invested is recovered tax-free. It is usually necessary to use the simplified method to figure the taxable portion of tier 2 benefits. To use the *Simplified Method Worksheet*, the tax preparer must know the age of the taxpayer, how many payments were received in the tax year, and how much has been recovered tax-free since 1986. When the taxpayer has recovered their cost, the entire tier 2 benefit becomes taxable.

The difference between Form RRB 1099 for tier 1 and tier 2 is that the form for tier 1 is known simply as Form RRB 1099. Tier 2 is a retirement; therefore, it has the letter "R" following the 1099 (Form RRB 1099-R).

Part 3 Review

To obtain the maximum benefit from each part go online now and watch the video.

Part 4 Schedule 1: Additional Income

Schedule 1, Part 1 of **Form 1040** ensures taxpayers report **additional income** beyond their primary sources such as wages and salaries. This section is intended to provide tax authorities with the income information they need to ensure accurate assessment and compliance with tax laws. Additional income can come from diverse sources including rental income, interest earned, dividends received, capital gains from investments, royalties, and various forms of self-employment income. Understanding Schedule 1 Part 1 is crucial for taxpayers to fulfill their reporting obligations accurately and avoid potential penalties or scrutiny from tax authorities. It serves as a comprehensive framework for capturing the full spectrum of income, contributing to the fairness and integrity of the tax system.

SCHEDULE 1 (Form 1040)	**Additional Income and Adjustments to Income**	OMB No. 1545-0074
Department of the Treasury Internal Revenue Service	Attach to Form 1040, 1040-SR, or 1040-NR. Go to *www.irs.gov/Form1040* for instructions and the latest information.	**20**23 Attachment Sequence No. **01**

Name(s) shown on Form 1040, 1040-SR, or 1040-NR		Your social security number

Part I   Additional Income

1	Taxable refunds, credits, or offsets of state and local income taxes	**1**	
2a	Alimony received	**2a**	
b	Date of original divorce or separation agreement (see instructions): _____		
3	Business income or (loss). Attach Schedule C	**3**	

Portion of Schedule 1

Schedule 1, line 1: Taxable Refunds

If a taxpayer claims state income taxes were paid as an itemized deduction in the prior tax year, one would report the state income tax refund (part of the state taxes claimed in the previous year) as income in the year it was received. If the state income tax refund is taxable, report it on Form 1040, Schedule 1, line 1. Tax refunds are reported to the taxpayer on Form 1099-G, not to be confused with unemployment, which is also reported on the same form number. The state sends Form 1099-G to all refund recipients by January 31 of the current year.

To understand how a state income tax refund may be taxable, the tax professional must understand the "tax benefit rule," which states:

> If a taxpayer recovers an amount that was deducted or credited against tax in a previous year, the recovery must be included in income to the extent that the deduction or credit reduced the tax liability in the earlier year. However, if no tax benefit was derived from a prior year deduction or credit, the recovery does not have to be included as income.

Recovery of Items Previously Deducted

A recovery is a return of an amount the taxpayer deducted or took a credit for in a prior year. The most common recoveries are state tax refunds, reimbursements, and rebates of deductions itemized on Form 1040, Schedule A. The taxpayer may also have recoveries of nonitemized deductions (such as payments on previously deducted bad debts) and recoveries of items for which the taxpayer previously claimed a tax credit. Taxpayers who used a deduction or credit to reduce their tax liability in the previous year must include those reductions as income on their current tax return.

Schedule 1, line 2: Alimony Received

Alimony is a payment or series of payments to a spouse or former spouse required under a divorce or separation instrument that must meet certain requirements. Alimony payments are deductible by the payer and are includable as income by the recipient. Alimony received should be reported on Form 1040, Schedule 1, line 2. Alimony paid should be deducted as an adjustment on Form 1040, Schedule 1, line 19. The Tax Cuts and Jobs Act changed the alimony rule; alimony will no longer be an adjustment to income or a source of income if the divorce or separation agreement was completed after December 31, 2018.

Payments are alimony or separate maintenance if *all* the following are true:

➢ Payments are required by a divorce or separation agreement
➢ The taxpayer and the recipient spouse do not file a joint return
➢ Payments are in cash (including checks or money orders)

- ➢ Payments are not designated in the instrument as "not alimony"
- ➢ Spouses are legally separated under a decree of divorce or separate maintenance agreement and are not members of the same household
- ➢ Payments are not required after the death of the recipient spouse
- ➢ Payments are not designated as child support

The following are not considered alimony or separate maintenance payments.

- ➢ Payments designated as child support
- ➢ A noncash property settlement, such as giving the spouse the house
- ➢ Payments that are the spouse's part of community property income
- ➢ Payments used for property upkeep of the alimony payer's house
- ➢ Use of property and voluntary payments not required by the written decree

These payments are neither deductible by the payer nor includable in income by the recipient. There are different rules for payments under a pre-1985 instrument. See Publication 504

Divorced or Separated Individuals.

Payments made by cash, check, or money order for the taxpayer's spouse's medical expenses, rent, utilities, mortgage, taxes, tuition, etc., are considered third-party payments. If the payments are made on behalf of the taxpayer's spouse under the terms of the divorce or separation agreement, they may be considered alimony.

If the payer must pay all mortgage payments (both principal and interest) on a jointly owned home and if the payments otherwise qualify, they may deduct one-half of the payments as alimony payments. The spouse will report one-half as alimony received.

The deductibility of real estate taxes and insurance depends on how the title is held. Additional research may be needed to determine how to handle the taxpayer's situation.

Example: In November 1984, Kael and Braxton executed a written separation agreement. In February 1985, a decree of divorce was substituted for the written separation agreement. The decree of divorce did not change the terms for the alimony that Kael had to pay Braxton because it is treated as having been executed before 1985 since the terms of the alimony are still the same as the original agreement made in 1984.

Schedule 1, line 3: Business Income or Loss

Use Schedule C for business income if an individual operated a business as a sole proprietor. An activity will qualify as a business if the primary purpose for engaging in such activity is for income or profit and if the proprietor is continually and regularly involved in such activity. Schedule C will be discussed in a later chapter.

Schedule 1, line 4: Other Gains or Losses

Use Schedule D to report capital gains and losses. Use Form 4797 to report other capital gains and losses not reported on Schedule D, line 13. Use Schedule D to figure out the overall gain and loss from transactions reported on Form 8949 and to report gain from Form 2439 or 622 or Part I of Form 4797. Capital gains and losses will be discussed in a later chapter.

Schedule 1, line 5: Rental Income Form 1040

To report income or loss from rental real estate, royalties, partnerships, S corporations, estates, trusts, and residual interests in Real Estate Mortgage Investment Conduits (REMICs), use Schedule E. Rental income is any payment received for the use or occupation of real estate or personal property. Payment received by the taxpayer is reportable. Schedule E will be discussed in a later chapter.

Schedule 1, line 6: Farm Income or Loss

Schedule F would be used to report farm income or loss. Schedule F will be discussed in a later chapter.

Schedule 1, line 7: Unemployment Compensation

Unemployment compensation is taxable, and the taxpayer may elect to have taxes withheld for income tax purposes. To make this choice, the taxpayer must complete Form W-4V, *Voluntary Withholding Request*. The recipient of unemployment compensation will receive Form 1099-G, which reports the income.

If the taxpayer had to repay unemployment compensation for a prior year because they received unemployment while employed, they would subtract the total amount repaid for the year from the total amount received and enter the difference on Form 1040, Schedule 1, line 7. On the dotted line, next to the entry on the tax return, write "Repaid" and enter the amount repaid.

Paid Medical Family Leave

Paid family leave is an element of a state disability insurance program, and workers covered by State Disability Insurance (SDI) could be covered for this benefit. The maximum claim is six weeks; this is reported as unemployment on the individual's tax return. In some states, paid family leave and unemployment could be reported on separate forms. Be aware of how the taxpayer's state reports the two programs. Both are considered a form of unemployment compensation that must be reported on Form 1040, Schedule 1, line 7.

Señor 1040 Says: A good tax professional may have to add the totals of paid family leave with unemployment to report the correct amount of unemployment.

Schedule 1, line 8a – 8z: Other Income

Use Form 1040, Schedule 1, line 8, to report any income not reported on the previous lines of the tax return or schedules. If necessary, attach a statement to give the required details concerning the income. The type of income should be identified on the dotted line.

Income that is not reported on line 8:

1. Self employment
2. Notary public income
3. Income reported on Form 1099-MISC
4. Income reported on Form 1099-NEC, unless it is NOT self-employment income, such as a hobby
5. Form 1099-K

Examples of Other Income reported on line 8 are:

➢ Net operating loss (8a)
➢ Gambling winnings, including the lottery and raffles (8b)
➢ Form 1099-C, *Cancellation of Debt* (8c)
➢ Foreign income exclusion from Form 2555 (8d)
➢ Archer MSAs and Long-term Care Insurance Contracts Form 8853 (8e)
➢ Health Savings Account distributions, Form 8889 (8f)
➢ Alaska Permanent Fund dividend (8g)
➢ Jury duty pay (8h)
➢ Prizes and awards (8i)
➢ Activity not for profit income (8j)
➢ Stock options (8k)
➢ Income from the rental of personal property if taxpayer engaged in the rental for profit but was not in the business of renting such property (8l)
➢ Olympic and Paralympic medal and USOC prize money (8m)
➢ Section 951(a) inclusion (8n)
➢ Section 951A(a) inclusion (8o). Attach Form 8992
➢ Section 461(l) excess business loss adjustments (8p)
➢ Taxable distributions from an ABLE account (8q)
➢ Scholarships and fellowship grants not reported on W-2 (8r)
➢ Nontaxable amount of Medicaid waiver payments included on Form 1040, line 1a or 1d (8s)
➢ Pension or annuity from a nonqualified deferred compensation plan or a nongovernmental section 457 plan (8t)
➢ Wages earned while incarcerated (8u)
➢ Other income, such as bartering (8z)

See Publication 525 *Taxable and Nontaxable Income.*

> *Señor 1040 Says*: Form 1099-NEC, *Nonemployee Compensation,* is reported on line 8 unless it is not self-employment income.

Line 8a, Net Operating Loss

When a taxpayer is taking a net operating loss (NOL) from an earlier year, it would be reported on Schedule 1, line 8(a). An NOL is a loss, so enter the amount in parentheses as a negative number. See Publication 536, *Net Operating Losses (NOLs) for Individuals, Estates, and Trusts.*

Line 8b, Gambling Winnings

Gambling winnings from lotteries, lump-sum payment from the sale of a right to receive future lottery payments, bingo, slot machines, keno, poker, etc. are reported on Form W-2G. Form W-2G is now an evergreen form, with the taxpayer or preparer adding the last two digits of the filing year in the box marked "For calendar year."

Form W-2G would be given to a taxpayer when winnings are $1,200 or more from a bingo game or slot machine. Keno winnings of more than $1,500 and poker tournament winnings of $5,000 or more are reported. Winnings from all other gambling wagers or buy-in would be reduced at the option of the payer, if the wager is $600 or more, and at least 300 times the amount of the wager and if the winnings are subject to federal income tax withholding. Winnings are subject to federal income tax. Gambling losses are no more than the taxpayers' winnings and are reported on Schedule A, line 16.

Gambling winnings are reported to the taxpayer by the gambling organization (such as a casino) on Form W-2G, which shows both the amount won and withheld. The tax withheld (box 4) is reported with all other federal income tax withholding on Form 1040, page 2, line 25. "Backup" withholding on gambling winnings occurs when the payee does not give the payer their Social Security number. The withholding rate will be 24% and applies to winnings of more than $600.
If the winner is not a U.S. citizen, their withholding could be 30%, and they would receive Form 1042-S, *Foreign Person's U.S. Source Income Subject to Withholding.*

Line 8c, Cancellation of Debt

A debt is any amount owed to the lender; this includes, but is not limited to, stated principal, stated interest, fees, penalties, administrative costs, and fines. If a taxpayer's debt is canceled or forgiven, the canceled amount would generally be included as income. The amount of canceled debt can be all, or part, of the total amount owed. For a lending transaction, the taxpayer is required to report only the stated principal. If the cancellation of a debt is a gift, it would not be included as income. If a federal government agency, financial institution, or credit union forgives or cancels a debt of $600 or more, the taxpayer should receive a Form 1099-C

Cancellation of Debt. The amount to be included as income is listed in box 2 of Form 1099-C.
If the forgiven or canceled debt includes interest, the amount considered interest would be listed in box 3 and can only be included as income if it would have been deductible on the taxpayer's tax return.

Health Savings Accounts (HSAs) Form 8889 (8f).

Generally, medical expenses that have been paid during the year are not reimbursed by the plan until the taxpayer has met the deductible. The taxpayer may receive a tax-free distribution from the HSA to pay for or reimburse qualified medical expenses after the taxpayer has established an HSA. Distributions received for any other reason are subject to an additional 20% tax.

Alaska Permanent Fund Dividends line 8g

The Alaska Permanent Fund is a dividend that is paid to all qualifying residents of Alaska. The dividend is based upon a five-year average of the Permanent Fund's performance, which depends on the stock market and other factors. The dividend is taxable on the recipients' federal tax returns.

Activity Not Engaged in for Profit line 8j

Income received through activities from which the taxpayer does not expect to make a profit (such as money made from a hobby) must be reported on Form 1040, Schedule 1, line 8. Deductions for the business or investment activity cannot offset other income. To determine if the taxpayer is carrying on an activity for profit, you must consider the following factors:

➢ The taxpayer carries on the activity in a businesslike manner.
➢ The time and effort put into the activity indicate the taxpayer intended to make a profit.
➢ Losses are due to circumstances beyond the taxpayer's control.
➢ Methods of operation were changed to improve profitability.
➢ The taxpayer or the taxpayer's advisor(s) have the knowledge needed to carry on the activity as a successful business.
➢ The taxpayer was successful in making a profit in similar activities in the past.
➢ The activity makes a profit in some years.
➢ The taxpayer can expect to make a future profit from the appreciation of the assets used in the activity.
➢ The taxpayer depends on the income for their livelihood.

An activity is presumed to be carried on for profit if it produced a profit in at least three of the last five years, including the current year. Activities that consist of breeding, training, showing, or racing horses are presumed to be carried on for profit if they produced a profit in at least two of the last seven years. The activity must be substantially the same for each year within the period, and the taxpayer has a profit when the gross income from the activity exceeds the deductions.

Line 8k, Stock Options

There are three kinds of stock options:

➢ Incentive stock options
➢ Employee stock purchase plan options
➢ Non-statutory (non-qualified) stock options

The employer must report any excess of the fair market value (FMV) of the stock received, and will be reported in box 12 with the code *V*. For more information about employee stock options, see Internal Revenue Code (IRC) section 1.83-7, §421, §422, and §423 and related regulations.

Part 4 Review

To obtain the maximum benefit from each part go online now and watch the video.

Part 5 Other Taxable Income

Taxable income is more than just earned wages; it can include sources that are often overlooked. Some of these taxable income types will be reported on a W-2, but others may be reported to the taxpayer on a 1099-MISC or 1099-NEC. This section covers the most common type of other taxable income.

Advance Commission and Other Earnings

If the cash method is used and the taxpayer received an advance commission, that amount is included as income in the year received. If the taxpayer repays unearned commission in the same year it was received, then reduce the amount included by the repayment. If the repayment is in a later year, then the taxpayer would deduct the repayment on Schedule A as an itemized deduction.

Prepaid income, in most cases, is included as compensation in the year the taxpayer received the income. If the taxpayer is on the accrual method of accounting, the income is reported when it is earned in the performance of the services. See Publication 525.

Back Pay

If a taxpayer receives a settlement or judgment for back pay, it is included in their income. Back pay is treated as wages in the year paid, not the year it was supposed to have been paid. If a settlement was reached in 2022 for pay that should have been given in 2018, and the back pay is received in 2023, the back pay is reported as income for tax year 2023, not 2022 or 2018.
Taxpayer could receive one of the following:

➢ Form W-2
➢ Form 1099-INT
➢ Form 1099-MISC or 1099-NEC

Payments made to the taxpayer for damages, unpaid life insurance premiums, and unpaid health insurance premiums are reported to the taxpayer on Form W-2. There are special rules on how to report these wages to the Social Security Administration, and those guidelines are not covered in this course. See https://www.dol.gov/general/topic/wages/backpay.

Bartering

Bartering is an exchange of property or services. Goods and services acquired through bartering must be included as income at the value they held when they were received. The taxpayer should use Form 1099-B to report the exchange of services or property received. See Publication 525.

Severance Pay

When an employee receives a severance package, any payment for the cancellation of the employment contract is included in the employee's income. A severance package is considered wages and is subject to Social Security and Medicare taxes. See Publication 525.

Sick Pay

Pay received from an employer while the employee is sick or injured is part of the employee's salary or wages. Taxpayers must include sick pay benefits in their income that are received from any of the following sources:

➢ A welfare fund
➢ A state sickness or disability fund
➢ An association of employers or employees
➢ An insurance company if the employer paid for the plan

➢ Railroad sick pay

If the employee paid the premiums on an accident or health insurance policy, the benefits received under the policy are not taxable.

Sick pay is intended to replace regular wages while an employee is unable to work due to injury or illness. Payments received from the employer or an agent of the employer that qualify as sick pay must have federal withholding, just as any other wage compensation. Payments under a plan in which the employer does not participate (i.e., the taxpayer paid all the premiums) are not considered sick pay and are not taxable.

Sick pay does not include any of the following payments:

➢ Disability retirement payments
➢ Workers' compensation
➢ Payments to public employees as workers' compensation
➢ Medical expense payments
➢ Payments unrelated to absences from work
➢ Black lung benefit payments

Señor 1040 Says: Do not report any amounts as income that were reimbursed for medical expenses that were incurred after the plan was established.

See Publication 525 and IRC Sec 61(a)(1).

Tips

All tips received by the taxpayer are income, subject to federal income tax, and must be reported to employers regardless of whether they were received directly or indirectly. There are several ways an individual could receive tips such as tip-splitting, a tip-pooling arrangement, or some other method. The IRS states that all tips received from customers must be included as income regardless of what an employer considers to be a tip; an employer's characterization of a payment as a "tip" is not determinative for withholding purposes. Noncash tips, such as tickets, passes, or other items of value, are not reported to the employer.

Employees who receive tips should keep daily records of the tips received. A daily report will help the employee when it comes to filing their tax return. Employees should do the following:

➢ Report tips accurately to their employer
➢ Report all tips accurately on their tax return
➢ Keep a daily report of tips received and those paid out
➢ Provide their tip income report if their tax return is ever audited

If the server paid out tips, that amount should be documented on Publication 1244. The amount paid out is not reported on the payer's tax return and then subtracted out. There are two ways to keep a daily tip log. Employees should:

> ➢ Write information about their tips in a tip diary
> ➢ Keep copies of documents that show tips

 Señor 1040 Says: The taxpayer can use Publication 1244 to track their daily tips totals and amount reported to their employer. Taxpayer can download the publication @ https://www.irs.gov/forms-pubs/about-publication-1244

This daily record should be kept with tax and other personal records. The daily tip report should include:

> ➢ The date and time of work
> ➢ Cash tips received directly from customers or other employees
> ➢ Credit and debit card charges that customers paid directly to the employer
> ➢ Total tips paid out to other employees through tip pools or tip splitting
> ➢ The value of noncash tips received, such as tickets, passes, etc.

If more than $20 worth of tips are received per month from one employer, they must be reported to the taxpayer's employer on Form 4070: *Employee's Report of Tips to Employer.* The employer will withhold Social Security, Medicare, federal taxes, and state taxes from the employee's reported tips based on the total amount of the employee's regular wages and reported tips. Form 4070 should be filed with the employer no later than the 10th of each month. If the 10th of the month falls on a Saturday, Sunday, or legal holiday, the due date to report tips becomes the next business day.

Tips not reported to the employer are still required to be reported as income on Form 1040. If the taxpayer fails to report tips, the taxpayer may be subject to a penalty equal to 50% of the Social Security and Medicare taxes or railroad retirement tax owed on unreported tips. This penalty amount is an additional tax owed, although the taxpayer could try to avoid the penalty by attaching a statement to the return showing the reasonable cause for not reporting the tips. Taxpayer would use Form 4137: *Social Security Tax on Unreported Tip Income*, to report unreported tips to the IRS.

Do not include service charges in the tip diary. Service charges that are added to the customer's bill and paid to the employee are treated as wages, not tips. The absence of any of the following factors creates doubt as to whether a payment is a tip and indicates that the payment may be a service charge:

> ➢ The payment must be made free from obligation
> ➢ The customer must have an unrestricted right to determine the amount
> ➢ The payment should not be subject to discussion or defined by employer policy
> ➢ The customer has the right to determine who receives the payment

Example: Fish 'n' Chips for You specifies that an 18% service charge will be added to bills for parties of six or more. Julio's bill included the service charge for food and beverages for the party of eight he served. Under these circumstances, Julio did not have the unrestricted right to determine the amount of payment because it was dictated by Fish 'n' Chips for You. The 18% charge is not a tip; it is distributed to the employees as wages. Julio would not include that amount in his tip diary.

Employees who work in an establishment that must allocate tips to its employees or who fail to earn or report an amount of tips that is equal to at least 8% of the total amount of their gross receipts are subject to "allocated tips." In this case, the employer will assign them (or "allocate") additional tips to ensure they reach the 8% minimum. Allocated tips are calculated by adding the tips reported by all employees from food and drink sales (this does not include carryout sales or sales with a service charge of 10% or more). The employee's share is then determined using the sales based on hours worked.

Allocated tips are shown separately in box 8 of Form W-2 and are reported as wages on Form 1040, line 1c. Social Security and Medicare taxes have not been taken out of allocated tips, but are still subject to them, and must be reported on Form 4137: *Social Security Tax on Unreported Tip Income.* Employers must also report them by filing Form 8027: *Employer's Annual Information Return of Tip Income and Allocated Tips.* The purpose of Form 4137 is to calculate the Social Security and Medicare tax on tips that were not reported to the taxpayer's employer. Once calculated, report the amount of unreported Social Security and Medicare tax on Form 1040, Schedule 2, line 5. See Publication 525.

Disability Income

Disability income is the amount paid to an employee under the employee or employer's insurance or pension plan (under some plans, employees can also contribute) while the employee is absent from work due to a disability. Disability income reported as wages on Form W-2 is taxable, but income attributable to employee contributions would not be taxable. If the employee pays for the entire cost of the accident or health plan, they should not include any amount received as income. If the premiums of a health or accident plan were paid through a cafeteria plan, and the amount of the premium was not included as taxable income, then it is assumed that the employer paid the premiums, and the disability benefits are taxable.

If a taxpayer retires using disability payments before reaching the minimum retirement age of 59½, the payments will be treated as wages until the taxpayer reaches the minimum retirement age. Once a taxpayer is over the age of 59½, their disability payments will be taxed as a pension and not as regular income. Tax professionals should not confuse disability income (which may be taxable) with workers' compensation (which may not be taxable) for those who are injured at work.

Señor 1040 Says: The minimum retirement age is 59½ or the age at which the taxpayer could first receive an annuity or pension if he or she was not disabled. The taxpayer must report all their taxable disability payments until the taxpayer reaches the minimum retirement age.

Part 5 Review

To obtain the maximum benefit from each part go online now and watch the video.

Part 6 Fringe Benefits

A fringe benefit is any benefit provided by an employer to individuals in addition to their normal compensation. A person who performs services for the employer does not have to be an employee; they can be an independent contractor, partner, or director. The employer is the provider of the fringe benefit if it is provided for services performed for the employer, and the person who performs services for the employer is the recipient of the fringe benefit.

Fringe benefits received from an employer are considered compensation. They are taxable and must be included in income unless tax law specifically excludes the benefits, or the taxpayer paid fair market value for the benefit (in which it would no longer be a provision from the employer or a fringe benefit). The employer usually determines the amount of the fringe benefits and includes this amount on the employee's W-2. The total value of the fringe benefits should be shown in box 12. The employer is the provider of the benefit even if a customer of the employer provided the services. The employee who profits from the fringe benefit reports the provision as income.

Dependent Care Assistance

If the employer provides dependent care assistance under a qualified plan, the taxpayer may be able to exclude the amount from income. Dependent care benefits include the following:

➢ Amounts the employer paid directly to the care provider
➢ The fair market value of the care in a day-care facility provided or sponsored by the employer

The amounts paid are reported on Form W-2, box 10. To claim the exclusion, the taxpayer would complete Part III of Form 2441: *Child and Dependent Care Expenses*. The maximum the employer can pay per taxpayer (and spouse if filing jointly) is $5,000. See Publication 503.

Señor 1040 Says: Individuals who provide childcare in their own home are considered self-employed and should report their income on Schedule C. If the childcare is provided in the child's home, the providers are considered employees and should receive a W-2 from the child's parent or guardian, who should report the caretaker's income on Schedule H.

Group-Term Life Insurance

Generally, group-term life insurance coverage provided by an employer (current or former) to employees is not included as income up to the cost for coverage of $50,000 after being reduced by any amount the employee paid toward the purchase of the insurance.

If the coverage is worth more than $50,000, the employee must include the amount of money that the employer-provided insurance costs the employer as the employee's personal income. If the employer provided more than $50,000 of coverage, the includable amount is reported as part of the employee's wages in boxes 1, 3, and 5 of Form W-2. It is also shown separately in box 12 with code C on the W-2. Life insurance coverage should meet the following conditions:

➢ The employer provided a general death benefit that is not included in income.
➢ The employer provided it to a group of employees (usually 10 or more).
➢ The employer provided an amount of insurance to each employee based on a formula that prevents individual selection.
➢ The employer provided the insurance under a policy that was directly or indirectly carried. Even if the employer did not pay any of the cost, the employer is considered to carry it since the employer arranged for payment of its cost by the employees and charged at least one employee less than, and one employee more than, the cost of their insurance.

Group term life insurance that is payable on the death of the employee, employee's spouse, or dependent, and with a payment amount of less than $2,000, is considered a *de minimis* benefit.

The following types of insurance plans are not group term insurance:

➢ Insurance that does not provide general death benefits such as travel insurance or only provides accidental death benefits
➢ Life insurance on the life of the employee's spouse or dependent
➢ Insurance provided under a policy that provides a permanent benefit (an economic value that extends more than one year unless certain requirements are met) See Internal Revenue Code (IRC) section 1.79-1 for more information.

Health Savings Accounts (HSAs)

A Health Savings Account (HSA) is a form of pretax savings account set up to help set aside money to pay for future medical costs. If the taxpayer is an eligible individual, HSA contributions can be made by the employer, the taxpayer, or any of the taxpayer's family members. Medical expenses must not be reimbursable by the insurance or other sources, Taxpayer must be covered by a High Deductible Health Plan (HDHP) and not covered by another health plan.

Contributions made by the employer are not included in income. Distributions from the HSA that are used to pay for qualified medical expenses are included in income. Contributions to the account are used to pay current or future medical expenses of the account owner, spouse, and any qualified dependent.

Contributions by a partnership to a bona fide partner's HSA are not considered to be contributions by an employer. The contributions are treated as a distribution and are not included in the partner's gross income.

If the contributions by the partnership are for the partner's services rendered, they are treated as guaranteed payments that are included in the partner's gross income.

Contributions by an S corporation to a 2% shareholder-employee's HSA for services rendered are treated as guaranteed payments and are included in the shareholder-employee's gross income. The shareholder-employee may deduct the contribution made to the shareholder-employee's HSA. See Publication 969.

Transportation

If an employer provides a qualified transportation fringe benefit, a certain amount may be excluded from income. Providing any of the below can be a qualified transportation fringe benefit:

➢ A transit pass
➢ Qualified parking
➢ Transportation in a commuter highway vehicle (must seat at least 6 adults) between the taxpayer's home and workplace

Cash reimbursements by an employer for these expenses under a bona fide reimbursement arrangement are also excludable. However, cash reimbursement for a transit pass is excludable only if a voucher or similar item that can be exchanged only for a transit pass is not readily available for direct distribution to the taxpayer.
The exclusion for commuter highway vehicle transportation and transit passes fringe benefits cannot be more than a total of $280 a month, regardless of the total value of both benefits.

The exclusion for the qualified parking fringe benefit cannot be more than $280 a month, regardless of its value. For benefits with a value higher than the limit, the excess must be included as income. If the benefits have a value that is more than these limits, the excess is included as income. See IRC Sec 132(f).

Deductions for employee transportation fringe benefits such as parking and mass transit are denied, and no deduction is allowed for transportation expenses that are equivalent of commuting for employees. If the benefits have a value that is more than these limits, the excess is included as income. See IRC Sec 132(f).

Educational Assistance

If the taxpayer received educational assistance benefits from their employer under a qualified educational assistance program, up to $5,250 of eligible assistance can be excluded yearly, in which case it would not be included on the W-2 or be a part of a return. However, if the education was not work-related or if the taxpayer is a highly compensated employee, the assistance from the employer may be taxable. See Publication 970. See Sec. 127.

An employee who meets either of the following tests is a highly compensated employee:

➢ The employee was a 5% owner at any time during the year or the preceding year
➢ The employee received more than $130,000 in pay for the preceding year

The second test listed above can be ignored if the employee was not in the top 20% of the employees' pay ranking for the preceding year. All payments or reimbursements made under the adoption assistance program must be excluded from wages subject to federal income tax withholding.

A student in a degree program can exclude amounts received from a qualified scholarship or fellowship. Excludable income from a qualified scholarship or fellowship is any amount received that is used for the following:

➢ Tuition and fees to enroll at or attend an eligible educational institution
➢ Fees, books, and equipment required for courses at the eligible educational institution

Payments received for services required as a condition of receiving a scholarship or fellowship grant must be included in the taxpayer's income, even if the services are required of all students for the degree. Amounts used for room and board do not qualify for the exclusion. This includes amounts received for teaching and research. Include these payments on Form 1040, line 1. See Sec 127 and Pub 970.

Nontaxable Income

Although it may seem like taxes are collected on all income, there are several types of income that are exempt from taxation because of the nature of the reason behind the payment.

Child Support

Taxpayers who receive child support payments do not report the payments as income. Payments designed to be child support should be defined in legal documents such as divorce or separation agreements or any child custody documents.

Workers' Compensation

Amounts received as workers' compensation for an occupational sickness or injury are fully exempt from tax if they are paid under a workers' compensation act or some similar statute. The exemption also applies to the taxpayer's survivors. This exception does not apply to retirement plan benefits received based on age, length of service, or prior contributions to the plan, even if the taxpayer retired because of an occupational sickness or injury.

If the taxpayer returns to work after qualifying for workers' compensation, payments received while assigned to light duties are taxable. Report these payments as wages on line 1 of Form 1040.

Income paid under a statute that provides benefits only to employees with service-connected disabilities could be considered workers' compensation or disability for pension. The rest is taxable as annuity or pension income. If a taxpayer dies and their survivor benefits from the pension, the workers' compensation remains exempt from tax.

Welfare and Other Public Assistance Benefits

Benefit payments made by a public welfare fund to individuals with disabilities (such as blindness) should not be included as income. Welfare or public assistance payments from a state fund for the victims of a crime should not be included in the victims' income. Do not deduct medical expenses that are reimbursed by such a fund. Any welfare payments obtained fraudulently are not tax-exempt and must be included as income.

Veterans' Benefits

Veterans' benefits paid under any law, regulation, or administrative practice administered by the Department of Veterans Affairs (VA) should not be included as income.

For veterans and their families, the following benefits are not taxable:

➢ Education, training, and subsistence allowances
➢ Disability compensation and pension payments for disabilities paid either to veterans or their families
➢ Grants for homes designed for wheelchair living
➢ Grants for motor vehicles for veterans who lost their sight or the use of their limbs
➢ Veterans' insurance proceeds and dividends paid either to veterans or to their beneficiaries, including the proceeds of a veteran's endowment policy paid before death
➢ Interest on insurance dividends left on deposit with Veterans Affairs
➢ Benefits under a dependent-care assistance program
➢ The death gratuity paid to a survivor of a member of the armed forces who died after September 10, 2001
➢ Payments made under the compensated work therapy program
➢ Any bonus payment by a state or political subdivision because of services in a combat zone

How to Read the Tax Tables

Tax tables are charts that show how much tax is charged per income amount for each of the federal filing statuses. Tax tables apply to income that is less than $100,000 and each filing status has a separate table. If the taxpayer's income is over $100,000, the tax is calculated differently.

To read the tax table, you must find the income range in which your client's income falls and then look at the column that matches your client's filing status. If a client's income is the exact amount of one of the ranges, always round up and use the higher tax amount. Tax tables are found in the Form 1040 Instructions. Tax tables can also be accessed through the IRS website.

2023 Tax Table — Continued

If line 15 (taxable income) is—		And you are—			
At least	But less than	Single	Married filing jointly *	Married filing sepa-rately	Head of a house-hold
			Your tax is—		

72,000

At least	But less than	Single	Married filing jointly	Married filing separately	Head of household
72,000	72,050	11,153	8,203	11,153	9,547
72,050	72,100	11,164	8,209	11,164	9,558
72,100	72,150	11,175	8,215	11,175	9,569
72,150	72,200	11,186	8,221	11,186	9,580
72,200	72,250	11,197	8,227	11,197	9,591
72,250	72,300	11,208	8,233	11,208	9,602
72,300	72,350	11,219	8,239	11,219	9,613
72,350	72,400	11,230	8,245	11,230	9,624
72,400	72,450	11,241	8,251	11,241	9,635
72,450	72,500	11,252	8,257	11,252	9,646
72,500	72,550	11,263	8,263	11,263	9,657
72,550	72,600	11,274	8,269	11,274	9,668
72,600	72,650	11,285	8,275	11,285	9,679
72,650	72,700	11,296	8,281	11,296	9,690
72,700	72,750	11,307	8,287	11,307	9,701
72,750	72,800	11,318	8,293	11,318	9,712
72,800	72,850	11,329	8,299	11,329	9,723
72,850	72,900	11,340	8,305	11,340	9,734
72,900	72,950	11,351	8,311	11,351	9,745
72,950	73,000	11,362	8,317	11,362	9,756

Portion of Tax Table

The tax tables are not used by the following:

➢ Estates or trusts
➢ Individuals claiming the exclusion for foreign tax credits
➢ Taxpayers who file a short-period return
➢ Taxpayers whose income exceeds $100,000

Part 6 Review

To obtain the maximum benefit from each part go online now and watch the video.

Takeaways

Gross income, or "worldwide income," includes all income received from any source, anywhere in the world. This chapter covered the most common types of earned and unearned income. Later chapters will go into depth regarding the most common income reported on Schedule A, B, C, D, E, and F.

If the taxpayer repays an amount that was included in an earlier year as income, the taxpayer may be able to deduct the amount repaid from income for the year in which it was repaid. If the amount repaid is more than $3,000, the taxpayer may be able to take a credit against the tax for the year in which it was repaid. This credit is taken on Schedule A. Schedule A will be discussed in a later chapter. Generally, the taxpayer can claim a deduction or credit only if the repayment qualifies as an expense or loss incurred in the taxpayer's business or in a for-profit transaction.

Any individual with taxable compensation may be eligible to contribute to a traditional IRA. The individual may be able to contribute to a Roth IRA, establish a new traditional IRA, or fund the new IRA with funds transferred from either another traditional IRA or an employer-sponsored qualified retirement plan. In the taxable year in which an individual turns 72, the taxpayer cannot make future contributions to a traditional IRA.

TEST YOUR KNOWLEDGE!
Go online to take a practice quiz.

Chapter 5 Adjustments to Income

Introduction

In this chapter, students will learn how various expenses affect the taxpayer's income, and how to use this information to calculate the taxpayer's adjusted gross income (AGI). The Tax Cuts and Jobs Act (TCJA) has changed how adjustments are made at the federal level, while some states did not conform to the TCJA. Nonconforming states will have differences on the state return if applicable. For returns prior to TCJA, the tax professional may need to do additional research to file a correct return. TCJA mandates affect Schedule A, which will be discussed in a later chapter.

Objectives

At the end of this lesson, the student will:

➢ Understand how an adjustment to income can decrease the taxpayer's AGI
➢ Explain the differences between the education credits
➢ Define who qualifies to use Form 2106
➢ Know the different types of Health Savings Account

Resources

Form 1040	Publication 17	Instructions Form 1040
Form 1098-E	Publication 504	Instructions Form 1098-E
Form 2106	Publication 521	Instructions Form 2106
Form 3903	Publication 560	Instructions Form 3903
Form 8889	Publication 969	Instructions Form 8889
Form 8917	Publication 4334	Instructions Form 8917
Schedule SE	Tax Topics 451, 452, 455, 456, 458	Instructions Schedule SE
Schedule 1		

Part 1 Adjustments to Income

Adjustments are certain expenses that directly reduce the taxpayer's total income and are known in the industry as "above the line" tax deductions in the industry. Adjustments reduce total income to arrive at adjusted gross income (AGI), the total income from all sources minus any adjustments. Adjustments are calculated and reported using Form 1040, Schedule 1, lines 11 – 24z.

Schedule 1 (Form 1040) 2023 Page **2**

	Part II Adjustments to Income	
11	Educator expenses	11
12	Certain business expenses of reservists, performing artists, and fee-basis government officials. Attach Form 2106	12
13	Health savings account deduction. Attach Form 8889	13
14	Moving expenses for members of the Armed Forces. Attach Form 3903	14
15	Deductible part of self-employment tax. Attach Schedule SE	15
16	Self-employed SEP, SIMPLE, and qualified plans	16
17	Self-employed health insurance deduction	17
18	Penalty on early withdrawal of savings	18
19a	Alimony paid	19a
b	Recipient's SSN	
c	Date of original divorce or separation agreement (see instructions): _____	

Portion of Schedule 1

Changes Made by the Tax Cuts and Jobs Act

Due to the Tax Cuts and Jobs Act (TCJA), federal adjustments have been suspended from December 31, 2017, to December 31, 2025. Not all states conformed to the TCJA.

The TCJA eliminated Form 1040A and 1040EZ from 2018 to 2025. Here are some adjustments that will be discussed:

➢ Educator expenses
➢ IRA deductions
➢ Student loan interest deductions
➢ Tuition and fees

Educator Expenses

If the taxpayer was an eligible educator, they can deduct up to $300 of qualified expenses paid in 2023. An eligible educator is a teacher for kindergarten through twelfth –grade, or an instructor, counselor, principal, or aide who works in a school for at least 900 hours during a school year. If the taxpayer and spouse are filing jointly and are both eligible educators, the maximum deduction is $600. Neither spouse may deduct more than $300 of qualified expenses on line 11 of Form 1040, Schedule 1. The PATH act made this adjustment permanent.

Qualified expenses include ordinary and necessary expenses paid in connection with books, supplies, equipment (including computer equipment, software, and services), and other materials used in the educator's classroom. An ordinary expense is one that is common and accepted in the taxpayer's education field, and a necessary expense is one that is helpful and appropriate for the taxpayer's profession as an educator. An expense does not have to be required to be considered necessary.

Qualified expenses do not include homeschooling expenses or nonathletic supplies for health or physical education courses. The income adjustment amount must be reduced if the educator has any of the following:

➢ Excludable interest on qualified U.S. savings bonds series EE and I are reported on Form 8815
➢ Any distribution from a qualified tuition program that was excluded from income
➢ Any tax-free withdrawals from Coverdell education savings account(s)
➢ Any reimbursements received for expenses not reported in box 1 of the W-2

Form 2106: Unreimbursed Employee Business Expense

Due to the suspension of Form 2106 for tax years 2018 through 2025, most employees cannot use the form. Individuals who can still file Form 2106 include armed forces reservists, qualified performing artists, fee-basis state or local government officials, or individuals with a disability claiming impairment-related work expenses. These individuals may qualify to deduct unreimbursed employee business expenses as an adjustment to gross income. This is done by calculating the adjustment using Form 2106 and then reporting the calculated amount on Form 1040, Schedule 1, line 12.

To qualify, the taxpayer must meet all of the following requirements:

1. The taxpayer must be a performing artist who performed for at least two employers during the tax year
2. The taxpayer received at least $200 from each of at least two of these employers
3. The taxpayer's related performing arts business expenses are more than 10% of the gross income from the performance of those services
4. The taxpayer's adjusted gross income is not more than $16,000 before deducting these business expenses

If the taxpayer meets all the above requirements, they should complete Form 2106. If the taxpayer is married, they must file a joint return to claim the adjustment unless they lived apart during the tax year. When filing jointly, the couple must figure out requirements 1, 2, and 3 separately for each of them. However, requirement 4 applies to their combined AGI. If all the requirements are met, the amount on Form 2106, line 10, is entered on Form 1040, Schedule 1, line 12.

Schedule 1 Line 12

Included on line 12 are certain business expenses for reservists, performing artists and fee-basis government officials.

Reservists Expenses

If the taxpayer is a member of the U.S. military reserves, National Guard, or a member of the Public Health Service Reserve Corps, the expense for traveling more than 100 miles from their main home is deductible. To report these travel expenses, use Form 2106, Employee Business Expenses. Information from this form is then entered on Schedule 1, line 12. The deductible expenses are limited to the federal per diem rates for the city the taxpayer is traveling to.

Armed forces reservists are members of a reserve component of the following organizations:

➤ The United States Army, Navy, Marine Corps, Air Force or Coast Guard
➤ The Army National Guard of the United States
➤ The Air National Guard of the United States
➤ The Ready Reserve Corps of the Public Health Service

Sec IRC Sec 162(p) and IRS Pub 3.

Fee-Basis State or Local Government Official

Fee-basis state or local government officials qualify if they are employed by a state or a political subdivision of a state and are compensated in whole or in part on a fee basis. Under the Fair Labor Standards Act (FLSA), a "fee-basis" is defined as follows:

Administrative and professional employees may be paid on a fee basis. An employee will be considered to be paid on a "fee basis" within the meaning of these regulations if the employee is paid an agreed upon sum for a single job regardless of the time required for its completion. These payments resemble piecework payments with the important distinction that generally a "fee" is paid for the kind of job that is unique rather than for a series of jobs repeated an indefinite number of times and for which payment on an identical basis is made over and over again. Payments based on the number of hours or days worked and not on the accomplishment of a given task are not considered payments on a fee basis (Section 541.605).

If the fee-basis government official has qualifying expenses, use Form 2106. The expenses will be included on Schedule 1, line 12.

Health Savings Accounts

Health savings accounts contributions from both the employer and the employee are reported on Form 8889 and can be claimed as an adjustment to income on Form 1040, Schedule 1, line 13. Distributions made from the HSA that were paid for qualifying medical expenses are excludable from income. If the maximum possible amount of the HSA were contributed, then that amount would become taxable on the tax return.

A health savings account (HSA) is a tax-exempt trust or custodial account that is set up with a qualified HSA trustee to pay or reimburse certain medical expenses incurred by the employee. While this account is always paired with a medical insurance plan, an HSA is not health insurance. The HSA has tax advantages over a regular savings account. The taxpayer will receive a tax form stating the exact amount deposited into the account at the end of the year, and that amount is tax-deductible.

To qualify to contribute to an HSA as an eligible individual, the taxpayer must meet the following requirements:

➢ Have no other health coverage except permitted coverage
➢ Not enrolled in Medicare
➢ Not claimed as a dependent on another return
➢ Have a high deductible health plan (HDHP) on the first day of the month

Anyone can contribute to the plan for the taxpayer, and no permission or authorization from the IRS is necessary to establish an HSA. When an HSA is set up, the taxpayer will have to work with a qualified HSA trustee, which can be a bank, an insurance company, or anyone previously approved by the IRS to be a trustee of individual retirement accounts (IRAs) or Archer medical savings accounts (MSA). The HSA can be established through a trustee that is not a health plan provider.

2023 HSA Contribution Limits with an HDHP:

Type of Coverage	Contribution Limit
Self-only	$3,850
Family	$7,750

2024 HSA Contribution Limits with an HDHP:

Type of Coverage	Contribution Limit
Self-only	$4,150
Family	$8,300

The maximum annual out-of-pocket limit does not apply to deductibles and expenses for out-of-network services if the plan uses a network of providers. Only deductibles and out-of-pocket expenses for services within the network should be used to figure out whether the limit is reached.

Contributions to an HSA

Contributions made by the employer to the HSA on behalf of the employee are not included in the taxpayer's income. An employer's contributions to an employee's account using a salary deduction through a cafeteria plan are treated as an employer contribution. All contributions are reported on Form 8889 and must be filed with Form 1040.

Distributions from an HSA

Generally, medical expenses that have been paid for during the year are not reimbursed by the plan until the taxpayer has met the deductible. The taxpayer may receive a tax-free distribution from the HSA to pay for or reimburse qualified medical expenses after the taxpayer has established an HSA. Distributions received for any other reason are subject to an additional tax.

The Three Primary Types of HSAs

1. High-Deductible Health Plan (HDHP)

An HDHP has:

> ➢ A higher annual deductible than typical health plans
> ➢ A maximum limit on the total yearly deductible amount and out-of-pocket medical expenses

An HDHP can provide preventive care and other benefits with no deductible or deductible below the annual minimum. Preventive care can include:

> ➢ Routine exams and periodic health evaluations
> ➢ Routine prenatal and well-childcare
> ➢ Child and adult immunizations
> ➢ Stop-smoking programs
> ➢ Weight-loss programs

2. Archer Medical Savings Accounts (MSAs)

Archer MSAs are IRA-type savings accounts that taxpayers can use for medical expenses. They were created to help self-employed individuals and employees of certain small employers meet the medical costs of the account holder, the account holder's spouse, or the account holder's dependent(s). MSAs can be used when taxpayers have low-cost health insurance with a high-deductible health plan (HDHP). MSA contributions are tax-deductible.

The taxpayer can withdraw tax-free funds from the MSA to pay the portion of medical expenses not covered by insurance. The participants cannot pay their insurance premiums using funds in the MSA. Taxpayers who use Medicare, which counts as health insurance, can only use a Medicare MSA. If the taxpayer has no medical expenses in a tax year, the contributions remain in the account for future use. The maximum the taxpayer can contribute is 65% of the health-plan deductible for individuals (self-only plan) and 75% for families.

3. Health Flexible Spending Arrangements (FSAs)

A health FSA is usually funded through voluntary salary reduction and reimbursement for the employee's medical expenses. An FSA is not reported on the tax return, and the salary-reduction contribution limit is

$3,050 for 2023, and $3,200 for 2024. Regardless of the amount contributed, the taxpayer can receive a tax-free distribution to pay for qualified medical expenses. Self-employed individuals do not qualify for this reduction.

Part 1 Review

To obtain the maximum benefit from each part go online now and watch the video.

Part 2 Other Adjustments to Income

This part covers other adjustments that have been changed due to the Tax Cuts and Jobs Act. The two adjustments that have changed the most are moving expenses and alimony.

Form 3903: Moving Expenses

Under some circumstances, moving expenses can be claimed as adjustments to income. Moving expenses are reported on Form 1040, Schedule 1, line 14. Complete and attach Form 3903, *Moving Expenses*, to the tax return to claim this adjustment. The taxpayer does not have to itemize deductions to claim the adjustment. Although the Tax Cuts and Jobs Act made several changes to moving expenses, it is important for the tax professional to know how moving expense adjustments worked before and after the TCJA.

Moving Expenses Before the TCJA

To claim moving expenses as adjustments to income, the taxpayer must meet the following requirements:

➢ The move is closely related to the start of work
➢ The taxpayer meets the distance test
➢ The taxpayer meets the time test

Señor 1040 Says: Recordkeeping is vital to maintaining an accurate record of expenses for a move. The taxpayer should save receipts, bills, canceled checks, credit card statements, and mileage logs to correctly report the amount of moving expense.

Before the Tax Cuts and Jobs Act was enacted, moving expenses were claimed based on whether the move was made in conjunction with the taxpayer's job or business. The distance between the previous home and the new workplace must be at least 50 miles more than the distance between the previous home and the previous workplace. Also, if the taxpayer did not have any reimbursed moving expenses, they could report the expenses in the year they were incurred or when they were paid in full. The following moving expenses could be claimed as adjustments to income before the TCJA:

➢ The cost of packing and moving household goods and personal effects
➢ The cost of storing and insuring household goods once 30 days have passed
➢ The cost of connecting and disconnecting utilities
➢ The cost of one trip, including lodging but not meals, to the new home
➢ The cost of tolls and parking fees

The taxpayer would first report the moving expenses on Form 3903 and then on line 14 of Form 1040, Schedule 1. If the taxpayer had reimbursed moving expenses under an *accountable plan*, the expenses would be reported on the taxpayer's Form W-2 in box 12 and designated with code *P*. Reimbursed expenses reported with code *P* do not have to be reported on the tax return. If taxpayers were reimbursed for the moving expenses, they cannot claim the same moving expenses as adjustments to income on their tax return.

To be considered an accountable plan, the employer's reimbursement or allowance arrangement must meet the following requirements:

➤ The expenses must have a business connection, which means the taxpayer must have paid or incurred deductible expenses while performing services as an employee
➤ The taxpayer must adequately account to the employer for these expenses within a reasonable time
➤ The taxpayer must return any excess reimbursement or allowance within a reasonable time

Example: Donald lives in Seattle, WA, and accepted a job in Portland, ME. Donald's new employer reimbursed him using their accountable plan for his travel expenses from Seattle to Portland. Donald's employer would report the reimbursement with code *P* on his W-2, box 12.

Distance Test

The distance between a job's location and the taxpayer's main home is the shortest of the most traveled routes between them. The distance test considers only the location of the former home, and it does not account for the location of any new home. If the taxpayer had more than one job during the year, only use the "main job" location to calculate the distance for this test. To determine which job was the "main job," examine the following factors:

➤ The total time spent at each job
➤ The amount of work completed at each job
➤ The amount of money earned at each job

Whichever job had the highest or the majority of the above is the main job.

Time Test

The taxpayer must also meet a time test to qualify for moving expenses. According to the time test, if a taxpayer moves to another location and claims it was job-related, they must work in the new location for at least 39 weeks during the first 12 months of their stay to claim the moving expenses as adjustments to income.

Moving Expenses During the TCJA

One of the many changes made by the TCJA was to suspend adjustments for moving expenses with one exception: Active armed forces who have a military order to move or permanently change their station can claim moving expenses if they meet the normal qualifications. The moving mileage rate is 22 cents per mile. If the taxpayer has made multiple moves in one tax year, then a different Form 3903 will be used for each move.

A permanent station change can be any of the following:

➢ A move from the taxpayer's current home to their first post of duty
➢ A move from one permanent post to another
➢ A move from the taxpayer's last permanent post to a new home in the United States. The move must occur within one year of the end of active duty or within the allowable period designated by the Joint Travel Regulations, which is beyond the scope of this course.

Alimony Paid Beginning 2019

Alimony is a payment or a series of payments to a spouse or former spouse required under a divorce decree or a separation agreement that meets certain requirements. Any alimony a taxpayer receives should be reported on Form 1040, Schedule 1, line 2a. The amount of alimony paid should be reported on Form 1040, Schedule 1, line 19a, as an adjustment to income. The paying spouse must report the recipient's Social Security number on line 19b. Not all payments received from a spouse are considered alimony. For a description of what is considered alimony, see Publication 504.

The term "divorce or separation instrument" refers to the following:

➢ A decree of divorce or separate maintenance or a "written instrument incident" (see IRS Publication 504) to that decree
➢ A written separation agreement
➢ A decree or a type of court order requiring a spouse to make payments for the support or maintenance of the other spouse

Payments that are not alimony include:

➢ Child support
➢ Noncash property settlements
➢ Payments that are the taxpayer's spouse's part of community income
➢ Payments to keep up the payer's property
➢ Use of the payer's property
➢ Noncash property settlements, whether in lump sum or installments
➢ Voluntary payments

Divorce Agreement Post 2018

Alimony will no longer be an adjustment to income or a source of income if the divorce or separation agreement is completed after December 31, 2018. The new law applies if an agreement was executed on or before December 31, 2018, and then modified after that date. The new law applies if the modification does these two things:

➢ It changes the terms of the alimony or separate maintenance payments
➢ It says explicitly that alimony or separate maintenance payments are not deductible by the paying spouse or includable in the income of the receiving spouse

Agreements executed on or before December 31, 2018, follow the previous rules. If an agreement was modified after January 1, 2019, the new agreement should state that they are following the 2018 laws if the modifications did not change what is described above.

Community property laws may not apply to an item of community property income, and special rules may apply to community property states.

Example: Kathy and Lloyd live in Arizona and are a married couple. Kathy's father passed away in 2010. Her mother sold her country residence and moved into town to be closer to friends and church. Her mother had a trust and passed away in 2023. Kathy was a beneficiary of the trust and received $75,000 as an inheritance. Since Kathy and Lloyd live in a community property state, she would need to put her inherited money in a separate bank account to preserve her inheritance. If Kathy deposited the money into a joint account, the inheritance would become community property belonging to both Kathy and Lloyd. See Publication 504.

Individual Retirement Account (IRA) Deduction

Some individuals may participate in an Individual Retirement Account (IRA), a personal savings plan designed to provide tax advantages for saving toward retirement or education expenses. There are various types of IRAs available, including traditional, Roth, SIMPLE, and education IRAs.

It's crucial to differentiate between IRA contributions and deductions. Contributions are deposits into a taxpayer's IRA, while deductions are the portion of these contributions that can be subtracted from taxable income.

Taxpayers under the age of 72 with taxable compensation are eligible to contribute to an IRA, subject to certain conditions. For IRA purposes, compensation encompasses wages, salaries, commissions, tips, professional fees, bonuses, and other income received for personal services, including taxable alimony and separate maintenance payments.

The deductible amount of IRA contributions may be subject to limitations based on two primary factors:

➢ Whether the taxpayer or their spouse is covered by an employer-provided pension plan
➢ The modified adjusted gross income (MAGI) of the taxpayer

The maximum contribution to an IRA for a single taxpayer is either $6,500 or the amount of their taxable compensation, whichever is lower. For married couples where only one spouse has taxable compensation, the maximum joint contribution is $13,000. However, individual contributions cannot exceed $6,500 per account. If both spouses have compensation exceeding $7,500 each, they may each contribute up to $7,500.

Individuals 50 or older may make a "catch-up" contribution of $1,000 to their IRA. However, the total contribution for the tax year cannot exceed $7,500. Contributions must be made in cash, as property cannot be contributed to an IRA.

Exceeding the contribution limits ($6,500 or $7,500 for those 50 and older) incurs penalties. The taxpayer faces a tax on the excess contribution and its earnings each year until the excess is withdrawn. This penalty is not limited to the year the excess contribution was made and must be reported on Form 5329.

For the tax year 2024, the contribution limit is $7,000 ($8,000 for individuals aged 50 and over).

In addition to adjusting the taxpayer's gross income, interest earned on a traditional IRA account is accumulated tax-deferred until it is withdrawn, thus benefiting the taxpayer.
Suppose a taxpayer contributes more than $6,500 ($7,500 if age 50 or older) in one year to an IRA. In that case, the taxpayer will be penalized with a tax on the excess contribution and earnings each year until

the taxpayer withdraws the excess contribution. This penalty is not limited to the year the excess contribution is made. The excess contributions must be reported on Form 5329, *Additional Taxes Attributable to IRAs, Other Qualified Retirement Plans, Annuities, Modified Endowment Contracts, and MSAs*, Part II.

Spousal IRA

A nonworking spouse can contribute to a traditional IRA the same amounts as a working individual: $6,500 or $7,500 if 50 or older. The traditional IRA would be reduced by the amount of contributions that are completely funded by employee contributions.

Form 1098-E: Qualified Student Loans

Student loan providers will send Form 1098-E to borrowers who have paid $600 or more in interest. For the taxpayer to report their student loan interest, one of the following must apply:

➢ The loan has been subsidized, guaranteed, financed, or otherwise treated as a student loan under a federal, state, or local government program or a postsecondary education institution
➢ The loan is certified by the borrower as a student loan incurred solely to pay qualified higher education expenses

Reading Form 1098-E

2023 Form 1098-E

Box 1: Box 1 reports the total interest paid on the student loan for the current tax year, including any capitalized interest and loan origination fees.

Box 2: This box is checked if box 1 has loan origination fees and/or capitalized interest that, for some reason, were not included in box 1.

Academic Period

An academic period includes a semester, trimester, quarter, or other study period (such as a summer school session) as reasonably determined by an educational institution. In the case of an educational institution that uses credit hours or clock hours and does not have academic terms, each payment period can be treated as an academic period.

Student Loan Interest Deduction

Taxpayers with education loans can claim up to $2,500 of education loan interest paid in 2023 as adjustments to income. Student loan interest is reported on Form 1040, Schedule 1. The adjustment is allowed on qualifying loans for the taxpayer's benefit or the taxpayer's spouse or dependent when the debt was incurred. The adjustment phases out at income of $75,000 ($155,000 for MFJ). MFS individuals are unable to adjust student loan interest. If more than $600 were paid in interest on the student loan, Form 1098-E would be received.

The person for whom the expenses were paid must have been an eligible student; however, a loan is not a qualified student loan if both of the following are true:

➢ Any of the proceeds were used for other purposes
➢ The loan was from either a related person, a person who borrowed the proceeds under a qualified employer plan, or a contract purchased under such a plan

An eligible student is a person who meets the following conditions:

➢ Enrolling in a degree, certificate, or another program (including a studying abroad program approved for credit by the institution the student is registered with), leading to a recognized education credential at an eligible education institution
➢ Carried at least half of the normal full-time workload for the course of study the student is pursuing

See Publication 970, *Tax Benefits for Education*.

Part 2 Review

To obtain the maximum benefit from each part go online now and watch the video.

Part 3 Self-Employment Adjustments

Self-employed taxpayers must pay both the employer and employee portions of the Medicare and Social Security taxes. Since the self-employed person pays the entire amount, the taxpayer will make an adjustment to income equal to one-half of the total self-employment tax. This tax is figured on Schedule SE, and the adjustment is then carried to Form 1040, Schedule 1, line 15. If the taxpayer has W-2 wages, the taxpayer's net self-employment earnings are combined with their wages when determining the earning limit for the self-employment tax.

Self-Employment Tax

Self-employment tax does not apply to income earned as a shareholder of an S corporation or as a limited partner of a partnership (except for guaranteed payments). Self-employment tax is calculated on Schedule SE and must be paid if the following apply:

➢ Net earnings for the year from self-employment (excluding income as a church employee) were $400 or more
➢ Church-employee income for the year is more than $108.28

The self-employment tax rules apply even if the taxpayer receives Social Security and Medicare benefits. Special rules apply to workers who perform in-home services for elderly or disabled individuals. Caregivers are typically classified as employees of the individuals they provide care for. Self-employed individuals may have to make estimated quarterly payments to the IRS. See IRC Section 6017 and Schedule SE Instructions.

Self-Employment Retirement Plans

This adjustment pertains to self-employed individuals who offer retirement plans not only for themselves but also for their employees. The plans that can be deducted on this line are as follows:

➢ Simplified Employee Pension (SEP) plans
➢ Savings Incentive Match Plan for Employees (SIMPLE)
➢ Qualified plans, including HR (10) or Keogh plans, which are beyond this course's scope

SEP (Simplified Employee Pension)

A business of any size may establish a specific type of traditional IRA for their employees called a Simplified Employee Pension (SEP), also referred to as a SEP-IRA. A self-employed individual is also eligible to participate in this plan. There are three basic steps in starting a SEP:

➢ Must have a formal written agreement to provide benefits to all eligible employees
➢ Must give each eligible employee certain information
➢ A SEP-IRA must be set up for each employee

The formal written agreement must state that the employer will benefit all eligible employees under the SEP. The employer may adopt an IRS-provided model by filing Form 5305-SEP. Professional advice should be sought when setting up the SEP. Form 5305-SEP cannot be filed if any of the following apply:

➢ The company already has a qualified retirement plan other than a SEP
➢ The company has eligible employees whose IRAs have not been set up
➢ The company uses the service of leased employees who are not common-law employees
➢ The company is a member of one of the following trades or businesses:
  o An affiliated service group as described in section 414(m)
  o A controlled group of corporations as described in section 414(b)
  o A trade or business under common control as described in section 414(c)
➢ The company does not pay the cost of the SEP contributions

The contributions are made to IRAs (SEP-IRAs) of the eligible participants in that plan. Interest accumulates tax-free until the participant begins to make withdrawals. Contribution limits are based on net profits.

A taxpayer is eligible for a SEP if they meet the following requirements:

➢ Has reached age 21
➢ Has worked for the employer for at least 3 of the past five years
➢ Has received at least $600 in compensation from the employer during each of the last three tax years

The least of the following amounts is the maximum amount that an employer may annually contribute to an employee's IRA:

➢ $66,000 (for 2023)
➢ $69,000 (for 2024)
➢ 25% of the employee's compensation, or 20% for the self-employed taxpayer

Contributions made by the employer are not reported as income by the employee, nor can they be deducted as an IRA contribution. Excess contributions are included in the employee's income for the year and are treated as contributions. Do not include SEP contributions on the employee's Form W-2 unless the contributions are pre-tax contributions.

Example: Susan Plant earned $21,000 in 2023. Because the maximum employer contribution for 2023 is 25% of the employee's compensation, the employer can contribute $5,250 to her SEP-IRA (25% x $21,000).

SIMPLE Retirement Plan

A SIMPLE retirement plan is a tax-favored retirement plan that certain small employers (including self-employed individuals) can set up to benefit their employees.

A SIMPLE plan can be established for any employee who received at least $5,000 in compensation during the two years before the current calendar year and is reasonably expected to receive at least $5,000 during the current calendar year. Self-employed individuals are also eligible. The plan may also use less restrictive guidelines, but it may not use more stringent ones.

The employee's elective deferrals from salary reduction are limited to $15,500; or $18,500 (an additional $3,000) if age 50 or older (for 2023). For 2024 the limit is $16,000. Salary-reduction contributions are not treated as catch-up contributions. The employer can match employee deferrals dollar-for-dollar up to 3% of the employee's compensation.

SIMPLE IRA

A SIMPLE IRA is a plan that uses separate IRA accounts for each eligible employee. A SIMPLE plan is a written agreement (salary-reduction agreement) between the taxpayer and their employer that allows the taxpayer to choose to do either of the following:

➢ Reduce the taxpayer's compensation by a certain percentage each pay period
➢ Have the employer contribute the salary reductions to a SIMPLE IRA on the taxpayer's behalf. These contributions are called "salary-reduction contributions."

All contributions under a SIMPLE IRA plan must be made to SIMPLE IRAs and not to any other type of IRA. The SIMPLE IRA can be an individual retirement account or an individual retirement annuity. In addition to salary reduction contributions, the employer must make either matching contributions or non-elective contributions. The taxpayer is eligible to participate in their employer's SIMPLE plan if the taxpayer meets the following requirements:

➢ They received compensation from their employer two years before the current year
➢ They are reasonably expected to receive at least $5,000 in compensation during the calendar year in which contributions were made

The difference between the SIMPLE retirement plan and the SIMPLE IRA is that the retirement plan is part of a 401(k) plan, and the IRA plan uses individual IRAs for each employee. See Publication 560.

Self-Employed Health Insurance Deductions

Self-employed taxpayers can claim (as adjustments to income on Form 1040, Schedule 1, line 17) of the amount paid in 2023 for medical insurance and qualified long-term care insurance for the taxpayer and the taxpayer's family if any of the following apply:

> ➢ The taxpayer is a self-employed individual and makes a net profit
> ➢ The taxpayer is a partner who receives net earnings from self-employment on Schedule SE
> ➢ The shareholder owns more than 2% in an S corporation and have wages on Form W-2

Premiums are not deductible any month that the taxpayer or spouse was eligible to participate in an employer-subsidized health plan. The taxpayer's earned income could also limit the deduction. Schedule C would be the net profit minus the SE tax deduction (Schedule 2, line 4) and SEP deductions (Schedule 1, line 16). Self-employed individuals must have a net profit for the year to deduct their paid premiums as adjustments to income.

The self-employed health insurance deduction should be calculated using the *Worksheet for the Health Insurance Deduction* found in Publication 974.

If any of the following exceptions apply, the worksheet cannot be used:

> ➢ The taxpayer had more than one source of income subject to self-employment.
> ➢ The taxpayer filed Form 2555
> ➢ The taxpayer included their qualified long-term care insurance to calculate the deduction
> ➢ How to deduct health insurance premiums for the self-employed

Part 3 Review

To obtain the maximum benefit from each part go online now and watch the video.

Takeaways

Taxpayers have the option to claim various "deductions" directly on their tax return. These deductions, however, differ from itemized or standardized deductions, as they are referred to as adjustments to income. These adjustments modify the taxpayer's gross income and are commonly known as "above the line" deductions, appearing above the adjusted gross income section on the tax form.

An example of such an adjustment is an HSA (Health Savings Account), which is a specialized account reserved for covering qualified medical expenses of the account holder, their spouse, or dependents. Other adjustments to income that taxpayers may claim include deductible portions of self-employment tax, IRA deductions, self-employed health insurance expenses, and student loan interest from $600 to $2,500.

TEST YOUR KNOWLEDGE!
Go online to take a practice quiz.

Chapter 6 Other Taxes and Taxpayer Penalties

Introduction

This chapter provides an overview of taxes reported on Schedule 2. Some common taxes that a tax preparer will see are:

➢ Alternative Minimum Tax (AMT)
➢ Additional Medicare Tax
➢ Additional tax on IRAs
➢ Excess Social Security tax
➢ Household employment taxes
➢ Net investment income tax (NIIT)
➢ Self-employment tax (will be covered in a later chapter)
➢ Unreported tip income

Objectives

At the end of this chapter, the student will:

➢ Complete Form 1040, Schedule 2
➢ Explain when a taxpayer must repay the Premium Tax Credit
➢ Understand the taxability of excess Social Security
➢ Identify when a taxpayer must pay an additional tax on IRAs
➢ Clarify when to use Schedule H

Resources

Form 1040	Publication 17	Instructions Form 1040
Form 4137	Publication 334	Instructions Form 4137
Form 5329	Publication 560	Instructions Form 5329
Form 5405	Publication 575	Instructions Form 5405
Form 6251	Publication 590-B	Instructions Form 6251
Form 8919	Publication 594	Instructions Form 8919
Form 8959	Publication 721	Instructions Form 8959
Form 8962	Publication 939	Instructions Form 8962
Form 8965	Publication 974	Instructions Form 8965
Schedule 2	Tax Topic 556, 557, 558,	Instructions Schedule 2
Schedule H	560, 611, 653	Instructions for Schedule H

Part 1 Additional Taxes from Schedule 2

Schedule 2 (Form 1040), Part I, is used to report Additional Taxes. This section captures supplemental tax provisions that modify or expand upon the income tax liability determined on Form 1040. Schedule 2, Part 1 accounts for additional and specialized taxes, certain tax credits, and other adjustments to ensure taxpayers are compliant with all applicable tax laws and regulations.

This portion of Schedule 2 is critical for accurately calculating total tax liabilities, as it incorporates specific taxes like the Additional Medicare Tax on earned income, and tax recapture provisions aimed at upholding the integrity of the tax system. Tax professionals must thoroughly understand Part I to ensure their clients are fully compliant while taking advantage of all available tax planning opportunities.

SCHEDULE 2 (Form 1040) Department of the Treasury Internal Revenue Service	**Additional Taxes** Attach to Form 1040, 1040-SR, or 1040-NR. Go to *www.irs.gov/Form1040* for instructions and the latest information.	OMB No. 1545-0074 **2023** Attachment Sequence No. **02**
Name(s) shown on Form 1040, 1040-SR, or 1040-NR		Your social security number

Part I Tax

1	Alternative minimum tax. Attach Form 6251	**1**	
2	Excess advance premium tax credit repayment. Attach Form 8962	**2**	
3	Add lines 1 and 2. Enter here and on Form 1040, 1040-SR, or 1040-NR, line 17 . .	**3**	

Portion of Schedule 2

Line 1 Alternative Minimum Tax (Form 6251) See IRC Sec 55 -59

The alternative minimum tax (AMT) applies to taxpayers who qualify for certain deductions. The additional tax is on preference items, which is normally tax-free income, or when a large amount of itemized deductions is taken. If the taxpayer has deducted preference items and their income exceeds a certain amount, the AMT recalculates income tax after adding tax preference items back into adjusted gross income. As the name suggests, the AMT is the minimum tax possible, designed to ensure fairness in the tax system and prevent excessive tax avoidance by high-income individuals, despite whatever exclusions, credits, or deductions may have been taken. If an adequate amount of a taxpayer's income is from the preference items, and that income exceeds the preset amounts discussed below, they will have to pay AMT even if they had otherwise lowered their tax liability below zero. Form 6251 calculates the AMT and is reported on Schedule 2, line 1. AMT could offset personal and business taxes.

AMT is determined based on taxpayer's income. If a taxpayer with an excess amount of deductions received an amount of income that exceeds $81,300 (2023) (Individuals), $126,500 (2023) (Qualifying Surviving Spouse or Married Filing Jointly), or $63,250 (for taxpayers filing separately), then the AMT will be triggered and applied. The 2023 AMT rate was 26% on the first $220,700 worth of income for non-corporate taxpayers. If the taxpayer is above $220,700 then they are taxed at 28%. The AMT exemption begins to phase out for married filing couples at $1,156,300 and for all other filers the phaseout is $578,150. For Married Filing Separate taxpayers, the AMT threshold is $103,050.

For 2024, the AMT amount is $85,700 for individuals, $133,300 for married couples, and $66,650 for married filing separately. 2024 AMT begins to phase out for single filers at $609,350 and for married jointly filers at $1,218,700. The 28% rate applies to the excess Alternative Minimum Tax Income (AMTI) for all taxpayers with income of $232,600; for taxpayers filing separately the rate is $116,300.

The following taxpayers must file Form 6251:

1. If line 7 on Form 6251 is greater than line 10.
2. The taxpayer claimed a general business credit, and either line 6 in Part I of line 25 Form 3800 is more than zero.
3. The taxpayer claimed the qualified electric vehicle credit on Form 8834, using the personal part of the alternative fuel vehicle refueling property credit on Form 8911 or the prior year minimum tax on Form 8801.
4. The total of lines 2c through 3 on Form 6251 is negative and line 7 is greater than line 10, if lines 2c through 3 were not taken into account.

Taxpayers who need to file Form 8801, *Credit for Prior Year Minimum Tax*, could be an individual, estates or a trust. This form is used when the taxpayer has a credit carryforward to the next year, or if the taxpayer had claimed a qualified vehicle credit that was unallowed. Another cause could be the AMT liability, and adjustments or preferences that were not exclusion items. See IRC Code Section 53.

Line 2 Advanced Premium Tax Credit (Form 8962) Sec 36B

Although there is no penalty for not having health insurance, if the taxpayer purchased health care through the Marketplace, the individual must complete Form 8962 to calculate if they need to repay the premium tax credit repayment. Taxpayers who have purchased a federal or state government health care plan would use this form to calculate if they are responsible for repaying excess advanced payments from the premium tax credit (APTC).

Portion of Form 8962

Qualified individuals and families can claim the Premium Tax Credit (PTC) on Form 8962. This credit helps pay for qualifying health insurance if the taxpayer and their family (as defined below) are enrolled through the Health Insurance Marketplace, an exchange offering qualifying health plans. For more information, see Publication 974 and Instructions Form 8962. The Premium Tax Credit is reported on both Form 1040 and Form 1040NR.

Terms to know for PTC purposes:

➢ **Tax Family**: Tax family comprises the taxpayer and/or spouse and qualifying individual(s). The family's size is the number of qualifying individuals claimed on the tax return unless either the taxpayer or spouse is claimed as a dependent on another tax return.

➢ **Household Income**: Household income is the modified gross income of the taxpayer and spouse if filing jointly. Add the modified AGI of everyone claimed as a dependent and required to file a tax return due to the filing threshold. Household income does not include the modified AGI of dependents who file return just to receive their refund.

➢ **Modified AGI**: Modified AGI is the AGI plus specific income not subject to tax. That income is foreign earned income, tax-exempt interest, and the portion of Social Security benefits that are not taxable.

➢ **Coverage Family: The coverage family includes all individuals in the tax family enrolled in a qualified health plan and not eligible for minimum essential coverage (MEC) beyond the coverage in the individual market.** Individuals included in the coverage family may change from month to month. If an individual in the tax family is not enrolled in a qualified health plan or is enrolled in a qualified health plan but is eligible for minimum essential coverage, they are not included in the coverage family. The Premium Tax Credit is available to pay for the coverage of those included in the coverage family.

➢ *Monthly Credit Amount*: The amount of tax credit for a month. The PTC for the year is the sum of all monthly credit amounts. The monthly credit amount is the least of the following:
  o The enrollment premiums for the month for one or more qualified health plans in which any individual in the tax family was enrolled.
  o The applicable monthly amount of the Second Lowest Cost Silver Plan (SLCSP) premium after the monthly contribution amount has been subtracted.
  To qualify for the monthly credit amount, at least one tax family member must be enrolled in a qualified health plan on the first day of the month. The monthly credit will not apply if the tax family was not enrolled in a qualified health plan on the 1st of the month. See Instructions Form 8962.

➢ *Enrollment Premiums*: Total monthly premiums for one or more qualified health plans that any tax family member is enrolled in. Form 1095-A Part III, column A reports the enrollment premiums. The tax professional should ask to see all forms related to health coverage.

➢ *Applicable Second Lowest Cost Silver Plan (SLCSP)*: The Second Lowest Cost Silver Plan is, as the name suggests, the plan in the silver category (discussed further in the "Marketplace Plan Levels" Section) that costs the second least. It is not the least costly plan but the second-least costly plan. It is important to know the premium of the SLCSP offered in the taxpayer's area, because that premium is one of the things used to calculate the PTC. The SLCSP premium is a different premium than the enrollment premium described above.

➢ *Monthly Contribution Amount*: The monthly contribution is also used to calculate the Premium Tax Credit amount. The monthly contribution is the amount of income that taxpayers are responsible for paying as their monthly premiums.

➢ *Qualified Health Plan*: A qualified health insurance plan purchased through the Marketplace. Catastrophic health plans and stand-alone dental plans purchased through the Marketplace, as well as all plans purchased through Small Business Health Options Programs, are not qualified health plans.

Minimum Essential Coverage (MEC)

Minimum essential coverage includes government-sponsored programs, eligible employer-sponsored plans, individual market plans, and any other coverage that the Department of Health and Human Services designates as minimum essential coverage:

➢ Health plans offered in the individual market
➢ Government-sponsored programs
➢ Employer-sponsored plans
➢ Other health coverage plans designated as minimum essential coverage by the Department of Health and Human Services

Señor 1040 Says: Minimum essential coverage does not include coverage consisting solely of excepted benefits. Excepted benefits include stand-alone vision and dental plans (except pediatric dental coverage), workers' compensation coverage, and coverage limited to a specified disease or illness. A taxpayer may have any of these types of coverage and still qualify for the PTC on their qualified health plan.

The Individual Shared Responsibility Provision requires the taxpayer and each family member to do one of the following:

➢ Have qualifying health coverage
➢ Qualify for a health coverage exemption
➢ Make a shared responsibility payment when filing their federal income tax return

Many people already have minimum essential coverage and do not have to do anything more than maintain the coverage and report their coverage when they file their tax return. If the taxpayer is covered by any of the following types of plans, they are considered covered under the health care law and will not pay a penalty or get a health coverage exemption:

➢ Any Marketplace plan or any individual insurance plan already established
➢ Any job-based plan, including retiree plans and COBRA coverage
➢ Medicare Part A or Part C
➢ Most Medicaid coverage
➢ The Children's Health Insurance Program (CHIP)
➢ Most individual health plans bought outside the Marketplace, including "grandfathered" plans (not all plans sold outside the Marketplace qualify as minimum essential coverage)
➢ Dependents under the age of 24 who are covered under a parent's plan
➢ Self-funded health coverage offered to students by universities for plan or policy years that started on or before Dec. 31, 2014. The taxpayer should check with the university to confirm their plan is minimum essential coverage.
➢ Health coverage for Peace Corps volunteers
➢ Certain types of veteran's health coverage through the Department of Veterans Affairs
➢ Department of Defense Nonappropriated Fund Health Benefits Program
➢ Refugee Medical Assistance
➢ State high-risk pools for plan or policy years that started on or before December 31, 2014. The taxpayer should check with the high-risk pool to confirm their plan is minimum essential coverage

For a more detailed list of types of plans that may or may not be minimum essential coverage, see Instructions Form 8965, *Health Coverage Exemptions.*

Marketplace Plan Levels

The ACA requires that all new policies, including those plans that are sold on the exchange (except stand-alone dental, vision, and long-term care plans), comply with one of the four benefit categories set up by the Patient Protection and Affordable Care Act (PPACA). The PPACA coverage levels are based on the concept of "actuarial value," which is the share of health care expenses the plan covers for a typical group of enrollees. As plans increase in actuarial value, they would cover a greater share of an enrollee's medical expenses overall, though the details could vary across different plans. The levels of coverage provided for in the PPACA are central to the coverage that individuals will get under the health reform law.

The four Marketplace levels are:

Bronze	60%
Silver	70%
Gold	80%
Platinum	90%

The ACA provides reduced cost sharing for enrollees who select a plan from the silver tier in the federal or state marketplace. The cost-sharing reductions are achieved by requiring insurers to create variants of each standard silver plan, with each variant meeting a successively higher actuarial value. The federal government reimburses insurance companies for the loss of profit resulting from reducing costs for their customers. The reimbursement is known as a "subsidy."

Employer-sponsored Coverage

If the taxpayer and other family members had the opportunity to enroll in a plan offered by their employer for 2023, the taxpayer is considered eligible for MEC, even if the offer of coverage met a minimum standard of affordability and provided a minimum level of benefits. The coverage offered by an employer is generally considered affordable for the taxpayer and qualifying family members allowed to enroll in the coverage. A taxpayer's share of the annual cost for self-only coverage, which is sometimes referred to as the employee required contribution, is not more than 9.78% of household income.

Example: Don was eligible to enroll in his employer's coverage for 2023 but instead applied for coverage in a qualified health plan through the Marketplace. Don provided accurate information about his employer's coverage to the Marketplace, and the Marketplace determined that the offer of coverage was not affordable, and that Don was eligible for APTC. Don enrolled in the qualified health plan for 2023. Don got a new job with employer coverage that he could have enrolled in as of September 1, 2023, but chose not to. Don did not return to the Marketplace to determine if he was eligible for APTC from September through December 2023 and remained enrolled in the qualified health plan. Don is not considered eligible for employer-sponsored coverage for the months of January through August of 2023 because he gave accurate information to the Marketplace about the availability of employer coverage, and the Marketplace determined that he was eligible for APTC for coverage in a qualified health plan. The Marketplace determination does not apply, however, for the months September through December of 2023. This is because Don did not provide information to the Marketplace about his new employer's offer of coverage. Whether Don is considered eligible for employer-sponsored coverage and ineligible for the APTC for the months September through December of 2023 is determined under the eligibility rules described under Employer-Sponsored Plans. If the taxpayer cannot get benefits under an employer-sponsored plan until after a waiting period has expired, the taxpayer is not treated as being eligible for that coverage during the waiting period. See Publication 974.

Payments of the Premium Tax Credit

If the taxpayer purchased insurance through the Health Insurance Marketplace, they may be eligible for an Advanced Premium Tax Credit (APTC) to help pay for the insurance coverage. Receiving too little or too much in advance will affect the taxpayer's refund or balance due. To avoid owing a balance, the taxpayer should contact the insurance provider to report changes in income or family size to the Marketplace as soon as possible.

If the taxpayer and family members are enrolled in Marketplace coverage, Form 1095-A should be received from the Marketplace with the months of coverage and the amounts of APTC paid. If the taxpayer received a Form 1095-A showing APTC, Form 8962 must be filed, even if the taxpayer is not otherwise required to file. The taxpayer's Premium Tax Credit is determined by reference to the premium amount for the second lowest cost silver plan offered by an exchange in the rating area where the taxpayer resides.

The Premium Tax Credit is limited to the amount of premium paid for the chosen plan. The credit may be payable in advance, with the payments going directly to the insurance company. A taxpayer who is eligible for an advanced assistance payment may decline it and receive the full amount of the credit on their tax return. Eligibility and the amount of the credit itself are affected by the family size and household income. A married couple must file a joint return to claim the credit. If a married couple files Married Filing Separately, they are not eligible for the credit. If taxpayers file separately because they are victims of domestic abuse, see Notice 2014-23 for the criteria.

A taxpayer is allowed an advanceable and refundable credit to help subsidize the purchase of health insurance. The taxpayer must have household income of at least 100% but not more than 400% of the federal poverty line for their family size. The taxpayer must not receive health insurance under an employer-sponsored plan (including COBRA) or certain government plans such as Medicare.

Household income means an amount equal to the sum of the following items:

➢ The taxpayer's Modified Adjusted Gross Income (MAGI)
➢ The MAGI of all other individuals who are both of the following:
➢ Counted in family size
➢ Required to file an income tax return for the year under IRC §1 without regard to the exception for a child whose parents elect to use IRC §1(g)(7)

Remember, Modified Adjusted Gross Income (MAGI) is adjusted gross income, plus all the following:

➢ The amount excluded under IRC §911, *Foreign-Earned Income Exclusion*
➢ Tax-exempt interest income
➢ The excluded portion of Social Security benefits

Premium Tax Credit Repayment

The Premium Tax Credit helps pay health insurance premiums that were purchased through the Health Insurance Marketplace. If the advanced payments of this credit were made for coverage for the taxpayer, spouse, or dependents, Form 8962 would be used. If the advanced payments were more than the Premium Tax Credit, the taxpayer must repay the excess, reported on Schedule 2, line 46, and added to their tax liability. An additional tax liability could be caused by the taxpayer or spouse having an increase in income and not reporting the change to the Marketplace. If the advanced payments exceed the credit allowed, the income tax liability imposed for the tax year is increased by the difference.

Shared Policy Allocation

For any month during the year the taxpayer, spouse, or dependents did not have minimum essential coverage and do not have a coverage exemption, the taxpayer may need to make an individual shared responsibility payment on the tax return. The annual payment amount is either a percentage of taxpayer's household income or a flat dollar amount, whichever is greater. The national average premium is capped for a bronze level health plan on the Marketplace.

Part 1 Review

To obtain the maximum benefit from each part go online now and watch the video.

Part 2 Taxes for Self-Employed

A self-employed individual pays both the employer and the employee tax. This part will discuss which taxes a self-employed individual must pay, as well as how to pay their Social Security and Medicare tax. Other taxes are reported on Part II of Schedule 2.

Part II	Other Taxes			
4	Self-employment tax. Attach Schedule SE			4
5	Social security and Medicare tax on unreported tip income. Attach Form 4137	5		
6	Uncollected social security and Medicare tax on wages. Attach Form 8919	6		
7	Total additional social security and Medicare tax. Add lines 5 and 6			7

Portion of Schedule 2

Line 4 Self-Employment tax. Attach Schedule SE

This will be covered in *"Federal Schedule C"* chapter.

Line 5 Social Security and Medicare Tax on Unreported Tip Income (Form 4137)

Form 4137 is used to calculate the Social Security and Medicare tax on tips not reported to the taxpayer's employer. Unreported tips were covered in Chapter 4, "Federal Income."

Line 6 Uncollected Social Security and Medicare Tax (Form 8919)

If the taxpayer was an employee but was treated as an independent contractor by the employer, Form 8919, *Uncollected Social Security and Medicare Tax on Wages*, is used to figure and report the taxpayer's share of uncollected Social Security and Medicare taxes due on compensation. Filing this form ensures that the Social Security and Medicare taxes will be credited to the correct Social Security record.

Line 8 Additional Tax on IRAs and Other Tax-Favored Accounts

The calculated amount from Form 5329 is reported on Line 8 of Schedule 2. Form 5329 is used to report additional taxes on the following items:

- ➢ Early distributions from an IRA
- ➢ Early distributions from qualified retirement plans
- ➢ Excess contributions made to an IRA and other accounts such as:
  - o Archer MSA
  - o Health savings account
  - o ABLE Account
  - o Coverdell education savings account.
- ➢ The taxpayer did not tax their required minimum distribution.

The additional tax on an early distribution is included in the taxpayer's gross income and is an additional 10%, although there are some exceptions to the rule. The additional 10% tax on an early withdrawal does not apply to any of the following:

- ➢ A qualified disaster distribution

➢ A qualified HSA funding distribution from an IRA
➢ A distribution from a traditional or SIMPLE IRA that was converted to a Roth IRA
➢ An in-plan Roth rollover
➢ A distribution of certain excess IRA contributions

Required Minimum Distributions

IRA custodians, trustees, or the IRA issuer are required to provide IRA owners with an RMD statement indicating that a distribution is required. The taxpayer needs to withdraw the amount by April 1 of the year after they reach age 73. Failing to withdraw the RMD by the deadline may result in an additional tax liability of 50% of the excess accumulation. With reasonable cause, the taxpayer can request a waiver of the fee from the IRS by including a letter of explanation with Form 5329 with the tax return.

Excess accumulation relating to traditional IRA, Simplified Employee Pensions (SEP), Savings Incentive Match Plans for Employees of Small Employers (SIMPLE), and beneficiary Individual Retirement Accounts (IRAs) is defined as an amount remaining in the IRA because of an account owner or beneficiary failing to satisfy an RMD.

Line 9 Household Employment Taxes

Taxpayers who employ household workers may be required to pay and withhold employment taxes from their employees. Employment taxes include Social Security tax, Medicare tax, federal unemployment tax, federal income tax withholding, and state employment taxes. To determine if a household worker is considered self-employed for tax purposes, the worker must provide their own tools and offer services to the public in an independent business.

Some examples of household workers include babysitters, caretakers, cleaning people, domestic workers, drivers, health aides, housekeepers, maids, nannies, private nurses, private chefs, and yard workers. A worker who performs childcare services in their home is generally not the taxpayer's employee.

Example: Melchior has made an agreement to care for Jess's lawn. Melchior runs a lawn care business and offers his services to the public. Melchior provides his own tools and supplies, and he hires and pays his employees. Neither Melchior nor his employees are Jess's household employees.

Form 1040, Schedule H, *Household Employment Taxes*, must be used to report household employment taxes if the taxpayer pays any of the following wages to the employee:

➢ Social Security and Medicare wages of $2,600 or more
➢ Federal Unemployment Tax Act (FUTA) wages
➢ Wages from which federal income taxes were withheld

If the taxpayer pays more than $2,400 in a calendar year to a household employee, the taxpayer must pay Social Security and Medicare taxes for that employee and withhold (or pay) the employee's portion of those taxes.

The taxpayer, who is the employer, is not required to withhold federal income taxes for household employees unless the employee asks to have withholdings taken out and the employer agrees to withhold the taxes. The employer must have their employee(s) complete Form W-4, *Employee's Withholding Allowance Certificate*. As with other employment taxes, federal income taxes withheld may be reported on Schedule H. Schedule H is reported on Form 1040, Schedule 2, line 9. Schedule H can be a standalone form if the taxpayer is not filing a yearly tax return. If a paid tax preparer completed the form for the taxpayer, then they would complete the Paid Preparer Use Only section on Schedule H.

Line 10 First-Time Homebuyer Credit Repayment (Form 5405)

If the taxpayer purchased their primary residence in 2008 and qualified for the first-time homebuyer credit, and either disposed of the home or ceased using it as their primary residence, the taxpayer needs to repay the credit that was received on the 2008 tax return. The credit that was received in 2008 was an interest-free loan to the taxpayer and is to be repaid over a 15-year period. If the taxpayer purchased a home prior to April 8, 2008, and did not own another main home for 36 months prior to the date of purchase and received the credit, repayment of the loan is required.

If the taxpayer sold or converted the main home prior to repayment of the first-time homebuyer credit, the remaining portion of the loan must be repaid in the year the taxpayer sells or converts the property. This repayment is reported using Form 5405 on Form 1040, Schedule 2, line 10.

Example: In June 2008, Watson purchased his primary home. Watson moved out and converted his home to a rental in 2023; Watson will have to repay the remaining portion of the first-time homebuyer credit on his 2023 tax return because he sold it before the end of the 15-year repayment period. Tax year 2023 is the last payment the taxpayer needs to pay.

Line 11 Additional Medicare Tax (Form 8959)

The taxpayer may be subject to a 0.9% additional Medicare tax that applies to any Medicare wages, railroad retirement act compensation, and self-employment income that exceeds the filing status threshold. This tax is an employee tax, not an employer tax. The employer is responsible for withholding the additional tax once the taxpayer's compensation exceeds $200,000 (regardless of filing status) in a calendar year. The taxpayer cannot request that their employer stop withholding the additional tax. If the taxpayer has wages as well as self-employment income, the threshold is reduced on the self-employment income, but not below zero.

Filing Status	Threshold Amount
Married Filing Jointly	$250,000
Married Filing Separately	$125,000
Single	$200,000
Head of Household	$200,000
Qualifying Surviving Spouse	$200,000

The above threshold amounts are not indexed for inflation.

Example: Terri, a single filer, has $130,000 in self-employment income and $0 in wages. Terri is not liable for the Additional Medicare Tax and does not have to file Form 8959.

Example: George and Jean are married and filing a joint return. George has $190,000 in wages and Jean has $150,000 in compensation subject to railroad retirement taxes. Neither George nor Jean has wages or compensation that exceed $200,000 because their employers do not combine the wages and railroad retirement compensation to determine whether they are more than the $250,000 threshold for a joint return. George and Jean are not liable for the additional tax.

Example: Carl, a single filer, has $220,000 in self-employment income and $0 in wages. Carl must file Form 8959 as he is liable to pay the additional Medicare Tax on $20,000 of his $220,000 income ($220,000 minus the threshold of $200,000).

Line 12 Net Investment Income Tax (NIIT)

Reported using Form 8960, NIIT is a 3.8% tax on the lesser of net investment income or the excess of the taxpayer's modified adjusted gross income amount that is over the filing status threshold. NIIT generally includes income and gain from passive activities. For the purposes of the NIIT, a passive activity, as defined by §469 of the Internal Revenue Code, includes rental activity whether the taxpayer materially participated or not. Income is excluded from the NIIT if it is derived from a trade or business as defined under §162 of the Internal Revenue Code and is non-passive. Individuals who have NIIT and modified adjusted gross income (MAGI) over the following thresholds will owe 3.8%:

Filing Status	Threshold Amount
Married filing jointly & Qualifying Surviving Spouse	$250,000
Married filing separately	$125,000
Single & Head of Household (with qualifying person)	$200,000

Taxpayers should be aware that these threshold amounts are not indexed for inflation. If an individual is exempt from Medicare taxes, they may still be subject to NIIT if the taxpayer's modified adjusted gross income is over the thresholds.

NIIT includes gross income from interest, dividends, capital gains, rental and royalty income, and annuities, unless they are derived from the ordinary course of a trade or business that is:

1. Not a passive activity
2. A trade or business of financial instruments or commodities

The net investment income tax will not apply to any gain excluded from gross income for regular income tax purposes. The pre-existing statutory exclusion in IRC §121 exempts the first $250,000 (or $500,000 in the case of a married couple filing jointly) of gain recognized on the sale of a principal residence from gross income for regular income tax purposes and, thus, from the NIIT. For more information on NIIT, go to www.irs.gov and see the FAQs for the NIIT.

The following gains are examples of items that are taken into consideration when computing NIIT:

➤ Gains from sale of stocks, bonds, and mutual funds
➤ Capital gain distributions from mutual funds
➤ Gain from the sale of investment real estate, including the gain on the sale of a second home that is not the taxpayer's primary residence
➤ A gain from the sale of interest in partnerships and S corporations (to the extent that the partner or shareholder was a passive owner).

Distributions are considered when determining the modified adjusted gross income threshold. Distributions from a nonqualified retirement plan are included in net investment income. Form 8960 will be filed if the taxpayer has net investment income tax. For more information, refer to IRS Regulation Sections 1.1411-1 through 1.1411-10.

The Alaska Permanent Fund is a dividend that is paid to all qualifying residents of Alaska. The dividend is based upon a five-year average of the Permanent Fund's performance, which is based on the stock market and other factors. The dividend is taxable on the recipients' federal tax returns.

Additional Taxes

The following are other taxes reported on Form 1040, Schedule 2, line 17:

- ➤ Form 8611   *Recapture of Low-Income Housing Credit*
- ➤ Form 8828   *Recapture of Federal Mortgage Subsidy*
- ➤ Form 8853   *Archer MSAs and Long-Term Care Insurance Contracts*
- ➤ Form 4255   *Recapture of Investment Credit*
- ➤ Form 8889   *Health Savings Account*

Line 18 Total Additional Taxes

Add the amounts of 17a - z and report the total on line 18. This is the total amount of Additional Taxes. Report this amount on Form 1040, line 23, to add to the taxpayer's total tax liability.

Line 20 Net Tax Liability Installment

This line reports the amount calculated from Form 965-A. See Instructions Form 965-A.

Kiddie Tax (Form 8615)

The kiddie tax is a tax imposed on unearned income earned by individuals who are 18 years of age or under or dependent full-time students under age 24. Although Form 8615 is not included on Schedule 2 as an additional tax, it is an additional tax to the parent. If the parent claims their child's unearned income, the child will not file a tax return. Claiming the child's unearned income would change the parents' tax liability and could affect the taxpayer's adjusted gross income (AGI). The election is made annually. The parent can claim their child's unearned income if the child meets the following conditions:

1. The child had $2,500 or more of unearned income
2. The child is required to file a tax return
3. The child either:
   a. Was under age 18 at the end of 2023
   b. Was age 18 at the end of 2023 and didn't have earned income that was more than half of their support
   c. Was a full-time student at least age 19 and under age 24 at the end of 2023 and did not have earned income that was more than half of their support
4. At least one of the child's parents was alive at the end of 2023
5. The child does not need to file a joint return for 2023

A "child" as defined by the kiddie tax rules also includes legally adopted children and stepchildren. These rules apply whether the child is or is not a dependent. If neither of the child's parents were living at the end of the year, none of the rules apply.

Support includes all amounts spent to provide the child with food, lodging, clothing, education, medical and dental care, recreation, transportation, and similar necessities. To calculate the child's support, include support provided by parents and their child, and others who support the child. A scholarship received by the child is not considered support if the child is a full-time student.

The Setting Every Community Up for Retirement Act (SECURE ACT) of 2019 repealed the TCJA changes made for Kiddie Tax. For tax year 2020 and beyond, the law reverts the kiddie tax back to the parent's marginal tax rate. See Publication 919 and IRC Section 1(g).

Part 2 Review

To obtain the maximum benefit from each part go online now and watch the video.

Part 3 Taxpayer Penalty

Penalties and Interest Charges

Tax law imposes penalties to ensure that all taxpayers accurately report and pay their taxes. Both taxpayers and tax preparers can be subject to penalties, interest charges and even prosecution for underpayment of taxes due to fraud, incorrect preparation of a tax return, and other offenses.

Preparer penalties are enforced by the IRS under Revenue Code §6694, and in §6695 "*Understatement of taxpayer's liability by tax return preparer,*", "*Other assessable penalties with respect to the preparation of tax returns for other persons.*" These due diligence penalties affect both the taxpayer and the tax preparer. Tax professionals can receive penalties based on how they prepare their clients' returns. Preparer penalties were discussed in Chapter 1.

Penalties are treated as additions to taxes and are not deductible for federal income tax purposes. Taxpayers can receive penalties based on their filed tax return or not filing a return. Due diligence is the responsibility of both the taxpayer and the tax professional. Penalties and interest for a taxpayer could be assessed for not filing a tax return or filing an incorrect return. An incorrect return could be when the taxpayer understates their income or overstates their expenses.

If the taxpayer and tax professional prepare a tax return with an understatement of tax liability, both could be taking a frivolous stance where there is no credible possibility the IRS would accept the tax return in an audit. In this case, the penalty would be $1,000 or 50% of the income derived by the tax return preparer, whichever is more. The tax preparer may face a penalty of $5,000 or 50% of the income derived by the tax return if the attempt to understate the tax liability is intentional (IRC, §6695(a)).

If an individual owes taxes, the IRS will calculate penalties and interest on the amount owed. Penalties are calculated on the balance due. There are several separate types of penalties:

> ➢ Failure-to-file
> ➢ Failure-to-pay
> ➢ Failure to pay proper estimated tax
> ➢ Dishonored check

The interest accrues until the tax owed is paid in full. A late-payment penalty may be charged as well, but if the taxpayer shows a reasonable cause for not paying on time, they may be able to abate these penalties. The taxpayer must still make a good effort to properly estimate and pay the tax due on the due date.

Taxpayer Penalties

The following penalties are the most common for taxpayers.

Failure-to-File Penalty

The penalty for failing to file a return by the due date is 5% of the amount of tax due if the failure is for not more than one month, with an additional 5% for each additional month or fraction thereof, but not exceeding 25% of the total tax. The failure-to-pay penalty reduces the failure-to-file penalty for any month in which both penalties apply. However, if the return is more than 60 days late, the penalty will be $435 or 100% of the tax balance, whichever is less. The taxpayer will not have to pay the penalty if they show reasonable cause for not filing on time.

If the taxpayer files an extension, the tax is still due on the filing date, normally April 15.

A tax professional must be aware when their clients owe tax, and must inform them that penalties and interest will accrue on the unpaid tax. A taxpayer can apply for an installment agreement. See 26 U.S. Code Section 6651 and 26 Code of Federal Regulations section 301.665-1.

Failure-to-Pay Penalty

The IRS will calculate the Failure-to-Pay penalty based on how late the tax return is and how much unpaid tax is due. This penalty cannot be more than 25% of the unpaid tax. The taxpayer will not have to pay the fine if they show a good reason for not paying the tax on time. Add the failure-to-pay penalty to interest charges on late payments. The monthly or partial month rate is half the usual rate—25% instead of 50%—if an installment agreement is in effect for the month.

When the IRS issues an intent to levy, the tax rate increases to 1% if the taxpayer does not pay the amount within 10 days of the notice. When the IRS issues a notice and demands immediate payment, the rate will increase to 1% at the start of the first month, beginning after the notice and demand are issued. See 26 U.S. Code Section 6651 and 26 Code of Federal Regulations section 301.665-1.

Combined Penalties

If both the failure-to-file penalty and the failure-to-pay penalty apply in any month, the 5% (or 15%) failure-to-file penalty is reduced by the failure-to-pay penalty. However, if the taxpayer filed the return more than 60 days after the due date or extended due date, the minimum penalty is the smaller of $435 (for tax returns for 2020, 2021, and 2022) or 100% of the unpaid tax.

Underpayment of Estimated Tax by Individuals Penalty

The IRS operates on the assumption that all income is on a "pay as you go" basis. This is to ensure timely revenue collection by the agency and helps the taxpayer meet their tax obligations and avoid penalties. Therefore, self-employed taxpayers should make quarterly estimated payments. Taxpayers that owe additional tax payments for tax year 2022 may need to pay estimated payments for 2023 tax year.

The taxpayer may owe a penalty if the total of the withholding was filed on time, but the estimated payments did not equal the smaller of:

1. 90% of the tax owed on the 2023 tax return.
2. 100% of the taxpayer 2022 tax. The tax return covers a 12-month period.

The penalty is figured on Form 2210 or Form 2210-F for farmers or fishermen. See Instructions Form 2210 and Publication 505.

Dishonored Check

If the taxpayer writes a check to pay for the amount due and the check "bounces" (is not honored by the bank), the IRS may impose a penalty. A penalty will be assessed as well if the taxpayer does not have enough funds in the bank account to pay the balance due. The penalty is whichever is less: 2% of the amount of the check or $25 if the check is less than $1,250. See *IRC §6695(f)*.

If the taxpayer is required to make a payment by Electronic Funds Transfer (EFT) and makes the payment by another means, the penalty is 10% of the amount paid via non-EFT. An exception could be granted for reasonable cause, but not for willful neglect.

Paying or Receiving Interest

If taxpayers have a balance due on their current year tax return or owe taxes to the IRS for prior years and fail to pay the amount due by the due date, interest will be owed on the unpaid balance. Taxpayers cannot deduct the interest paid to the IRS on their return. When the taxpayer receives interest on a delayed refund or an amended return, that amount is considered earned income in the year received.

Information Reporting Penalties

If an individual files information returns and does not file them on time, they could receive penalties. An information return is typically filed by a business, rather than an individual taxpayer, such as filing W-2s or 1099s. The IRS charges penalties based on the due date of the information return.

For example, Diego prepares W-2s for his business client's company. For tax year 2023, the penalty for information returns filed up to 30 days late is $50 per information return or payee statement; for 31 days late through August 1, the penalty is $110 per return or statement. After August 1 or if the information return is not filed at all, the penalty amount is $280 per item. If the taxpayer or Diego intentionally disregards the payment dates, the penalty amount increases to $580 per failure to file. For tax year 2024, the amounts are $60, $120, $310, and $630 per failure to file.

Filing Late

Taxpayers who do not file their returns by the due date (including extensions) could be assessed a failure-to-file penalty. The penalty is based on the tax owed as of the due date and the time elapsed (without regard to extensions). The penalty is usually ½% of the balance due for each month or part of a month that a return is late, but not more than 25%. See IRC code 6651.

Late-Filed Return with a Refund

If the taxpayer was due a refund but did not file a return, the taxpayer generally must file within three years from the date the original return was due. If the taxpayer files the return more than 60 days after the due date or extended due date, the minimum penalty is $135 or 100% of the unpaid tax, whichever is less.

If the taxpayer could show reasonable cause for not filing a timely return, the penalty may not be assessed.

Reduced Refund

The taxpayer's refund may be reduced by an additional tax liability that has been assessed. A refund may also be reduced if the taxpayer owes past-due child support, debts to another federal agency, delinquent student loans, or state tax.

Penalty for Failure to Disclose Foreign Income

There are criminal and civil penalties for failure to disclose a foreign bank account report (FBAR). Criminal penalties would be charged if the taxpayer fails to report an asset or has an underpayment of tax. If the taxpayer is required to file Form 8938 by the due date, the penalty would be $10,000 or up to $50,000 depending on circumstances.

In addition to the penalty for failure to file Form 8938, the IRS could assess an additional penalty under IRC §6662 for failure to report the income attributable to an undisclosed foreign financial asset. The maximum additional penalty for not filing Form 8938 is $50,000. See Instructions Form 8938.

First-Time Abate Policy

The IRS has a policy for penalty relief called First Time Abate (FTA). Under certain conditions, the FTA penalty relief option for failure-to-file, and failure-to-pay penalties, does not apply if the taxpayer has not filed all returns and paid or arranged to pay all tax currently due. The taxpayer is considered current with an open installment agreement and if current installment payments are up to date.

Penalties are imposed on taxpayers who file late and who fail to pay tax in full on time. The late penalty is 5% of the unpaid taxes for each month or part of a month that the return is late, up to 25%. To reward past tax compliance and promote future tax compliance, the IRS waives these penalties for taxpayers who have demonstrated full compliance over the prior three years.

Failure to Provide Social Security Number

If the taxpayer does not include a Social Security number (SSN) or the SSN of another person where required on a return, statement, or other document, the taxpayer will be subject to a penalty of $50 for each failure. The taxpayer may also be subject to the $50 penalty if they do not give their SSN to another person when required on a return, statement, or other document. The taxpayer will not have to pay the penalty if they are able to show that the failure was due to reasonable cause and not willful neglect.

Example: Lauren has a bank account that earns interest. Lauren must give her SSN to the bank. The number must be shown on Form 1099-INT or other statement the bank sends Lauren. If Lauren does not give the bank her SSN, she will be subject to the $50 penalty. Lauren could also be subject to "backup" withholding of income tax.

Failure to Furnish Correct Payee Statements

Any person who does not provide an individual with a complete and correct copy of an information return (payee statement) by the due date is subject to a penalty of $250 for each statement. If any failure is corrected within 30 days of the due date, the penalty could be $50. See IRC Code 6722.

Interest Charges

April 15 is normally the deadline for taxpayers to file and pay any amount due on their individual return. Interest generally accrues on the unpaid tax from the due date until the amount is paid in full. If the taxpayer does not pay the balance due on time, the IRS will charge a late-payment penalty.

Penalty for Substantial Understatement

If the taxpayer understates their income or expenses they may be charged with a penalty. The understatement is substantial if it is more than the larger of 10 percent of the correct tax or $5,000 for individuals. The substantial underpayment penalty is 20 percent of the portion of the underpayment that was understated on the tax return.

Criminal Penalties

The taxpayer may be subject criminal prosecution for any of the following actions:

➢ Tax evasion
➢ Willful failure to file a return, supply information, or pay any tax due
➢ Fraud and false statements
➢ Preparing and filing a fraudulent return
➢ Identity theft

A taxpayer convicted of criminal fraud is subject to a fine of up to $100,000 or imprisonment of up to five years, or both, as well as having to pay the cost of the prosecution. For more information, see code section 7201.

Tax Evasion

Tax evasion is illegally avoiding paying taxes, failing to report taxes, or reporting income and expenses falsely or erroneously. The government imposes strict and serious penalties for tax evasion. The following are some common indicators the IRS looks for to validate tax evasion:

➢ Understatement of income
➢ Claiming fictitious or improper deductions
➢ Accounting irregularities
➢ Allocation of income
➢ Acts and conduct of the taxpayer

Fraud and Tax Evasion

If the taxpayer's failure to file is due to fraud, the maximum fine is $250,000 for individuals and $500,000 for corporations. An individual convicted of fraud and tax avoidance could be sentenced to up to five years.

Tax Avoidance

Tax avoidance is different from tax evasion. Tax avoidance is using legal methods to minimize the amount of income tax owed by a taxpayer or business. What distinguishes tax avoidance from tax evasion is the intent of the taxpayer. The intent to evade tax occurs when a taxpayer knowingly misrepresents the facts. The intent is the state of mind behind a person's judgment or decision to act. A taxpayer's intent is judged by others, and others judge a taxpayer's intent.

Negligence or Disregard

"Negligence" is the failure to make a reasonable attempt to comply with the tax law or to exercise ordinary and reasonable care in preparing a return. Negligence also includes a failure to keep adequate books and records. The taxpayer will not have to pay a negligence penalty if they have a reasonable basis for the position taken. "Disregard" includes any careless, reckless, or intentional disregard of rules or regulations. Negligence or ignorance of tax law does not generally constitute fraud.

Joint Return

The fraud penalty on a joint return may not apply to a spouse unless some part of the underpayment is due to the spouse's fraud. The spouse may need to file a separate return.

Section 7201 provides that "any person who willfully attempts in any manner to evade or defeat any tax imposed by this title or the payment thereof shall, in addition to other penalties provided by law, be guilty of a felony." In addition to criminal penalties, any person who violates Section 7201 may be guilty of a felony and upon conviction thereof, shall be fined not more than $100,000 or imprisoned not more than five years, or both, and the individual will be required to pay the cost of prosecution.

Adequate Disclosure

The taxpayer can avoid the penalty for disregarding rules or regulations if the taxpayer adequately disclosed a position that has at least a reasonable basis on the return. The exception will not apply if the taxpayer did not keep adequate books, or the item relates to a tax shelter.

Substantial Understatement of Income Tax Penalty

Understatement occurs when the tax shown on the tax return is less than the correct tax. The understatement is substantial if it is more than the larger of 10% of the correct tax or $5,000.

However, the amount of understatement can be reduced to the extent the understatement is due to:

➢ Substantial authority
➢ Adequate disclosure and a reasonable basis

Whether there is or was substantial authority for the tax treatment of an item depends on the facts and circumstances—consider the court opinions, Treasury regulations, revenue rulings, revenue procedures, and notices. Announcements issued by the IRS and published in the Internal Revenue Bulletin that involve the same or similar circumstances as the taxpayer will also be considered.

Frivolous Tax Return Penalty

The taxpayer may have to pay a penalty of $5,000 for filing a "frivolous return." A frivolous return does not include enough information to figure out the correct tax or contains information clearly showing that the tax reported is substantially incorrect.

Taxpayers may be motivated to file frivolous returns for any number of reasons, all of which can lead to IRS allegations of tax avoidance or evasion. The filing of a frivolous return can be intended to delay or interfere with the administration of federal income tax laws. This action includes altering or striking out the preprinted language above the space provided for the taxpayer's signature. This penalty is added to any other penalty provided by law.

A frivolous return can lead to penalties for the taxpayer and the preparer and should never be considered as a legitimate tax strategy.

Part 3 Review

To obtain the maximum benefit from each chapter you should complete the part review

Takeaways

"Other taxes" consist of different types of taxes. Some taxes have forms attached directly to Form 1040, while others are reported on Form 1040, Schedule 1, 2 and 3. The IRS has expanded Schedule 2 by detailing certain additional taxes, which have their own line on Schedule 2. For example, on page 2 of Schedule 2, line 17 is for additional tax items such as Health Savings Account, Archer Medical Savings Account, and recapturing deductible credits.

AMT is a separate tax that is added to the income tax. Under tax law, certain deductions could benefit taxpayers who qualify for the tax deduction. The purpose of the minimum tax credit is to prevent the double taxation of deferral preference adjustments. AMT is a tax imposed in addition to the regular income tax to recapture the reductions resulting from the use of special tax relief provisions of the tax law. The repayment of the Premium Tax Credit is based on the amount of the premium paid and the taxpayer's income.

There are significant civil and sometimes criminal penalties for filing late, incorrect or fraudulent tax returns and information returns or failing to file required returns. Taxpayers and preparers should be careful to avoid these mistakes whether deliberately or unintentionally.

TEST YOUR KNOWLEDGE!
Go online to take a practice quiz.

Chapter 7 Payments and Tax Credits

Introduction

Unlike a deduction, which reduces the income subject to taxation, credits can directly reduce the taxpayer's tax liability to zero. Depending on the type of credit, the amount will reduce the tax liability below zero, resulting in a refund for the taxpayer. There are two types of credits: refundable and nonrefundable. The refundable credits reduce the tax liability below zero, resulting in a refund. In some instances, after reducing the tax liability to zero, the remaining amount will be carried over to the next year until the full amount is used. Not all nonrefundable credits can be carried over.

Objectives

At the end of this chapter, the student will be able to:

➤ Explain how a nonrefundable credit affects the taxpayer's tax liability
➤ Name the refundable credits
➤ Understand the qualifications for the Earned Income Credit (EIC)
➤ Identify who qualifies for the additional child tax credit
➤ Know the rules for the refundable portion of the American opportunity credit (AOC)
➤ Recognize when a dependent qualifies for the Other Dependent Credit (ODC)

Resources

Form 1040	Publication 17	Instructions Form 1040
Form 1098-T	Publication 503	Instructions Form 1098-T
Form 1116	Publication 505	Instructions Form 1116
Form 2441	Publication 514	Instructions Form 2441
Form 8396	Publication 524	Instructions Form 8396
Form 8801	Publication 596	Instructions Form 8801
Form 8812	Publication 972	Instructions Form 8812
Form 8863	Publication 4933	Instructions Form 8863
Form 8867	Publication 4935	Instructions Form 8867
Form 8880	Tax Topic 601, 602, 607, 608, 610	Instructions Form 8880
Form 8959	Schedule 3	Instructions Form 8959
Schedule EIC	Instructions Schedule 3	Instructions Schedule EIC
Schedule R		Instructions Schedule R

Part 1 Nonrefundable Credits

Nonrefundable credits reduce the taxpayer's income tax. The credits are computed in the order they appear on Form 1040, Schedule 3, Part I.

Foreign Tax Credit

The foreign tax credit is intended to reduce the double tax burden that could occur when a foreign source of income is taxed by both the foreign country and the United States. Generally, the credit for foreign taxes paid or accrued to a foreign country or U.S. possession will qualify for the tax credit reported on Form 1040, Schedule 3, line 1. If the taxpayer claims a foreign tax credit using Schedule 3,

Form 1116, *Foreign Tax Credit*, it must be attached to the tax return. The other way that the taxpayer could claim the credit is as an itemized deduction on Schedule A under "other taxes."

Do not complete Form 1116 if the taxpayer qualifies for any of the following:
- ➢ All foreign gross income is from interest and dividends and reported on Form 1099-INT, 1099-DIV, or Schedule K-1
- ➢ Total foreign taxes were not more than $300 ($600 if married filing jointly)
- ➢ All foreign source gross income was "passive category income"

SCHEDULE 3
(Form 1040)
Department of the Treasury
Internal Revenue Service

Additional Credits and Payments

Attach to Form 1040, 1040-SR, or 1040-NR.
Go to *www.irs.gov/Form1040* for instructions and the latest information.

OMB No. 1545-0074

2023

Attachment
Sequence No. **03**

Name(s) shown on Form 1040, 1040-SR, or 1040-NR | Your social security number

Part I Nonrefundable Credits

1	Foreign tax credit. Attach Form 1116 if required	**1**
2	Credit for child and dependent care expenses from Form 2441, line 11. Attach Form 2441	**2**
3	Education credits from Form 8863, line 19	**3**
4	Retirement savings contributions credit. Attach Form 8880	**4**
5a	Residential clean energy credit from Form 5695, line 15	**5a**
b	Energy efficient home improvement credit from Form 5695, line 32	**5b**
6	Other nonrefundable credits:	
a	General business credit. Attach Form 3800	**6a**
b	Credit for prior year minimum tax. Attach Form 8801	**6b**
c	Adoption credit. Attach Form 8839	**6c**
d	Credit for the elderly or disabled. Attach Schedule R	**6d**
e	Reserved for future use	**6e**
f	Clean vehicle credit. Attach Form 8936	**6f**
g	Mortgage interest credit. Attach Form 8396	**6g**
h	District of Columbia first-time homebuyer credit. Attach Form 8859	**6h**
i	Qualified electric vehicle credit. Attach Form 8834	**6i**
j	Alternative fuel vehicle refueling property credit. Attach Form 8911	**6j**
k	Credit to holders of tax credit bonds. Attach Form 8912	**6k**
l	Amount on Form 8978, line 14. See instructions	**6l**
m	Credit for previously owned clean vehicles. Attach Form 8936	**6m**
z	Other nonrefundable credits. List type and amount:	**6z**
7	Total other nonrefundable credits. Add lines 6a through 6z	**7**
8	Add lines 1 through 4, 5a, 5b, and 7. Enter here and on Form 1040, 1040-SR, or 1040-NR, line 20	**8**

Schedule 3

Form 2441: Child and Dependent Care

Dependent care benefits are payments the employer paid directly to either the taxpayer or the care provider for taking care of qualifying dependent(s) while the taxpayer worked. Dependent care benefits are pre-taxed contributions made based on the fair market value of care in a daycare facility provided by or sponsored by the employer under a Flexible Spending Arrangement (FSA).

"Care" is the cost of attending a facility to qualifying individual(s) outside the taxpayer's home. It does not include food, lodging, education, clothing, or entertainment. If a dependent care facility provides the care, the center must meet all the applicable state and local regulations. A dependent care facility is a place that offers care for more than six individuals who do not live there and receives a fee, payment, or grant for providing those services for any individual. This includes the cost of a day camp, but not the cost of an overnight camp, summer school, or tutoring program.

When the expenditures are work-related, the taxpayer can take a nonrefundable credit of up to 35% of the qualifying expenses for the care of a qualified dependent. The percentage of credit goes down as income goes up, with a minimum of 20% of eligible expenses allowed. Expenses are limited to $3,000 for one child and $6,000 for two or more qualified dependents. Child and dependent care are reported on Form 2441 and flow to Form 1040, Schedule 3, line 2.

A qualifying person is:

➢ A qualifying child under 13 and claimed as a dependent. If a child turns 13 during the tax year, the taxpayer can still prorate their care for the portion of the year the child was not 13
➢ A disabled spouse who wasn't physically or mentally able to care for themself
➢ Any disabled person who wasn't physically or mentally able to care for themself and whom the taxpayer can claim as a dependent unless one of the following is true:
  o The disabled individual had a gross income of $4,700 or more
  o The disabled individual filed a joint return
  o The disabled individual or spouse, if filing a joint tax return, could be claimed as a dependent on another individual's 2023 tax return

To be able to claim the child and dependent care expenses, the taxpayer must meet all the following requirements:

➢ The care must be for one or more qualifying persons who are identified on Form 2441
➢ If filing a joint return, the taxpayer (and spouse if filing a joint return) must have earned income during the year
➢ The taxpayer must pay child and dependent care expenses to allow the taxpayer and spouse to work, or look for work
➢ The taxpayer must make payments for child and dependent care to someone who cannot be claimed as a dependent on the taxpayer's return
➢ The filing status may be Single, Head of Household, or Surviving spouse with a dependent child. If married, they must file a joint return (unless an exception applies)
➢ The taxpayer must fill out Form 2441 to identify the provider's name, TIN, the cost of care, and the address of the location where the care was provided and attach the form to their tax return
➢ If the taxpayer excludes or deducts dependent care benefits provided by a dependent care benefit plan, the total amount excluded or deducted must be less than the dollar limit for qualifying expenses ($3,000 per child up to $6,000)

Below is the portion of the current chart used to calculate the child and dependent care credit. Calculate the credit amount by multiplying the percentage on the right against the credit's monetary limit ($3,000-$6,000) and which percentage, based on the taxpayer(s) combined income. For tax year 2023, the American Rescue Plan Act of 2021 (ARPA) significantly impacted the Child and Dependent Care Credit by making it more generous. ranges from 20% to 35%. The following is just a snapshot of certain portions of the percentage chart.

Income	Percentage
$0 – $15,000	35%
$23,001 – $25,000	30%
$33,001 – $35,000	25%
$43,001 – No limit	20%

For example, a taxpayer and his spouse each made $50,000 for a combined income of $100,000, and they paid $8,500 for childcare for one child. Because they paid $8,500 for childcare and only for one child, they will be allowed to use $3,000 of that expense to calculate their credit amount. This is because that is the credit limit no matter how much they paid for childcare. Because their combined income was under $125,000, they will calculate their credit amount using the 20% section from the chart. Therefore, the 20% deduction is calculated as follows: $3,000 ´ .20 = $600. Their credit amount is $600.

If all other details were the same, but they had only spent $2,000 on childcare, their credit amount would be 20% of that two thousand, not three. This is because they did not spend enough to reach the credit limit, meaning their credit amount would be $1,000 ($2,000 ´ .20 = $400).

Child of Divorced or Separated Parents

In addition to meeting the qualifying person requirements, additional rules apply for divorced or separated parents. The parent who has physical custody of the child for the more significant portion of the year is the only parent who can claim the credit, regardless of how much support the other parent provides or if the dependency exemption is released.

Earned Income Test

The taxpayer and spouse (if filing jointly) must have earned income to claim the credit. Earned income includes wages, salary, tips, other taxable employee compensation, and net earnings from self-employment. A loss from self-employment reduces income. If the taxpayer has nontaxable combat pay not included in earned income, they may include the income to calculate the child and dependent credit. If both the taxpayer and spouse have nontaxable combat pay, both will have to make the election. A good tax professional should calculate the credit both ways for the taxpayer to determine which results in the higher credit amount.

Señor 1040 Says: Remember Child and Dependent Care Expenses are a different credit than the Additional Child Tax Credit.

Work-Related Expense Requirement

Child and dependent care expenses must be work-related to qualify for the credit. You can consider work-related expenses only if the following are true:

➢ Dependent care allows the taxpayer(s) to work or look for work
➢ The expenses are for a qualifying person's care

Example 1: Darlene works during the day, and her spouse, Craig, works at night and sleeps while Darlene is working. Their five-year-old son, Trevor, goes to daycare so Craig can sleep. Their expenses are work-related because the care allows Craig to sleep to perform his job adequately.

Example 2: Darlene and Craig get a babysitter on Craig's night off, so they can go out to eat and spend some time together. This expense is not work-related because the care is not directly facilitating Darlene or Craig's ability to work or look for work.

Married Taxpayer Filing Separately

Usually, married couples file a joint return to take the child and dependent care credit. However, if the taxpayer and spouse are legally separated or living apart, they may still take the credit. If the following apply, the taxpayer would be able to claim the credit:

➢ The taxpayer's home was the qualifying individual's home for more than half the year
➢ The taxpayer paid more than half the cost of home upkeep for the year
➢ The taxpayer's spouse did not live in their home during the last six months of the year

Rules for Students' Spouses Who Are Not Able to Care for Themselves

A married couple is treated as having earned income for any month that one was a full-time student or attended a school during any five months of the tax year (the months do not have to be consecutive) or is physically or mentally disabled or unable to care for themself. This definition of "school" does not include night school or a correspondence school.

If the taxpayer or spouse was a full-time student for at least five months or was disabled, they are considered to have earned an income of $250 per month (or $500 if more than one qualifying person was cared for during the tax year). This is done to help taxpayers who have little-to-no earned income qualify for the Child and Dependent Care Credit, because credits can only be claimed if the taxpayer or spouse has earned income.

Employer Dependent Care Assistance

If the employer provides dependent care benefits excluded from income (such as those received under a cafeteria plan), the taxpayer must subtract that amount from the applicable dollar limit of the Child and Dependent Care Credit. Dependent care benefits include the following:

➢ Amounts the employer paid directly to the taxpayer or the taxpayer's provider while the taxpayer worked
➢ The fair market value of care in a daycare facility provided or sponsored by the employer
➢ Pre-tax contributions made under a dependent flexible spending arrangement

Box 10 reports dependent care benefits on the taxpayer's W-2. If a partner received benefits, they would appear in box 13 on the K-1, Form 1065 with code O.

The amount excluded from income is limited to the smallest of the following:

> ➢ The total amount of dependent care benefits received during the year
> ➢ The total amount of qualified expenses incurred during the year
> ➢ The taxpayer's earned income
> ➢ The spouse's earned income
> ➢ $5,000, or $2,500 if married filing separately

> *Señor 1040 Says:* Make sure to always check if there is an amount in box 10 of the W-2 for Dependent Care Payments.

If dependent care assistance exceeds the amount paid for dependent care, the excess amount becomes income to the taxpayer and is reported on line 1 of Form 1040. The letters "DCB" (dependent care benefit) should be written on the dotted line in the space before the entry block for line 1.

The taxpayer can also pay for the care provided in the home with the dependent care benefits. The taxpayer may have to withhold taxes (FICA and FUTA) for the dependent care provider if dependent care is in the taxpayer's home. The taxpayer is not required to withhold taxes if the dependent care provider is self-employed.

Expenses Not for Care

Care expenses do not include the taxpayer expenses for food, lodging, clothing, education, or entertainment. Expenses for a child in nursery school, preschool, or similar programs for children below the kindergarten level are considered expenses for care. Expenses to attend kindergarten or higher schooling are not expenses for childcare. In certain situations, expenses for before- or after-school care are expenses for care; there are exceptions. Do not use the summer school and tutoring programs as dependent care expenses. The cost of sending the dependent to an overnight camp is not considered work-related; however, the cost of a day camp might be a work-related expense.

Payments to Relatives or Dependents

Payments that enable the taxpayer to work made to relatives living in the taxpayer's home can be counted as dependent care unless the relative is a dependent that the taxpayer claims.

Dependent Care Provider Information

The following information is needed to complete Form 2441 regarding the individual or organization that provides care for the qualifying person:

> ➢ The individual or organization provider's name
> ➢ The individual or organization provider's address
> ➢ The individual or organization provider's identification number (EIN or SSN)

The taxpayer should show due diligence by keeping and maintaining the provider's completed Form W-10, *Dependent Care Provider's Identification and Certification*. The taxpayer could supply a statement from the employer if the employer's dependent care plan is the provider. The statement could be a year-end invoice that provides the above information needed.

> *Señor 1040 Says:* Encourage the taxpayer to maintain records in relation to their childcare provider and store the documents with their tax returns.

Tax Tip: If the dependent care provider cares for the dependent in the taxpayer's home, the provider may be considered a household employee. As a tax professional, ask questions about dependent care and document your questions and the answers from the taxpayer.

Form 8863: Education Credits

Education credits are available for taxpayers who pay expenses for postsecondary education. To claim the education credit, the student must receive Form 1098-T from the student's school and provide that form to the tax preparer. The two education credits are the American opportunity tax credit (AOTC) and the lifetime learning credit; both are reported on Form 8863, *Education Credits*. Lifetime learning is a nonrefundable credit, and the AOTC is a partially refundable credit. The student must meet the following requirements to be eligible for the education credits:

➤ Qualified education expenses were for higher education
➤ Paid qualifying education expenses for the eligible student
➤ The student is either a taxpayer, spouse, or a qualifying dependent

Tax Tip: If the qualifying dependent pays their own tuition, it is considered paid by the taxpayer.

American Opportunity Tax Credit (AOTC)

The American opportunity tax credit (AOTC) is a credit of up to $2,500, up to 40% of which may be refundable. The credit is based on 100% of the first $2,000 and 25% of the next $2,000 of qualified expenses. To qualify for the AOTC, the taxpayer's MAGI must be less than $180,000 for taxpayers filing MFJ and $90,000 for all others.

Qualified expenses include tuition and fees for enrollment at an eligible post-secondary program and expenses for books, supplies, and equipment needed for a course of study, regardless of whether the student purchases the materials from the education institution. The student must carry at least half the normal full-time workload for the course of study the student enrolled in. The student must also be free of federal or state felony offenses for the possession or distribution of a controlled substance. The refundable portion of the education credit is reported on Form 8863, line 8, and reported on Form 1040, page 2, line 29.

For example, Donna and Doug are first-year students at an eligible post-secondary program. They must have certain books and other reading materials to use in their mandatory first-year classes. Doug bought his books directly from a friend, and Donna purchased hers at the college bookstore. Although Donna and Doug purchased their books from different sources, the cost of both purchases is a qualifying education expense since books qualify for the American opportunity credit.

The American opportunity credit can be claimed for a student who has not completed their first four years of postsecondary education determined by the post-secondary program. The student qualifications to claim AOTC include all the following:

➢ The student did not complete the first four years of postsecondary education
➢ For at least one academic period beginning in 2023, the student:
   o Was enrolled in a program that leads to a degree, certificate, or other recognized credential
   o Carried at least one-half of the normal full-time workload for their course of study
➢ The student did not have a felony conviction for possessing or distributing a controlled substance

Tax Tip: When interviewing the taxpayer to determine if they qualify for the American opportunity credit, be sure to ask the following questions:

➢ Did the student receive Form 1098-T?
➢ Has the American opportunity credit been claimed for this student for four tax years before 2023?
➢ Was the student enrolled at least half-time for at least one academic period that began (or treated as begun) in 2023 at an eligible education institution in a program leading toward a postsecondary degree, certificate, or other recognized postsecondary education credential?
➢ Did the student complete the first four years of postsecondary education before 2023?
➢ Was the student convicted of a felony for possession or distribution of a controlled substance before the end of 2023?

Asking and documenting these questions are part of the tax professional's due diligence.

Lifetime Learning Credit

The Lifetime Learning Credit (LLC) is a tax credit available to the taxpayer, their spouse, or their dependent, designed to assist with qualified tuition and related expenses for eligible students enrolled in an eligible educational institution. The maximum allowed credit is $2,000 per tax return. Qualified expenses include tuition and fees required for enrollment at an eligible post-secondary program. Expenses incurred to acquire or improve the taxpayer's job skills are eligible expenses.

An expense related to a course that involves sports, games, or hobbies is not a qualified expense unless it is part of the student's degree program. Taxpayers must reduce their qualified expense by any education assistance received from the post-secondary program, scholarships, or amounts to compute the lifetime learning credit.

The lifetime learning credit is not based on the student's workload. Expenses for graduate-level courses are eligible. The amount of credit a taxpayer can claim does not increase based on the number of students for whom the taxpayer paid qualified expenses. The student does not have to be enrolled at least half-time in the course of study to be eligible for the credit. The nonrefundable portion of the education credits is reported on Form 8863, line 19, and is carried to Form 1040, Schedule 3, line 3. To qualify for the lifetime learning credit, the taxpayer's modified adjusted gross income (MAGI) should be less than $180,000 for taxpayers filing MFJ or less than $90,000 for all others.
Remember, modified adjusted gross income (MAGI) is adjusted gross income, plus all the following:

➢ The amount excluded under IRC §911, *Foreign-Earned Income Exclusion*
   o Foreign housing exclusion
   o Foreign housing deduction
➢ Exclusion of income for residents of American Samoa and Puerto Rico

Double Benefit Not Allowed

The taxpayer cannot claim overlapping educational expenses, including any of the following:

➢ Deduct higher education expenses on their income tax return and claim an education credit based on the same expenses
➢ Claim more than one credit based on the same qualified education expenses
➢ Claim a credit based on expenses paid with a tax-free scholarship, grant, or employer-provided education assistance
➢ Claim a credit based on the same expenses used to figure the tax-free portion of a distribution from a Coverdell education savings account (ESA) or a qualified tuition program (QTP)

Adjustment to Qualified Education Expenses

If taxpayers pay qualified education expenses with certain tax-free funds, they cannot claim a credit for those amounts. Taxpayers must reduce the qualified education expense by the amount of any tax-free education assistance.

Tax-free education assistance includes the following:

➢ The tax-free parts of scholarships and fellowships
➢ The tax-free portion of Pell grants
➢ Employer-provided education assistance
➢ Veterans' education assistance
➢ Other nontaxable (tax-free) payments (other than gifts or inheritances) received as educational assistance

Scholarships and Fellowships

A scholarship is generally an amount paid or allowed for the benefit of a student attending a post-secondary program. The student may be either an undergraduate or a graduate student. A fellowship is paid for the benefit of an individual to aid in the pursuit of study or research. How the student pays for their expenses with the fellowship money determines the taxable portion. A scholarship or fellowship qualifies as tax-free if the following conditions are met:

➢ The fellowship or scholarship does not exceed qualifying expenses
➢ The funds are not designated for other purposes such as room and board and cannot be used for qualified education expenses
➢ It does not represent payment for teaching, research, or other services required as a condition for receiving the scholarship

Señor 1040 Says: When a student receives a scholarship, make sure that it is not taxable to the student. Do research on how the funds were used by the student. If they were not used for qualifying expenses, the funds could be taxable to the student.

Who Claims the Expenses?

If there are qualified education expenses for the taxpayer's dependent for a year, the taxpayer can claim an education credit for the dependent's expenses for the current year. For the taxpayer to claim an education credit for their dependent's expenses, the student must be their dependent. The taxpayer does this by listing the dependent's name and other required information on Form 1040.

Expenses Paid by the Dependent

If the taxpayer claims an exemption on their tax return for an eligible student who is the taxpayer's dependent, expenses paid or deemed paid by the dependent are treated as if the taxpayer paid them. Include these expenses when figuring the amount of the taxpayer's education credit.

Expenses Paid by the Taxpayer

If the taxpayer claimed an exemption for a dependent who is an eligible student, only the taxpayer could include any expenses paid when figuring the amount of the education credit. If neither the taxpayer nor anyone else claims an exemption for the dependent, the dependent can include any expenses paid when figuring the education credit.

Expenses Paid by Others

Someone other than the taxpayer, the taxpayer's spouse, or the taxpayer's dependent (such as a relative or former spouse) may make a payment directly to an eligible post-secondary program to pay for an eligible student's qualified education expenses. In this case, treat the student as receiving the payment from the other person and, in turn, paying the college. The taxpayer paid the expenses if they claimed an exemption on their return for the student.

Example: In 2023, Laura Hardy directly pays the college for her grandson's qualified education expenses. Thomas is treated as receiving the money as a gift from his grandmother and, in turn, paying his qualified education expenses himself. Unless someone else claims Thomas's exemption, only Thomas can use the payment to claim the education credit. If Thomas's parents claim an exemption for Thomas, they may be able to use the expenses to claim an education credit. If anyone else claims an exemption for Thomas, Thomas cannot claim an education credit.

Academic Period

An academic period includes a semester, trimester, quarter, or another period of study determined by the college or university.

Eligible Education

An eligible post-secondary program is any college, university, vocational school, or other postsecondary educational institution eligible to participate in a student aid program administered by the Department of Education. It includes virtually all accredited, public, nonprofit, and proprietary (privately owned profit-making) postsecondary colleges. The education institution should tell the taxpayer if it is an eligible college or university.

Certain colleges and universities outside the United States also participate in the U.S. Department of Education's Federal Student Aid (FSA) programs. You can find a list of these foreign schools on the Department of Education's website at www.fafsa.ed.gov/index.htm. Click "Find my school codes," complete the two items on the first page, click "Next," and then follow the remaining instructions to search for a foreign school.

Be aware that not all eligible education institutions treat certain Coverdell education savings accounts (529 Plans) the same way, nor do they consider the same things when determining if a scholarship or fellowship grant is not taxable.

To determine if you can use the Coverdell education savings account for a college, university, vocational school, or another postsecondary education institute, the school must participate in a student aid program administered by the U.S. Department of Education. The education institution can be an accredited public, nonprofit, or proprietary postsecondary institution. Beginning in 2018, this includes any private, religious, or public school for kindergarten through 12th grade as determined by state law.

To determine if scholarships and fellowship grants are tax-free, the education institution must have a regular facility where it carries on its educational activities, maintain a curriculum, and normally have a regularly enrolled student body.

Claiming Credits for More than One Eligible Student

The taxpayer can claim only one credit (per student) for each eligible student but can claim different credits for different students. A taxpayer who pays qualified education expenses for more than one student and each dependent qualifies for different credits; this is acceptable.

Form 8863, Part III, must be completed for each individual claiming education credits on their tax return before completing Part I and Part II. Form 1098-T must be given to the tax preparer; making sure to receive the form is part of the tax professional's due diligence.

Form 1098-T

To help figure the education credit reported on Form 8863, the student should receive Form 1098-T from their school. Generally, an eligible education institution (such as a college or university) must send Form 1098-T (or an acceptable substitute) to each enrolled student by January 31 of each year. An institution reports payments received (box 1) or billed (box 2) for qualified education expenses. Form 1098-T should provide other information from the school, including adjustments made for prior years, the amount of scholarships, grants, reimbursements, or refunds provided, and whether the student was enrolled at least half-time or was a graduate student.

The eligible educational institution may ask for a completed Form W-9S, *Request for Student's or Borrower's Taxpayer Identification Number and Certification*, or some similar statement to obtain the student's name, address, and taxpayer identification number.

All filers of Form 1098-T may truncate the student's identification number on payee statements. When completing the tax return, you must use the institution's EIN. Tax preparers should review their clients' Form 1098-T and keep a copy in the taxpayer's file.

☐ CORRECTED			

FILER'S name, street address, city or town, state or province, country, ZIP or foreign postal code, and telephone number	1 Payments received for qualified tuition and related expenses $	OMB No. 1545-1574 20**24** Form **1098-T**	**Tuition Statement**
	2		
FILER'S employer identification no.	STUDENT'S TIN	3	**Copy B** **For Student**
STUDENT'S name		4 Adjustments made for a prior year $	5 Scholarships or grants $	This is important tax information and is being furnished to the IRS. This form must be used to complete Form 8863 to claim education credits. Give it to the tax preparer or use it to prepare the tax return.
Street address (including apt. no.)		6 Adjustments to scholarships or grants for a prior year $	7 Checked if the amount in box 1 includes amounts for an academic period beginning January– March 2025 ☐	
City or town, state or province, country, and ZIP or foreign postal code				
Service Provider/Acct. No. (see instr.)	8 Checked if at least half-time student ☐	9 Checked if a graduate student ☐	10 Ins. contract reimb./refund $	

Form **1098-T**   (keep for your records)   www.irs.gov/Form1098T   Department of the Treasury - Internal Revenue Service

Box 1: The school enters the amount of qualified tuition and related expenses from all sources during the calendar year here. The amount in box 1 is the total amount received by the taxpayer minus any reimbursements or refunds made during the tax year. Do not reduce this amount by the amounts of scholarships or grants (reported separately in box 5).

Box 2: Reserved.

Box 3: Reserved.

Box 4: Adjustments made for a prior year. Enter reimbursements or refunds of qualified tuition and expenses made in 2023 related to payments received for any prior year after 2002. See Instructions Form 1098-T.

Box 5: This box shows the total amount received for scholarships or grants administered and processed during the calendar year. Remember, if the amount in box 5 is larger than the amount in box 1, do not claim the education credit for the taxpayer.

Box 6: Adjustments to Scholarships or Grants for a prior year. Enter the amount of any reduction reported for any prior year after 2002.

Box 7: If this box is checked, the amount in box 1 or 2 includes amounts the taxpayer paid before the end of the current year for the next year's tuition.

Box 8: A checkmark in this box indicates that the student was at least a half-time student during any academic period that began during the tax year. Although each university determines who and what is considered a "part-time student," the part-time student workload must be equal to or exceed the standards established by the Department of Education under the Higher Education Act.

Box 9: If this box is checked, the taxpayer is a graduate student. A graduate student must be enrolled in a program or programs leading to a graduate-level degree, graduate-level certificate, or another recognized graduate-level educational credential.

Box 10: If the insurer of the qualified tuition and related expenses made reimbursements to the student, enter the amount here.

Some eligible educational institutions combine all fees for an academic period into one amount. The student should contact the school if the student does not receive or have access to a statement showing amounts for qualified education expenses and personal expenses. The institution must provide this information to the taxpayer and report the amount paid or billed for qualified education expenses on Form 1098-T.

Tuition Payments Statement

When an eligible education institution provides a reduction in tuition to an employee of the institution or a spouse or dependent child of an employee, the amount of the reduction may or may not be taxable. If the reduction is taxable, the employee receives funds and then uses them to pay the educational institution on behalf of the student.

Form 8880: Retirement Savings Contributions Credit

The Retirement Savings Contributions Credit is based on the first $2,000 contributed to IRAs, 401(k)s, and certain other retirement plans. Use Form 8880, *Credit for Qualified Retirement Savings Contributions*, to calculate the credit. The taxpayer can make contributions until the tax return's due date; filing an extension does not change the due date for making these contributions. This credit reduces the taxpayer's income tax dollar-for-dollar and is reported on Form 1040, Schedule 3, line 4.

To claim this credit for 2023, the taxpayer's MAGI must be less than $36,500 if Single or MFS, $54,750 if filing Head of household, or $73,000 if married filing jointly or Surviving spouse with qualifying dependent. If a taxpayer claims the credit, attach Form 8880 to Form 1040.

Form 5695: Residential Energy Credits

If taxpayers made energy-saving improvements to their main home in the United States, they might be able to claim the residential energy efficient property credit and report it on Form 1040, Schedule 3, line 5. The credit and its ability to carry forward any portion are still available from 2022 to 2032. The following residential energy-efficient property credits are available for the 2023 tax year if the taxpayer made such improvements to the main home located in the United States:

➢ Qualified solar electric property costs
➢ Qualified solar water heating property costs
➢ Qualified small wind energy property costs
➢ Qualified geothermal heat pump property costs
➢ Qualified biomass fuel property costs

If the taxpayer is a condominium owner or a tenant-stockholder in a cooperative housing corporation and has paid their proportionate share of the cost, the taxpayer could qualify for the credit. There is a 30% credit for installing qualified solar water-heating property, qualified solar electric property, geothermal heat pumps, and small wind-energy property. The credit applies for property placed in service from 2022 to 2032.

The Energy Efficient Home Improvement credit is reported on Part II of Form 5695. The taxpayer may be able to take a credit equal to 30 percent of:

1. The amount paid or incurred for qualifying energy efficiency improvements installed in 2023
2. The amount of the residential energy property costs paid or incurred in 2023
3. The amount for home energy audits during in the current tax year

The credit is limited to the following:

> ➤ A total combined credit limit of $1,200
> ➤ A credit limit of $600 for all exterior windows and skylights
> ➤ A credit limit of $250 for any exterior door and total for all qualifying exterior doors
> ➤ A combined credit limit of $2,000 for heat pump and heat pump, water heaters; biomass stoves and boilers
> ➤ A credit limit of $150 for home energy audits

Any subsidized energy financing cannot be used to figure the energy credit. See Instructions Form 5695.

Part 1 Review

To obtain the maximum benefit from each part go online now and watch the video.

Part 2 Other Nonrefundable Credits

Lines 6 a-z report other current nonrefundable credits on Form 1040, Schedule 3. LTP has chosen to cover those that are the most common credits.

Line 6b: Credit for prior year minimum tax; attach Form 8801.

Line 6c: Adoption credit; attach Form 8839.

Adoption Credit or Exclusion

The maximum adoption credit amount a taxpayer can receive from their employer for 2023 is $15,950. Suppose the taxpayer's modified adjusted gross income (MAGI) is between $239,230 and $279,230; in that case, the credit may be reduced based on income. A taxpayer can use the adoption credit for foreign and domestic adoptions in most circumstances. Some states have determined that if a child has special needs, the taxpayer may receive the maximum amount of the credit unless they claimed some expenses in a prior year. The tax credit phaseout for 2024 was for adjusted gross income (MAGI) from $252,150 to $292,150.

Line 6d: Credit for the Elderly or Disabled

Schedule R: Credit for the Elderly or Disabled

The Credit for the Elderly or Disabled is a nonrefundable credit based on the taxpayer's filing status, age, and income. A person is permanently and totally disabled if the taxpayer cannot engage in any substantial gainful activity due to a physical or mental condition or if a qualified physician determined that the condition has lasted or can be expected to last continuously for at least a year or until death. If the taxpayer is under 65, a physician's statement must be attached to the tax return. The statement must certify that the taxpayer was permanently and totally disabled on the date of retirement.

The base amount is reduced by most nontaxable pension and Social Security benefits and by half of the AGI that exceeds the base amount. To claim this credit, the taxpayer must meet the following criteria:

> ➤ Be age 65 or older by the end of the tax year
> ➤ Meet the following conditions if under the age of 65 at the end of the tax year:

o Retired on permanent and total disability: they must have been permanently and totally disabled on or before January 1, 1976, or January 1, 1977, if the taxpayer retired before 1977
o Received taxable disability benefits in the current tax year
o Have not reached the employer's mandatory retirement age (when the employer's retirement program requires an employee to retire) on or before January 1 of the tax year in question

If the taxpayer is under the age of 65, they must have a physician's statement certifying that they were permanently and totally disabled on the date of retirement. Do not file the statement with the taxpayer's Form 1040; however, the taxpayer must keep it for their records. The instructions for Schedule R include a template statement taxpayers can provide to their physicians to complete and keep for their records. The taxpayer's income cannot exceed the limits listed below to qualify for the credit, so many taxpayers will not be able to take advantage of it.

Señor 1040 Says: Be aware that when preparing a Schedule R to determine a taxpayer's eligibility for the elderly or disabled credit, the Social Security income must be considered as well even though it is not taxable.

Income Limits for Schedule R

If the taxpayer's income exceeds the following limits, the taxpayer cannot claim the credit.

If filing status is:	The taxpayer cannot take the credit if the amount from Form 1040, or Form 1040-SR, line 11, is:	Or the taxpayer received:
Single, Head of Household, or Surviving spouse with qualifying dependent	$17,500 or more	$5,000 or more of nontaxable Social Security or other nontaxable pensions, annuities, or disability income
Married Filing Jointly if only one spouse qualifies for the credit	$20,000 or more	$5,000 or more of nontaxable Social Security or other nontaxable pensions, annuities, or disability income
Married Filing Jointly if both spouses qualify for the credit	$25,000 or more	$7,500 or more of nontaxable Social Security or other nontaxable pensions, annuities, or disability income
Married Filing Separately and the taxpayer did not live with spouse any time during the year	$12,500 or more	$3,750 or more of nontaxable Social Security or other nontaxable pensions, annuities, or disability income

Example 1. Adam retired on disability as a salesperson, and he now works as a daycare provider assistant earning minimum wage. Although he does different work, Adam is a daycare provider assistant on ordinary terms for minimum wage. Thus, he cannot take the credit because he is engaged in a substantial gainful activity.

Example 2. Jess retired on disability and took a job with a former employer on a trial basis. The trial period lasted for some time, during which Jess was paid at a rate equal to minimum wage. Due to Jess's disability, he performed light-duty of a nonproductive, make-work nature. Unless the activity is both substantial and gainful, Jess is not engaged in a substantial, gainful activity. The activity was gainful because Jess's payment was at or above the minimum wage rate. However, the activity was not substantial because the duties were of a nonproductive, make-work nature. More information is needed to determine if Jess can engage in a substantial gainful activity.

How to Calculate the Credit

If the taxpayer checked box 6, the total amount entered on line 11 would be $5,000. If the taxpayer checked boxes 2, 4, or 9, then enter the total amount of disability income received. If the taxpayer checked box 5, enter the total amount of disability income received from the taxpayer and spouse on line 11.

Line 6f: Qualified plug-in motor vehicle credit; attach Form 8936

2-Wheeled Plug-in Electric Vehicle

The taxpayer could qualify for a credit for purchasing a qualified 2-wheeled electric vehicle that was acquired before 2022 and:

- ➢ Can go 45+ miles per hour
- ➢ Is propelled by an electric motor with a rechargeable battery with a capacity of not less than 2.5 kilowatt hours
- ➢ Is manufactured primarily for use on public streets, roads, and highways
- ➢ Has a gross vehicle weight of less than 14,000 pounds

See Instructions Form 8936.

Qualified 4-Wheel Plug-in Electric Drive Motor Vehicle (EV)

The taxpayer could receive credit for purchasing a 4-wheel vehicle (placed in service before 2023), with gross weight of less than 14,000 pounds and a rechargeable battery with at least 4-kilowatt hours capacity. The vehicle must be manufactured primarily to be used on public streets, roads, and highways. The owner is the only one that can claim the credit. If the vehicle is leased, only the lessor and not the lessee can claim the credit. The vehicle must be used primarily in the United States and the final assembly of the car must occur in North America. See IRC Code Section 30D.

Line 6g: Mortgage interest credit; attach Form 8396.

Taxpayers claim the mortgage interest credit if a state, local governmental unit, or agency under a qualified mortgage credit certificate program issues them a Mortgage Credit Certificate (MCC). If the mortgage is equal to or smaller than the certified indebtedness amount (known as the loan) shown on the MCC, multiply the certified credit rate shown on the MCC by all interest paid on the mortgage during the year.

Child Tax Credits Schedule 8812

The child tax credit (CTC) is a nonrefundable credit for taxpayers who have a qualifying child. For tax year 2023, the credit reverted to $2,000 per child under the age of 17. The refundable portion is $1,600.

The maximum phaseout amounts are $400,000 for married taxpayers filing a joint return and all others is $200,000. The taxpayer's tax liability and modified AGI limits the child tax credit. If the child were not issued a valid Social Security number, they would not qualify the taxpayer for either credit. This credit is reported on Form 1040, line 19.

To be a qualifying child for the child tax credit, the child must be a citizen, national, or resident of the United States. The qualifying child must have an SSN for the taxpayer to claim the child for the Child Tax Credit and/or the Advanced child tax credit. If the dependent does not qualify for the child tax credit, the taxpayer cannot include that dependent in the calculation for the credit. However, the dependent may still qualify for the Other Dependent Credit (ODC).

The Additional Child Tax Credit (ACTC) is a refundable credit available for taxpayers with qualifying children. Use Schedule 8812, Parts II-III to calculate the additional child tax credit. This credit is reported on Form 1040, line 27, and Schedule 3 should be completed.

Qualifying Child for Child Tax Credit

For a child to qualify for the child tax credit, they must meet the following conditions:

➢ The child is the son, daughter, stepchild, eligible foster child, brother, sister, stepbrother, stepsister, half-brother, half-sister, or a descendant of any of these
➢ The child did not provide over half of their support
➢ The child lived with the taxpayer for more than half of 2023
➢ The child is claimed as a dependent on the taxpayer's return
➢ The child does not file a joint return for the year or only files to claim a refund of withheld income tax or if the dependent paid estimated payments
➢ The child was a U.S. citizen, U.S. national, U.S. resident alien, or adopted by a U.S. citizen, U.S. national, or U.S. resident alien

Qualifying Person for the ODC

An individual qualifies for the Other Dependent Credit (ODC) if they meet the following conditions:
➢ The taxpayer claims the qualifying dependent on their tax return
➢ The dependent is ineligible for the CTC or the ACTC
➢ The dependent was a U.S. citizen, U.S. national, U.S. resident alien, or adopted by a U.S. citizen, U.S. national, or U.S. resident alien
➢ They have a TIN on or before the due date of the 2023 tax return
➢ The maximum phaseout amounts are $400,000 for married taxpayers filing a joint return and all others are $200,000

Example: Levi is claiming his 10-year-old nephew Fernando, who lives in Mexico and qualifies as Levi's dependent. Because Fernando is not a U.S. citizen, U.S. national, or a U.S. resident alien, Levi cannot use Fernando to claim the Other Dependent Credit (ODC) unless Levi adopts him, and Fernando comes to live with Levi in the United States.

Improperly Claiming the CTC, ODC, or ACTC

If the IRS determines the taxpayer has claimed any of these credits in error, they may be prohibited from claiming these credits for two years. If the error is determined to be fraud, they may be prohibited from claiming the credit for 10 years. The taxpayer may also have to pay penalties and interest. If the tax preparer committed the error and the IRS determines that the error was intentional, the tax preparer will be charged penalties and interest and may be prohibited from preparing returns for as long as the IRS decides it is appropriate. ODC has been added to both the due diligence questionnaire and part III of Form 8862, *Information to Claim Certain Credits After Disallowance*.

Part 2 Review

To obtain the maximum benefit from each part go online now and watch the video.

Part 3 Payments and Refundable Tax Credits

In the tax industry, the term "refundable credit" refers to a credit that allows the taxpayer to lower their tax liability dollar-for-dollar to zero and below, potentially resulting in a refund. When the refundable credit exceeds the amount of taxes owed, it could result in a tax refund.

A refundable tax credit is a tax credit that is treated as a payment and can be refunded to the taxpayer by the IRS. Refundable tax credits offset certain taxes that are normally not reduced. The credits can create a federal tax refund higher than the amount of money a person had withheld during the year. Refundable tax credits are applied toward a person's tax obligation, and the overpayment could be refunded back to the individual. Withholding for federal income taxes and estimated taxes could be refundable, since they are prepayments toward a person's annual tax liability that can be refunded to the taxpayer if withholding was overpaid.

Federal Income Tax Withheld

Form 1040, page 2, line 25, reports the federal income tax withheld from all income reported by forms such as the W-2, W-2G, 1099-R, 1099-NEC, SSA-1099, and Schedule K. The amount of tax withheld is on Form W-2 in box 2 and on the Form 1099 series in box 4. If the taxpayer had federal tax withheld from Social Security benefits, it is in box 6 of Form SSA-1099. If the taxpayer had additional Medicare tax withheld by their employer, that amount shows on Form 1040, Schedule 2, line 11. Calculate the additional Medicare tax on Form 8959 and attach it to the return.

Estimated Tax Payments

Form 1040, page 2, line 26, reports any estimated tax payments made in the current tax year and any overpayments applied from the prior year's tax return. If a taxpayer and their spouse have divorced during the current tax year and made estimated payments together, enter the former spouse's SSN in the space provided on the front of Form 1040. The taxpayer should attach a statement to Form 1040 explaining that the divorced couple made the payments together; that statement should also contain proof of payments, the name, and SSN of the individual making the payments.

Estimated tax payments are also referred to as quarterlies since the payments are due in four equal payments. If the due dates fall on a Saturday, Sunday, or a legal holiday, estimated payments are due on the next business day. Estimated payments are due on the following dates:

> ➢ April 15
> ➢ June 15
> ➢ September 15
> ➢ January 15 (of the following year)

Amount Overpaid

The taxpayer can receive their overpayment as a paper check from the U.S. Treasury Department or through a direct deposit from the U.S. Treasury Department into a checking or savings account. After filing the tax return electronically, the taxpayer can go to www.irs.gov and click "Where's My Refund?" to receive information about their return within 24 hours after it has been electronically accepted by the IRS. If the overpayment amount is different than what the taxpayer was expecting, the taxpayer should receive an explanation from the IRS within two weeks after depositing the refund.

Form 1040, page 2, line 34, states if there was an overpayment of current-year taxes and indicates how the taxpayer would like to receive the overpayment refund. The desired refund amount should be entered on line 35a. The taxpayer can select a portion of the amount as a refund and forward the rest as estimated tax payments for the following tax year. Use line 36 to enter the desired estimated payments. The taxpayer can also elect to carry forward their entire refund amount. If the taxpayer wants to carry forward overpayments to the following year, enter the amount they would like to have applied on Form 1040, line 36. Suppose a couple filed MFJ, and a taxpayer's spouse wants the overpayment applied to her account. In that case, the refund amount is divided between the taxpayer's account and the spouse's separate account. The taxpayer can include up to three bank accounts on Part I in Form 8888. Use Part II to use the refund to purchase U.S. Series I Savings Bonds.

Tax Tip: The IRS will allow the taxpayer to have their direct deposit divided between multiple accounts, but not all tax software supports the use of Form 8888 to do so.

Example: Pat made estimated payments for the current tax year of $11,000 and overpaid her quarterlies by $4,500. Pat wants $2,000 refunded, so enter $2,000 on line 36. Pat would like the remaining $2,500 applied to next year's estimated payments, so enter the $2,500 amount on line 35a.

If the taxpayer wants to deposit the entire overpayment directly, submit a valid routing number and account number. A routing number is a nine-digit number that indicates which financial institute receives the direct deposit refund. The account number is specific to the taxpayer's bank account. The first two digits of the routing number must be 01 through 12 or 21 through 32. Some financial institutions have a separate routing number for direct deposits. If there is no entry on Form 1040, Page 2, line 35b or line 35d, the taxpayer will receive a paper check.

The routing number on a deposit slip may differ from the routing number on the bottom of a personal check. If the tax preparer is entering the numbers from the bottom of the check, make sure you do not enter the check number when entering the account number. On Form 1040, be sure to indicate whether the account is a checking or savings account.

ROBERT SAMPLE
JOAN SAMPLE
123 MAIN ST.
PORTLAND, ME 04101

9999

Date ___11/30/2011___

Pay to the Order of ___Sample Check___ $ 158.00

___one hundred and fifty eight___ _____ 00/100 Dollars

TD Bank
America's Most Convenient Bank®

For ___SAMPLE___   ___Joan Sample___

⑈123454321⑈ ⑈0123454321⑊ 9999

Routing Number   Account Number

If any of the following happen, the financial institution will reject the direct deposit, and the IRS will send a paper check to the taxpayer instead:

➤ Any numbers or letters on lines 35b or 35d are crossed out, or some type of correction material (such as correction tape or white-out) has been used

➤ The taxpayer's financial institution(s) will not allow a joint return to be deposited to an individual account; The U.S. Treasury Department is not responsible if the financial institution rejects the direct deposit.

➤ Three direct deposits have already been made to that account

➤ The name on the account does not match the name on the tax refund

➤ The name on the account is not the same as the name on the tax return

Señor 1040 Says: The IRS is not responsible for a lost refund if the account information is entered incorrectly. The taxpayer is responsible for making sure that his or her routing number and account number are accurate, and that the financial institution will accept the direct deposit.

Direct Deposit

Taxpayers may have refunds deposited into their checking or savings accounts. The tax professional must have the taxpayer's account number, routing number, and the financial institution's name to directly deposit the refund. The information is found at the bottom of the taxpayer's check. Be careful not to include the check number.

Form 8888, *Allocation of Refund*, allows the taxpayer to divide their refunds and deposit them into multiple accounts. A qualified account can be a checking or savings account or other accounts such as a money market account or an IRA. The taxpayer should not try to deposit money directly into an account not in their name. This form is limited to three accounts and can also be used to purchase U.S. Series I Savings Bonds.

Direct Deposit Limits

The IRS has imposed a limit of three direct deposits that can be electronically deposited into a single financial account or loaded on a pre-paid debit card. Any further deposits will be converted to a paper check and mailed to the taxpayer within four weeks. Taxpayers will receive a notification via mailed letter that their account has exceeded the direct deposit limit.

The IRS has implemented the direct deposit limit to safeguard taxpayer funds and to prevent unauthorized individuals from exploiting the system by obtaining multiple refunds through fraudulent means. Also, the new restrictions shield taxpayers from unscrupulous tax preparers who may try to misuse Form 8888 to unlawfully acquire a portion of the taxpayer's refund as their preparation fee. Tax preparers engaging in such practices are subject to penalties and fines.

Señor 1040 Says: The IRS will send refunds under $1 only if requested in writing.

If the taxpayer files a joint return and either the taxpayer or the spouse has an offset of bad debt to pay, the other spouse may be an injured spouse. If the IRS took one spouse's refund to pay the other spouse's tax liability, the injured spouse would file Form 8379 to see if they meet the conditions to get their portion of the refund back from the IRS.

Amount Paid with a Request for Extension

If the taxpayer used Form 4868 to file an extension and is making a payment, report the payment amount with the extension on Form 1040, Schedule 3, line 10. Do not include the taxpayer's fees when the individual pays by debit or credit card.

Señor 1040 Says: If the taxpayer itemizes his deductions and paid by credit or with debit card, the convenience fees are no longer a deduction on Schedule A.

Excess Social Security or Railroad Retirement Tax Withheld

When a taxpayer has more than one employer, it is possible that the employers will withhold too much for Social Security or Railroad Retirement Tax Act (RRTA) benefits. If that is the case, the taxpayer may claim the excess payment on Form 1040, Schedule 3, line 11, as a refundable credit. If, however, one employer withholds too much tax for Social Security or Railroad Retirement Tax Act, the employer makes the adjustment for the employee. Even if the employer does not refund the extra withholding to the employee, the taxpayer cannot adjust their income tax form but must instead file Form 843 to claim the refund.

The taxpayer is entitled to the credit if they had more than one employer and exceeded the withholding limits for 2023 of $160,200 in wages subject to Social Security and tier 1 RRTA withholding taxes of $9,932.40 or less. All wages are subject to Medicare tax withholding.

Earned Income Credit (EIC)

The earned income credit (EIC), also referred to as earned income tax credit (EITC), is a refundable tax credit for low-to-moderate-income working individuals and families. When the EIC exceeds the amount of taxes owed, it results in a refundable credit. Report the EIC on Form 1040, page 2, line 27.

Twenty-eight states and the District of Columbia have an EITC program. Most use federal eligibility rules, and their version of the credit parallels major elements of the federal structure. In most states and localities, the credit is refundable (as is federal), although, in a few areas, the EITC is used only to offset taxes owed. For more information, go to www.irs.gov/eitc. The taxpayer must have earned income during the tax year to be eligible for the earned income tax credit. If a married couple is filing a joint return, and only one spouse worked, both could still meet the earned income requirement.

Remember, earned income is revenue the taxpayer received for working and includes the following types of income:

➢ Wages, salaries, tips, and other types of taxable employee pay
➢ Net earnings from self-employment
➢ Gross income received as a statutory employee
➢ Union strike benefits
➢ Long-term disability benefits received before reaching the minimum retirement age

Unearned income includes the following:

➢ Interest and dividends
➢ Pensions and annuities
➢ Social Security and railroad retirement benefits (including disability benefits)
➢ Alimony and child support
➢ Welfare benefits
➢ Workers' compensation benefits
➢ Unemployment compensation
➢ Income while an inmate
➢ Workfare payments (see Publication 596)

A taxpayer and their spouse, if filing jointly, must have a valid SSN to qualify for the earned income tax credit. If the SSN says, "Not valid for employment," and if the SSN was issued solely so the taxpayer or spouse could receive aid from a federally funded program, they do not qualify to receive earned income credit. If the SSN says, "Valid for work only with INS authorization," or "Valid only with DHS authorization," then the SSN is valid, but only if the authorization has not expired.

Community Property

Taxpayers who live in a community property state could qualify for Head of Household if the couple has lived apart for at least the last six months of the year. A taxpayer's earned income for EIC does not include any amount earned by their spouse, even though income belongs to the spouse under the state's community property laws and is not earned income for EIC purposes. The taxpayer, however, must include it with all their earned income on the federal tax return. The same rules apply to taxpayers living in Nevada, Washington, and California who are Registered Domestic Partners (RDP's).

The IRS may ask the taxpayer to provide additional documentation to prove that the qualifying dependents belong to the taxpayer. The IRS might ask for the following documents:

➢ Birth certificate
➢ School records
➢ Medical records

During the initial interview, tax professionals should inform their clients what they might need if the IRS audits their claim for EIC. If a taxpayer receives an audit letter, the letter will include the taxpayer's name, address, telephone number, and the name of the IRS employee responsible for the taxpayer's audit. This process will delay the client's refund. If the taxpayer is found to have fraudulently claimed the EIC, the taxpayer will be denied the credit for the current tax year and for the next nine years after that.

Earned Income Rules

To qualify for EIC, the taxpayer's adjusted gross income (AGI) must be below a certain amount, and the taxpayer (and spouse if married filing jointly) must meet the following requirements:

➢ Have a valid Social Security number (if filing MFJ, the spouse must also have a valid SSN)
➢ Have earned income from employment or self-employment income
➢ Not file as Married filing separately (MFS)
➢ File MFJ as a U.S. citizen, as a resident alien all year, or as a nonresident alien married to a U.S. citizen
➢ Not file Form 2555 or Form 2555-EZ
➢ Not have investment income over $11,000
➢ Have a qualifying child who meets the four dependent tests (age, relationship, residency, and joint return; see "Qualifying Child" below)
   o Be at least age 25 and under age 65 at the end of the year
   o Live in the United States for more than half the year
   o Not qualify as a dependent of another person
➢ The 2023 AGI must be less than:
   o $56,838 ($63,698 MFJ) with three or more qualifying children
   o $52,918 ($59,478 MFJ) with two qualifying children
   o $46,560 ($53,120 MFJ) with one qualifying child
   o $17,640 ($24,210 MFJ) with no qualifying children

Valid Social Security Number

The qualifying child must have a valid Social Security number (SSN) issued by the Social Security Administration (SSA) unless a child died in the same year they were born. Social Security cards with the legend "not valid for employment" are issued to aliens who are not eligible to work in the United States but who need an SSN so they can get a federally funded benefit such as Medicaid. Suppose the immigration status of a taxpayer or spouse has changed to U.S. citizen or permanent resident. In that case, the taxpayer should ask the SSA for a new Social Security card without the legend. If the SSN says, "valid for work only with INS authorization or DHS authorization," this is considered a valid SSN, and the taxpayer may qualify for the credit. Taxpayers with an ITIN do not qualify for EIC.

Uniform Definition of a Qualifying Child

The Working Families Tax Relief Act of 2004, amended in 2008, added the joint return test and standardized the definition of a qualifying child for the five child-related tax benefits. The tax law also defined exceptions and special rules for dependents with a disability, children of divorced parents, and adopted children (always treated as the taxpayer's child), including a child lawfully placed with the taxpayer for adoption.

Taxpayers that have missing or kidnapped children that a non-family member abducted may still claim the child. The IRS treats a kidnapped child as living with the taxpayer for more than half of the year if the child lived with the taxpayer for more than half of the part of the year before the date of the kidnapping, even if that length of time does not amount to half of a year. For example, if a child was kidnapped on March 1, the parent can still claim the child if they lived with the taxpayer for at least half of the two months (January and February) preceding the date of the kidnapping.

Although there are five tests to claim a dependent, a qualifying child must meet only four of the dependent tests to qualify for the EIC:

➢ Relationship
➢ Age
➢ Residency
➢ Joint return

To review the rules and guidelines for these tests, please refer to the chapter "Filing Status, Dependents, and Deductions."

Foster Child

To receive the EIC, a person is the taxpayer's foster child if the child is placed with the taxpayer by a judgment, decree, other order of any court of competent jurisdiction, or by an authorized placement agency such as a state or local government agency, a tax-exempt organization licensed by a state, an Indian tribal government, or an organization authorized by an Indian tribal government to place Indian children.

Example: Allison, who is 12 years old, was placed in the taxpayer's care two years ago by an authorized agency responsible for placing children in foster homes. Allison is the taxpayer's eligible foster child because she was placed there by an authorized licensed agency.

A Qualifying Child of More than One Person

Sometimes a child meets the rules to be a qualifying child of more than one person. However, only one person can use a qualifying child to claim the EIC. If two eligible taxpayers have the same qualifying child, they can decide who will take all the following related tax benefits:

➢ The child's exemption
➢ The child tax credit
➢ Head of Household filing status
➢ The credit for child and dependent care expenses
➢ The exclusion for dependent care benefits
➢ The Earned Income Credit

Only one taxpayer can claim these benefits, and they must claim either all of them or none of them. Do not divide the benefits between the two competing taxpayers. The tie-breaker rule applies if the taxpayer and the other person(s) cannot agree and if more than one person claims the EIC or other benefits using the same child. However, the tie-breaker rule does not apply if the other person is the taxpayer's spouse and files a joint return.

If the taxpayer and another person both have the same qualifying child, but the other person cannot claim the EIC because the taxpayer is not eligible or because their earned income or AGI was too high, the child is a qualifying child for the taxpayer. Suppose a taxpayer's EIC is denied because the qualifying child is treated as the qualifying child of another person for the current tax year. In that case, one may claim the EIC if there is another, separate qualifying child. However, the taxpayer cannot take the EIC using the qualifying child that another individual claimed.

Example: Pedro has two children, Nora from his first marriage to Darla and a son named Francisco from his current spouse Martha. Even if Pedro and Darla agree to let Darla claim the EIC for Nora, Pedro can still claim the EIC for his son Francisco, and Pedro is not prohibited from claiming Francisco simply because he chose to give up his claim to Nora.

Tiebreaker rules

The tie-breaker rules covered in *Chapter 4 Income* also apply to the EIC.

Example: 25-year-old Jeannie and her five-year-old son, Billy, lived with Jeannie's mother, Sarah, all year. Jeannie is unmarried, and her AGI is $8,100. Her only source of income was from a part-time job. Sarah's AGI was $20,000 from her job. Billy's father did not live with Billy or Jeannie. Billy is a qualifying child of both Jeannie and Sarah since he meets the relationship, age, residency, and joint return tests. Jeannie and Sarah must decide who will claim Billy as their dependent. If Jeannie does not claim Billy as a qualifying child for the EIC or Head of household filing status, Jeannie's mother can claim Billy as a qualifying child for each of those tax benefits for which she qualifies. Remember that the dependent test for support does not apply to the EIC.

Special Rule for Divorced or Separated Parents

The special rules covered in Chapter 4 that apply to divorced or separated parents trying to claim an exemption for a dependent do not apply to the EIC. For more information, see Publication 501 and Publication 596.

The Taxpayer as a Qualifying Child of Another Person

To review how to determine if a taxpayer is a qualifying child of another person, refer to the chapter "Income" in this textbook. If the taxpayer (or spouse filing a joint return) is a qualifying child of another person, the taxpayer or spouse cannot claim the EIC. This rule is true even if the person for whom the taxpayer or spouse is a qualifying child does not claim the EIC or meet all the rules to claim the EIC. Write "No" beside line 64a (Form 1040) to show that the taxpayer does not qualify.

Example: Max and his daughter, Letty, lived with Max's mother all year. Max is 22 years old and attended a trade school full time. Max had a part-time job, earned $5,100, and had no other income. Because Max meets the relationship, age, and residency tests, he is a qualifying child of his mother, and she can claim the EIC if she meets all the other requirements. Because the taxpayer is his mother's qualifying child, he cannot claim the EIC for his daughter.

EIC for Taxpayers without Qualifying Children

Taxpayers who do not have qualifying children may also be eligible for the EIC. To be eligible for the EIC, the taxpayer must meet the following conditions:

➢ The taxpayer must be at least 25 years old and under the age of 65 at the end of 2023. If the taxpayer is filing a joint return; however, it is not required that both the taxpayer and the spouse meet the age requirement
➢ The taxpayer must not be dependent on another person
➢ The taxpayer must not be the qualifying child of another person
➢ The taxpayers must have resided in the United States for more than half of the year
➢ Maximum income for 2023 tax year should be no more than $17,640 or $24,210 if married filing jointly

Schedule EIC Worksheets

Taxpayers eligible for the EIC with qualifying children must complete Schedule EIC. Schedule EIC requires including the child's name, Social Security number, year of birth, the number of months lived in the home located in the United States, and the child's relationship to the taxpayer. Schedule EIC must be attached to the taxpayer's Form 1040. The taxpayer's income must be less than the threshold amounts to qualify for EIC. Worksheets are available to help with the calculations of the EIC, and completion of the EIC worksheets is essential to determining the amount of credit a taxpayer may claim on their return. The completed worksheet should be placed in the client's file and not be attached to the federal tax return. The IRS has the EIC worksheets on its website. If the taxpayer is self-employed, the taxpayer must complete EIC Worksheet B, found in Instructions Form 1040.

All other taxpayers would calculate their earned income by using Worksheet A of the Form 1040 Instructions.

EIC Disallowed

There are circumstances when the IRS does not allow the EIC. Some of the most common reasons for disallowance of the EIC include:

➢ Claiming a child who does not meet all the qualifying child tests
➢ The Social Security numbers are mismatched or incorrect

- ○ Example: A couple is married during the current tax year, and they file their tax return under the spouse's married name; however, the wife did not change her name with the Social Security Administration, so her Social Security number is assigned with her maiden name listed, making the information on the return incorrect.
- ➢ Filing as Single or Head of Household when the taxpayer is married
- ➢ Over- or underreporting income

If the taxpayer's EIC has been denied or reduced for any year after 1996 for any reason other than a mathematical error, the taxpayer will have to complete Form 8862, *Information to Claim Earned Income Credit after Disallowance,* and attach it to their tax return. When interviewing the taxpayer, the tax preparer should ask if the taxpayer has ever received a notice from the IRS or filed Form 8862 in any year after 1996. If the taxpayer has received a notice that the EIC was denied or reduced from a previous tax year, the preparer should complete Form 8862 to claim the credit again if the taxpayer is eligible.

The purpose of Form 8862 is to claim the EIC after it has been disallowed or reduced in an earlier year. Form 8862 must be attached to the tax return if all the following apply:

- ➢ The EIC was reduced or disallowed for any reason other than a mathematical or clerical error for a year after 1996
- ➢ The taxpayer wants to claim the EIC and meet all the requirements

The taxpayer must attach Schedule EIC and Form 8862 to the return if the taxpayer needs to reclaim any previously disallowed credits for any qualifying children. The taxpayer may be asked for additional information before a refund is issued. If the IRS contacts the taxpayer to request additional information, and the taxpayer does not provide the necessary information or documentation, the taxpayer will receive a statutory notice of deficiency from the IRS. The notice explains that an adjustment will be assessed unless the taxpayer files a petition in the tax court within 90 days. If the taxpayer fails to reply to the IRS or file a petition within 90 days, the IRS will deny their petition for the EIC and assess how much tax they might owe.

EIC Taxpayer Penalties

The IRS may penalize the taxpayer if it determines that the taxpayer has been negligent or has disregarded rules or regulations relating to the EIC. The taxpayer may be prohibited from claiming EIC for the next two years if they are found negligent. If the taxpayer has fraudulently claimed the credit, the taxpayer will be prohibited from claiming the credit for the next 10 years. The tax preparer may be assessed penalties for not performing their due diligence.

Example: Brittni claimed the EIC on the 2022 tax return that she filed in February 2023. The IRS determined that she was not entitled to the EIC due to fraud. She received a statutory notice of deficiency in September 2023, explaining the adjustment amount that would be assessed unless she filed a petition in the tax court within 90 days. The IRS determined that Brittni did not file her petition, and she was prohibited from claiming the EIC on her return for 10 years until 2033. In that year, if she is eligible, she will need to complete and attach Form 8862 to her return to claim the credit again.

Claiming a Child in Error

The most common error is claiming a child that is not a qualifying child and does not meet the tests. The knowledge requirement for paid tax preparers states that the preparer must apply a reasonable standard (as defined by Circular 230 and the Form 8867 Instructions) to the information received from the client. If the information provided by the client appears to be incorrect, incomplete, or inconsistent, the paid preparer must make additional inquiries of the client until they are satisfied that they have gathered correct and complete information.

Example 1: Cindy tells Jack, her tax preparer, that she is 22 years old and has two sons, 10 and 11. Jack may need to ask Cindy the following questions:
- ➢ Are these Cindy's biological children, foster sons, or adopted sons?
- ➢ Was Cindy ever married to the children's father?
- ➢ Were the children placed in Cindy's home for adoption or as foster children?
- ➢ Did the father live with Cindy?
- ➢ How long have the children lived with Cindy?
- ➢ Does Cindy have any records to prove that the children lived with her, such as school or medical records?

Example 2: Maria tells Andres, her tax preparer, that last year she filed Single and claimed the EIC for her child, but that this year she has two children to claim for EIC. Andres may need to ask Maria the following questions:

- ➢ You claimed one child last year. What changed?
- ➢ How many months did the children live with you?
- ➢ Do you have any records to prove the children lived with you, such as school or medical records?

Nontaxable Combat Pay Election for EIC

Nontaxable combat pay for armed forces members is only considered earned income for the EIC if they elect to include nontaxable combat pay in earned income to increase or decrease the EIC. Figure the credit with and without the nontaxable combat pay before making the election. If the taxpayer makes the election, they must include all nontaxable combat pay as earned income. Examples of nontaxable military pay are combat pay, basic allowance for housing (BAH), and the basic allowance for subsistence (BAS). Combat pay is reported on Form W-2 in box 12 with code Q.

Part 3 Review

To obtain the maximum benefit from each part go online now and watch the video.

Takeaways

A tax credit reduces the amount of tax the taxpayer is liable for. Unlike a deduction, which reduces the amount of income subject to tax, a tax credit directly reduces the taxpayer's liability. A tax credit is a sum deducted from the total amount a taxpayer owes. There are two categories of tax credits: nonrefundable and refundable.

There are a variety of credits and deductions for the taxpayer. This lesson covered a few credits that allow taxpayers to lower their tax liability to zero and below and possibly receive a refund from the credits. A refundable credit is a tax credit treated as a payment and can thus be refunded to the taxpayer by the IRS. Refundable credits can help offset certain types of taxes that normally cannot be reduced and can even produce a federal refund.

Taxpayers and tax preparers may be subject to penalties for improperly claiming tax credits. It is important that the tax preparer carefully performs their due diligence in gathering taxpayer information and preparing a return.

TEST YOUR KNOWLEDGE!
Go online to take a practice quiz.

Chapter 8 Itemized Deductions

Introduction

There are two personal deductions: Standard Deductions and Itemized Deductions. A *standard deduction* is a set amount that the taxpayer can claim based on their filing status. Itemized deductions are certain personal expenses the IRS allows taxpayers to deduct. Itemized deductions are computed on the tax return using Schedule A, *Itemized Deductions*. The taxpayer should choose whichever option is best for their tax situation.

Itemized deductions are beneficial if the total amount exceeds the standard deduction. Some taxpayers must itemize deductions because they do not qualify for the standard deduction. Taxpayers not eligible for the standard deduction include nonresident aliens and individuals who file a tax return for less than 12 months. When a married couple files individual returns, if one spouse itemizes deductions, the other spouse must also itemize deductions. This is required even if standard deductions deliver the best option for them. See Publication 501, *Exemptions, Standard Deduction, and Filing Information*.

Objectives

At the end of this chapter, the student will know:

> ➢ Which deductions are limited to the 7.5% floor
> ➢ Which taxpayers are eligible to use Form 2106 after December 31, 2017, until December 31, 2025
> ➢ Which taxpayers are eligible to use Form 3903 after December 31, 2017, until December 31, 2025

Resources

Form 1040	Publication 17	Instructions Form 1040
Form 2106	Publication 463	Instructions Form 2106
Form 4684	Publication 502	Instructions Form 4684
Form 4952	Publication 526	Instructions Form 4952
Form 8283	Publication 529	Instructions Form 8283
Schedule A	Publication 530	Instructions for Schedule A
Publication 1771	Publication 936	Tax Topics 501–506, 508–515
Publication 597		

Part 1 Itemized Deductions

Itemized deductions encompass a variety of expenses the taxpayer can subtract from their adjusted gross income (AGI) to lower their taxable income. Common categories include medical expenses, state and local taxes, mortgage interest, and charitable contributions.

It's crucial that taxpayers maintain meticulous records for claiming itemized deductions. They should keep receipts, invoices, and documentation for all deductible expenses. Documentation should include dates, amounts, and descriptions of expenses, as well as any relevant supporting documents. Before opting for itemized deductions, compare them with the standard deduction. Depending on the taxpayer's financial situation, the standard deduction may be more advantageous. Consider factors such as changes in income, life events, and potential tax law changes when deciding whether to itemize deductions.

TCJA and Itemized Deductions

The Tax Cuts and Jobs Act (TCJA) has eliminated the overall limitation of itemized deductions based on the taxpayer's adjusted gross income. TCJA also changed the limitations that can impact the total itemized deduction amount; for example, the total amount that can be deducted from the state and local income tax on Schedule A, line 5, is now capped at $10,000 ($5,000 for MFS); taxpayers may not be able to claim all of their expenses as deductions.

For example, in 2017, George's itemized deductions for his state and local taxes was $17,000. George's financial situation did not change, and he expected to be able to deduct the same amount in 2018. However, even though George would still have qualified for a $17,000 itemized deduction under the old rules, George will only receive a $10,000 deduction on line 5 under the TCJA. His deduction amount is capped. Taxpayers should itemize or consider doing so if they meet the following criteria:

➢ Would get a higher amount of deductions by itemizing
➢ Had large unreimbursed medical or dental expenses that amounted to more than 7.5% of their adjusted gross income
➢ Paid mortgage interest
➢ Paid points to discount the interest rate
➢ Had casualty or theft losses that were declared during a federal disaster
➢ Made contributions to qualified charities and have receipts for recordkeeping.
➢ Have itemized deductions amounting to more than the standard deduction to which the taxpayer is entitled
➢ Paid state and local taxes (may be capped)
➢ Paid property taxes (may be capped)

Itemizing While Married Filing Separate

If taxpayers are filing MFS and one spouse itemizes, the other spouse is obligated to itemize. This is true even if the spouse's total deductions may be less than the standard deduction to which the individual would otherwise be entitled. If one spouse later amends the return, the other spouse must also amend their return. To formally agree to the amendments, both taxpayers must file a "consent to assessment" for any additional tax that one might owe as a result of the amendment. In the case of a spouse who qualifies to file as Head of Household, this rule will not apply. The spouse who qualifies as Head of Household is not required to itemize deductions even if the spouse who is required to file MFS decides to itemize their deductions. However, if the spouse filing Head of Household decides to itemize deductions, the spouse filing MFS is required to itemize deductions.

Señor 1040 Says: If the taxpayer is MFS and both the spouse and taxpayer elect to deduct sales tax and the spouse elects to use the optional sales tax tables, the taxpayer must use that table to figure the state and local general sales tax deduction (SALT).

Medical and Dental Expenses

Medical care expenses can be deducted if these amounts are paid for the diagnosis, cure, treatment, or prevention of a disease or condition affecting any part or function of the body. Procedures such as facelifts, hair transplants, hair removal, and liposuction are generally not deductible. Cosmetic surgery is only deductible if it is to improve a deformity arising from or directly related to a congenital abnormality, a personal injury from an accident or trauma, or a disfiguring disease. Medications are only deductible if prescribed by a doctor. The taxpayer can deduct any medical and dental expenses that exceed 7.5% of the taxpayer's AGI as shown on Form 1040, page 1, line 10. The 7.5% has been made a permanent floor.

Examples of deductible medical expenses include:

➢ Medical insurance premiums
➢ Dental treatment
➢ Prescription medicines
➢ Medical mileage
➢ Ambulance
➢ Seeing eye guide dogs care cost
➢ Eye exams
➢ Eyeglasses
➢ Hospital fees
➢ Lab fees
➢ X-rays
➢ Personal protective equipment (PPE)

Some home improvements may be deducted if their main purpose is to provide a medical benefit. The deduction is limited to the difference between the increase in the fair market value of the home and the cost of the improvements.

Examples of nondeductible medical expenses include over-the-counter medications, bottled water, diaper services, expenses for general health items, health club dues (unless related to a specific medical condition), funeral expenses, illegal operations and treatments, weight-loss programs (unless recommended by a doctor for a specific medical condition), and swimming pool dues. However, prescribed therapeutic swimming costs are deductible.

Other nondeductible items are insurance premiums paid for life insurance; loss of earnings, limbs, or sight; guaranteed payments for days the taxpayer is hospitalized for sickness or injury; and the medical insurance coverage portion of the taxpayer's auto insurance. Cafeteria plans are not deductible unless the premiums are included in box 1 of Form W-2.

The medical mileage rate for 2023 is 22 cents per mile for the full year. For 2024 the mileage rate is 21 cents per mile.

Spouse and Dependent Medical Expenses

The taxpayer is allowed to claim medical expenses that were paid for their spouse. To claim the expenses, they must have been married at the time the spouse received medical treatment. If the taxpayer and spouse do not live in a community property state and file separate returns, each would claim only their paid medical expenses. If the taxpayer and spouse live in a community property state and file separate returns, the medical expenses must be divided equally if they were paid out of community funds.

The taxpayer is allowed to claim medical expenses that were paid for their dependent(s). To claim these expenses, the individual must have been a dependent at the time the medical treatment was completed or when the expenses were paid. An individual would qualify as a dependent if all the following are true:

➤ The individual was a qualifying child or a qualifying relative
➤ The individual was a U.S. citizen or a resident of the United States, Canada, or Mexico
➤ The dependent's gross income was less than $4,700

Medical expenses can be deducted for any individual who is a dependent of the taxpayer, even if the taxpayer cannot claim the exemption for the individual on his or her return.

Example: James, age 66, has an AGI of $35,000; 7.5% of $35,000 is $2,625.00, and James had medical expenses of $2,700; therefore, James would be able to deduct $75.00 for medical expenses. The $75.00 is the difference between his expenses and the 7.5% "floor" needed to deduct medical expenses.

Example: Ryan, age 35, has an AGI of $40,000; 7.5% of $40,000 is $3,000, and Ryan had medical expenses of $2,500; therefore, Ryan will not be able to deduct his medical expenses since they are not over $3,000.

Medical Expense Reimbursement

Taxpayers can deduct only medical expenses paid during the taxable year. If the taxpayer receives a reimbursement for a medical expense, the taxpayer must reduce their total medical deduction for the year. If taxpayers are reimbursed for more than their medical expenses, they may have to include the excess as income. If the taxpayer paid the entire premium for medical insurance, the taxpayer would not include the excess reimbursement as gross income.

Premiums paid for qualified long-term care insurance contracts can be deducted within limits for long-term care insurance.

2023 Long-Term Care premium limits were:

Age 40 or under	$480
Age 41–50	$890
Age 51–60	$1,790
Age 61–70	$4,770
Age 71 or over	$5,940

Fees paid to retirement or nursing homes designed for medical care and/or psychiatric care are deductible. Meals, lodging, and prescriptions are deductible only if the individual is in the home primarily to get medical care. If the main reason the individual is in the home is personal, meals and lodging are not deductible.

Improvements made to the taxpayer's home due to a medical condition may increase the fair market value of the house. Some examples are:

➤ Construction of entrance or exit ramps
➤ Widening doorways or hallways
➤ Lowering cabinets and countertops
➤ Installing lifts

➢ Modifying stairways
➢ Adding handrails or grab bars in the home

If the cost of the improvement is more than the new fair market value, then the difference is a medical expense.

Example: Caroline had a lift installed in her two-story house for medical reasons. The cost of the lift was $12,000. The increase in the fair market value of the home was $10,000. Therefore, she can deduct $2,000 as a medical expense.

Taxes Paid

Certain taxes such as state, local, or foreign taxes, real estate taxes, and personal property taxes can be deducted by the taxpayer. Property taxes can only be deducted by the owner of the property. Real estate taxes are deductible on Schedule A for all property owned by the taxpayer. Unlike mortgage interest, this deduction is not limited to personal residences. Deeded time-shares may have a deductible real estate tax as well.

State and Local General Sales Tax (SALT)

State and local tax amounts withheld from wages are reported on line 5 of Schedule A, and the taxpayer may deduct the amounts of the following state and local taxes to reduce the taxpayer's federal tax liability:

➢ State and local taxes withheld from wages during the current tax year
➢ State estimated tax payments made during the current year
➢ State and local taxes paid in the current tax year for a prior tax year
➢ Mandatory contributions made to the California, New Jersey, or New York Non-occupational Disability Benefit Fund
➢ Mandatory contributions made to the Rhode Island Temporary Disability Fund or Washington State Supplemental Workmen's Compensation Fund
➢ Mandatory contributions to the Alaska, California, New Jersey, or Pennsylvania state unemployment funds
➢ Mandatory contributions to state family leave programs such as the New Jersey Family Leave Insurance (FLI) program and the California Paid Family Leave program

Interest and penalties for paying taxes late are never a deduction. For tax returns after December 31, 2017, and before January 1, 2026, the state and local tax (SALT) is capped at $10,000 or $5,000 if the taxpayer is married filing separate.

General Sales Tax

If the taxpayer elects to deduct state and local sales tax, the taxpayer will check box 5a on Schedule A. The taxpayer can deduct either actual expenses or an amount figured using the Optional State Sales Tax Tables. If the Optional State Sales Tax Tables are chosen, the taxpayer must check the sales tax tables for their local jurisdictions and follow the calculation instructions found at. If the filing status is MFS and one spouse elects to use the sales tax, the other spouse must use the sales tax method as well. The taxpayer must keep actual receipts showing general sales taxes paid. See Schedule A Instructions.

Señor 1040 Says: The taxpayer can either deduct state and local general sales taxes or state and local income taxes; not both.

Real Estate Taxes

State, local, or foreign real estate taxes paid for real estate owned by the taxpayer are deducted on line 5b of Schedule A only if the taxes are based on the assessed value of the property. If the taxpayer's real estate taxes are included in the mortgage and paid out of an escrow account, the amount paid by the mortgage company is the deductible amount.

After December 31, 2017, the taxpayer is no longer able to deduct foreign personal or real property taxes. If the taxes are based on the assessed value of the property, state and local real estate taxes paid on real estate owned by the taxpayer are deducted on line 5b of Schedule A. Items such as leasing solar equipment that has been added to the taxpayer's property tax bill is not a real estate tax deduction.

If the monthly mortgage payment includes an amount placed in an escrow account for real estate taxes, the taxpayer may not be able to deduct the total amount placed in escrow. The taxpayer can only deduct the real estate taxes that the third party actually paid to the taxing authority. If the third party does not notify the taxpayer of the amount of real estate tax paid, the taxpayer should contact the third party or the taxing authority to obtain the correct amount to report on the return. If the taxpayer bought or sold real estate during the year, the real estate taxes charged to the buyer should be reported on the settlement statement and in box 5 of Form 1099-S.

Personal Property Taxes

Personal property taxes are deducted on line 5c of Schedule A. The taxpayer should deduct state or local tax that is imposed yearly based on the value of the property. After December 31, 2017, the taxpayer must deduct personal property taxes on line 5c of Schedule A. The taxpayer should be careful not to include refunds, rebates, interest, or penalties as taxes paid.

Example: Lourdes pays a yearly registration fee for her car. Part of her fee is based on value, and the other part is based on the weight of the car. Lourdes can only deduct the part of the fee that was based on the value of the car, not the part based on the weight of the car.

Other Taxes

The taxpayer can claim a credit for foreign taxes as a nonrefundable credit on Form 1040, Schedule 3, line 1, or take it as an itemized deduction on Schedule A under "other taxes." The taxpayer may or may not have to complete Form 1116, *Foreign Tax Credits*. After December 31, 2017, the taxpayer must deduct other taxes on line 6 of Schedule A. Other taxes consist of foreign taxes earned from overseas investments and not from real property owned abroad.

Nondeductible Taxes and Fees

Nondeductible miscellaneous taxes and fees include:

➢ Federal income tax and most excise taxes
➢ Employment tax, such as Social Security, Medicare, federal unemployment, and railroad retirement taxes
➢ Fines and penalties
➢ License fees (such as for a marriage or driver's license)
➢ Certain state and local taxes such as gasoline tax, car inspections, and other improvements to personal property

Home Mortgage Interest and Points

Home acquisition debt refers to the mortgage and other funds a taxpayer took out to buy, build, or substantially improve a qualified home. A qualified loan or home mortgage is a loan used to acquire the taxpayer's primary residence or a second home, and the loan must be secured by the individual property. In order for the mortgage interest to be deductible, the loan must be secured and can be a first or second mortgage, a home improvement loan, or a home equity loan. The deductibility of interest expense is determined based on how the loan proceeds are used, which is referred to as interest tracing. For loans acquired before the TCJA went into effect on December 15, 2017, the interest on up to $1 million of debt ($500,000 for Married filing separately) incurred for acquiring, constructing, or substantially improving the residence is deductible.

If the taxpayer has a primary home and a second home, the home acquisition and home equity debt dollar limit apply to the total mortgage on both homes.

For home loans secured after December 15, 2017, the deductible amount is limited to $750,000 ($375,000 for Married filing separately). Taxpayers may use the 2017 threshold amounts if the following are true:

➢ The home acquisition debt was taken on prior to December 16, 2017
➢ They entered into a written, binding contract on or before December 15, 2017, in order to close on a principal residence before January 1, 2018
➢ They purchased the property before April 1, 2018.

If a taxpayer refinances a home acquisition loan that was acquired before the TCJA went into effect, the refinanced loan is subject to the same provisions as the original, pre-TCJA loan, but only up to the amount of the balance of the original loan. Any additional debt not used to buy, build, or substantially improve the home is not a home acquisition debt. For example, Cheryl took out a home equity line of credit for $100,000. She used $10,000 to remodel the master bedroom and then used the rest to go on a world cruise. The $10,000 could be used as home acquisition debt, but she is unable to use the world cruise as home acquisition debt. That could be considered income to Cheryl. See Publication 936.

Grandfathered Debt

If the taxpayer took out a mortgage on their home before October 14, 1987, or refinanced the loan, it may qualify as grandfathered debt. Grandfathered debt does not limit the amount of interest that can be deducted. All the interest paid on this loan is fully deductible home mortgage interest. However, the grandfathered debt amount could limit the home acquisition debt. For example, Sergio took out a first mortgage of $200,000 to buy a house in 1986. The mortgage was a seven-year balloon note, and the entire balance on the note was due in 1993. Sergio refinanced the debt in 1993 with a new 30-year mortgage. The refinanced debt is treated as grandfathered debt for the entire 30 years of the loan.

The main home is the property where the taxpayer lives the most. The second home is a similar property. The main or second home could be a boat or recreational vehicle. Both must provide basic living accommodations, which include a sleeping space, a toilet, and cooking facilities. Mortgage interest and points are reported to the taxpayer on Form 1098 and entered on line 8 of Schedule A. Form 1098, *Mortgage Interest Statement*, usually includes the amounts of mortgage interest paid, real estate taxes, and points (defined below). Mortgage companies will often "sell" mortgages during the year. If this occurs, the taxpayer could receive a Form 1098 from each mortgage company.

Señor 1040 Says: Remember to ask your clients if they paid more than one mortgage company. If they have more than one Form 1098, ask if this was for a second mortgage or if they bought and sold homes during the year.

Mortgage interest paid to an individual not reported on Form 1098 is reported on line 8b of Schedule A. The recipient's name and Social Security number or employer identification number is required. Failure to provide this information may result in a $50 penalty.

Points, often called loan origination fees, maximum loan charges, loan discounts, or discount points, are prepaid interest. Points that the seller pays for on behalf of the borrower are treated as being paid by the borrower. This allows the borrower, not the seller, to deduct these points as interest.

The full amount of paid points cannot be deducted 100% in the year of purchase or refinance. Points are generally deducted annually, over the life of the mortgage. To be reported on Form 1098, points need to meet the following conditions:

1. Clearly designated on HUD-1 or HUD Closing Settlement points with titles
   a. Loan discount
   b. Discount points
   c. Points
2. Computed as a percentage of the specified principal loan amount
3. Charged as a business practice of where the loan was issued and does not exceed the rates generally charged in the area
4. Paid for the acquisition of the taxpayer's principal residence
5. Paid directly by the taxpayer. Points were paid directly if either one applies:
   a. Funds were not borrowed from the lender by the taxpayer
   b. The seller paid the points on behalf of the taxpayer

Points paid when borrowing money for a refinance are normally deductible over the life of the loan. If the taxpayer pays off a mortgage early, the taxpayer can deduct the remaining points in the year the loan was paid off. Points are currently deductible only if paid from the taxpayer's funds. Financed points must be deducted over the life of the loan. If the taxpayer refinances and ends the loan, the remaining points are deducted when the life of the loan ends.

Mortgage Insurance Premiums

Mortgage insurance protects a mortgage lender in the event that a borrower defaults on their mortgage payments. It is typically required by lenders when a borrower makes a down payment that is less than 20% of the home's purchase price.
There are two principal types of mortgage insurance:

Private Mortgage Insurance (PMI): This type of insurance is typically required for conventional loans and is provided by private insurance companies. PMI protects the lender against loss if the borrower defaults on the loan.

Mortgage Insurance Premium (MIP): This type of insurance is required for certain government-backed loans, such as FHA (Federal Housing Administration) loans and USDA (United States Department of Agriculture) loans. MIP serves a similar purpose to PMI but is specifically designed to protect the government agency that insures the loan.

Mortgage insurance premiums are typically added to the borrower's monthly mortgage payments until the loan-to-value ratio (LTV) reaches a certain threshold, at which point the insurance may be canceled. However, for FHA loans, MIP payments may be required for the entire term of the loan.

Mortgage insurance allows borrowers to obtain financing with a lower down payment, making homeownership more accessible to those who may not have sufficient savings for a larger down payment. However, it adds an additional cost to the monthly mortgage payment, which borrowers should consider when budgeting for homeownership. As of the 2020 tax year, mortgage insurance premiums are no longer a deduction.
Form 1098

The IRS has made the mortgage interest statement evergreen.

Part 1 Review

To obtain the maximum benefit from each part go online now and watch the video.

Part 2 Charity and Casualty and Theft Losses

There are two ways to donate to a qualifying charitable organization: cash and noncash. The taxpayer could receive a tax benefit based on the amount of the contribution and the taxpayer's adjusted gross income.

Casualty is when the taxpayer has lost property by destruction that is sudden or unexpected.

Theft is when an individual takes another individual's belongings with the intent to deprive the owner.

Gifts to Charity

Contributions of money or property, such as clothing, made to "qualified domestic organizations" by individuals and corporations are deductible as charitable contributions. Dues, fees, or bills paid to clubs, lodges, fraternal orders, civic leagues, political groups, for-profit organizations, or similar groups are not deductible. Gifts of money or property given to an individual are also not deductible, even if they were given for noble reasons. Raffle tickets or church bingo games would not be a deductible expense (they may count as gambling expenses). If the taxpayer received a benefit (for example, a gift of $60) from a donation, the donation amount must be reduced by the value of the benefit.

Cash Contributions

Cash contributions include those paid by cash, checks, electronic funds transfer, debit card, credit card, or payroll deduction. Regardless of the amount, cash contributions are only deductible if the taxpayer keeps one of the following:

> ➤ A bank record that shows the name of the eligible organization, the date of the contribution, and the amount of the contribution. Bank records may include:
>   - A canceled check
>   - A bank or credit union statement
>   - A credit card statement
> ➤ A receipt or a letter or other written communication from the qualified organization showing the name of the organization, the date of the contribution, and the amount of the contribution.
> ➤ The payroll deduction records, or a pledge card or other document prepared by the organization. The document from the organization must show the name of the organization.

The tax professional should not overlook charitable contributions made through payroll deductions. They should appear on the taxpayer's last check stub or W-2. Make sure that the payroll deductions are not pretax contributions. Pretax contributions are not deductible. Advise your clients to make donations with checks, not cash. Make sure they get a receipt for all cash donations.

For payroll deduction contributions, one must keep the following:

> ➤ A pay stub, Form W-2, or other document furnished by the taxpayer's employer that shows the date and amount of the contribution
> ➤ A pledge card or other document prepared by or for the qualified organization that shows its name

The written communication must include the charity's name, the contribution date, and the amount. If the contribution was more than $250, the taxpayer should receive a statement from the charitable organization. When figuring donations of $250 or more, do not combine separate donations. The charitable organization must include the following on the letter or statement:

> ➤ The amount of money contributed and a description and estimated value of any property that was donated
> ➤ Whether or not the organization provided goods or services to the taxpayer in return

If the taxpayer overstates their charitable deductions resulting in understatement of their tax liability, the taxpayer could be assessed a penalty of 20% of the total deduction amount if more than 10% of the amount is owed. Additionally, the taxpayer may have to pay an underpayment penalty if the understatement amount exceeds $5,000.

Other Than by Cash or Check

If the taxpayer gives items such as clothing or furniture, they can deduct the fair market value (FMV) at the time of the donation. The FMV is what a willing buyer would pay to purchase when both the buyer and seller are aware of the conditions of the sale. If the noncash deduction amount is over $500, the taxpayer must fill out Form 8283.

If the contribution is a motor vehicle, boat, or airplane, the organization accepting the donation must issue the taxpayer Form 1098-C with the required information for the taxpayer to attach to Form 8283. If the deduction for any single item is over $5,000, the taxpayer must get an appraisal of the donated property. The vehicle identification number (VIN) must be reported on Form 8283, and if the car was sold in an auction the amount of the contribution is what the vehicle was sold for. See Instructions Form 8283.

When taxpayers donate noncash items, they must keep a list of the items donated as well as obtain and keep receipts. Donated items are priced according to their resale value, not the price of the item when it was purchased. See Instructions Schedule A.

If noncash charitable contributions are made with a value of more than $500, the taxpayer must complete Form 8283, *Noncash Charitable Contributions*, and attach it to the return. Use Section A of Form 8283 to report noncash contributions for which the taxpayer claimed a deduction of $5,000 or less per item (or group of similar items). Also, use Section A to report contributions of publicly traded securities. Complete Section B, Form 8283, for each deduction over $5,000 claimed for one item or group of similar items. A separate Form 8283 must be submitted for separate contributions of over $5,000 to different organizations. The organization that received the property must complete and sign Part IV of Section B.

The IRS may disallow deductions for noncash charitable contributions if they are more than $500 and if Form 8283 is not submitted with the return. See Publication 526 and Schedule A Instructions.

Contributions of Property Placed in Trust

When property has been placed in a trust and the trustees make a charitable deduction from the trust, the deduction is not allowed. If the property was placed in a remainder trust, then the deduction would be allowed. See IRC Code Section 170(f)(13).

Car Expenses

If the taxpayer claims expenses directly related to the use of their car when providing services to a qualified organization, the taxpayer must keep reliable written records of expenses. For example, the taxpayer's records might show the name of the organization the taxpayer was serving and the dates the car was used for a charitable purpose. The taxpayer would use the standard mileage rate of 14 cents a mile; records must show the miles driven for the charitable purpose.

Canadian, Israeli, and Mexican Charities

The taxpayer may be able to deduct contributions to certain charitable organizations under the income tax treaty the United States has with Mexico, Canada, and Israel. For contributions to be deductible, these organizations must meet tests like the ones used to qualify U.S. organizations. The organization should be able to tell the taxpayer if they meet the necessary test. See Publication 526.

Taxpayer Must Keep Records

Records document the amount of the contributions the taxpayer made during the year. The types of records to keep depends on the amount of the contributions and whether they include any of the following:

> ➢ Cash contributions
> ➢ Noncash contributions
> ➢ Out-of-pocket expenses when volunteering

Organizations are usually required to give a written statement if they receive a payment that is more than $75 and is partly a contribution and partly a payment made in exchange for goods or services. The statement should be kept with the taxpayer's records. See Revenue Procedure 2006-50, 2006-47 I.R.B. 944.

Other Itemized Deductions

The following items can be claimed on Schedule A, line 16:

> ➢ Gambling losses up to the extent of gambling winnings
> ➢ Casualty and theft losses from income-producing property
> ➢ An ordinary loss attributable to a contingent payment debt instrument or an inflation-indexed debt instrument
> ➢ Amortizable premiums on taxable bonds purchased before October 23, 1986
> ➢ Certain unrecovered investments in a pension
> ➢ Impairment-related work experience of persons with disabilities
> ➢ Deductions for repayment of amounts under a claim of right if over $3,000. See Publication 525

See Instructions Schedule A.

Gambling Losses

The taxpayer must report the full amount of any gambling winnings for the year. The taxpayer will deduct gambling losses for the year on line 16, Schedule A (Form 1040). The taxpayer may claim gambling losses up to the amount of gambling winnings. Taxpayers cannot reduce gambling winnings by gambling losses and report the difference; they must report the full amount of their winnings as income and claim their losses up to the amount of winnings as an itemized deduction. Therefore, the taxpayer's records should show winnings separately from losses. The taxpayer must keep an accurate diary or similar record of losses and winnings. The diary should contain at least the following information:

> ➢ The date and type of specific wagers or wagering activity
> ➢ The name and address or location of the gambling establishment
> ➢ The names of other persons present with the taxpayer at the gambling establishment
> ➢ The amount(s) won or lost

Casualty and Theft Losses

A casualty is the damage, destruction, or loss of property resulting from an identifiable event that is sudden, unexpected, or unusual. A loss on deposits can occur when a bank, credit union, or other financial institution becomes insolvent or bankrupt. When property is damaged or destroyed as a result of hurricanes, earthquakes, tornadoes, fires, vandalism, car accidents, and similar events, it is called a casualty loss. A casualty loss must be sudden and unexpected, so damages that occur over time do not qualify. Theft losses can occur as a result of the unlawful taking and removal of the taxpayer's money or property with the intent to deprive the owner.

A casualty loss amount equals the least of the following:

➢ The decrease in the fair market value (FMV) of the property as result of the event (in other words the difference between the property's fair market value immediately before and after the casualty).

➢ The adjusted basis in property before the casualty loss, minus any insurance reimbursement

➢ After calculating a casualty or theft loss and subtracting any reimbursements, one must figure how much of the loss is deductible. To claim a loss as a deduction, each loss amount must have been greater than $100 or greater than 10% of the amount on Form 1040, line 8b, reduced by $100.

After December 31, 2017, theft losses can no longer be claimed, and casualty losses can only be claimed if they are the result of an event that was officially declared a federal disaster by the President of the United States. Apart from this, casualty losses are still calculated using the same methods explained above. Form 4684, Casualty and Theft must still be attached to the tax return. If the taxpayer has a net qualified disaster loss on Form 4684, line 15, and has not itemized deductions, the taxpayer may qualify for an increased standard deduction.

Prior to January 1, 2018, if a casualty or theft loss occurred, the taxpayer completed Form 4684, *Casualty and Theft*, and attached it to the return. The loss calculated on Form 4684 was transferred to line 15 of Schedule A. The IRS allowed taxpayers who used Schedule A to deduct these losses with limited coverage.

Disasters and Casualties

If damage from a casualty is to personal, income-producing, or business property, taxpayers may be able to claim a casualty loss deduction on their tax return. Taxpayers must generally deduct a casualty loss in the year it occurred. However, if the property was damaged as a result of a federally declared disaster, taxpayers can choose to deduct that loss on their return for the tax year immediately preceding the year in which the disaster happened. A federally declared disaster is a disaster that took place in an area declared by the President to be eligible for federal assistance. Taxpayers can amend a tax return by filing Form 1040X, *Amended U.S. Individual Income Tax Return*.

Disaster Relief

The following website is where a taxpayer and tax professional can find the list of presidentially declared disaster areas: https://www.irs.gov/newsroom/tax-relief-in-disaster-situations.

Reconstructing Tips for the Disaster Claim

Reconstructing records after a disaster may be essential for tax purposes and for obtaining federal assistance or insurance reimbursement. After a disaster, taxpayers might need certain records to prove their loss. The more accurately a loss is estimated, the more loan and grant money may be available.

Below are tips to help the taxpayer gather the necessary information to reconstruct their records regarding their personal residence and real property. Real estate refers not just to the land but also to anything built on, growing on, or attached to it.

➢ Take photographs or videos as soon as possible after the disaster. This establishes the extent of the damage.

- ➢ Contact the title company, escrow company, or bank that handled the purchase of the home to get copies of the original documents. Real estate brokers may also be able to help.
- ➢ Use the current property tax statement for land-versus-building ratios if available. If they are not available, owners could get copies from the county assessor's office.
- ➢ The basis or fair market value of the home needs to be established. This can be completed by reviewing comparable sales within the neighborhood or by contacting an appraisal company or visiting a website that provides home valuations.
- ➢ Ask the mortgage company for copies of appraisals or other information needed regarding cost or fair market value in the area.
- ➢ Insurance policies list the value of the building, which initiates a base figure for replacement value insurance.
- ➢ If improvements were made to the home, contact the contractors who did the work to see if records are available. Get statements from the contractors that state their work and its cost.
    - ○ Get written accounts from friends and relatives who saw the house before and after any improvements. See if any of them have photos taken at get-togethers.
    - ○ If there is a home improvement loan, get paperwork from the institution that issued the loan. The amount of the loan may help establish the cost of the improvements.
- ➢ If no other records are available, check the county assessor's office for records that might address the value of the property.

Business Records

- ➢ To create a list of lost inventories, get copies of invoices from suppliers. Whenever possible, the invoices should date back at least one calendar year.
- ➢ Check for photos on mobile phones, cameras, and videos of buildings, equipment, and inventory.
- ➢ Get copies of statements from the bank for information on income. The deposits should reflect what the sales were for the given time period.
    - ○ Get copies of last year's federal, state, and local tax returns. This includes sales tax reports, payroll tax returns, and business licenses from the city or county. These should reflect gross sales for a given time period.
- ➢ If there are no photographs or videos available, sketch an outline of the inside and outside of the business location and then start to fill in the details of the sketches. For example, for the inside of the building, record where equipment and inventory were located. For the outside of the building, map out the locations of items such as shrubs, parking, signs, and awnings.
    - ○ If the business was pre-existing, go back to the broker for a copy of the purchase agreement. This should detail what was acquired.
    - ○ If the building was newly constructed, contact the contractor or planning commission for building plans.

Other Helpful Agencies

There are several resources that can help determine the fair market value of most cars on the road. The following are available online:

- ➢ Kelley Blue Book: www.kbb.com
- ➢ National Automobile Dealers Association: www.nadaguides.com
- ➢ Edmunds: www.edmunds.com

Call the car dealer where the vehicle was purchased and ask for a copy of the contract. If this is not available, give the dealer the details and ask for a comparable price. If the taxpayer is making payments on the car, another source is the lien holder.

It can be difficult to reconstruct records showing the fair market value of some types of personal property. Here are some things to consider when categorizing lost items and their values:

> ➢ Look on mobile phones for pictures that were taken in the home that might show the damaged property in the background before the disaster
> ➢ Check websites that could establish the cost and fair market value of lost items
> ➢ Support the valuation with photographs, videos, canceled checks, receipts, or other evidence
> ➢ If items were purchased using a credit or debit card, contact the credit card company or bank for past statements

If there are no photos or videos of the property, a simple method to help remember which items were lost is to sketch pictures of each room that was impacted:

> ➢ Draw a floor plan showing where each piece of furniture was placed – include drawers, dressers, and shelves
> ➢ Sketch pictures of the room looking toward any shelves or tables showing their contents
> ➢ Take time to draw shelves with memorabilia on them
> ➢ Be sure to include garages, attics, closets, basements, and items on walls

These do not have to be professionally drawn if they are functional.

Figuring Loss

Taxpayers may need to reconstruct their records to prove a loss and the amount thereof. To compute loss, determine the decrease in FMV of the property resulting from the casualty or disaster or determine the adjusted basis of the property – this is generally the amount that the property is now worth after disaster events have added to or lessened the value of the amount that was originally paid for the property.

Taxpayers may deduct whichever of these two amounts is smaller after subtracting the amount of any reimbursement provided to the taxpayer. If the reimbursement is larger than the adjusted basis of the loss, then the taxpayer will have a gain and not a subtraction. Certain deduction limits apply. See Publication 547, *Casualties, Disasters and Thefts*, for details on limits and Publication 551, *Basis of Assets*, for basis information.

If the casualty loss deduction causes a taxpayer's deductions for the year to be more than their income for the year, there may be a net operating loss. For more information, see Publication 536, *Net Operating Losses (NOLs) for Individuals, Estates and Trusts*.

Determining the Decrease in Fair Market Value

Fair market value (FMV) is generally the price for which the property could be sold to a buyer. The decrease in FMV used to figure the amount of a casualty loss is the difference between the property's fair market value immediately before and after the casualty. FMV is generally determined through an appraisal.

Casualty and Theft Losses of Income-Producing Property

Taxpayers can no longer claim a business casualty loss of income-producing property as an itemized deduction. If preparing a tax return from before 2018, use the following information to complete Form 4684:

> ➢ Loss from other activities from Schedule K-1 (Form 1065-B), box 2
> ➢ Amortizable bond premium on bonds acquired before October 23, 1986
> ➢ Deduction for repayment of amounts under a claim of right if over $3,000 (see Publication 525)
> ➢ Certain unrecovered investments in a pension
> ➢ Impairment-related work expenses for a disabled person (see Publication 529)

The loss of income-producing property, such as a rental, is calculated depending on if the property was stolen or destroyed. The loss minus the adjusted basis of the property, any salvage value, and the insurance reimbursements expected to receive.

Insurance Payments

If a taxpayer receives funds from an insurance contract for daily living expenses due to damage, destruction, or denied access to their primary residence, such amounts received compensate or reimburse the living expenses for the taxpayer and their household. See IRC Code Section 123.

Investment Interest Form 4952

Investment income is income that comes from interest payments, dividends, and capital gains collected upon the sale of a security or other assets, and any other profit made through an investment vehicle of any kind. Generally, individuals earn most of their total net income each year through regular employment income.

An investment interest expense is any amount of interest that is paid on loan proceeds used to purchase investments or securities. Investment interest expenses include margin interest used to leverage securities in a brokerage account and interest on a loan used to buy property held for investment.

The deductions for investment expenses could be limited by the at-risk rules and the passive activity loss limits. Interest related to passive activities or to securities that generate tax-exempt income is not included. The investment expense deduction is limited to investment income. Interest and ordinary dividend income are examples of investment income. Property held for investment purposes includes property that produces interest, dividends, annuities, or royalties that were not earned in the ordinary course of a trade or business. Alaska Permanent Fund dividends are not investment income.

Investment interest does not include any qualified home mortgage interest, or any interest taken into account in computing income or loss from a passive activity. The deduction for investment interest expense is limited to the amount of net investment income.

Example: Sandy had interest income of $800. She also had ordinary dividend income of $325. Sandy's investment interest expense for the year was $695. Sandy will be allowed to deduct the full amount of investment interest expense on her Schedule A since her investment income exceeds her investment interest expense.

When claiming investment interest, Form 4952 should be completed and attached to the tax return. Form 4952 does not have to be completed if the following apply:

➤ Taxpayer interest expense is not more than the investment income from interest and ordinary dividends minus qualified dividends
➤ The taxpayer has no other deductible investment expenses
➤ The taxpayer had non-disallowed interest expense for the year

Report Investment interest on Schedule A, line 9. See Publication 550.

Señor 1040 Says: Alaska Permanent Fund dividends, including those reported on Form 8814, are not investment income.

Fines or Penalties

The taxpayer cannot deduct their fines or penalties paid to a governmental unit for violating a law. This includes all fines and penalties paid in an actual settlement or a potential liability. Fines or penalties include parking tickets, tax penalties, and penalties deducted from teachers' paychecks after an illegal strike.

Part 2 Review

To obtain the maximum benefit from each part go online now and watch the video.

Part 3 Form 2106: Employee Business Expenses and Other Expenses

Prior to January 1, 2018, the following section is no longer reported on the federal return. This section is to help those who prepare returns where the states did not conform to the Tax Cuts and Jobs Act. Schedule A is still used to calculate the state deduction amount. The following states did not conform:

➤ Alaska
➤ Arkansas
➤ California
➤ Georgia
➤ Hawaii
➤ Iowa
➤ Minnesota
➤ Montana
➤ New York

Form 2106 is still used by Armed Forces reservists, qualified performing artists, fee-basis state or local government officials, and employees who will be claiming impairment-related work expenses such as traveling more than 100 miles from home to perform their services. See Instructions Form 2106.

With the suspension of miscellaneous itemized deductions under section 67(a), which began December 31, 2017, employees who do not fit the classifications in the previous paragraph may not use Form 2106. The information in the next section has been provided to assist those preparing taxes in the states that did not conform to section 67(a) and still need to calculate the federal deduction to arrive at the state deduction amount.

An employee may deduct unreimbursed expenses that are paid and incurred during the current tax year. The expenses must be incurred for conducting trade or business as an employee, and the expenses must be ordinary and necessary. An expense is considered ordinary if it is common and accepted. It is considered necessary if it is helpful and appropriate in the taxpayer's trade or business. Self-employed taxpayers do not use Form 2106 to report their business expenses.

An employee may deduct any of the following unreimbursed business expenses on Schedule A as a miscellaneous deduction subject to the 2% AGI limitation:

➢ Employee's business bad debt
➢ Education that is employment related
➢ Licenses and regulatory fees
➢ Malpractice or professional insurance premiums
➢ Occupational taxes
➢ Passport for a business trip
➢ Subscriptions to professional journals and trade magazines related to the taxpayer's trade or business
➢ Travel, transportation, entertainment, gifts, and car expenses related to the taxpayer's trade or business
➢ Tools used in a trade or business
➢ Memberships for professional associations
➢ Uniforms, work clothing, or protective wear, as well as their cleaning and maintenance

Do not include any educator expenses on Form 2106.

Taxing Employee Expenses

Tax treatment of employee business expenses depends on whether the expenses are categorized as reimbursed expenses or non-reimbursed expenses. Business expenses incurred by an employee under a reimbursement arrangement with an employer are normally not shown on the tax return. Unreimbursed business expenses are deductible as miscellaneous itemized deductions. The definition of trade or business does not include the performance of services as an employee.

The taxpayer may deduct certain expenses as miscellaneous itemized deductions on Schedule A. The taxpayer may deduct the expenses that exceed 2% of their adjusted gross income. The calculation is determined by subtracting 2% of the AGI from the total amount of qualifying expense.

Tax Home

The taxpayer's main place of doing business is considered their tax home. If the taxpayer does not have a regular or principal place of business due to the nature of work, the taxpayer's tax home may be the place where the taxpayer lives regularly. The length of occupancy must be considered when determining the taxpayer's principal place of business. See Tax Topic 511.

Temporary Assignment or Job

The taxpayer may regularly work at their tax home and at another location. If the assignment is temporary, the taxpayer's tax home does not change. If the assignment is indefinite, the taxpayer must report any income amounts received from his or her employer for living expenses, even if they were considered travel expenses. An indefinite assignment is a job that is expected to last a year or more, even if it does not end up lasting that long.

To determine the difference between a temporary and an indefinite assignment, look at when the taxpayer began working. A temporary assignment usually lasts for one year or less, although a temporary assignment could turn into an indefinite assignment, requiring the tax home to change. An indefinite assignment can be a series of short assignments at the same location for a certain amount of time. If the time spent at that location becomes sufficiently long, the temporary assignment could become indefinite.

If the taxpayer is a federal employee participating in a federal crime investigation or prosecution, the taxpayer is not limited to the one-year rule but must meet other requirements to deduct the expenses.

If the taxpayer returns home from a temporary assignment, the taxpayer is not considered to be away from home. If the taxpayer takes a job that requires a move with the understanding that they will keep the job after the probationary period, the job is considered "indefinite." The expense for lodging and meals is not deductible.

Meals

Deductions can be determined by using the actual meal expense for the standard meal allowance. If there is no reimbursement for meal expenses, then only 50% of the standard meal allowance is deductible, and that 50% is subject to the 2% floor. Employees who travel out of town for extended periods of time may elect to take a per diem rate. The federal per diem rate depends on the location.

A transportation worker is defined as an individual whose work involves moving people or goods by plane, bus, ship, truck, etc. Transportation workers can deduct a special per-day allowance for meals and incidentals if their work requires that they travel away from home to areas with different federal per diem rates. Unlike other traveling employees, a Department of Transportation (DOT) worker is allowed to deduct up to 80% of the meal.

Travel and Transportation Expenses

If the taxpayer travels away from their tax home for business, the expenses could be deducted on Form 2106. Business-related travel expenses must be ordinary and necessary expenses incurred while traveling away from home for the business or job. Expenses cannot be lavish or extravagant. A taxpayer is traveling away from home if:

➢ The taxpayer's duties require one to be away from the general area of their tax home for substantially longer than an ordinary day's work
➢ The taxpayer needs sleep or rest to meet the demands of his or her work while away from home

Travel by airplane, train, or bus is generally deductible. Fares paid for taxis, airport limousines, buses, or other types of transportation used between the airport, bus station or hotel, can be deducted including those used between the hotel and the client visited. Necessary trips are also deductible. Cleaning expenses, business calls, tips, and other necessary expenses related to the trip are also deductible.

Employees who drive their own vehicles are permitted to deduct either the actual expenses or the standard mileage rate for unreimbursed mileage. If the taxpayer is partially reimbursed, only the portion that is unreimbursed is reportable. See Publication 463, *Travel, Entertainment, Gift, and Car Expenses.*

Entertainment

Entertainment expenses must be ordinary and necessary. This includes activities generally considered to provide entertainment, recreation, or amusement to clients, customers, or employees. Expenses for entertainment that are lavish or extravagant are not deductible. An expense is not considered lavish or extravagant if the expense is reasonable based on facts and circumstances related to the business.

Entertainment expense deductions are limited to 50% of the actual expense and are further reduced by the 2% floor. "Entertainment" includes any activity that generally is considered to provide diversion, amusement, or recreation. It does not include club dues and membership fees to country clubs, airline clubs, and hotel clubs. The taxpayer may deduct entertainment expenses only if they are ordinary and necessary. Deducting entertainment expenses must meet either the "directly related" test or the "associated" test.

To pass the "directly related" entertainment test, expenses must meet the following conditions:

➢ Expenses must be directly related to business either before, during, or after the entertainment, or associated with the active conduct of business
➢ The taxpayer and client engaged in business during the entertainment period
➢ The entertainment occurred simultaneously with the business activity, and occurred with more than a general expectation of getting income or some other business benefit in the future

To meet the "associated" test, the entertainment must be associated with the active conduct of the taxpayer's trade or business and occur directly before or after a substantial business discussion. Daily lunch or entertainment expenses with subordinates or coworkers are not deductible, even if business is discussed.

Business Gifts

Gifts can be given to the client directly or indirectly. The taxpayer can deduct up to $25 per client per year for business gifts. Items do not include those that cost $4 or less, have the taxpayer's name imprinted on them, and are distributed (for example, pens, pencils, cases, etc.). Any item that could be considered a gift or entertainment is considered entertainment. Packaged food and beverage items are treated as gifts.

Business Recordkeeping

If audited, taxpayers must prove their deductions to the IRS. It is important to keep all receipts related to the tax return. Records of expenses should include the following:

➢ Amount paid
➢ Time, date, and place
➢ The purpose of the business discussion or the nature of the expected business benefit
➢ People in attendance

Reimbursements

Reimbursements paid by an employer's accountable plan are not reported in box 1 of Form W-2. Excess reimbursements paid by a nonaccountable plan are included in the employees' wages in box 1 of the W-2. See Instructions Form 2106.

Other Expenses

The taxpayer can deduct certain other expenses as miscellaneous itemized deductions subject to the 2% of adjusted gross income limit. The following are examples of deductible expenses:

➢ Expenses to manage, conserve, or maintain property held for producing taxable gross income (such as office space rented to maintain investment property)
➢ Attorney fees and legal expenses paid to collect taxable income
➢ Appraiser fees to determine the value of a donated party
➢ Fees paid to determine the value of a casualty loss

The taxpayer can deduct investment fees, custodial fees, trust administration fees, and other expenses paid for managing investments that produce taxable income.

Tax Preparation Fees

Tax preparation fees are deductible to the taxpayer. If the taxpayer paid the preparation fee by using a debit or credit card and a convenience fee was charged, the taxpayer cannot deduct the convenience fee as a part of the overall cost of preparing the return.

Education

The taxpayer can deduct qualifying education tuition and expenses. The education must be required by the employer or the law to keep one's salary, status, or job or to maintain or improve skills required in the taxpayer's present job in order to be deductible. Education that qualifies the taxpayer for his or her first job in a specific field is not deductible on Schedule A, nor is education that enables the taxpayer to change jobs; however, these may be deductible as a lifetime learning credit.

Deductible expenses include tuition, textbooks, registration fees, supplies, transportation (standard mileage or actual expenses), lab fees, the cost of writing papers or dissertations, student cards, insurance, and degree costs.

Part 3 Review

To obtain the maximum benefit from each part go online now and watch the video.

Takeaways

The taxpayer must decide whether to use the itemized deduction or the standard deduction. The standard deduction is a dollar amount that reduces the amount of income on which the taxpayer is taxed. The itemized deduction can be greater than the standard deduction. Some taxpayers must itemize their deductions because they do not qualify to use the standard deduction or because one's spouse chose to itemize their deductions.

Understanding and leveraging itemized deductions can result in substantial tax savings. By knowing what qualifies for a deduction, keeping accurate records, and strategically timing your expenses, you can optimize your tax situation. Stay informed about changes in tax laws and consult with a tax professional to ensure you're maximizing your deductions and minimizing your tax liability.

TEST YOUR KNOWLEDGE!
Go online to take a practice quiz.

Chapter 9 Schedule C

Introduction

This chapter presents an overview of Schedule C, the tax form used to report business income and expenses. Business income or loss from a business run as a sole proprietorship is reported on Schedule C, then flows to Schedule 1, line 3. Typically, Schedule C is used by a business run as a sole proprietorship.

Objectives

At the end of this lesson, the student will:

➢ Be able to identify the accounting methods and periods used by businesses and how they affect tax preparation
➢ Understand the guidelines that determine whether a person is an independent contractor or an employee
➢ Recognize what determines start-up costs
➢ Identify how to classify employees

Resources

Form 1040	Publication 15	Instructions Form 1040
Form 1099-NEC	Publication 15-A	Instructions Form 1099-NEC
Form 3115	Publication 334	Instructions Form 3115
Form 4562	Publication 463	Instructions Form 4562
Form 4797	Publication 535	Instructions Form 4797
Form 8829	Publication 536	Instructions Form 8829
Schedule C	Publication 538	Instructions for Schedule C
Schedule SE	Publication 544	Instructions Schedule SE
Publication 560	Publication 551	Publication 946
Publication 587		Publication 527

Part 1 Business Entity Types

There are many different types of business entities with their own sets of rules, regulations, and guidelines within the U.S. tax laws. The following entity types could apply to Schedule C, E, and/or F.

Sole Proprietorship

Sole proprietorship is not a legal entity. A sole proprietor is an individual owner of a business or a self-employed individual. It is a popular business structure due to its simplicity, ease of setup, and nominal start-up costs. A sole proprietor would register the business name with the state and city, obtain local business licenses, and then open for business. A drawback of being a sole proprietor is that it does not afford the owner the legal protections of a corporation or other formal business entities, and the owner is 100% personally liable for the business's income and/or debt.

A sole proprietorship reports the income and expenses from the owner's business on Schedule C, *Profit or Loss from a Business*. An individual is self-employed if the following apply:

> ➢ Conducts a trade or business as a sole proprietorship
> ➢ Is an independent contractor
> ➢ Is in business for themselves

Self-employment can include work in addition to regular full-time business activities. It can also include certain part-time work done at home or in addition to a regular job.

Minimum Income Reporting Requirements for Schedule C Filers

If the taxpayer's net earnings from self-employment are $400 or more, the taxpayer is required to file a tax return. If net earnings from self-employment were less than $400, the taxpayer may still have to file a tax return if they meet other filing requirements.

Husband and Wife Qualified Joint Venture (QJV)

A husband and wife cannot be sole proprietors of the same business. If they are joint owners, they are partners and should file a partnership return using Form 1065, *U.S. Partnership Return of Income.* They can be partners, but "sole" means one, and for the purposes of a business, the IRS does not recognize spouses as one.

If the taxpayer and spouse each materially participated in the business as the only members of a jointly owned and operated business, and if they file a joint return, they can elect to be taxed as a qualified joint venture (QJV) instead of a partnership. This election does not generally increase the total tax on the joint return, but it does give the self-employment credit for each taxpayer's Social Security earnings.

To make the QJV election, the spouses must divide all their income and expenses between them and file two separate Schedule Cs. Once the election has been made, it can only be revoked with IRS permission. The election will remain in effect if the spouses file as a qualified joint venture. If the taxpayer and spouse do not qualify in one year, then they will need to resubmit the paperwork to qualify as a qualified joint venture for the next year.

If the spouses own an unincorporated business and if they live in a state, foreign country, or a U.S. possession that has community property laws, the income must be treated as either a sole proprietorship or a partnership. Alaska, Arizona, California, Idaho, Louisiana, Nevada, New Mexico, Texas, Washington, and Wisconsin are the only states with community property laws.

Single-member Limited Liability Company (LLC)

For federal income tax purposes, a single-member LLC is not a separate entity. The single-member LLC would report income directly on the related schedule as a sole proprietor. A sole member of a domestic LLC would need to submit Form 8832 to the IRS prior to filing a corporation return if it is electing to treat the LLC as a corporation.

Accounting Periods

An accounting period is the fixed time covered by the company's financial statements. A tax year is an annual accounting period used for keeping records and reporting income and expenses. An accounting period cannot be longer than 12 months, and options include:

> ➢ The standard calendar year

> ➤ A fiscal year, which is a 12-month period that can end on the last day of any month except December

Taxpayers generally choose the calendar-year accounting period for their individual income tax returns. Business owners must choose their accounting period before filing their first business tax return.

Calendar Year

A calendar tax year is the 12 consecutive months from January 1 to December 31. Sole proprietors must adopt the calendar year if any of the following apply:

> ➤ The taxpayer does not keep books or records
> ➤ The taxpayer has no annual accounting period
> ➤ The taxpayer's present tax year does not qualify as a fiscal year
> ➤ The taxpayer's use of the calendar tax year is required under the Internal Revenue Code (IRC) or the Income Tax Regulations

Fiscal Year

A fiscal year is 12 consecutive months ending on the last day of any month except December. A "52 to 53-week tax year" is a fiscal year that varies from 52 to 53 weeks. It does not have to end on the last day of the month. For more information on fiscal years, who might choose them, and why, see Publication 538.

Change in Tax Year

To change the type of tax year used, the taxpayer would file Form 1128, *Application to Adopt, Change, or Retain a Tax Year*. See Instructions Form 1128.

Accounting Methods

Accounting methods are sets of rules used to determine when income and expenses are reported on a return. The accounting method chosen for the business must be used throughout the life of the business. If the owner wants to change the accounting method, approval from the IRS must be obtained. The two most common methods are cash and accrual. Businesses that have inventory must use the accrual accounting method.

The following are acceptable accounting methods:

> ➤ The cash method
> ➤ The accrual method
> ➤ Special methods of accounting for certain items of income and expenses
> ➤ The combination (hybrid) method, using elements of two or more of the above

Taxpayers should choose whichever system best reflects the frequency and regularity of their income and expenses. If the taxpayer does not choose an appropriate accounting method consistent with their income situation, the IRS may recalculate the income to reflect the correct accounting method, which could involve penalties and interest. Taxpayers must use the same accounting method when figuring their taxable income and keeping their books. However, business owners can use a different accounting method for each business they operate. See Publication 538, *Accounting Periods and Methods*.

Cash Method

When a taxpayer uses the cash method, all items must be reported as income in the year in which they are actually or constructively received. Income is constructively received when it becomes or is made available to the taxpayer without restrictions, such as through a bank account; the income does not necessarily have to be in the taxpayer's physical possession.

When using the cash method, all expenses are deducted in the year they are paid. This is the method most individual taxpayers use. Exceptions to the rule include prepaid expenses—for example, insurance or tuition. If expenses were paid in advance, they are generally deductible only in the year to which the expense applies.

Example: In the beginning of 2022, Chandler paid his business insurance expenses in advance for 2022, 2023, and 2024. For his 2022 tax return, he will only be able to claim the portion of those expenses that were used for 2022. He will only be able to claim the portion of the expense used for 2023 and 2024 on his tax returns for those respective years.

The cash method is the simplest accounting method, and taxpayers must use this method if they do not keep regular or adequate books.

The following three types of taxpayers are unable to use the cash method:

➢ C corporations
➢ Partnerships that have a C corporation as a partner
➢ Tax shelters

Accrual Method

If the accrual method is used, income is reported when earned, whether it has been actually or constructively received. Similarly, expenses are deducted when acquired rather than when paid. Businesses with inventory are required to use the accrual method to track the business' cost-of-goods-sold. Once this accounting method has been chosen, the taxpayer cannot change to a different accounting method without IRS permission.

If a business owner chooses the accrual method, the amount of gross income would be reported at the earliest of the following events:

➢ When payment was received
➢ When the income is due
➢ When the business earned the income
➢ When title was passed to the business

Example: Ruben is a calendar-year taxpayer who uses the accrual method and owns a dance studio. He received payment on October 1, 2022, for a one-year contract for 48 one-hour lessons beginning on October 1, 2022. Ruben gave eight lessons in 2022. Ruben would include one-sixth (8/48) of the payment in his 2022 income and the remaining five-sixths (40/48) would be reported in his 2023 tax year because, under the accrual method, income is reported when it has been earned, not when it has been actually or constructively received.

Combination (Hybrid) Method

The taxpayer can choose any combination of cash, accrual, and special methods of accounting if the combination clearly shows the taxpayer's income and expenses and if the method is used consistently. The combination (or hybrid) method is often used when a company has inventory that is not essential to accounting for income. The combination method cannot be used in the following cases:

➢ If inventory is necessary to account for income, the accrual method must be used
➢ If the cash method for figuring income is used, the cash method must also be used for expenses. It cannot be combined with another method
➢ If the taxpayer uses an accrual method for reporting expenses, then the accrual method of income must be used for everything else as well
➢ If the taxpayer uses a combination method that includes the cash method, treat that combination method as the cash method

Independent Contractors

An independent contractor is an individual who is hired by employers on a per-contract basis where the employer only has the right to control or direct the result of the work but cannot dictate what or how the result will be achieved. This classification offers the taxpayer certain tax benefits and gives them full responsibility for their employment taxes. An independent contractor can itemize all ordinary and necessary business expenses by using the appropriate schedule.

To be considered an independent contractor, the taxpayer should set their own hours and work schedule, be responsible for having their own tools or equipment, and usually work for multiple individuals or companies.

If a taxpayer is an independent contractor, the taxpayer would not fill out Form W-4, *Employee's Withholding Allowance Certificate,* nor will taxes be withheld from the taxpayer's paycheck. The independent contractor is responsible for paying self-employment tax (Social Security and Medicare) and making estimated tax payments to cover both the self-employment tax and their income tax.

Taxpayers are considered employees and not independent contractors if the following apply:

➢ Must comply with their employer's work instructions
➢ Receive training from the employer or the employer's designee
➢ Provide services that are integral to the employer's business
➢ Provide services that are personally rendered
➢ Hire, pay, and supervise workers for the employer
➢ Have an ongoing working relationship with the employer
➢ Must follow set hours of work
➢ Work full time for the employer
➢ Work on the employer's premises
➢ Work in a sequence set by the employer
➢ Submit regular reports to the employer
➢ Receive payments of regular amounts at regular intervals
➢ Receive payments for business or travel expenses
➢ Rely on employer to provide tools and materials
➢ Do not have a major investment in resources for providing services
➢ Do not make a profit or suffer a loss from services provided

    ➢ Work for one employer at a time
    ➢ Do not offer services to the general public
    ➢ Can be fired by the employer
    ➢ May quit anytime without incurring liability
    ➢ Are statutory employees

If the taxpayer qualifies as a statutory employee for income tax purposes, the box titled "Statutory Employee" on Form W-2, *Wage and Tax Statement*, will be checked. Income and expenses must be ordinary and necessary business expenses, and are reported on Schedule C.

Statutory Employees

A statutory employee is an independent contractor who is nevertheless still treated as an employee due to some statute. This applies to the following occupational groups, all of whom qualify as statutory employees under U.S. law:

    ➢ Agent drivers or commissioned drivers limited to those who distribute food, beverages (other than milk products), and laundry or dry-cleaning services for someone else
    ➢ Full-time life insurance salespeople who work for one company
    ➢ A home worker who adheres to the guidelines set forth by their employer, utilizing materials provided by the employer and returning them as instructed by the employer
    ➢ Traveling or city salespeople who sell for one principal employer. The goods sold must be merchandise for resale or supplies for use in the buyer's business operation. The customers must be retailers, wholesalers, contractors, or operators of hotels, restaurants, or other businesses dealing with food or lodging.

To make sure the salespeople are employees under the usual common-law rules, individuals must be evaluated separately. If a salesperson does not meet the tests for a common-law employee, then they may be considered a statutory employee. See Publication 15 and Publication 535.

An employee must meet specific criteria to meet the definition of statutory employee. Tax preparers should watch for incorrectly marked Forms W-2 and advise people with incorrectly marked forms to have their employers reissue a corrected Form W-2. If the taxpayer does not wish to do this, the tax professional should prepare the return using the information reported on Form W-2.

Statutory Nonemployees

Statutory non-employees are treated as self-employed for federal tax purposes, including income and employment taxes. The following are considered statutory non-employees:

    ➢ Direct sellers
    ➢ Qualified real estate agents
    ➢ Certain types of caretakers

Identification Numbers

Taxpayers can use their SSN or taxpayer identification number (TIN) on the appropriate schedule. However, the taxpayer must have an employer identification number (EIN) if either of the following applies:

➤ The taxpayer pays wages to one or more employees
➤ The taxpayer files pension or excise tax returns

Taxpayers can obtain an EIN by completing Form SS-4, *Application for Employer Identification Number*. A new EIN must be obtained if either the entity type or the ownership of the business changes. If the business has employees, the employer (or their delegate) must see the SSN to verify the name and number as it appears on the Social Security card. The employer (or their delegate) must have each employee complete Form W-4. See Publication 17 and SS-4 Instructions.

Schedule SE: Self-Employment Tax

Social Security and Medicare taxes become a little more complicated for self-employed taxpayers. Normally, the standard 12.4% tax for Social Security and 2.9% tax for Medicare is split between employees and their employer; an employee pays half this amount, and the employer matches it. Self-employed individuals, however, are simultaneously the employee and the employer and thus must pay the full 15.3% tax for Social Security and Medicare by themselves. This is called the self-employment tax (SE), and self-employed taxpayers must pay it because they do not have Social Security and Medicare taxes withheld from their earnings.

The self-employment tax is not as overwhelming as it might seem. For example, the 15.3% self-employment tax is figured from 92.35% of the taxpayer's net profit; it is not figured from their gross income or even from their total net profit, just 92.35% of it. Taxpayers who have net profit of less than $400 do not need to pay self-employment tax. If net earnings are more than $400, self-employment tax needs to be paid. Self-employed taxpayers can deduct half of the self-employment tax as an adjustment to income on Schedule 1, line 15.

Reported on Schedule 2, line 4, the SE tax applies to everyone who has self-employment income with net earnings of $400 or more. Self-employment income consists of income from self-employed business activities that are reported on Schedule C, E, and F, as well as income received by clergy and employees of churches and religious organizations. There are three ways to figure net earnings from self-employment:

➤ The regular method
➤ The nonfarm optional method
➤ The farm optional method

The regular method must be used unless the taxpayer qualifies to use either one or both optional methods. To calculate net earnings (sometimes referred to as "actual earnings") using the regular method, multiply the self-employment earnings by 92.35% (.9235).

Taxpayers who would like to make estimated tax payments to cover the self-employment tax they expect to owe must send the estimated tax payments on the following due dates:

➤ April 15
➤ June 15
➤ September 15
➤ January 15 of the next calendar year

If any of these dates fall on a holiday or weekend, the payment is due the next business day. The dates for 2024 differ for this reason, with payments due as follows:

➢ April 15
➢ June 17
➢ September 16
➢ January 15, 2025

Schedule C

Schedule C, *Profit or Loss from Business*, is used for the sole proprietor or the sole owner of an LLC to report the business income and expenses for the current tax year. If the business owner owns multiple businesses, then a separate Schedule C must be filed for each business.

Completing Schedule C

Schedule C is a very detailed form that categorizes the income and expense of the business. The first portion requires basic information about the business and its type.

Line A: Enter the business or professional activity that provided the principal source of income reported on line 1 of Schedule C. If the taxpayer owned more than one business, each business must complete a separate Schedule C or appropriate form. If the general field or activity is wholesale or retail trade or services connected with production services, state the type of customer or client. For example, "wholesale of hardware to retailers," or "appraisal of real estate for lending institutions."

Line B: Enter the six-digit code found in the instructions for Schedule C to designate the type of business. If the taxpayer's company type is not listed, find a similar principal business or professional activity code. No matter how unsure you are about which code to use, try not to use business code 999999, *Unknown Business*; businesses with this code are significantly more likely to be audited by the IRS due to the lack of information provided by using that code.

Line C: Enter the business name.

Line D: Enter the employer ID number (EIN). The taxpayer would have obtained this number by filling out and submitting Form SS-4 online to the IRS. If there is no EIN, enter the taxpayer's SSN at the top of the page where indicated. Remember: as a sole proprietorship, the company only needs an EIN in the following cases:

➢ The company has a qualified retirement plan
➢ The company is required to file an employment, an excise, or an alcohol, tobacco, or firearms return
➢ At least part of the company involves paying gambling winnings

Line E: Business address. Enter the physical address of the business, not a P.O. box number. If the business has a suite or room number, make sure that it is entered as well. If the business was conducted from the taxpayer's home, and if it is the same address used on Form 1040, page 1, do not complete this line.

Line F: Select which accounting method was used by the business during the tax year.

Line G: Material Participation

"Material participation" is when an owner of a passive activity takes part in the business's operations even though they typically would not. A business is a passive activity if the owner does not regularly participate in its daily operations. Rental activity is the most common type of passive activity, but it is far from the only kind. If the business experienced a passive activity loss, the loss may be limited by reducing the percentage of the business's income that can be taxed, but only if the taxpayer can show that they materially participated in the business.

To be able to limit losses by claiming "material participation," the taxpayer must meet any of the seven material participation tests from the requirements listed below. These generally cover any work done in connection with an activity in which one owned an interest at the time the work was completed. However, work is considered participation if it is work that the owner would not customarily do in the same type of activity, and if one of the main reasons for doing the work was to avoid the disallowance of losses or credits from the activity under the passive activity rules.

If the taxpayer meets any of these tests, check "Yes" on line G; otherwise, check "No." For the purposes of the passive activity rules, any of the following requirements must be met to be considered to have materially participated:

1. The taxpayer substantially participated in the activity on a regular and continuous basis for more than 500 hours during the tax year
2. The taxpayer substantially participated in the activity of all individuals, even including those who do not own an interest in the activity
3. The taxpayer participated during the tax year as much as any other person in the company
4. Taxpayer participated for more than 100 hours during the tax year but did not materially participate
5. The taxpayer materially participated in the activity for any five of the prior 10 tax years
6. The taxpayer is in a personal service activity in which the taxpayer materially participated for any three prior tax years. A personal service activity is an activity that involves performing personal services in the fields of health, law, engineering, architecture, accounting, consulting, or any other trade or business in which capital is not a material income-producing factor
7. Taxpayer meets the test if any person other than the taxpayer did the following:
   a) Received compensation for performing management services in connection with the activity
   b) Spent more hours during the tax year doing other activities than he or she spent performing management services in connection with the activity, regardless of whether the person was compensated for the service

Line H: If the business was started or acquired in the current tax year, check the box.

Line I: If the taxpayer made any payments that would require the taxpayer to file Form(s) 1099, check yes; otherwise, check no.

Schedule C, Part I, Income

Gross Income Receipts

Self-employment income is income earned from the performance of personal services that cannot be classified as wages because an employer-employee relationship does not exist between the payer and the payee because they are the same person. Self-employment tax is imposed on any U.S. citizen or resident alien who has self-employment income. If one is self-employed in a business that provides services (where products are not a factor), the gross income goes on line 7 of Schedule C and includes amounts reported on Form 1099-MISC, Form 1099-K, and Form 1099-NEC.

Different Kinds of Income

The taxpayer must report on their tax return all income received in business unless it is excluded by law. In most circumstances, income will be in the form of cash, checks, and credit card charges. Bartering is another form of income, and its fair market value must be included as income.

Example: Ernest operates a plumbing business and uses the cash method of accounting. Jim owns a computer store and contacts Ernest to discuss fixing the clogged pipes in his store in exchange for a laptop for Ernest's business. This is business-to-business bartering. If Ernest accepts the deal, he must report the fair market value of the laptop as income because it was the "income" he received in exchange for his service.

Miscellaneous Income

If a taxpayer is self-employed in a business involving manufacturing, merchandising, or mining, the gross income on line 7 of Schedule C is the total sales from that business, minus the cost of goods sold, and plus any income from investments and incidental or outside operations or sources. If the taxpayer is involved in more than one business, a separate Schedule C is filed for each business (for example, newspaper delivery and computer consulting). Other income commonly includes bank interest, rebates, and reimbursements from government food programs for a daycare provider.

Line 1: Enter the gross receipts for the year from the trade or business. Include all amounts received, even if the income was not reported on Form(s) 1099.

Line 2: Enter returns and allowances for the year from the trade or business. Even though this amount will be subtracted later, make sure it is entered here as a positive number. A sales return is a refund given to the taxpayer's customers who returned defective, damaged, or unwanted products.

Line 6: Report all amounts from finance reserve income, scrap sales, bad debts recovered, interest (on notes and accounts receivable), state gasoline or fuel tax refunds received during the current tax year. Prizes and awards related to the trade or business and other miscellaneous business income are also reported on line 6.

Schedule C, Part II, Expenses

To be a deductible business expense, the tangible or nontangible item must be either ordinary or necessary. An ordinary expense is an expense that is common, standard, and accepted in the taxpayer's industry. A necessary expense is one that is helpful and appropriate for the taxpayer's trade or business. An expense does not have to be indispensable to be considered necessary. The taxpayer needs to keep records of their expenses no matter how minimal the payment is. Documentation is the key if the taxpayer is ever audited for proof of expenses.
The following examples are expenses that can be deducted:

Line 8: Advertising. Advertising is communicating with the public to promote a product or service that the business provides. All advertising expenses can generally be deducted if the expenses are related to the business. Advertising for purposes of influencing legislation is not deductible as this is considered lobbying.

Line 9: Car and Truck Expenses. Expenses used for business can be deducted as a business expense. Vehicle expenses include gasoline, oil, repairs, license tags, insurance, and depreciation. For tax year 2023 the business travel expense rate is 65.5 cents per mile. This is a slight increase from the 2022 rates, which were 58.5 cents per mile from January to June and 62.5 cents per mile from July to December. The standard mileage rate for each business mile can be used for the taxpayer's owned or leased vehicle. The standard mileage rate cannot be used if five or more cars or light trucks are used at the same time. Five or more cars are considered a fleet.

The taxpayer may choose between using the actual expenses incurred by using the vehicle or using the standard mileage rate. Report the expense amount on Schedule C, Part II, line 9. The taxpayer should include the following in their daily business mileage log:

- ➢ Beginning mileage
- ➢ Ending mileage
- ➢ Commuting mileage

Business meals for 2023 are 50 percent deductible only if the properly applied rules from Revenue Procedure 2019-48 are used. The rule is for expenses incurred after December 31, 2020, and before January 1, 2022, the food and/or beverages must be provided by a restaurant.

A restaurant means a business that prepares and sells food and beverages to retail customers for immediate consumption, regardless of whether the food or beverages are consumed on the restaurant's premises. A restaurant does not include a business that primarily sells prepackaged food or beverages not for immediate consumption, such as:

- ➢ A grocery store
- ➢ Specialty food store
- ➢ Beer, wine, or liquor store
- ➢ Drugstore
- ➢ Convenience store
- ➢ Newsstand
- ➢ A vending machine or kiosk

See Notice 2021-25.

Remember, ordinary business-related meals are 50% deductible if business travel is either overnight or long enough to require the taxpayer to stop for sleep or rest to properly perform their duties. The taxpayer should note the destination and the reason for travel on a daily business mileage document. Business meals for 2023 revert to prior to 2021 rules, which is 50% deductible, and most entertainment expenses are not deductible at all.

Line 10: Commissions and Fees. A commission is a service charge for providing advice on an investment purchase for the taxpayer. The commission must be ordinary and necessary for the type of business the taxpayer claims. Expenses paid for services rendered by a non-employee could be considered commissions or fees. If more than $600 is paid to one individual, Form 1099-NEC and/or 1099-MISC must be filed, and a copy of the form should be issued to the independent contractor by January 31 of the following year. A copy must also be sent to the IRS along with Form 1096. See Instructions Form 1099(s).

Line 11: Contract Labor. Contract labor includes payments to individuals that are not employees, such as independent contractors. Report the payment amounts on this line.

Line 12: Depletion. Depletion is only deducted when a taxpayer has an economic interest in mineral property such as oil, gas, and standing timber reported on this line.

Line 13: Depreciation. Depreciation is the annual deduction that is allowed or allowable on all qualified business property reported on this line. If the taxpayer has timber depletion, they will use Form T. See Publication 535.

Line 14: Employee Benefit Programs. Employee benefit programs are an expense for the business owner and include retirement plans, disability insurance, life insurance, education assistance, and vacation and holiday pay. Expenses for employees such as accident plans, health plans, dependent-care expenses, and group life insurance plans can be deducted on this line.

Line 15: Insurance. The following business insurance premiums may be deducted on this line:

➤ Liability insurance
➤ Malpractice insurance
➤ Casualty insurance, such as fire or theft
➤ Workers' compensation insurance
➤ Disability insurance that covers the business's overhead expenses if the sole proprietor becomes unable to work
➤ Bond insurance
➤ Insurance to cover inventory and merchandise
➤ Credit insurance
➤ Business interruption insurance

A taxpayer who is self-employed may qualify to deduct up to 100% of the medical insurance premiums paid for themselves and qualifying family members. To take the deduction, the insurance plan must be established under the business, and the business must make a profit. Self-employed individuals should use *Form 7206 Self-Employed Health Insurance Deduction* to report and calculate their deduction for health care insurance costs.

Line 16: Interest. The following are examples of deductible interest reported on this line:

➤ The portion of mortgage interest related to the business
➤ If an auto is used in business, business percentage of the auto loan interest
➤ Interest capitalization
➤ Interest on business purchases

See Publication 535.

Line 17: Legal and professional fees. The following are examples of deductible legal and professional expenses on this line:

➤ Bookkeeping and accounting fees
➤ Tax preparation fees for business tax preparation
➤ Business-related attorney's fees

See Publication 334 and 535.

Line 18: Office Expense. Office expenses that are not included in home office expenses are deducted here. The following are examples of deductible expenses on this line:

- ➢ Postage
- ➢ Office supplies

Line 19: Pension and profit-sharing plans. Deduct the contribution portion of an employee's pension or profit-sharing plan that is paid as a benefit to the employee using this line. See Publication 560.

Line 20: Rent or lease. Schedule C, Part II, line 20a, is used for the lease of vehicles, machinery, and equipment rentals. Part II, line 20b, is used for leasing other rental property, such as rent for an office, building, or warehouse. See Publication 560.

Line 21: Repairs and maintenance. Repairs and maintenance of equipment, offices, buildings, or structures are deductible expenses and should include the cost of labor and supplies on this line.

Line 22: Supplies. Ordinary and necessary expenses that are not included in inventory should be deducted on this line.

Line 23: Taxes and licenses. The following are examples of deductible expenses on this line:

- ➢ License and regulatory fees for the trade or business
- ➢ Real estate and personal property taxes on business assets
- ➢ State and local sales taxes imposed for the selling of goods or services
- ➢ Social Security and Medicare taxes paid to match employee wages
- ➢ Paid federal unemployment tax
- ➢ Federal highway use tax
- ➢ Contributions to a state unemployment insurance fund or to a disability benefit fund if the contributions are considered taxes under state law

Do not deduct the following:

- ➢ Federal income tax, including the self-employment tax
- ➢ Estate and gift taxes
- ➢ Taxes used to pay for improvements, such as paving and sewers
- ➢ Taxes on the taxpayer's primary residence
- ➢ State and local sales taxes on property purchased for use in the business
- ➢ State and local sales taxes imposed on the buyer that were required to be collected and paid to state and local governments
- ➢ Other taxes and licenses fees not related to the business

See Publication 535.

Line 24a: Travel. The following are examples of ordinary and necessary business travel expenses that can be deducted on this line:

- ➢ Business airfare
- ➢ Hotels for business trips

➢ Taxi fares and tips while on business

Example: Gladys lives in Seattle, Washington, and is a paid tax practitioner. She went to the Latino Tax Fest to learn the latest tax law and updates. The Fest was held on Tuesday, Wednesday, and Thursday. Gladys flew from Seattle to Las Vegas, Nevada, on Sunday and then flew home on Friday. Her ordinary and necessary expenses are the above costs that were incurred during the days of the convention, not the costs that were incurred on Sunday, Monday, and Friday. Her meals and hotel room on Sunday, Monday, and Friday are not a business expense. See Publication 463.

Line 24b: Meals. Include expenses for meals while traveling away from home. Meals must be food or beverage provided by a restaurant.

Line 25: Utilities. Utility expenses include water, gas, electric, and telephone costs. Business telephone expenses do not include the base rate for any personal phone lines into the taxpayer's house, even if they are used for business. If the taxpayer has additional costs related to the business use of the phone, such as long-distance calls, the taxpayer can deduct those expenses. If the taxpayer has a dedicated second phone line for business, all expenses may be deducted regarding the second phone line.

Line 26: Wages. The gross amount paid in wages (minus employment credits) to employees is deducted from the business's gross income. If a self-employed taxpayer paid themselves out of the profits of the business, those "wages" are not deductible as an expense on line 26. This is considered a draw and is not a deductible expense.

Line 27: Other Expenses. Other expenses are deducted in Part V of Schedule C, and the total amount of any deductions in Part V is reported here. Other expenses include any expense that is not described elsewhere and is both ordinary and necessary in the operation of the taxpayer's business.

Part 1 Review

To obtain the maximum benefit from each part go online now and watch the video.

Part 2 Business Use of the Home

Report the total amount of expenses from business use of the home on Line 30 of Schedule C. If the taxpayer chooses to use the simplified method, they cannot claim more than 300 –square feet for storage of inventory or product samples. If the taxpayer runs a daycare, then use Form 8829.

Form 8829: Expenses for Business Use of Your Home

Self-employed taxpayers may be able to use Form 8829, *Expenses for Business Use of Your Home*, to claim deductions for certain expenses for business use of their home. To qualify for these deductions, the taxpayer must show that they used a space (such as an office) in the home exclusively and regularly for business. The amount of deduction a taxpayer can receive is based on what percent of the house's total square footage is being used for the business.

Example: Monica has an office she uses exclusively to manage and run her catering business. To receive a deduction for her home business expenses, Monica would divide the square footage of her office by the total square footage of her home to find the percentage of expense she can deduct. If her office is 130 square feet and her home is 1,000 square feet, then the percentage of her expenses she can deduct would be 13%.

Daycare providers would use Form 8829 to report expenses based on the number of hours spent caring for children or disabled dependents. The time also includes time spent cleaning the house before and after children arrive or leave as well as time spent preparing activities for the children.

If childcare providers do not use their entire home for childcare, they will use a combination of hours and square feet to determine business use. The home portion does not have to meet the exclusive-use test if the use is for an in-home daycare facility.

Business expenses that apply to a part of the taxpayer's home may be a deductible business expense if the part of the home was exclusively used on a regular basis in all the following ways:

> ➢ As the principal place of business for any of the taxpayer's trade or business
> ➢ As a place of business used by patients, clients, or customers to meet or deal during the normal course of trade or business
> ➢ In connection with the trade or business if the office is a separate structure not attached to the taxpayer's home

There are exceptions to the requirement that the space be used on a "regular" basis, such as certain daycare facilities and storage spaces used for inventory or product samples. The tax professional must determine whether the office in the home qualifies as the taxpayer's principal place of business.

To qualify an office in the home as the primary place of business, the following requirements must be met:

> ➢ The taxpayer uses the home exclusively and regularly for administrative or management activities of the taxpayer's trade or business
> ➢ The taxpayer has no other fixed location where the taxpayer conducts substantial administrative or management activities of their trade or business

Administrative or Management Activities

There are many activities that can be considered administrative or managerial in nature. Some of the most common include:

> ➢ Billing customers, clients, or patients
> ➢ Keeping books and records
> ➢ Ordering supplies
> ➢ Setting up appointments
> ➢ Writing reports or forwarding orders

If the following activities are performed at another location, the taxpayer would be disqualified from being able to claim the home office deduction:

> ➢ The taxpayer conducts administrative or management activities at other locations other than the home
> ➢ The taxpayer conducts administrative or management activities at places that are not fixed locations, such as in a car or a hotel room
> ➢ The taxpayer occasionally conducts administrative or management activities at an outside location
> ➢ The taxpayer conducts substantial non-administrative or non-management business activities at another fixed location other than home

> ➤ The taxpayer has suitable space to conduct administrative or management activities outside of their home but chooses to work at home

Example: Fernando is a self-employed plumber. Most of Fernando's time is spent installing and repairing plumbing at customers' homes and offices. He has a small office in his home that he uses exclusively and regularly for the administrative and management activities of his business, such as calling customers, ordering supplies, and keeping his books. Fernando writes up estimates and records of work completed at his customers' premises but does not conduct any substantial administrative or management activities at any fixed location other than his home office. Fernando does not do his own billing. He uses a local bookkeeping service to bill his customers.

Because it is the only fixed location where he does his administrative and managerial activities, Fernando's home office qualifies as his principal place of business for deducting expenses for its use. The fact that a bookkeeper does his billing is not important, as it does not change or impact where Fernando does his business administrative and managerial activities.

Simplified Option for Home Office Deduction

Taxpayers may use a simplified option to figure the home office business deduction. Revenue Procedure 2013-13 provides an optional safe harbor method that taxpayers may use, which is an alternative to the calculation, allocation, and substantiation of actual expenses for purposes of satisfying the Internal Revenue Code section 280A. These rules do not change the home office criteria for claiming business use but instead simplify the ruling for recordkeeping and calculation.

The major highlights of the simplified option are as follows:

> ➤ Standard deduction of $5-per-square-foot of home used for business with a maximum 300-square-feet ($1,500)
> ➤ Allowable home-related itemized deductions claimed in full on Schedule A
> ➤ No home depreciation deduction or later recapture of depreciation for the years the simplified option is used

When selecting a method, the taxpayer must choose to use either the simplified method or the regular method for any taxable year and can make that choice by using their selected method on their tax return. However, once the method has been chosen for the year, it cannot be changed. If the methods are used in different tax years, the correct depreciation table must be used. Year-by-year determination is acceptable.

The deduction under the safe harbor method cannot create a net loss; it is limited to the business' gross income reduced by deductions unrelated to the home office deduction. Any excess is disallowed and cannot be carried over or back, unlike the carryover of unallowed expenses that is available to offset income from that activity in the succeeding year when using the actual expense method. Regardless of the method used to claim home office expenses, the space must be regularly and exclusively used as the taxpayer's principal place of business. If the taxpayer used the simplified method for tax year 2022, and they chose not to use it for 2023, the taxpayer may have an unallowed expense from a prior year carryover to the current year. See Instructions Form 8829.

Regular and Exclusive Use

The portion of the home that is used must be used exclusively for conducting business.

Example: Nadine teaches piano lessons in her home. She has a piano in her spare bedroom and a grand piano in her living room. She uses the piano in her spare bedroom to teach her students and the grand piano for the students' recitals. Nadine does not use the spare bedroom for anything else except teaching students and storing music books related to her students. Her spare bedroom is used exclusively and regularly for business, but her grand piano is not; it is only used for recitals for her students. Therefore, she would only be able to claim the spare bedroom as a deduction and not the living room.

Like everything with tax law there are exceptions to the rule; the taxpayer does not have to meet the exclusive use test if either of the following applies:

➢ If the taxpayer uses part of their home for storage of inventory or sample product(s), they may deduct business use of the home expense if the following conditions are met:

   ○ The taxpayer sells products wholesale or retail as their trade or business
   ○ The taxpayer keeps inventory in their home for the trade or business
   ○ The home is the only fixed location for the trade or business
   ○ The storage space is used on a regular basis
   ○ The space used can be identifiable as a separate suitable space for storage
➢ The taxpayer uses part of the home as a daycare facility

Principal Place of Business

If the taxpayer conducts business outside of the home and uses their home substantially and regularly to conduct business, they may qualify for a home office deduction. The taxpayer can also deduct expenses for a separate freestanding structure such as a studio or a barn, but the regular and exclusive use test still applies. To determine if the place used is the primary place of business, the following factors must be considered:

➢ The relative importance of the activities performed at each location where the taxpayer conducts their business
➢ The amount of time spent at each location where the taxpayer conducts business

Expenses

When using Form 8829, there are two categories for expenses, direct and indirect. Direct expenses are for the business portion of the home. Indirect expenses are for keeping up and running the home. Direct expenses include:

➢ Business portion of casualty losses
➢ Insurance: direct insurance covers the business, while indirect insurance covers the entire home. A direct insurance policy is referred to as an umbrella policy
➢ Business rent
➢ Business repairs for the home
➢ Business portion of real estate taxes
➢ Business portion of home mortgage interest

Indirect expenses include:

➢ Security system: The cost to maintain and monitor the system is considered an indirect cost. However, the taxpayer may depreciate the percentage of the system that relates to their business

➢ Utilities and services: Including electricity, gas, trash removal, and cleaning services
➢ Telephone: The basic local service charge, including taxes for the first line into the home, is a nondeductible personal expense. Long-distance phone calls and the cost of a secondary home phone line used exclusively for business are both deductible expenses

Depreciation: If the taxpayer owns the home, the business portion could be depreciable. See Publication 587. Before calculating the depreciation deduction, the following information is needed:

o The month and year the taxpayer began using the home for business
o The adjusted basis and fair market value of the home at the time the taxpayer began using it for business; the cost of the home plus any improvements, minus casualty losses or depreciation deducted in earlier years; land is never considered part of the adjusted basis
o The cost of improvements before and after the taxpayer began using the home for business
o The percentage of the home used for business

The following expenses are not deductible:

➢ Bribes and kickbacks
➢ Charitable contributions
➢ Demolition expenses or losses
➢ Dues paid to business, social, athletic, luncheon, sporting, airline, and hotel clubs
➢ Lobbying expenses
➢ Penalties and fines paid to a governmental agency for violating the law
➢ Personal, living, and family expenses
➢ Political contributions
➢ Repairs that add value to the home or increase the property life

Business Auto Expenses

Taxpayers can deduct ordinary and necessary transportation expenses if they incur them while procuring income. If taxpayers use a personal vehicle for maintaining business activities, the deduction of the expenses is either by actual expenses or the standard mileage rate. For tax year 2023 the business travel rate is 65.5 cents per mile. The standard mileage rate for each business mile can be used for a vehicle owned or leased by the taxpayer.

The taxpayer can deduct the ordinary and necessary business-related expenses of traveling away from home. The taxpayer must properly allocate expenses between rental and nonrental activities. Information needed to record auto expenses accurately:

➢ Beginning mileage
➢ Ending mileage
➢ Commuting mileage
➢ Business mileage (Include notes about the destination and reason for travel)

Schedule C, Part III, Cost of Goods Sold

The cost of goods sold is used when a business has inventory or produces a product. Inventory must be calculated at the beginning and end of the year.

The following items are used to calculate a business's cost of goods sold:

Line 35: Beginning inventory. The beginning inventory is the closing inventory from the prior year. If this is the taxpayer's first business year, then beginning inventory is the amount of the cost of goods purchased.

Line 36: Purchases. The amount of reported purchases is the completed products or raw materials used for manufacturing, merchandising, or mining plus the cost of shipping minus the cost of items removed for personal use.

Line 37: Cost of labor. The cost of labor used in the actual production of the goods. The cost of labor is not wages, which are reported on Schedule C, Part II, line 26, *Wages*. The cost of labor is mainly used in manufacturing or mining, since the labor can be properly charged to the cost of goods sold. A manufacturing business can properly allocate indirect and direct labor to the expense of the cost of goods. A direct expense would be the labor to fabricate raw material into a saleable product.

Line 38: Materials and Supplies. Materials used in the actual production or processing of the goods such as hardware and chemicals are charged to the cost of goods sold.

Line 39: Other Costs. A proportion of overhead expenses related to creating a product. Containers and freight used for raw materials are examples of other costs.

Line 41: Ending Inventory. The inventory as counted at the end of the tax year is used as the beginning inventory for the following year's return.

Inventory is an itemized list of goods, with valuations, held for sale or consumption in a manufacturing or merchandising business. Inventory should include all finished or partly finished goods and only those raw materials and supplies that have been acquired for sale or that will physically become a part of merchandise intended for sale. How companies valuate inventory varies from business to business. See Publication 334.

Schedule C, Part IV, Information on Your Vehicle portion of Schedule C

To claim vehicle related expenses, the taxpayer enters the vehicle's information in Part IV. Commuting is generally considered travel between home and work. Part IV is used to calculate the standard mileage rate for the taxpayer's vehicle. If more than one vehicle was used, attach a statement containing the same information included in Schedule C, Part IV. The following circumstances may not meet the commuting rules:

➢ The taxpayer has at least one regular location away from home, and the travel is to a temporary work location in the same trade or business. See Pub 463
➢ The travel is to a temporary work location outside the location where he or she lives and normally works
➢ The home is the principal place of business, and the travel is to another work location in the same trade or business, regardless of whether the location is regular or temporary and regardless of the distance. See IRC Section 280A(c)(1)(A)

For more information on recordkeeping rules for vehicles, see Publication 463.
Schedule C, Part V, Other Expenses

Other expenses are deducted in Part V, Schedule C. Other expenses include any expense that is not included elsewhere and is ordinary and necessary in the operation of the taxpayer's business. Once all other expenses have been reported, figure the total amount, and report it on line 48 and line 27a.

List the type and amount of each expense separately in the spaces provided. If more space is needed, use another sheet of paper. Other expenses can include the following:

➢ Amortization that began in 2022; attach Form 4562
➢ Bad business debt that was previously reported as income. If the bad debt is paid off after writing the amount off as a deduction or expense, the business must include on their next return the reduction amount that they had received as income
➢ At-risk loss deduction
➢ Business start-up costs
➢ Costs of making commercial buildings energy efficient
➢ Deductions for removing barriers to the elderly and individuals with disabilities
➢ Excess farm loss
➢ Film and television production expenses
➢ Forestation and reforestation costs

Do not include the following as other expenses:

➢ Charitable contributions
➢ Cost of business equipment or furniture
➢ Replacements or permanent improvements to property
➢ Personal, living, and family expenses
➢ Fines or penalties paid to a government for violating any law

Bad Debts from Sales or Services

The business owner accrues bad debt when the charges for sales or service become uncollectable from a customer. Bad debt that is unrelated to business is not a reportable entry. When using the cash method of accounting, bad debts cannot be deducted unless the amount was previously included as income.

Start-Up Costs

Start-up costs are the expenses incurred before a business begins due to starting or purchasing a business. Taxpayers can elect to deduct up to $5,000 of start-up costs and up to $5,000 of organizational expenditures that were paid or incurred during the tax year in which the trade or business began. Start-up or organizational expenditures not deductible in the year in which the trade or business began must be capitalized and amortized over the 15 years following the business or trade's beginning. See Publication 535.

The following are examples of start-up costs:

➢ Survey of market
➢ Advertisements for the opening of the business
➢ Training wages
➢ Travel and other expenses incurred to secure distributors, suppliers, etc.
➢ Consulting fees and professional fees connected with starting a business
➢ Legal fees
➢ Net operating loss (NOL)

A net operating loss is incurred when business expenses and expenditures exceed business income. Sometimes the loss is great enough to offset income from other tax years. For more information, see Publication 536, *Net Operating Losses (NOLs) for Individuals, Estates and Trusts*.

Work Opportunity Tax Credit (WOTC)

An employee may claim the work opportunity credit for wages paid to workers from 10 targeted groups. See IRC Code section 51 and 52 for a description of targeted groups. The credit is calculated on Form 5884 and reduces the taxpayer's deduction for wages and salaries. The work opportunity credit is a business credit, and the credit can be claimed against both regular and alternative minimum tax liabilities.

The credit is normally 40% of the first $6,000 of qualified wages during the first year of employment, then reduced to 25% of the first $6,000 if the employee works less than 400 hours. The employee needs to work at least 120 hours for the employer to qualify. See IRC code section 51.

This credit has been extended to 2020 and before 2026 for qualifying wages. Qualifying wages do not include:

➢ Wages paid to or earned for any employee during any period the employee was paid by a federally funded on-the-job training program
➢ Wages paid for a summer youth employee for services performed when the employee lived outside an empowerment zone
➢ Wages paid to a designated community resident for services by a summer youth employee before or after any 90-day period between May 1 and September 15

See Instructions Form 5884.

Research Credit

A sole proprietor, partnership, or corporation that does not have publicly traded stock could claim the research credit. Any unused credit will be carried forward and deducted in the next year. To be able to claim this credit the research activities must directly contribute to the enhancement or creation of new or improved aspects of the function, performance, reliability, or quality of a product, process, software, or technology within the company. Capitalized expenses are reduced by the amount of the research credit that exceeds the amount allowable as a deduction for the expenses. For expenditures paid or incurred in the tax year 2023, the amount is capitalized and eligible for amortization over five years and is reduced by the excess (if any) of the research credit for the tax year.

Part 2 Review

To obtain the maximum benefit from each part go online now and watch the video.

Part 3 Qualified Business Income

Qualified Business Income (QBI)

The qualified business income deduction (QBI) is a tax deduction that allows eligible self-employed and small-business owners to deduct up to 20% of their qualified business income on the tax return. To be eligible, the taxpayer's total taxable income for 2023 must be under $182,100 for all filers except married filing jointly. The joint filers' income needs to be less than $364,200 to qualify.

Qualified Business Income (QBI) is the net amount of income, gain, deduction, and loss for any qualified taxpayer business. Qualified items of income, gain deduction, and loss include items that are effectively connected with the conduct of a U.S. trade or business and are included in determining the business's taxable income for the tax year.

The Section 199A Qualified Business Income Deduction, enacted as part of the Tax Cuts and Jobs Act in 2017, was meant to provide a tax benefit to smaller flow-through businesses in response to the large decrease in the C corporation tax rate from 35% to 21%.

To calculate the Sec. 199A deduction start by determining the QBI, which is determined separately for each of the taxpayer's qualified businesses. Certain investment items are excepted from QBI, including short-term and long-term capital gains and losses, dividends, and interest income not properly allocable to a trade or business. QBI also does not include reasonable compensation payments to a taxpayer for services rendered to a qualified business, guaranteed payments to a partner for services rendered to a business, and, to the extent provided in regulations, a Sec. 707(a) payment to a partner for services rendered to the business (Sec. 199A(c)).

20% Deduction for a Pass-Through Qualified Trade or Business

The combined QBI amount serves as a placeholder: it is the amount of the Section 199A deduction before considering a final overall limitation. Under this overall limitation, a taxpayer's QBI deduction is limited to 20% of the taxpayer's taxable income in excess of any net capital gain. The combined QBI amount is the sum of the deductible QBI amounts for each of the taxpayer's qualified businesses. The deductible QBI amount of a qualified business is generally 20% of its QBI, but the deductible QBI amount may be limited when the business is a specified service trade or business or by a wage and capital limitation. See Sec. 199A(b).

The calculation of a taxpayer's Sec. 199A deduction depends on whether the taxpayer's taxable income is below a lower taxable income threshold ($170,100, or $340,100 if filing a joint return). When computing taxable income for this purpose, the Sec. 199A deduction is ignored. If a taxpayer has income below the lower threshold, calculating the Sec. 199A deduction is straightforward. The taxpayer first calculates the deductible QBI amount for each qualified business and combines the deductible QBI amounts to determine the combined QBI amount. If the taxpayer has only one qualified business, the combined QBI amount is the deductible QBI amount for that business. The taxpayer then applies the overall taxable income limitation to the combined QBI. Thus, the taxpayer's Sec. 199A deduction is equal to the lesser of the combined QBI amount or the overall limitation (20% × taxpayer's taxable income in excess of any net capital gain).

Issues in Calculating the Deduction

If the taxpayer has taxable income above the higher threshold amount, two issues arise in the calculation of the Sec. 199A deduction. First, if the taxpayer has a business that meets the definition of a specified service trade or business (see below), it will not be treated as a qualified business, and the income of the business of the taxpayer will not be included in QBI. Thus, the Sec. 199A deduction will be denied in full for the business. Second, if a business is a qualified business (i.e., it is not a specified service trade or business), the deductible QBI amount for the business is subject to a W-2 wage and capital limitation. Taxpayers with taxable income that is over the phaseout amount are unable to use the Sec. 199A deduction for the business income that is a specified service trade or business.

Specified Service Trade or Business

A specified service trade or business is defined in Sec. 199A(d)(2) as "any trade or business which is described in section 1202(e)(3)(A) (applied without regard to the words 'engineering, architecture,') ... or which involves the performance of services that consist of investing and investment management, trading, or dealing in securities (as defined in section 475(c)(2)), partnership interests, or commodities (as defined in section 475(e)(2))."

Sec. 1202(e)(3)(A) defines a "qualified trade or business" as:

> "...any trade or business involving the performance of services in the fields of health, law, engineering, architecture, accounting, actuarial science, performing arts, consulting, athletics, financial services, brokerage services, or any trade or business where the principal asset of such trade or business is the reputation or skill of 1 or more of its employees or owners."

Thus, service trades or businesses (e.g., engineering, architecture, manufacturing, etc.) that are not specified service trades or businesses are eligible for the deduction regardless of the taxpayer's taxable income, but businesses providing specified services (e.g., law, accounting, consulting, investment management, etc.) of taxpayers who have taxable income above the higher taxable income threshold limit are excluded from the deduction.

Taxpayers with Income Above the Threshold

If a taxpayer has taxable income above the higher taxable income threshold and owns a business that is not a specified service trade or business, the QBI deductible amount for the business is subject to a limitation based on W-2 wages or capital (capital here is measured as the unadjusted basis of certain business assets) (Sec. 199A(b)(2)(B)). The deductible QBI amount for the business is equal to the *lesser* of 20% of the business's QBI or the *greater* of 50% of the W-2 wages for the business or 25% of the W-2 wages plus 2.5% of the business's unadjusted basis in all qualified property. Thus, two alternative limitations under Sec. 199A(b)(2) may limit the deductible QBI amount for each business that is included in a taxpayer's combined QBI amount (a pure 50% wage test or a combined 25% wage and capital test).

QBI and the W-2

W-2 wages are total wages subject to wage withholding, elective deferrals, and deferred compensation paid during the tax year that are attributable to QBI (Sec. 199A(b)(4)). However, amounts not properly included in a return filed with the Social Security Administration on or before the 60th day after the due date (including extensions) for that return are not included (Sec. 199A(b)(4)(C)). A partner's allocable share of W-2 wages is required to be determined in the same manner as the partner's share of wage expenses.

QBI and Property

The basis of qualifying property is calculated as the unadjusted basis immediately after acquisition of that property. Qualifying property is tangible property or depreciable property that was held by and available for use in the business at the close of the tax year, or was used in the production of QBI at any time during the year, and the "depreciable period" has not ended before the close of the tax year (Sec. 199A(b)(6)).

The depreciable period starts on the date the property is first placed in service and ends the last day of the last full year of the applicable recovery period under Sec. 168 (disregarding Sec. 168(g)) or 10 years after the beginning date, whichever is later. This rule allows "qualified property" to include property that has exhausted its modified accelerated cost recovery system (MACRS) depreciation period if it is still in its first 10 years of service. The statute directs Treasury to provide anti-abuse rules to prevent the manipulation of the depreciable period of qualified property through related-party transactions and for determining the unadjusted basis immediately after the acquisition of qualified property in like-kind exchanges and involuntary conversions.

Service Trade Disqualifier

A taxpayer potentially loses all or part of the Sec. 199A deduction if taxable income rises too high and the income is from a specified service business. The income phase-out amounts are as follows (adjusted for inflation in 2022):

- ➤ All other $170,050 - $220,050 partial phase out of Sec. 199A
                               $220,051 + complete phase out of Sec. 199A
- ➤ MFJ $340,100 - $440,100 partial phase out of Sec. 199A
                               $440,101+ complete phase out of Sec. 199A

A taxpayer potentially loses all or part of the Sec. 199A deduction if taxable income rises too high and the income is from a specified service business. This includes "fields of health, law, accounting, actuarial science, performing arts, consulting, athletics, financial services, brokerage services, or any trade or business where the principal asset of the business is the reputation or skill of one or more of its employees or owners."

The terminology "within the United States" means taxpayers only receive the 20% deduction on business income earned exclusively in the U.S. and on rental income from property located inside the U.S. The taxpayer only counts W-2 wages for businesses or real estate located within the U.S. If depreciable property figures into the formula, the property must be located inside the U.S. Therefore, if an entrepreneur has qualified business income from within and outside the U.S., separate the two before calculating the Sec. 199A deduction.

Pass-Through Entities

The pass-through deduction is available regardless of which deduction method is chosen—itemized or standard deduction. The deduction cannot exceed 20% of the excess of a taxpayer's taxable income over net capital gain. If QBI is less than zero, it is treated as a loss from a qualified business in the following year.

For pass-through entities other than sole proprietorships, the deduction cannot exceed whichever of the following is greater:

- ➤ 50% of the W-2 wages with respect to the qualified trade or business ("W-2 wage limit")
- ➤ The sum of 25% of the W-2 wages paid with respect to the qualified trade or business *plus* 2.5% of the unadjusted basis of all "qualified property" immediately after acquisition

Qualified property is any tangible, depreciable property that is held by and available for use in a qualified trade or business.

For a partnership or S corporation, each partner or shareholder is treated as having W-2 wages for the tax year in an amount equal to their allocable share of the W-2 wages of the entity for the tax year. A partner's or shareholder's allocable share of W-2 wages is determined in the same way as the partner's or shareholder's allocable share of wage expenses. For an S corporation, an allocable share is the shareholder's pro rata share of an item. However, the W-2 wage limit begins phasing out in the case of a taxpayer with taxable income exceeding $340,100 for married individuals filing jointly ($170,050 for other individuals). The application of the W-2 wage limit is phased in for individuals with taxable income exceeding the thresholds.

Reporting and Taxability of Form 1099-K, Payment Card, and Third-Party Network Transactions

Third-party settlement organizations charge a fee for being the facilitator of a transaction. The reporting requirements are $600 or more.

Effective January 1, 2022, third-party payment providers must begin reporting to the IRS business transactions totaling $600 or more, (ARPA section 9674(a); IRC section 6050W(e)). This new provision is meant to apply to transactions for goods and services only, but an individual taxpayer may receive a 1099-K for a nontaxable personal transaction. How do the new reporting guidelines distinguish between business and personal third-party transactions?

When an individual sets up their third-party network transaction app such as PayPal, Zelle, Venmo, etc., they choose either a personal or a business account. When a payment is made to a personal profile, the payor could tag that transaction as payment for goods and services, which would be determined to be a business transaction, and yet it could be a personal payment for goods and services.

If payments are considered taxable business income, they need to be reported on the appropriate tax forms (Schedule C, etc.) even if the payment processor does not issue a 1099. The burden is on the taxpayer to substantiate and report these appropriately.

Starting December 31, 2022, Third-Party Settlement Organizations (TPSOs) must report transactions exceeding a minimum threshold of $600 in aggregate payments, as mandated by Notice 2023-10.

Form 1099-K is utilized to report payments received for goods or services during the year, including those from credit, debit, or stored value cards (payment cards), as well as payment apps or online marketplaces, commonly known as TPSOs. TPSOs are responsible for completing Form 1099-K and distributing copies to both the IRS and the taxpayer.

Payments received from family and friends, intended as gifts or personal reimbursements, should not be included on Form 1099-K. Taxpayers should utilize Form 1099-K, alongside other financial records, to accurately determine and report taxable income when filing their tax returns.

If customers or clients make payments directly via credit, debit, or gift cards, a Form 1099-K will be provided by the payment processor or settlement entity, irrespective of the number or amount of transactions.

A payment app or online marketplace is obliged to issue a Form 1099-K if payments for goods or services exceed $20,000 or involve more than 200 transactions. However, they may opt to issue Form 1099-K for lower amounts. Regardless of receiving a Form 1099-K, all income must still be reported on tax returns.

Reportable payments encompass those for goods sold, services provided, or property rented, and can originate from various platforms including payment apps, online marketplaces, auction sites, and freelance marketplaces. Taxpayers may receive multiple Form 1099-K if they accept payments across different platforms.

Payments received from friends and family for personal expenses or gifts are not taxable income and should not be reported on Form 1099-K. Examples include cost-sharing for rides or meals, birthday or holiday gifts, and reimbursements for rent or household bills. It is advisable to categorize these payments as non-business within payment apps where feasible.

Employee Retention Credit

An employer may qualify for a refundable employment tax equal to 50% of qualified wages. The eligible employer who pays employees after March 21, 2020, and before January 1, 2022, may qualify for the Employee Retention Credit. The credit is 50% of the employees' wages up to $10,000 per employee. To receive the refunded money, the employer will need to file Form 7200, *Advance of Employer Credits Due to COVID-19*. In fall 2023, the IRS, in response to an increase in improper ERC claims, enacted a moratorium on new claims received on or after Sept. 14, 2023; the moratorium was initially effective until at least Dec. 31, 2023, but the IRS has not announced if or when it will again accept ERC claims. This credit has expired but the taxpayer can still amend their 2021 tax return and 941s. See Instructions Form 7200.

Recordkeeping

This section will cover basic recordkeeping for all business returns. A tax professional should emphasize to their clients the importance of recordkeeping and advise them to keep separate business and personal accounts. If a taxpayer has a loss on their business return, remind the taxpayer of the hobby rules. The taxpayer does not want to lose expense deductions due to poor recordkeeping; this is where the tax professional should spend time with their clients to educate them on how to track income and expenses. A good recordkeeping system includes a summary of all business transactions. These transactions are recorded in journals and ledgers and can be kept electronically or as hard copies (paper). If paper records are maintained, they must be stored in a secure manner, such as being kept in a locked filing cabinet or safe. Electronic records must be backed up in case of a computer failure, and should be password protected for security and privacy.

Benefits of Recordkeeping

Everyone in business must keep appropriate and accurate records. Recordkeeping will help the taxpayer:

- ➢ Monitor the progress of their business
- ➢ Prepare an accurate financial statement
- ➢ Classify receipts
- ➢ Track deductible business expenses
- ➢ Prepare the tax return
- ➢ Support reported income and expenses on the tax return

Records show the taxpayer if the business is improving, which items sell the best, and insights to increase the success of the business. Records are needed to prepare accurate financial statements, which include profit and loss, balance sheets, and any other financial statements.

Taxpayers should identify receipts at the time of purchase. It is easier to get into the habit of tracking receipts when received rather than dealing with them when preparing the tax return. A tax professional should teach clients how to identify and track receipts.

Kinds of Records to Keep

The taxpayer should choose the recordkeeping system that is best for their business. The system should match the accounting method of the taxpayer's tax year. The recordkeeping system should include a summary of all the taxpayer's business transactions. For example, recordkeeping should show gross income as well as deductions and credits for the business. Supporting documentation for consistently reoccurring transactions, such as purchases, sales, and payroll, should be maintained. It is important to retain documentation that supports the entries in the journal, ledgers, and the tax return. Records for travel, transportation, and gift expenses fall under specific recordkeeping rules. For more information see Publication 463. There are also specific employment tax records the employer must keep. See Publication 51 (Circular A).

Assets used in business can be property, such as machinery and equipment used to conduct business. Records of the asset are used to figure depreciation and the gain or loss when the asset is sold. Records should include the following information:

> ➢ When and how the business asset was acquired
> ➢ The purchase price of the business asset
> ➢ The cost of any business improvements
> ➢ Section 179 deduction
> ➢ Business deductions taken for depreciation
> ➢ Business deductions taken for casualty losses, such as losses resulting from fires, storms, or natural disasters
> ➢ How the business asset was used
> ➢ When and how the business asset was disposed
> ➢ The selling price of the asset or the business
> ➢ The expense of the business asset

The following are examples of records that might show the information from the above list:

> ➢ Business purchase and sales invoices
> ➢ Business purchase of real estate closing statements (HUD-1)
> ➢ Canceled business checks
> ➢ A business's bank statements

Maintaining Records

Tax records should be kept as needed for administering any Internal Revenue Code provision. Business records should be kept that document income and deductions appearing on the return. These should be kept for the duration of the period of limitations. Generally, this is three years, although certain records must be kept longer.

Employment records must be kept for at least four years after the date the tax becomes due or is paid. Records that pertain to assets such as property should be kept if the taxpayer owns property that is a business asset. Other creditors, such as an insurance company, may require the business records to be kept longer than required by the IRS.

Part 3 Review

To obtain the maximum benefit from each part go online now and watch the video.

Takeaways

Business income is derived from a multitude of sources and reported using Schedules C, E, and F. How business income is calculated, and which deductions and expenses are reported can vary based on the type of business, the accounting method used, and many other considerations. It is fundamental that the tax professional be familiar with these concepts when preparing business returns. There are four common tax errors for business taxpayers:

1. Not paying enough estimated tax
2. Neglecting to deposit employment taxes, or depositing late
3. Filing tax returns and payroll returns late
4. Not separating business and personal expenses

See Publication 15, 505, 535, and Circular E for more information.

TEST YOUR KNOWLEDGE!
Go online to take a practice quiz.

Chapter 10 Schedule E and Capital Gains and Losses

Introduction

Schedule E tax is used by taxpayers in the United States to report **Supplemental Income and Loss** from rental real estate, royalties, partnerships, S corporations, estates, trusts, and residual interests in real estate mortgage investment conduits (REMICs).

Rental income is any payment received by landlords and real estate investors for the use or occupation of real estate or personal property. Specifically for rental real estate, Schedule E allows taxpayers to report:

➢ Rental income received from real estate properties they own
➢ Allowable expenses related to operating those rental properties, such as mortgage interest, property taxes, maintenance costs, insurance, etc.
➢ Depreciation deductions related to the rental properties

Taxpayers use Schedule E to report rental income and deduct allowable expenses related to operating the rental properties, such as mortgage interest, property taxes, maintenance costs, and depreciation, to calculate their net rental profit or loss for the tax year. This net amount is then transferred to their individual income tax return (Form 1040).

Each Schedule E can report up to three rental properties. If the taxpayer has more than three rental properties, additional Schedule E forms must be used. Schedule E should not be used to report personal income and expenses, or for income from renting personal property that is not a business. To report other types of income, the taxpayer should use Schedule 1, lines 8 - 24b.

In addition to reporting rental real estate income and expenses, Schedule E is also used to report income or losses from partnerships, estates, trusts, and S-corporations.

Capital gains and losses refer to the increase or decrease in the value of an asset, such as stocks, bonds, real estate, or other investments, over the period of time that the asset is owned. A capital gain occurs when an asset is sold for a higher price than its original purchase price, resulting in a profit. A capital loss occurs when an asset is sold for a lower price than its original purchase price, resulting in a loss.

Understanding capital gains and losses is important for investors as they have tax implications. Capital gains are generally taxed as income, while capital losses can be used to offset other capital gains.

Objectives

At the end of this lesson, the student will:

➢ Know the types of income reported on Schedule E
➢ Understand the difference between repairs and improvements
➢ Know where to find the rental property depreciation chart
➢ Know the holding periods for different types of property
➢ Understand the difference between short-term and long-term capital gains
➢ Be able to identify capital assets
➢ Know how to determine basis before selling an asset

> ➢ Understand when the primary residence is excluded from capital gain

Resources

Form 1040	Publication 17	Instructions Form 1040
Form 4562	Publication 527	Instructions Form 4562
Form 4797	Publication 534	Instructions Form 4797
Form 6198	Publication 544	Instructions Form 6198
Form 8582	Publication 925	Instructions Form 8582
Form 8949	Publication 946	Instructions for Schedule E
Schedule E	Publication 523	Instructions Form 1099-B
Form 1099-B	Publication 551	Instructions Form 6252
Form 6252	Tax Topic 409, 414, 415, 425,	Instructions Form 8949
Schedule D	703, 704	Instructions for Schedule D

Part I Reporting Rental Income

If the taxpayer rents buildings, rooms, or apartments and provides heat and electricity, trash collection, etc., the taxpayer should report the income and expenses in Part I of Schedule E. Do not use Schedule E to report a not-for-profit activity.

If the taxpayer provided significant services primarily for the tenant's convenience, such as regular cleaning, changing linens, or maid service, the taxpayer reports the rental income and expenses on Form 1040, Schedule E, *Supplemental Income and Loss.* Significant services do not include the furnishing of heat and light, cleaning of public areas, trash collection, etc. If the taxpayer provides significant services, the taxpayer may have to pay self-employment tax on the income.

Types of Rental Income

Cash or the fair market value of property received for the use of real estate or personal property is taxable rental income. Individuals who operate on a "cash basis" report their rental income as income when it is constructively received and deduct expenses as they are paid. In addition to normal rent, many other things may be considered rent.

Advance Rent

Advance rent is any amount collected by the taxpayer before the time it is due. This income is reported in the year the taxpayer receives it, regardless of the taxpayer's accounting method and when the income was due.

Example: On March 18, 2023, Matthew signed a 10-year lease to rent Martha's property. During 2023, Martha received $9,600 for the first year's rent and $9,600 as rent for the last year of the lease. Martha must include $19,200 as rental income in 2023 ($9,600 + $9,600 = $19,200).

Canceling a Lease

If the tenant paid the landlord to terminate a lease, the amount received is considered rent. The amount paid by the tenant is included in the year received, regardless of the accounting method.

Expenses Paid by Tenant

If the occupant pays any of the owner's expenses, the payments are rental income. The taxpayer must include them as income and can deduct the rental expenses if they are deductible.

Example: Anet pays the water and sewage bill for Fernando's rental property and deducts the amount from her rent payment. Under her terms of the lease, Anet is not required to pay those bills. Fernando would deduct the amount Anet paid for the water and sewage bill as a utility expense and include the amount as rental income.

Property or Services (instead of rent)

If the taxpayer receives property or services as rent instead of money, the fair market value of the property or service is included as rent income.

Example: Lynn enjoys painting, and she is Leonard's tenant. Lynn offers to paint the rental property in lieu of paying two months' rent. Leonard accepts the offer. Leonard will include in his rental income the amount that Lynn would have paid for two months' rent. Leonard can deduct the same amount that was included as rent as a rental expense.

Security Deposits

Do not include a security deposit as income when received if the owner returns it at the end of the lease. If the owner keeps part or all of the security deposit during any year because the tenant did not perform under the terms of the lease, the owner must include the amount as income for that year. If a security deposit is to be used as the final rent payment, it is advance rent. The taxpayer would include it in income in the year received.

Rental Property Also Used as Home

If the taxpayer rented their primary residence for fewer than 15 days yearly, do not include the rent received as income. Rental expenses are not deductible either.

Fair Rental Value of Portion of Building Used as a Home

Fair rental value for property is an amount that a person who is not related to the owner would be willing to pay for rental use. If any part of the building or structure is occupied by the taxpayer for personal use, the gross rental income includes the fair rental value of the part occupied for personal use. See Publication 946, *Residential Rental Property.*

Room Rental

If a taxpayer rents out rooms of their primary residence, expenses that arise from the rental activity must be ordinary and necessary to be deductible. All income is taxable. The taxpayer needs to prorate expenses based on the room's square footage. To get the percentage, take the entire square footage of the home and divide by the room's square footage. For example, Jenny's home is 1,800-square-feet, and the room she rents out is 180-square-feet. The percentage she would use to deduct expenses is 10%. 180/1,800=10%.

Part Interest

If the taxpayer is a partial owner in a rental property, the taxpayer must report their percentage of the rental income from the property.

Lease with Option to Buy

If the rental agreement offers the tenant the right to purchase the property, the payments received under the agreement are considered rental income. If the tenant exercises the right to purchase the property, the payments received for the period after the date of sale are considered part of the selling price.

Husband and Wife Qualified Joint Venture (QJV)

A husband and wife cannot be sole proprietors of the same business. If they are joint owners, they are partners and should file a partnership return on Form 1065, *U.S. Return of Partnership Income.* They can be partners, but "sole" means one. For purposes of a business, the IRS does not recognize spouses as one.

If the taxpayer and spouse each materially participated in the business as the only members of a jointly owned and operated business and file a joint return, they can elect to be taxed as a qualified joint venture instead of a partnership. Generally, this election does not increase the total tax on the joint return, but each taxpayer gets credit towards their individual Social Security account for their share of the business profits. If Form 1065 was filed for a prior year, the partnership terminates the year immediately preceding the year the joint venture election takes effect.

To make the election, the taxpayers must divide all income and expenses and each file a separate Schedule E. Once the election is made, it can only be revoked with IRS permission. The election remains in effect for as long as the spouses file as a qualified joint venture. If the taxpayer and spouse do not qualify in one year, then the next year they will need to redo the paperwork to become a qualified joint venture.

Community Income Exception

If the spouses own an unincorporated business and they live in a state, foreign country, or a U.S. possession that has community property laws, the income and deductions are reported as follows:

1. If only one spouse participates in the business, all the income from that business is self-employment earnings of the spouse who carried the business
2. If both spouses participate, the income and the deductions are allocated to the spouses based on their distributive shares
3. If either or both spouses are partners in a partnership, see Publication 541
4. If the taxpayer and spouse elected to treat the business as a qualifying joint venture, both taxpayer and spouse must each file a separate Schedule E and a separate Schedule SE

Community property law states are Arizona, California, Idaho, Louisiana, Nevada, New Mexico, Texas, Washington, and Wisconsin.

Types of Property

Just as a filing status must be determined, rental property needs to be classified as well. A single- family residence is any building situated on one lot with a single dwelling, sharing no common wall, foundation, or other interconnection. Types of single-family residences are homes, mobile homes, and mansions. Use code 1 for these structures.

Multi-family residence is a classification of housing with multiple separate housing units for residential inhabitants contained within one building. This includes duplexes, tri-plexes, condos, and/or apartments. Use code 2 for these structures.

Commercial buildings include offices, hotels, malls, retail stores, etc. Use code 4 for these structures. Land is never depreciated. If the taxpayer earns income from renting out the land, they may need to report this. Use code 5 for this use. Items considered rent income include renting the land to a farmer to grow crops; this would not be reported on Schedule F, but Schedule E. Basis for land is the price determined by the county as land value. It is also found on the property statement.

A royalty payment is income derived from the use of the owner's property. It must relate to the use of a valuable right. A valuable right could be associated with items such as precious minerals (gold, silver, etc.) and crude oil.

Self-rental is when the owner of the property rents the business to their own business. This is regarded as material participation, so any net income for the property is deemed nonpassive.

Types of Expenses

Deductible rental expenses are expenditures that are incurred in renting the property. The taxpayer would deduct all ordinary and necessary expenses such as:

Advertising – line 5

An ad in a local paper, online, or other means of advertising intended to cause a potential renter to inquire about the property are all considered advertising. The amount of the fees paid for advertising is entered on line 5.

Auto and Travel – line 6

Taxpayers can deduct ordinary and necessary auto and travel expenses related to rental activity. The taxpayer should keep track of the miles to and from the rental. Ordinary and necessary mileage is incurred when the owner collects rent, works on the rental, etc. The standard mileage rate is used for the current tax year. Taxpayer can claim the mileage only if they:

1. Owned the vehicle and used the standard mileage rate for the first year placed in service
2. Leased the vehicle and are using the standard mileage rate for the entire lease period

Señor 1040 Says: The taxpayer cannot deduct car rental or lease payments, depreciation, or the actual auto expense if the standard mileage rate is used.

Cleaning and Maintenance – line 7

The day-to-day maintenance of the property is an allowed expense provided it is only for common areas and day-to-day cleanliness. These expenses are also limited to the days that are allowable rental days and not personal use days.

Commissions – line 8

Fees or commission paid to agents who collect rent, maintain the rental, or find tenants could be reported on line 8.

Insurance – line 9

Insurance for the rental property and the rider policy if the taxpayer has one are reported on line 9.

Legal and Other Professional Fees – line 10

The taxpayer can claim fees paid to an accountant for managing their accounts and for tax advice and tax return preparation. Legal fees charged in connection with buying or selling a rental property cannot be claimed. Fees involved with setting up the rental property are not deductible.

Management Fees – line 11

Property management services are reported on line 11 and may lower the taxpayer's liability. The taxpayer may claim the entire cost of the services but must keep all invoices or statements the property management company issues as evidence supporting the deduction's eligibility.

One of the obligations of a property manager or management company is to maintain contracts, agreements and other paperwork between the tenant and the landlord. This can be particularly useful at tax time, especially for property owners needing financial record-keeping assistance. The property management company can help prepare the necessary documentation for the tax professional to contribute to a more accurate tax return.

Mortgage Interest Paid to Banks – line 12

The taxpayer can claim the interest charged on money borrowed to buy the rental property, but not the entire mortgage payment. If the taxpayer borrowed money against the rental and did not use it for the rental, interest is not a deduction on Schedule E.

Other Interest – line 13

If the taxpayer paid interest on the rental income to an individual and did not receive Form 1098, enter the amount on line 13 and not on line 12. Attach to the return a statement that shows the name and address of the person who received the income. On the dotted line next to line 12 enter "See attached."

Repairs – line 14

The taxpayer can claim costs for repairs and general maintenance to the property. If the taxpayer is doing the work themselves, they can only claim the materials and not the time it took to repair the property. If the work is an improvement and not a repair, the taxpayer cannot claim the cost as an expense. In this case, the cost would be considered an asset, and will be covered in the depreciation chapter.

Supplies – line 15

"Materials and supplies" are tangible property used or consumed in business operations that fall within any of the following categories:

> ➤ Tangible items that cost less than $200
> ➤ Personal property with a useful economic life of 12 months or less
> ➤ Spare parts that have been acquired to maintain or repair a unit of tangible property

The cost of such items may be deducted in the year the item is used or consumed. To use this deduction, the taxpayer should keep records of when items are used or consumed for the rental property.

Cleaning and repair supplies are fully deductible, and some materials are as well. Supplies used in maintenance or to complete repairs are reported under supplies and not added to line 14. Materials on the other hand are generally not "used up" and sometimes become a part of the property. Materials used for improvements are usually depreciated, but materials used for repairs are considered supplies and can be deducted.

For example, if the taxpayer replaced the roof on their rental property, nails and tar would be considered repair supplies, while roof shingles would be considered an improvement. The supplies get deducted, and the materials are added to the basis, and depreciated separately over 27.5 years.

If the roof replacement was a repair and not an improvement (replacing a leaky roof), the roof shingles would be considered repair supplies, and would be deducted in the year the expenses were incurred.

Taxes – line 16

This line reports the property tax paid on the property. Like the primary home, one cannot claim bonds or other add-on taxes that are not related to the property.

Utilities – line 17

Utilities that can be claimed are those paid by the taxpayer, such as water, electricity, etc. If the renter is the one paying these expenses, they are not deductible by the landlord.

Depreciation – line 18

Depreciation is the annual deduction one must take to recover the cost or other basis of business or investment property having a useful life. Depreciation starts when the taxpayer puts the property into service. Any deduction for the appreciation of a property ends when the owner has sold or discontinued using the property as a rental.

Other Expenses – line 19

Any ordinary and necessary expenses not included on lines 5-18 are reported on line 19.

Expenses That Cannot be Claimed

The taxpayer cannot claim deductions for capital expenses, private expenses, or expenses that do not relate to the rental. Capital expenses are the costs of buying a capital asset or increasing its value; for example, the cost of buying the property and making improvements. Private expenses are things purchased for their own benefit, rather than to generate rental income.

Rental income expenses that cannot be used on the taxpayer's personal income tax return include:
- ➢ Purchase price of a rental property
- ➢ Capital portion of mortgage repayments
- ➢ Interest on money borrowed for any purpose other than financing a rental property
- ➢ The costs of making additions or improvements to the property
- ➢ The costs of repairing or replacing damaged property, if the work increases the property's value
- ➢ Real estate agent fees (commissions) charged as part of buying or selling the property

Claiming Deductions When Renting Out the House or Part of the Home

The usual rule for deductions when the taxpayer rents out their house or a portion of it, is to claim expenses related to the rental activity only. Expenses the taxpayer may be able to claim include electricity, gas, telephone and internet, insurance, or rates that are related to the rental portion. If the taxpayer is living in the house, these expenses will need to be apportioned. The taxpayer cannot claim private living costs or capital expenses. Private living costs include the taxpayer's day-to-day costs, such as food, electricity, or gas. Capital expenses include buying furniture for the rented room or the cost of improving that portion of the property. The taxpayer can claim depreciation on capital expenses. Renting Out the House - Apportionment

If the taxpayer rents out the house on an occasional basis, the taxpayer can claim the percentage of expenses for the time the house is rented. This may apply if the taxpayer rents out the house or property while away for a short period of time. The percentage of expenses claimed must match the amount of time in the tax year the house was rented out.

Renting Out a Room - Apportionment

If the taxpayer is renting out part of the home, the taxpayer can only claim expenses that relate to that part of the property. The taxpayer can only claim expenses for the time the room was rented out and occupied. Expenses could be claimed as a percentage based on the total area of the home and the rented room area.

Expenses Lines 5 - 19

Expenses reported on Schedule E are:

- ➢ Advertising
- ➢ Cleaning and maintenance
- ➢ Depreciation
- ➢ Rental insurance premiums

➢ Real estate taxes

Transportation and Travel Expenses, Line 6

Taxpayers can deduct ordinary and necessary local transportation expenses if they incur them while collecting rental income or to manage, conserve, or maintain the rental property. If taxpayers use a personal vehicle for maintaining rental activities, the deduction of the expenses is either by actual expenses or the standard mileage rate. For tax year 2023 the business travel rate is 65.5 cents per mile. For tax year 2024, the rate is 67 cents per mile.

The taxpayer can deduct the ordinary and necessary expenses of traveling away from home if the primary purpose of the trip was to collect rental income or to manage, conserve, or maintain rental property. The taxpayer must properly allocate expenses between rental and nonrental activities. Information needed to record auto expenses accurately:

➢ Beginning mileage
➢ Ending mileage
➢ Commuting mileage
➢ Business mileage (notes about the destination and reason for travel should be made)
➢ Separate records for each rental property

If the taxpayer rents only part of the property, the expenses must be allocated between the part rented and the part that is not rented.

Insurance Premiums Prepaid, Line 9

If the owner prepays an insurance premium for more than one year in advance, the payment will be applied for the year it was used.

Example: Gary paid $1,200 for his insurance on April 15, 2023, for 2023 and 2024. Gary will apply $600 for insurance in 2023 and $600 for insurance in 2024. He cannot take the entire amount in 2023.

Legal and Other Professional Fees, Line 10

These fees include legal and other professional fees such as tax preparation and expenses paid to resolve a tax underpayment related to rental activities. Federal taxes and penalties are not deductible.

Mortgage Interest, Line 12

Mortgage interest paid on a rental building could be deducted in the year paid. If the taxpayer owns a partial interest in a rental property, part of the rental expenses for that property can be deducted based on the taxpayer's percentage interest.

Points

Points are used to describe certain charges paid or treated as paid by a borrower to obtain a home mortgage. Points are not added to the basis of the property. Points can also be called loan origination fees. A portion of points paid for the purchase of a rental property are deductible, using the OID method. See Publication 527.

Taxes Line 16

State and local real estate taxes paid for rental income owned by the taxpayer are deducted on line 16 of Schedule E. If the taxpayer's real estate taxes are included in the mortgage and paid out of an escrow account, the amount paid by the mortgage company is the deducted amount.

Depreciation Line 18

Depreciation is a capital expense. Depreciation begins when the property has been placed in service.

Depreciation is the annual deduction for recovery of the purchase price of a fixed-asset expenditure. Property used for business should be depreciated. The amount of depreciation taken each year is determined by the basis of the property, the recovery period for that property, and the depreciation method. The recovery period for residential rental property under MACRS is 27.5 years and is used for property placed in service after 1986.

Depreciation for rental property (in the year placed in service) is reported on Form 4562, *Depreciation and Amortization*, and flows to Schedule E.

Depreciation that was not taken in one year cannot be taken in a following year. However, an amended return (Form 1040X) can be filed for the year in which it was not taken (if no more than three years prior). If depreciable property is sold, its basis for determining gain or loss will be reduced by depreciation "allowed or allowable," even if not deducted. Land is never depreciated.

Section 179 deductions cannot be used to depreciate rental property.

Property That Can Be Depreciated
Most types of tangible property can be depreciated. Examples of tangible property are:

> ➢ Buildings
> ➢ Vehicles
> ➢ Machinery
> ➢ Furniture
> ➢ Equipment
> ➢ Storage facilities

Land is tangible property and can never be depreciated. Some intangible items that can be depreciated are:

> ➢ Copyrights
> ➢ Patents
> ➢ Computer software if its life value is more than one year

Property that needs to be depreciated must meet the following requirements:

> ➢ Must be the taxpayer's own property
> ➢ Must be used in the taxpayer's business or income-producing activity
> ➢ Property must have a determinable useful life
> ➢ The property is expected to last more than one year

Passive Activity Limits

Passive activity is when the taxpayer did not materially participate in the business during the tax year. The two types of passive activity are:

1. Trade or business in which the taxpayer did not materially participate during the tax year
2. Rental activities, regardless of the taxpayer participation

Material participation is involvement in the activity of the business on a regular, continuous, and substantial basis. The taxpayer can claim a passive loss only against active income. Any excess passive activity loss can be carried forward to future years until used, or until it can be deducted in the year when the taxpayer disposes of the activity in a taxable transaction.

Rental real estate activities are passive activities; exceptions may apply for certain real estate professionals. Rental activity is when the taxpayer receives income mainly for the use of tangible property, rather than for services. Deductions or losses from passive activities are limited. Taxpayers cannot offset their income with passive activity income; passive activity income can only offset passive activity loss. The excess loss or credit is carried forward to the next tax year.

At-Risk Rules

The at-risk rules place a limit on the amount that can be deducted as a loss from rental real estate activity. Losses from holding real property (other than mineral property) placed in service before 1987 are not subject to the at-risk rules.

Generally, any loss from an activity subject to the at-risk rules is allowed only to the extent of the total amount at risk in the activity at the end of the tax year. The amount the taxpayer is considered at-risk in an activity is the sum of cash and the adjusted basis of other property contributed to the activity, and certain amounts borrowed for use in the activity.
The taxpayer may need to complete Form 6198 to figure their loss if:

➢ The taxpayer has a loss from the activity that is a trade or business or for production of income
➢ The taxpayer is not at-risk in this activity

Active Participation

If a taxpayer owned at least 10% of the rental property and made management decisions in a significant and bona fide sense, they are considered to have active participation. Management decisions include approving new tenants, deciding on rental terms, approving expenditures, and similar decisions. In most cases, all rental real estate activities are passive activities. For this purpose, a rental activity is an activity from which income is received mainly for the use of tangible property rather than for services.

Example: Christian is single and had the following income and losses during the tax year:

Salary	$56,954
Lottery winnings	$10,000
Rental loss	($3,450)

The rental loss resulted from a residential rental house that Christian owned. Christian made all the management decisions including collecting rent, making repairs, or hiring someone to complete the repairs, and approving the current tenant. Christian actively participated in the rental property management; therefore, he can use the entire loss of $3,450 to offset his other income.

Local Benefit Taxes

A deduction cannot be taken for taxes for local benefits that increase the value of the rental property. Examples of taxes for local benefits are those for putting in streets, sidewalks, or water and sewer systems. These taxes are capital expenditures that cannot be depreciated. The taxes may be added to the basis of the property. Local benefit taxes may be deducted if they are for maintenance, repairing, or paying interest charges for the benefits.

Expenses Accrued While Fixing the Rental

The taxpayer can deduct ordinary and necessary expenses for managing, supporting, or maintaining rental property from the time it is made available for rent.

Rental of Equipment

The taxpayer could deduct the rent paid for equipment that is used for rental purposes. However, if the lease contract is a purchase contract, the taxpayer cannot deduct these payments.

Uncollected Rent

If the taxpayer uses the cash basis, the taxpayer cannot deduct uncollected rent since the cash-basis taxpayer was never included in income. If the taxpayer is an accrual-basis taxpayer, the taxpayer must report the income when it is earned. If the taxpayer is unable to collect the rent, one may be able to deduct it as a bad-debt business expense.

Vacant Rental Property

If the taxpayer holds property for rental purposes, the taxpayer may be able to deduct ordinary and necessary expenses for managing, sustaining, or maintaining rental property from the time it became available for rent. Loss of rental income is not deductible.

Repairs and Improvements

Repairs

Maintaining the condition of the rental property. Repairs do not add to the value of the property or substantially prolong its life. The following are examples of repairs:

> ➢ Repainting the property inside and out
> ➢ Fixing gutters or floors
> ➢ Fixing leaks
> ➢ Plastering a hole in a wall
> ➢ Replacing broken windows

If repairs are made during an extensive remodeling of the property, the whole job, including the repairs, is an improvement. Improvements add value to the property and prolong the property's useful life. Improvements to property must be capitalized. The capitalized costs can generally be depreciated as if the improvements were separate property.

Example: Janice purchased an old Victorian house. The house needed many repairs, such as re-plastering, repainting, replacing broken windows, replacing roof tiles, and fixing leaks. After taking several months to complete the repairs, Janice was finally able to place the property on the market for rent. The remodeling of the property is considered an improvement, not a repair.

Improvements

Any expense that is paid to improve the property must be capitalized. An improvement adds value or prolongs the property life, restores the property, and/or adapts the property to a new or different use. Examples include:

> *Betterment* includes expenses for fixing a pre-existing defect or condition or for enlarging or expanding the property

> *Restoration* includes expenses for replacing a substantial structural part of the property, repairing damage to the property, or rebuilding the property to a like-new condition

Adaptation includes expenses for altering the property to a use that is not consistent with the intended ordinary use of the property

Recordkeeping

Keeping records is a way to show proof of any deduction that has been claimed on the tax return. Taxpayers should keep the tax records for at least five years from the date of filing the tax return and claiming the deduction. The individual should keep all receipts, loan documents, and the buyers closing statement of the assets that are reported on the tax return.

The taxpayer must also keep records regarding expenses and days of rental use. Records should be kept if the taxpayer or a member of the family used the rental property for personal purposes. The taxpayer should keep records of dates and times they personally spent on repairing or maintaining the property.

Not Rented for Profit

If the property is not rented with the intent of making a profit, the expenses can be deducted only up to the amount of income. In this situation, the income is reported on Schedule 1, line 8a - z. The mortgage interest, real estate taxes, and casualty losses are deducted on the appropriate lines of Schedule A. If the taxpayer rents the home fewer than 15 days a year, the taxpayer does not need to report any of the rental income and cannot deduct any of the expenses.

Fair Rental Price

A fair rental price for property is an amount that a person who is not related to the taxpayer would be willing to pay. The rent charged is not a fair rental price if it is substantially less than rent charged for other similar properties. Ask the following questions when comparing one property to another:

> ➢ Is it used for the same purpose?
> ➢ Is it approximately the same size?
> ➢ Is it in approximately the same condition?
> ➢ Does it have similar furnishings?
> ➢ Is it in a similar location?

If any one of the answers are no, the properties are not similar.

Use as Main Home Before or After Renting

Do not count personal days when the property was used as a main home before or after renting or offering it for rent in either of the following situations:

1. The taxpayer rented or tried to rent the property for 12 or more consecutive months
2. The taxpayer rented or tried to rent the property for a period of less than 12 consecutive months, and the period ended because the property was sold or exchanged

This special rule does not apply when dividing expenses between rental and personal use.

Dividing Expenses for Property Changed to Rental Use

Expenses for both personal and rental use must be divided between the two. Any reasonable method can be used to divide the expense. For example, it may be reasonable to divide the cost of some items, such as water, based on the number of people using them. However, the two most common methods for dividing expenses are:

1. Dividing an expense based on the number of rooms in the home
2. Dividing an expense based on the square footage of the home

Property Changed to Rental Use

If the taxpayer converts their primary home or other property (or a part of it) to rental use at any time other than at the beginning of the year, the taxpayer must divide the yearly expenses (such as depreciation, taxes, and insurance) between rental use and personal use. The taxpayer can deduct as rental expenses only the portion of the expenses that was for the part of the year the property was used or held for rental purposes. The taxpayer cannot deduct insurance or depreciation for the part of the year the property was held for personal use. The taxpayer can deduct home mortgage interest and real estate taxes as an itemized deduction on Schedule A for the part of the year the property was used for personal purposes.

Rental of Vacation Homes and Other Dwelling Units

If the taxpayer uses a dwelling as both a home and a rental unit, expenses must be divided between personal use and rental use. The taxpayer uses a dwelling as a home if one uses it for personal use more than the greater of:

➢ 14 days
➢ 10% of the total days it is rented to others at a fair rental price

Personal use consists of any day the unit is used by:

➢ The taxpayer or other person who has an interest in the home unless rented to another owner as the main home under a shared equity financing agreement
➢ A family member or member of any other family who has an interest in the home unless the family member uses the dwelling as their main home and pays fair rental price
➢ Anyone under an arrangement that lets the taxpayer use some other dwelling unit even if that person pays a fair rental price

> ➤ Anyone who uses the dwelling at less than a fair rental price

Days spent substantially working full-time to repair or maintain the property do not count as personal days. If the taxpayer occupies any part of a building or structure for personal use, its gross rental income includes the fair rental value of that part.

Dividing Expenses for Vacation Homes and Other Dwelling Units

If a unit is used for both rental and personal use, the expenses must be divided between the two. Any day that the unit is rented at the fair market value and used for both rental and personal use, the expenses are considered business use. Any day that the unit is available for rent but not actually rented is not a day of rental use.

Example: A ski lodge is available for rent from November 1 through March 31 (a total of 151 days, using 28 days for February). The taxpayer's family uses it for 14 days in October. No one rents it in the first week of November or at any time in March. The person who rented it the first week in December was called home for a family emergency. The taxpayer's daughter used it for two days in December. The remainder of the year, the lodge was closed and not used by anyone.

Rental Days: 151 − 38 = 113

The lodge was available for 38 days in which it was not rented. Days used by taxpayer and/or the taxpayer's family on which fair rental price was received count as rental days. The use by the taxpayer's daughter in December is recorded as rental days.

Total Use: 113 + 14 = 127

Personal Use: Percentage on rental is 113/127 = 89%. The deductible portion of any expenses is 89%. If the taxpayer does not have a profit from the rental, deductible expenses are limited.

Real Estate Professional

Generally, rental activities are passive activities even if the taxpayer materially participates. However, the activity may not be passive if all of these are true:

> ➤ The taxpayer is a real estate professional
> ➤ During the year the individual materially participated in the rental activities
> ➤ The taxpayer participates more than 750 hours in performing personal services in the trade or business
> ➤ The taxpayer spends half of the time performing personal services in real property

Qualified activities include developing, redeveloping, constructing, reconstructing, acquiring, converting, operating, managing, leasing, or selling real property. A taxpayer materially participates in an activity if for the tax year they were involved in its operation on a regular, continuous, and substantial basis during the year. If the taxpayer meets these requirements, the rental business is not a passive activity. If the taxpayer has multiple properties, each one is treated separately unless the taxpayer chooses to treat them as one activity. Personal services that were performed as an employee cannot be counted. If the taxpayer files a joint return, the hours cannot be added together to fulfill the requirements.

Limited Partnership Interests

If the taxpayer held property in a limited partnership as a limited partner, the taxpayer does not materially participate in rental real estate. Failure to meet the minimum-hours threshold may result in the passive activity amount being limited. Proper recordkeeping is the key to making sure that if the taxpayer is audited, they do not lose their passive activity loss (PAL).

Rental Property Sales

When rental property or other business assets are sold, the gain or loss must be reported on Form 4797, *Sales of Business Property*. If the property sold includes land, both the land and the property must be reported on Form 4797. Each property is reported separately in the appropriate part of Form 4797. The different sections of Form 4797 are as follows:

Part I: Used to report sales of the section 1231 portion of a real estate transaction. This includes land and all long-term property sold at a loss. A transaction reported here does not need to be reported in Part III.

Part II: Used to report sales of business property that are not reported in Part I or Part III.

Part III: Used to calculate the recapture of depreciation and certain other items that must be reported as ordinary income on the disposition of property. The property includes sections 1245, 1250, 1252, 1254, and 1255 property sales. This includes most long-term property that was depreciated and sold at a gain.

Depreciation should be calculated (and deducted on the appropriate form) for the period prior to the sale. If the taxpayer sells or exchanges property used partly for business or rental purposes and partly for personal purposes, the taxpayer must figure the gain or loss on the sale or exchange as though two separate pieces of property were sold. The taxpayer must divide the selling price, selling expenses, and the basis of the property between the business or rental part and the personal part. The taxpayer must subtract depreciation that was taken or could have taken from the basis of the business or rental part. Gain or loss on the business or rental part of the property may be a capital gain or loss or an ordinary gain or loss. Any gain on the personal part of the property is a capital gain. The taxpayer cannot deduct a loss on the personal part.

Depreciation is the annual deduction that allows taxpayers to recover the cost or other basis of their business or investment property over a certain number of years. Depreciation begins when a taxpayer places property in service for use in a trade or business or to produce income. The property ceases to be depreciable when the taxpayer has fully recovered the property's cost or other basis or when the property has been retired from service, whichever comes first.

Property Owned

To claim depreciation, one must be the owner of the property, even if the property has debt. Leased property can be claimed only if ownership in the property includes the following:

- ➢ The legal title to the property
- ➢ The legal obligation to pay for the property
- ➢ The responsibility to pay maintenance and operating expenses
- ➢ The duty to pay any taxes on the property
- ➢ The risk of loss if the property is destroyed, condemned, or diminished in value through obsolescence or exhaustion

Example: Amanda made a down payment on a rental property and assumed Terrance's mortgage. Amanda owns the property and can depreciate it.

If the property is a business or investment property held by the taxpayer as a life tenant, the taxpayer may depreciate the property.

Property Having a Determinable Useful Life

Property must have a determinable useful life to be depreciated. It must be something that wears out, decays, is used up, becomes obsolete, or loses its value from natural causes.

Property Lasting More than One Year

To depreciate property, the useful life must be one year or more.

Example: Ms. Lady maintains a library for her tax business. She purchases yearly technical journals to use in her tax business. The library would be depreciated, but the technical journals do not have a useful life of more than one year. The technical journals can be taken as a yearly business expense.

Property used in Business or Income-Producing Activity

To claim depreciation on property one must use it in their business or an income-producing activity. If the taxpayer uses the property to produce an investment use, then the income is taxable. One cannot depreciate property that one uses solely for personal activities.

If the property has a multiple-use business and personal purpose, the portion used for business will be depreciated. For example, the taxpayer cannot deduct deprecation on a car used only for commuting to and from work or used for personal shopping trips and family vacations. Records must be kept showing business and personal use of the property.

Inventory cannot be depreciated. Inventory is any property that is held primarily for sale to customers in the ordinary course of business. If the owner is in the rent-to-own business, certain property held in that business may be considered as depreciable instead of inventory. See Publication 946.

Containers for the products one sells are part of inventory and are not depreciable. Containers used to ship products can be depreciated if the life expectancy is more than one year and meet the following requirements:

1. Qualify as property used in business
2. Title to the containers does not pass to the buyer

Property That Cannot Be Depreciated

Land does not wear out; therefore, it cannot be depreciated. The cost of land generally includes clearing, grading, planting, and landscaping. Although land is never depreciated, certain improvements to the land can be depreciated, such as landscaping.

Excepted Property

The following property cannot be depreciated even if the requirements are otherwise met:

1. Property placed in service and disposed of in the same year
2. Equipment used to build capital improvements
3. Section 197 intangibles that must be amortized
4. Certain term interests

The Beginning and Ending of Depreciation

Depreciation begins when the property is placed in service for use in a trade or business or to produce income. Depreciation ends when the cost (or other basis) has been fully recovered or when it has been retired from service, whichever comes first.

Placed in Service

Property is placed in service when it is ready and available for a specific use for a business activity, an income-producing activity, a tax-exempt activity, or a personal activity. Even if the property is not being used, it is still placed in service when it is ready and available for its specific use.

Example 1: Joel purchased a machine in December of last year for his business. The machine was delivered but not installed. Joel had the machine installed and ready for use in February of the current tax year. The machine would be placed in service in February of the current year.

If the property has been converted from personal to business use, the "placed in service" date is the date it was converted to business use or to an income-producing activity. In other words, depreciation begins when the property has been placed in service.

Example 2: Nicolas purchased a home as his primary residence in 2016, and in 2021 he converted it to a rental property. He placed the home in service in 2021; therefore, Nicolas would start depreciation when it was placed in service as an income-producing property.

Royalties

Royalty income is reported on Schedule E as ordinary income. The following are examples of royalty income:

➤ Copyrights on literary, musical, or artistic works
➤ Patents on inventions
➤ Gas, oil, and mineral properties
➤ Depletion, if the taxpayer is the owner of an economic interest in mineral deposits or oil and gas wells
➤ Coal and iron ore

Like rental income, expenses reduce this income. If the taxpayer was self-employed as a writer, inventor, artist, etc., income and expenses should be reported on Schedule C.

If the taxpayer is in business as a self-employed writer, artist, or musician, or if they hold an operating oil, gas, or mineral interest, the income and expenses would be reported on Schedule C. Royalties from copyrights and patents, oil and gas, and mineral properties are taxable as ordinary income and are reported on page 1 of Schedule E.

Taxable rental income and taxable income from royalties are reported on Schedule E and reported on Schedule 1, line 5. However, income from renting hotel rooms or other retail property where the renter provides significant additional services is not reported on Schedule E; it is reported as business income on Schedule C.

Partnership or S Corporation Income

Income a taxpayer receives from a partnership, or an S corporation is taxable. Neither the partnership nor the S corporation pays taxes. The taxes are "passed through" to the partners or shareholders, who report the income, as well as some of the expenses, on their individual tax returns. This income is reported on Schedule E, page 2.

Taxpayers should receive a Schedule K-1 from the partnership or S corporation, which will show the income and expenses the taxpayers would report on their individual returns.

Part II on page 2 of Form 1040, Schedule E is used to report income from partnerships and subchapter S corporation shareholders, as detailed in Schedule K-1. If the taxpayer actively participates in their partnership's business, it is nonpassive income or nonpassive loss. Partnership income is reported to each partner on Schedule K-1.

Part 1 Review

To obtain the maximum benefit from each part go online now and watch the video.

Part 2 Capital Gains and Losses

Introduction

Almost everything a taxpayer owns and uses for personal or investment purposes is a capital asset. When a capital asset is sold, the difference between the basis in the asset and the amount the item is sold for is either a capital gain or a capital loss. A capital gain is the profit that results from selling an investment (stocks, bonds, or real estate) for more than the purchase price. Capital gains may refer to investment income that arises in relation to real assets (such as property), financial assets (such as shares of stocks or bonds), and intangible assets (such as goodwill). A capital loss arises if the proceeds from the sale of a capital asset are less than the purchase price. The taxpayer can deduct up to a $3,000 loss ($1,500 if filing MFS). The capital loss that exceeds the limit amount may be taken in future years.

Capital Assets

Capital assets are items held for personal use, pleasure, or investment purposes. Some examples of capital assets are:

- ➢ Stocks or bonds held in a personal account
- ➢ A house owned and used by the taxpayer and family
- ➢ Household furnishings
- ➢ A car used for pleasure and/or work
- ➢ Coin or stamp collections
- ➢ Gems and jewelry
- ➢ Gold, silver, or other metal types
- ➢ Timber grown on taxpayer personal property or investment property

A capital asset can be any property held by the taxpayer; however, the following would be considered noncapital assets:

➢ Property held mainly for sale to customers or property that will physically become a part of merchandise for sale to customers (e.g., inventory)
➢ Depreciable property used in trade or business, even if 100% depreciated
➢ Real property used in trade or business
➢ Accounts or notes receivable acquired in the ordinary course of a trade or business for services rendered, or the sale of stock in trade or other property included in inventory
➢ A copyright, a literary, musical, or artistic composition, a letter or memorandum, or a similar property that is:
　○ Created by personal efforts
　○ Prepared or produced for the taxpayer in the case of a letter, memorandum, or similar property
　○ Received from an individual who created the property or for whom the property was prepared under circumstances entitling the taxpayer to the basis of the person who created the property, or for whom it was prepared or produced
➢ U.S. government publications received from the government for free or for less than the normal sales price
➢ Any financial instruments for commodities derivative held by a commodities derivatives dealer
➢ Hedge fund transactions, but only if the transaction is clearly identified as a hedging transaction before the close of the day on which it was acquired or originated
➢ Supplies of a type regularly used or consumed in the ordinary course of trade or business
➢ Property deducted under the de minimis safe harbor for tangible property

The rate at which the gain on the sale of a capital asset will be taxed depends on the type of capital asset, the holding period, and the taxpayer's tax bracket. If the taxpayer has a capital loss, the loss will be netted against any realized gain. If the taxpayer has a net loss in excess of $3,000, they will be able to deduct up to $3,000 of the loss against the taxpayer's ordinary income in the year of the sale. The unused capital loss would then be carried forward to subsequent years and used to help offset net capital gains or ordinary income up to $3,000 a year until the loss is depleted. If the taxpayer is filing as Married filing separately, the limit is $1,500.

Basis of Property

Basis is a way of determining the cost of an investment in property and is determined by how it was acquired. If the property was purchased, the purchase price is the basis. Any improvements made to the property are then added to that basis. The purchase price plus improvements constitutes the adjusted basis. Other items that add to the basis are the expenses of acquiring the property (commissions, sales tax, and freight charges). There are also items that reduce the basis, which include depreciation, nontaxable distributions, and postponed gain on home sales. This is also referred to as cost basis.

Basis is the amount of the investment in the asset for tax purposes. To calculate the gain or loss, basis is needed on the sale or disposition of the asset. Recordkeeping must be accurate to adjust the basis of the property when it is sold.

If a single transaction includes multiple properties, the total cost must be allocated among the separate properties according to the fair market value established by each property's basis. As a result of the allocation, for tax purposes, the basis of each property is its original unadjusted basis. This rule applies in determining basis for depreciation purposes or a gain or loss, on a transaction.

Holding Period

The holding period (the length of time an individual "held" or owned a property) determines whether the capital gain or loss is short-term or long-term. The holding period starts on the day after the date the taxpayer acquired the property. The holding period ends the day the taxpayer sold the property. Short-term property is property held for one year (365 days) or less. Long-term property is property held for more than one year. For example, if the taxpayer purchased property on September 20, 2021, and sold it on September 20, 2022, the taxpayer would have a short-term capital gain or loss. However, if the taxpayer waited one more day and sold the property on September 21, 2022, the transaction would be a long-term capital gain or loss. It is important to correctly determine the holding period because the maximum tax rate is based on the holding period. To calculate the total net gain or loss, combine the net short-term gains or losses with the net long-term gains or losses.

Adjusted Basis

To arrive at the adjusted basis, the taxpayer must make allowable adjustments to the basis of the property. The taxpayer would figure the gain or loss on a sale, exchange, or other disposition of property, or would figure the allowable depreciation, depletion, or amortization. The result is the property's adjusted basis.

Increases to Basis

To increase the property basis, the improvements must have a useful life of more than one year. Examples of capital improvements that would increase the property basis are an addition to the primary home, replacing the entire roof, and paving the driveway. Each one of these items may have a different class life (useful life) for depreciation. Each has to be depreciated by the rules for the associated property. Each depreciation class should have separate recordkeeping.

Decreases to Basis

There are certain items that will cause the property to decrease its basis. Those items include certain vehicle credits, IRC section 179 deductions, residential energy credits, casualty and theft losses, and insurance reimbursement. See Publication 551.

Sale of Personal Residence

The Taxpayer Relief Act of 1997 repealed IRC section 1034, *Deferral of Gain on Sale of Residence*, and amended section 121, *The Once-in-a-Lifetime Exclusion of Gain*. Previously, IRC section 1034 allowed taxpayers to defer the gain on the sale of a principal residence if a replacement residence was purchased within two years and if the replacement residence's price was equal to or exceeded the adjusted selling price of the former residence. Now, however, the current law under IRC section 121 is considerably more generous. The sale of the primary residence is reported on the taxpayer's tax return only if there is a taxable gain or if the property was used for business.

To qualify for the exclusion, the taxpayer must meet certain "ownership and use" tests during the last five-year period ending on the date of the sale. They must have:

➢ Owned the home for at least two years (the ownership test)

➢ Lived in the home as the main home for at least two years (the use test)

A taxpayer can meet the ownership and use test during different two-year periods if they meet both tests during the five years before the date of the sale.

Exclusion

If all the following are true, a taxpayer can exclude the entire gain of the sale of their main home up to $250,000 or up to $500,000 if Married Filing Jointly or a Surviving Spouse:

➢ The taxpayer is married and filing a joint return for the year
➢ Either the taxpayer or the spouse meets the ownership test
➢ Both the taxpayer and the spouse meet the use test

If the taxpayer's divorce decree allows the taxpayer's former spouse to live in the home the taxpayer owns, the taxpayer is considered to have also lived there for the purposes of claiming the exclusion. The exclusion is limited to one sale every two years on sales after May 6, 1997.

Other Facts and Circumstances for a Partial Exclusion

The amount of gain a taxpayer can exclude must be prorated if the sale of a home is due to a job relocation, health reasons, or other unforeseen circumstances of the homeowner (or the homeowner's spouse if they file a joint return), and if any the following are also true:

➢ Both spouses meet the residence and look-back requirements and one or both spouses meet the ownership requirement
➢ The taxpayer meets the residence, ownership, and look-back requirements
➢ A widow(er) taxpayer:
    1. Sells the home within two years of the spouses' death
    2. Has not remarried when the house is sold
    3. Has not taken the home exclusion in the past two years before the current home sale, nor has the spouse
    4. Meets the two-year ownership and residence requirements (including the late spouse's times of ownership and residence, if relevant)

Use worksheet in Publication 523, to determine if the taxpayer qualifies.

Sales of residences other than the taxpayer's main residence are treated differently than sales of primary residences for tax purposes. If the taxpayer sells a residence that is not their principal residence, a capital gain or loss would be reported on Form 8949. While a loss on a main residence is not deductible, a loss on a residential rental house may be deductible.

Because the exclusion only pertains to residences, if the taxpayer used part of their home for business or rental purposes, some of the gain may not qualify for the exclusion. Any gain due to depreciation claimed after May 6, 1997, cannot be excluded.

Example: Bill Burns had taken depreciation in prior years for an office in the home before changing it back to a bedroom and using it for personal purposes for two out of the five years prior to the sale. In this instance, Mr. Burns can exclude all the gain from the sale of the house, except for gain from depreciation after May 6, 1997.

If the taxpayer cannot exclude all of the gain, you would treat the sale as two transactions: one business and one personal.

Example: On February 1, 2019, Amy bought a house. She moved in on that date and lived in it until May 31, 2020, when she moved out of the house and put it up for rent. The house was rented from June 1, 2020 to March 31, 2021. Amy moved back into the house on April 1, 2021, and lived there until she sold it on January 31, 2022. During the five-year period ending on the date of the sale (February 1, 2019 to January 31, 2022), Amy owned and lived in the house for more than two years.

Five-Year Period

Period	Used as Home	Used as Rental
2/1/19 – 5/31/20	16 months	
6/1/20 – 3/31/21		10 months
4/1/21 – 1/31/22	10 months	
Totals	26 months	10 months

Because she lived in the home for more than two years, Amy can exclude gain up to $250,000. However, as mentioned above, she cannot exclude the part of the gain equal to the depreciation she claimed for renting the house after May 6, 1997.

Surviving Spouse Taxpayer

The Mortgage Forgiveness Debt Relief Act of 2007 allows a surviving spouse to exclude up to $500,000 of the gain from the sale of a principal residence owned jointly. The sale needs to occur within two years from the death of the spouse. Exceptions apply.

Incapacitated Taxpayers

Taxpayers who own a residence are still considered to reside in that residence even if they become physically or mentally incapable of self-care and are placed in a care facility licensed by a state or governmental subdivision such as a nursing home. If the incapacitated taxpayer dies while in the nursing the taxpayer could qualify for the IRC section 121 by living in the house at least one year during the five years required to sell their primary home to not pay the capital gains from the sale of the house.

Divorced Taxpayers

If the taxpayer is divorced, and the primary residence is transferred to the taxpayer, the time during which the taxpayer's former spouse owned the residence is added to the taxpayer's period of ownership. A taxpayer who owns a residence is considered to have used it as a principal residence while the taxpayer's spouse or former spouse is granted use of the residence under the terms of the divorce or separation instrument.

Calculating the Sales Price

Anytime the taxpayer sells a home, land, stock, or other security, the taxpayer will receive either Form 1099-S, *Proceeds from Real Estate Transactions*, or Form 1099-B, *Proceeds from Broker and Barter Exchange Transactions*.

Forms 1099-S and 1099-B are "reporting documents" that indicate the gross proceeds or sales price. If the taxpayer sold one stock several times, Form 1099-B might only report the total gross proceeds of multiple transactions instead of individually. The taxpayer can divide the gross proceeds by the total number of shares sold to arrive at an average price per share. The taxpayer can then multiply the price per share by the number of shares sold on each occasion to arrive at the sales price.

Installment Sales

An installment sale is a sale of property in which the taxpayer receives a payment after one year of the sale. An installment sale is an arrangement where some or all of the selling price is paid in a later year. Owners who sell homes and finance the purchase themselves often do so as an installment sale. This is beneficial because the taxpayer does not have to pay taxes on the entire gain in the year of sale. It can also benefit the taxpayer by keeping the gain from pushing them into a higher tax bracket. For taxpayers looking for a steady stream of income over a period of time, the installment sale can provide this income.

The gain from an installment sale is usually reported in the year it is received. However, the taxpayer can elect to report all of the gain in the year of sale, which can be beneficial if the taxpayer had other capital losses to offset the gain. The income from the sale is reported on Form 6252, *Installment Sale Income*. Interest income is reported on Schedule B as it is received. The gain is reported on Form 4797 if it is a business gain. Personal gain is reported on Form 8949.

If a taxpayer has a loss, it cannot be reported as an installment sale. Personal losses are not deductible. If it is a business loss, the entire loss will be reported on Form 4797 in the year of the sale. The interest earned is still reported on Schedule B.

Inherited Property

The basis of inherited property is the property's fair market value (FMV) at the date of death or at an alternate valuation date if chosen by the executor of the estate. The election to use the alternate valuation date is irrevocable. The alternate date is generally six months after the decedent's death or some earlier date of sale or distribution. Alternate valuation can be elected only if the property use decreased both the value of the gross estate and the combined estate, and there was a generation-skipping transfer of tax liability. The holding period is always considered long-term regardless of how long the taxpayer actually owned the property because it includes the holding period of the deceased.

Gift of Property

To determine the basis of property received as a gift, it is necessary to know the donor's adjusted basis of the gift when given to the taxpayer, the fair market value at the time it was given to the taxpayer, and the amount of gift tax that was paid. The taxpayer's basis for figuring gain at the time of the sale or for figuring the disposition of the asset at the time of the sale is the donor's adjusted basis, plus or minus any changes during the period the taxpayer held the property. The taxpayer's basis for figuring loss is the fair market value when received, plus or minus any required adjustments to the basis made during the period the taxpayer held the asset.

The amount of gift tax paid that is included in the basis of the asset depends on the date the gift was received.

Example: Jess received an acre of land as a gift. At the time the gift was given, the land had a fair market value of $8,000. Ezra purchased the land for $10,000, which then becomes the property's adjusted basis. Jess received the property; no further events occurred to increase or decrease the basis. Jess is thinking of selling the property for $12,000; if Jess sells the land, he will have a $2,000 gain. Jess must use Ezra's adjusted basis ($10,000) at the time of the gift as the basis to figure gain. If Jess sells the property for $7,000, he will have a $1,000 loss because he must use the fair market value ($8,000) at the time of the gift to figure loss. If the sales price is between $8,000 and $10,000, he will have neither a gain nor a loss.

Reporting Capital Gains and Losses

Form 8949 is used to report the sales and exchanges of capital assets. It also allows the taxpayer and the IRS to reconcile what has been reported to the IRS on Forms 1099-B or 1099-S.

Individual taxpayers report the following information on Form 8949:

➢ The sale or exchange of a capital asset
➢ Gains from involuntary conversions
➢ Nonbusiness bad debts
➢ Worthless stocks or bonds

When using Form 8949, the taxpayer separates short-term and long-term capital gains and losses. If the disposed property was inherited, it is treated as a long-term asset. Remember, when figuring the holding period, the calculation starts one day after the property has been received. Short-term losses and gains are reported on Form 8949, Part I. Long-term losses and gains are reported on Form 8949, Part II.

Example: Rachel purchased 300 shares of Imperial Soap for $1,000. She sold the stock this year for $1,200. Rachel realized a gain of $200, not the $1,200 in proceeds she received from the sale. Only the $200 is included in gross income since the $1,000 is Rachel's return of capital.

Codes for Form 8949

Below are the definitions that tell the IRS if the sale was short-term or long-term. The codes also determine if the asset basis was reported to the IRS or not. The taxpayer will have received either Form 1099-B or a substitute statement with the codes. These codes are used for Box A-F on Form 8949.

A: Short-term basis reported to the IRS

B: Short-term basis not reported to the IRS

C: Short-term basis not reported on Form 1099-B

D: Long-term basis reported to the IRS

E: Long-term basis not reported to the IRS

Capital Assets Held for Personal Use

When a taxpayer sells their primary residence, it could be a reportable transaction. Factors that could trigger the transaction are:

1. Sales amount
2. Filing status
3. Claiming a portion of the house as a home office

If the taxpayer and spouse sold their primary residence and the gain was over $500,000 ($250,000 for all other filing statuses) the amount is reported on Schedule D. If the gain is $500,000 or less ($250,000 for all other filing statuses) it may not be taxable. See IRC section 121.

If the taxpayer converted the depreciable property to personal use, all or part of the gain on the sale or exchange would be recaptured as ordinary income. Recaptured means the gain realized by the sale of capital property that is depreciable and must be reported. A loss from the sale or exchange of a personal use asset is not deductible.

Example: Sally sold her main home in 2022 for $320,000 and received Form 1099-S showing the $320,000 gross proceeds. The selling expense was $20,000 and her home basis was $100,000. Sally would be able to exclude the entire $200,000 gain from her income.

$320,000	Sales price
-$100,000	Basis
-$20,000	Selling expenses
$200,000	**Capital gain (excluded from income)**

Part 2 Review

To obtain the maximum benefit from each part go online now and watch the video.

Takeaways

There are two types of residential activities: rental-for-profit activity and not-for-profit rental activity. This chapter discussed the types of income and expenses reported on Schedule E and the different property types. Special rules limit the amount of rental expense deductions that may be taken by an individual taxpayer on a residence that is rented out for part of a year and used for personal use during other parts of the year. For passive activity rules, income must be classified as active, passive, or non-passive. Active income is attributable to the direct efforts of the taxpayer, such as salary, commissions, wages, etc.

The original basis for property is its cost, except as otherwise provided by law. The cost is the amount paid for such property in cash or other property. The basis includes acquisition costs such as commissions, legal fees, recording fees, and sales taxes, as well as installation and delivery costs. The cost of property includes not only the amount of money or other property paid, but also the amount of mortgage cost paid, and liability incurred in connection with the purchase. This applies whether the taxpayer assumes the liability by taking over the payments or merely purchases the property at the asking price. When the property is disposed, any remaining amount of mortgage or liability of which the seller is relieved is treated as part of the amount realized. Real estate taxes are included as part of the property's basis if the buyer assumes the seller's obligation to pay them.

Capital gains and losses are classified as long-term or short-term. If the asset has been held for more than one year before the asset was disposed, it is considered to be a long-term capital gain or loss. If the asset is held for less than one year, it is considered a short-term capital gain or loss.

TEST YOUR KNOWLEDGE!
Go online to take a practice quiz.

Chapter 11 Schedule F and Depreciation

Introduction

Income received from the operation of a farm or from rental income from a farm is taxable. Farmers determine their taxable income from farming and related activities by using Schedule F. Profit or loss from farm income is first reported on Schedule F and then "flows" to Form 1040, Schedule 1, line 6. A farm could qualify to be a qualified joint venture (discussed in Schedule C chapter).

Depreciation is an annual deduction that allows taxpayers to recover the cost or other basis of their business or investment property over a specified number of years. Depreciation is an allowance for the wear and tear, decline, or uselessness of a property and begins when a taxpayer places property in service for use in a trade or business. The property ceases to be depreciable when the taxpayer has fully recovered the property's cost or other basis or when the property has been retired from service, whichever comes first. Depreciation is reported on Form 4562.

Objectives

At the end of this lesson, the student will:

 ➤ Understand basic farm income
 ➤ Know when a taxpayer should file Schedule F
 ➤ Know when property cannot be depreciated
 ➤ Recognize when depreciation begins and ends
 ➤ Be able to identify which method of depreciation to use for property

Resources

Schedule F	Publication 17	Instructions Schedule F
Form 1040	Publication 51 (Circular A)	Instructions Form 1040
Form 3115	Publication 225	Instructions Form 3115
Form 4562	Publication 334	Instructions Form 4562
Form 4797	Publication 463	Instructions Form 4797
Form 4835	Publication 536	Instructions Form 4835
Form 8866	Publication 538	Instructions Form 8866
Form 8990	Publication 534	Instructions Form 8990
Publication 544	Publication 551	Publication 946

Part I: Schedule F

Livestock income from breeding, draft, sport, or dairy purposes such as beef, pork, and racehorses, is reportable on Schedule F. Individuals who breed dogs, or cats to sell need to report their income and expenses for domestic animals on Schedule F.

Taxpayers are in the business of farming if they cultivate, operate, or manage a farm for profit, either as an owner or tenant. A farm can produce livestock, dairy, poultry, fish, or fruit. It can also include truck farms, plantations, ranches, ranges, and orchards. See Publication 225.

A farmer must keep records to prepare an accurate tax return. Tax records are not the only type of records needed for a farming business. The taxpayer should keep records that measure the farm's financial performance.

Income reported on Schedule F does not include gains or losses from sales or other farm assets dispositions such as:

➢ Land
➢ Depreciable farm equipment
➢ Buildings and structures
➢ Livestock held for draft, breeding, sport, or dairy purposes

Taxpayers are in the business of farming if they cultivate, operate, or manage a farm for profit, either as an owner or tenant. See Publication 225.

Where to Report Sales of Farm Products

When livestock, produce, grains, or other products raised on the taxpayer's farm are for sale or bought for resale, the entire amount received from the sale of the products is income and reported on Schedule F.

When farm products are bought for resale, the profit or loss is the difference between the selling price and the basis in the product. The year that the payment was received is the year that the income is reported.

Item Sold	Schedule F	Form 4797
Farm products raised for sale	X	
Farm products bought for resale	X	
Farm products not held primarily for sale, such as livestock held for draft, breeding, sport, or dairy purposes (bought or raised)		X

Example: Avery purchased 20 feeder calves for $6,000, in the prior tax year, with the intent to resell them. Avery sold them in the current tax year for $11,000. The $11,000 sale is reported as sales, and the $6,000 purchase price is reported as basis, resulting in $5,000 reported as profit on the current tax return.

$11,000 Sales price (reported on Schedule F, line 1a)
–$ 6,000 Purchase price (basis, reported on Schedule F, line 1b)
 $5,000 Profit (reported on Schedule F, line 1c)

Livestock held for draft, breeding, sport, or dairy purposes may result in ordinary capital gain or loss when sold depending upon the circumstances and needs to be reported on Form 4797. Animals that are not held for primary sale are considered business assets of the farm.

Completing Schedule F

As with any tax return or other reporting document, it is important to interview the taxpayer before entering the required information. The SSN or the EIN must be entered in the appropriate area. Like Schedule E, Schedule F has specific codes. Line B is for the principal agricultural activity codes. Select the code that best describes the source of the majority of the taxpayer's income. For example, Allen owns a dairy farm. He receives income from milk production and selling male calves. Allen receives most of the income from milk production, so this would be the dairy farm's principal agricultural activity. Principal Agricultural Activity Codes are located on Schedule F, Part IV.

Line C Accounting Method: The two accounting methods for farm income are Cash and Accrual. Hybrid is not an option for farm income. Check the appropriate box. Using the cash accounting method, the taxpayer would complete Parts I and II. Income is reported in the year in which it was actually or constructively received. If payment on an expenditure such as a prepaid expense creates an intangible asset that has a useful life that extends beyond 12 months of the end of the taxable year, that expense may not be deductible. See Publication 225.

If the accrual method is used, Parts II, III, and Part I, line 9 must be completed. Income is reported in the year it was earned, and expenses are deducted in the year they are incurred, even though they were paid in a prior year. Taxpayers who use the accrual method will use the cash basis for deducting business expenses owed to a related cash-basis taxpayer. See Publication 538.

Certain farming collectives are unable to use the cash method of accounting.

A farming syndicate may be a partnership, LLC, S corporation, or any other enterprise other than a C corporation if:

➢ The interests in the business have at any time been offered for sale in a way that would require registration with any federal or state agency
➢ More than 35% of the losses during any tax year are allocable to limited partners or limited entrepreneurs. A limited partner is one who can lose only the amount invested or required to be invested in the partnership. A limited entrepreneur is a person who does not take any active part in managing the business.

Line E is a yes-or-no question. Line E asks if the taxpayer materially participated in the activity. The taxpayer must meet the seven tests to qualify for material participation. To qualify for material participation in farming, the taxpayer must own an interest at the time work is performed in connection with the activity.

Line F asks if any payments made in the current tax year require filing Form 1099s. See General Instructions for Certain Information Returns if more information is needed. If the taxpayer paid more than $600 in rents, services, and prizes, then see the specific instructions for the individual Form 1099-MISC or 1099-NEC.

Schedule F Profit or Loss Framing

Similar to Schedule C & E, Schedule F has specific line items for income and expenses that are farm industry related. This section is designed for the tax preparer to become aware of types of farm income. For more information, see Instructions Schedule F.

Sales Caused by Weather-Related Conditions

If the farmer sells or exchanges more livestock, including poultry, than normal due to a drought, flood, or other weather-related conditions, the farmer may qualify to postpone reporting the income until the following year.

All the following conditions must be met:

> ➤ The principal trade or business is farming
> ➤ The accounting method is the cash method
> ➤ The taxpayer must be able to show that under their usual business practices, they would not have sold or exchanged the additional animals in that year except for the weather-related conditions
> ➤ The weather-related condition caused an area to be designated as eligible for assistance by the federal government

If sales or exchanges were made before the area became eligible for federal assistance due to weather-related conditions, the taxpayer could qualify if the weather-related condition caused the area to be eligible for assistance. In order for an area to qualify for federal disaster related assistance, the president of the United States must declare the area as a disaster.

Señor 1040 Says: A weather-related sale or exchange of livestock (other than poultry) held for draft breeding or dairy purposes may be an involuntary conversion. See Publication 225.

Example: Bernie is a calendar-year taxpayer, and he normally sells 100 head of beef cattle a year. As a result of a disaster, Bernie sold 250 head during the current tax year. Bernie realized $70,200 from the sale. Due to the drought, the affected area was declared a disaster area eligible for federal assistance in the same year. Bernie can postpone a portion ($42,120) of the income until the following year. ($70,200 ÷ 250 = $280.80 × 150 = $42,120).

Rents (Including Crop Share)

Rent received for farmland is rental income and not reported on Schedule F. However, if the farmer materially participates in the farming operations on the land, the rent received is farm income. If the taxpayer pastures someone else's livestock and takes care of them for a fee, the income is from the farming business. That income must be reported as "other" income on Schedule F. If the pasture is strictly rented out without providing services, the income is to be reported on Schedule E as rental income.

Rent received in the form of crop shares is income in the year the shares were converted to cash or the equivalent. The accounting method used—cash or accrual—does not matter. Whether the material participation in operating the farm is crop sharing or livestock, the rental income is included in self-employment income.

Crop-sharing lease arrangements that involve a loss may be subject to the limits under the passive-loss rules.

Income Averaging for Farmers

Taxpayers can use income averaging to figure their tax for any year in which they were engaged in a farming business as an individual, a partner in a partnership, or a shareholder in an S corporation. Services performed as an employee are disregarded in determining whether an individual is engaged in a farming business. However, a shareholder of an S corporation engaged in a farming business may treat as farm income compensation received from the corporation that is attributable to the farming business. Corporations, partnerships, S corporations, estates, and trusts cannot use income averaging.

Elected Farm Income (EFI)

EFI is the amount of income from the farming business that the taxpayer elects to be taxed at base-year rates. EFI can be designated as any type of income attributable to the farming business. However, EFI cannot be more than the taxable income, and EFI from a net capital gain attributable to the farming business cannot be more than the total net income. If the taxpayer is using income averaging, that is figured on Schedule J. See Publication 225.

Line 1 Sale of Purchased Livestock and Other Resale Items

Income from farming reported on Schedule F includes amounts taxpayers receive from cultivating, operating, or managing a farm for gain or profit, either as an owner or tenant. Income is included but not limited to:

> ➢ Income from operating a nursery specializing in growing ornamental plants
> ➢ Income from the sale of crop shares if the taxpayer materially participated in producing the crop
> ➢ Operating a stock, dairy, poultry, fish, fruit, or truck farm
> ➢ Income from operating a plantation, ranch, range, orchard, or grove

Both the actual cash received, and the fair market value of goods or income constructively received, are reported on lines 1 through 8. If the taxpayer ran the farm and received rents based on crop share or farm production, that income is reported as rents. If the taxpayer sold livestock due to drought, flood, or other weather-related conditions, the taxpayer could elect to report the income from the sale in the year after the year of sale.

For example, Caleb uses the cash method, and sold three Holstein heifers due to weather-related circumstances in the current tax year. Caleb chose to report the income in the next year after the sale. For Caleb to make the election, all the following must apply:

1. Caleb's main business is farming
2. Caleb can show he sold the livestock due to a weather-related event
3. Caleb's farm area qualified for federal aid

Items Purchased for Resale

If the cash method is used, deduct the ordinarily deducted cost of the livestock and other items purchased for resale only in the year of sale. Deduct this cost, including freight charges for transporting the livestock to the farm, on Part I of Schedule F.

Example: Sandy uses the cash method of accounting in the current year. Sandy purchased 50 steers in the current year, which she will sell in the next year. She cannot deduct the cost of the steers on her current return. She will deduct the cost in Part I of her next year Schedule F.

Line 3 Cooperative Distributions

Distributions from a farm cooperative are reported on Form 1099-PATR on line 3a. If the taxpayer receives more than one Form 1099-PATR, they must report the total distribution from all cooperatives.

Distributions include:

> ➤ Patronage dividends
> ➤ Nonpatronage distributions
> ➤ Per-unit retain allocations
> ➤ Redemptions of nonqualified written notices of allocation
> ➤ Per-unit retain certificates

Line 4 Agriculture Payments

Government payments received on Form 1099-G or Form CCC-1099-G are reported on line 4a. Any of the following sources are reported:

> ➤ Price loss coverage payments
> ➤ Agriculture risk coverage payments
> ➤ Coronavirus Food Assistance Program Payments
> ➤ Market Facilitation Program Payments
> ➤ Market gain from the repayment of a secured Commodity Credit Corporation (CCC) loan for less than the original loan amount
> ➤ Diversion payments
> ➤ Cost-share payments
> ➤ Payments in the form of materials (such as fertilizer or lime) or services (such as grading or building dams)

The taxpayer reports crop insurance proceeds in the year received. Federal crop disaster payments are treated as crop insurance proceeds. If there was crop damage in 2021, the taxpayer can elect to include certain proceeds in their 2022 income. To make this election, check the box on 6c.

Crop insurance proceeds received in a prior year, and elected to be treated in the current year's income, would be reported on line 6d. All other income that does not have a designated line on which to report it is reported on line 8. These types of income could include, but are not limited to:

> ➤ Illegal federal irrigation subsidies
> ➤ Bartering income
> ➤ Income from Form 1099-C
> ➤ State gasoline or fuel tax refunds received in current tax year

See Schedule F Instructions for a complete list.

Line 5 CCC (Commodity Credit Corporation Loans)

Loans are generally not reported as income. However, if the production was pledged in part to secure a CCC loan, then treat the loan as if it were a sale of the crop and report the loan proceeds as income in the year received. Approval is not needed from the IRS to adopt this method of reporting CCC loans. Once the CCC loan is reported as income for the year received, all CCC loans in that year and subsequent years are reported the same way.

If pledged crops are forfeited to the CCC in full payment of the loan, then the individual may receive a Form 1099-A, *Acquisition or Abandonment of Secured Property*. In box 6 of Form 1099-A, one would see

"CCC," and the amount of the outstanding loan would also be indicated on the form. See Publication 225.

Line 8 Other Types of Income

> ➢ Bartering income
> ➢ Income from canceled debt
> ➢ State gasoline or fuel tax refunds received
> ➢ Income from line 2 that includes Biofuel Producer Credit (Form 6478)
> ➢ Income from line 8 that includes Biodiesel and Renewable Diesel Fuels Credit (Form 8864)
> ➢ The amount of credit for federal tax paid on fuels claimed on the 2023 Schedule 3
> ➢ Recapture of excess depreciation on listed property, including Section 179 expense deduction
> ➢ Inclusion amount on leased property when the business drops 50% or less
> ➢ Any recapture of a deduction or credit for clean-fuel vehicle
> ➢ Any income from breeding fees
> ➢ Gain or a loss on commodity sales
> ➢ Any payroll tax credit amount from the employer payroll

Income from the farming business is the sum of any farm income or gain minus any farm expenses or losses allowed as deductions in figuring taxable income. However, it does not include gain or loss from the sale or other disposition of land or from the sale of development rights, grazing rights, or other similar rights.

Canceled Debt

If a debt is canceled or forgiven other than as a gift or bequest to the taxpayer, in most cases, the individual must include the canceled amount in gross income for tax purposes. Discharge of qualified farm indebtedness is one of the exceptions to the general rule. It is excluded from taxable income; report the canceled amount on Schedule F, line 10, if the canceled debt was incurred in the farming business. If the debt is a nonbusiness debt, report the canceled amount as "other income" on Schedule 1, line 8c. See Publication 225 and 982.

Schedule F Part II Farm Expense Cash and Accrual Method

Part II reports expenses that are typically deductible. Current costs are expenses that do not have to be capitalized or included in inventory costs. The deduction for the cost of livestock feed and certain other supplies may be limited.

Certain expenses paid throughout the year may be part personal and part business. Some shared expenses could include expenses for gasoline, oil, fuel, water, rent, electricity, telephone, automobile upkeep, repairs, insurance, interest, and taxes. Shared expenses need to be allocated correctly between personal and business. The personal portion is not deductible; the business portion would be deducted on Schedule F.

Ordinary and necessary costs of operating a farm for profit are deductible business expenses.

If the taxpayer has an operating loss, the taxpayer may not be able to deduct this loss. The following are not deductible:

> ➢ Personal or living expenses

> ➢ Expenses used to raise a family
> ➢ Animal expenses used by the taxpayer to raise the animal
> ➢ Repaid expenses
> ➢ Inventory losses
> ➢ Personal losses

Prepaid farm supplies are amounts paid during the tax year for the following items:

> ➢ Feed, seed, fertilizer, and similar farm supplies not used or consumed during the year. Do not include amounts paid for farm supplies that would have been consumed if not for a fire, storm, flood, other casualty, disease, or drought.
> ➢ Poultry (including egg-laying hens and baby chicks) bought for use (or for both use and resale) in the farm business. Include only the amount that would be deductible in the following year if the taxpayer had capitalized the cost and deducted it ratably over the lesser of 12 months or the useful life of the poultry.
> ➢ Poultry bought for resale and not resold during the year

Line 10, Car and Truck Expenses

Only expenses that are used for business can be deducted as a business expense. Items include gasoline, oil, repairs, license tags, insurance, and depreciation. The standard mileage rate for the 2024 tax year is 67 cents per mile, up 1.5 cents from 2023. The standard mileage rate for each mile of business use can be used for the taxpayer's owned or leased vehicle. The standard mileage rate cannot be used if five or more cars or light trucks are used at the same time. See Instructions Schedule F.

Line 14, Depreciation

When property is acquired to be used in the farm business and expected to last more than one year, do not deduct the entire cost in the year. The cost is recovered over more than one year and deducted each year on Schedule F as depreciation or amortization. Depreciation will be covered in a later chapter. See Instructions Form 4562.

Line 17, Fertilizer and Lime

In the year paid or incurred, the cost of fertilizer, lime, and other materials applied to farmland to enrich, neutralize, or condition the land can be a deductible expense. The cost to apply the raw material is also an expense.

Line 19, Gasoline, Fuel, and Oil

Some expenses paid during the tax year are part personal and part business. These can include expenses for gasoline, fuel and oil, water, utilities, automobile upkeep, repairs, insurance, and taxes. The taxpayer cannot mix business and personal portions to be reported. The business portion is deductible on the tax return.

Line 20, Insurance

The ordinary and necessary cost of insurance for the farm business is a business expense. Premiums can include payment for the following types of insurance:

- ➢ Fire, storm, crop, theft, liability, and other insurance on farm business assets
- ➢ Health and accident insurance for farm employees
- ➢ Workers compensation insurance set by state law that covers claims for job-related bodily injuries or diseases suffered by employees on the farm, regardless of fault
- ➢ Business interruption insurance

Self-employed health insurance can be deducted as well as medical, dental, and qualified long-term care insurance coverage for the taxpayer, the spouse, and dependents when figuring adjusted gross income. See Publication 535.

Line 21, Interest

Interest paid on farm mortgages and other obligations incurred in the farm business can be deductible. If the cash method of accounting is used, deduct interest paid during the tax year. Interest paid with other funds received from the original lender through another loan, advance, or other arrangement similar to a loan cannot be deducted until payments are made on the new loan. Under the cash method, if interest is prepaid before it is due, the deduction is taken in the tax year in which the interest is due. See Instructions Form 8990.

Line 22, Labor Hired

Reasonable wages paid for regular farm labor, piecework, contract labor, and other forms of labor hired to perform the farming operations can be paid in cash or in noncash items such as inventory, capital assets, or assets used in business. The cost of boarding farm labor is a deductible labor cost. Other deductible costs incurred for farm labor could include health insurance, workers compensation insurance, and other benefits. Reduce the tax deduction that was claimed on the following:

- ➢ Form 5884, Work Opportunity Credit
- ➢ Form 8844, Empowerment Zone Employment Credit
- ➢ Form 8845, Indian Employment Credit
- ➢ Form 8932, Credit for Employer Differential Wage Payments
- ➢ Form 8994, Employer Credit for Paid Family and Medical Leave

Line 25, Repairs and Maintenance

Most expenses for repair and maintenance are deductible. However, repairs or an overhaul to depreciable property that increases the asset's value or adapts it to a different use is a capital expense. See Publication 225.

Line 29, Taxes

Real estate and property taxes on farm business assets such as farm equipment, animals, farmland, and farm buildings can be deducted in the year paid. The taxes on the part of the farm used for personal use are not a deductible expense on the business; those expenses may be deductible on Schedule A.

State and local general sales tax on non-depreciable farm business items are deductible as part of the cost of those items. Include state and local general sales tax imposed on the purchase of the assets for use in the farm business as part of the cost that is depreciable.

Individuals cannot deduct state and federal income taxes as farm business expenses. Individuals can deduct state and local income taxes only as an itemized deduction on Schedule A. Federal income tax is not a deduction. One-half of the self-employment tax is figured as an adjustment to income on Form 1040. See Instructions Schedule F.

Line 32 Other Expenses

Travel Expenses

Ordinary and necessary expenses can be deducted if they are incurred while traveling away from home for farm business. Lavish and extravagant expenses cannot be deducted. For tax purposes, the farm business's location is considered the location of the farm, and the taxpayer is traveling away from the farm if:

➢ Duties require the taxpayer to be absent from the farm for substantially longer than an ordinary workday
➢ Sleep and rest are required to meet the demands of work while away from home

Following are some examples of deductible travel expenses:

➢ Air, rail, bus, and car transportation
➢ Meals and lodging
➢ Dry cleaning and laundry
➢ Telephone and fax
➢ Transportation between hotel and temporary work or business meeting location
➢ Tips for any expenses

Remember, ordinary business-related meals are deductible if business travel is overnight or long enough to require the taxpayer to stop for sleep or rest to properly perform his or her duties.

The following list includes some but not all expenses that may be deducted as farm expense on Part II of Schedule F. These expenses must be for business purposes and paid in the year used (if using the cash method) or incurred (if using the accrual method).

➢ Accounting fees
➢ Advertising
➢ Business travel and meals
➢ Commissions
➢ Consultant fees
➢ Crop-scouting expenses
➢ Dues to cooperatives
➢ Educational expenses (to maintain and improve farming skills)
➢ Farm-related attorney fees
➢ Farm magazines
➢ Ginning
➢ Insect sprays and dusts
➢ Litter and bedding
➢ Livestock fees
➢ Marketing fees
➢ Milk assessment

➢ Record-keeping expenses
➢ Service charges
➢ Small tools expected to last one year or less
➢ Stamps and stationery
➢ Subscriptions to professional, technical, and trade journals that deal with farming

Marketing Quota Penalties

Marketing quota penalties can be deducted as an "other expense" on Schedule F. These penalties are paid for marketing crops in excess of farm marketing quota. If the penalty is not paid but the purchaser of the crop deducts it from the payment, include the payment in gross income. Do not take a separate deduction for the penalty. See Publication 225.

Capital Expenses

A capital expense is a payment, or a debt incurred for the acquisition, improvement, or restoration of an asset that is expected to last more than one year. Include the expense in the basis of the asset. Uniform capitalization rules also require the asset to be capitalized or included in certain inventory expenses. See Publication 225.

Business Use of Home

Business use of the home can be deducted if part of the home is exclusively and regularly used as:

➢ The principal place of business for any trade or business
➢ A place to meet or deal with patients, clients, or customers in the normal course of the trade or business
➢ In connection with a trade or business, if using a separate structure that is not attached to the home

An office in the home will qualify as the principal place of business for deducting expense for its use if both of the following requirements are met:

➢ The taxpayer uses it exclusively and regularly for the administrative or management activities of the trade or business
➢ The taxpayer has no other fixed location where one conducts substantial administrative or management activities of the trade or business

The IRS has provided a simplified method to determine expenses for business use of the home. This was covered in Schedule C chapter. See Publication 587.

Business Start-Up and Organizational Costs

The taxpayer can elect to deduct up to $5,000 of business start-up costs and $5,000 of organizational costs paid or incurred after October 22, 2004. The $5,000 deduction is reduced by the amount of the total start-up or organizational costs exceeding $50,000. Any remaining costs must be amortized. See Publication 225.

Crop Production Expenses

The uniform capitalization rules require the taxpayer to capitalize expenses incurred in producing plants. However, for certain taxpayers who are required to use the accrual method of accounting, the capitalization rules do not apply to plants with a pre-productive period of two years or less. See Publication 225.

Timber

Capitalize the cost of acquiring timber; do not include the cost of the land. Generally, the taxpayer must capitalize the direct costs incurred in reforestation; however, they can elect to deduct some forestation and reforestation costs.

Christmas Tree Cultivation

If the taxpayer is in the business of planting and cultivating Christmas trees to sell when they are more than six years old, they can capitalize the expenses incurred for planting and stump culture and add them to the basis of the standing trees. The taxpayer would recover these expenses as part of the adjusted basis when the trees are sold as standing trees, or as a depletion allowance when the trees are cut.

Breeding Fees

If the accrual method is used, breeding fees need to be capitalized and allocated to the cost of the basis of the calf, foal, etc. Breeding fees can be an expense on Schedule F. If the breeder guarantees live offspring or other veterinary procedure costs as the cost basis of the offspring.

Other Nondeductible Expenses

Personal expenses and certain other items on the tax return cannot be deducted even if they are farm related. The taxpayer cannot deduct certain personal and living expenses, including rent and insurance premiums paid on property used as the taxpayer's primary residence. The cost of maintaining personal vehicles or other items used for personal use or the cost of purchasing or raising produce or livestock consumed by the taxpayer and his or her family is not deductible.

Losses from Operating a Farm

If the farm expenses are more than the farm income, the taxpayer has a loss from the operation of the farm. The amount of the loss that is deductible from taxable income may be limited. To figure the deductible loss, the following limits must be applied:

- ➢ The at-risk limits
- ➢ The passive activity limits

If the deductible loss after applying the limits is more than the income for the year, there may be a net operating loss. See Publication 536.

Not-for-Profit Farming

If the taxpayer operates a farm for profit, all ordinary and necessary expenses of carrying on the business of farming can be deducted on Schedule F. If the farming activity or other activity the taxpayer is engaged in or invests in is not-for-profit, the income from the activity is reported on Schedule 1, line 6. The expenses are no longer deducted on Schedule A. Losses from not-for-profit farming can be limited.

Estimated Payments Exception

If the taxpayer files their tax return yearly by March 1 and does the following, the penalty will be waived.

1. File the tax return and pay the tax due by March 1
2. Taxpayer had no liability for the prior year and the current year was for the 12 months
3. Taxpayer would not be charged a penalty if the total tax on the current year minus the amount of withholding tax paid is less than $1,000

Benefits of Recordkeeping

Everyone in business must keep appropriate and accurate records. Recordkeeping will help the taxpayer:

➤ Monitor the progress of their business
➤ Prepare an accurate financial statement
➤ Classify receipts
➤ Track deductible business expenses
➤ Prepare their tax return
➤ Support reported income and expenses on the tax return

Records show the taxpayer if the business is improving, which items sell the best, and insights to increase the success of the business. Records are needed to prepare accurate financial statements, which include profit and loss, balance sheets, and any other financial statements.

Taxpayers should identify receipts at the time of purchase. It is easier to get into the habit of tracking receipts when they are received rather than dealing with them when preparing the tax return. A tax professional should teach clients how to identify and track receipts.

Kinds of Records to Keep

The taxpayer should choose the recordkeeping system that is best for their business. The system should match the accounting method of the taxpayer's tax year. The recordkeeping system should include a summary of all the taxpayer's business transactions. For example, recordkeeping should show gross income as well as deductions and credits for the business. Supporting documentation for ongoing transactions, such as purchases, sales, and payroll, should be maintained. It is important to retain documentation that supports the entries in the journal, ledgers, and the tax return. Records for travel, transportation, and gift expenses fall under specific recordkeeping rules. For more information see Publication 463. There are also specific employment tax records the employer must keep. See Publication 51 (Circular A).

Assets used in business can be property, such as machinery and equipment used to conduct business. Records of the asset are used to figure depreciation and the gain or loss when the asset is sold. Records should show the following information:

➤ When and how the business asset was acquired
➤ The purchase price of the business asset
➤ The cost of any business improvements

➢ Section 179 deduction
➢ Business deductions taken for depreciation
➢ Business deductions taken for casualty losses, such as losses resulting from fires, storms, or natural disasters
➢ How the business asset was used
➢ When and how the business asset was disposed
➢ The selling price of the asset or the business
➢ The expense of the business asset

The following are examples of records that might show the information from the above list:

➢ Purchase and sales business invoices
➢ Business purchase of real estate closing statements (HUD-1)
➢ Canceled business checks
➢ Business bank statements

Maintaining Records

Tax records should be kept as needed for the administration of any provision of the Internal Revenue Code. Business records should be kept that support an item of income or deduction appearing on the return until the period of limitations is finished. Generally, that is three years, although certain records must be kept longer than that.

Employment records must be kept for at least four years after the date the tax becomes due or is paid. Records that pertain to assets such as property should be kept if the taxpayer owns the business asset. Other parties, such as an insurance company, may require business records to be kept longer than the periods required by the IRS.

Part 1 Review

To obtain the maximum benefit from each part go online now and watch the video.

Part 2 Defining Depreciation and Depreciation Methods

Depreciation is an annual allowance for the wear and tear of certain property that includes the process of allocating the cost of a tangible asset to expense over its estimated useful life. To be depreciable, tangible property must have a limited life. Tangible property can be divided into two categories: real property and personal property. Real property is land, land improvements, buildings, and building improvements. Land does not have a limited life; therefore, it does not qualify for depreciation. Personal property is usually business machinery and equipment, office furniture, and fixtures. The term "personal property" should not be confused with property owned by an individual for personal use.

Depreciation

Depreciation is a way of accounting for the costs associated with durable goods used in a business, for investment, or for a hobby. The recovery period is determined by the IRS and the taxpayer deducts the cost of the item over the property class life. Only the cost corresponding to the percentage of use attributable to deductible purposes can be depreciated; costs attributed to personal use can never be depreciated. Depreciation starts when the asset is placed into service and ends when the property is disposed of or worn out.

Basis is a way of determining the cost of an investment in property and is decided by how it was acquired. If the property was purchased, the purchase price is the basis. Any improvements made to the property are then added to that basis. The purchase price plus improvements constitutes the adjusted basis. Other items that add to the basis are the expenses of acquiring the property (commissions, sales tax, and freight charges). There are also items that reduce the basis, which include depreciation, nontaxable distributions, and postponed gain on home sales. This is also referred to as "cost basis." Depreciation is reported on Form 4562.

Section 179

Section 179 is an internal revenue code that allows the taxpayer an immediate deduction on certain business assets. Business owners can take the purchase price of business equipment in the year of purchase and depreciate the asset 100%. Federal law allows an expense election up to $1,050,000 of the cost of certain business property. For tax year 2023, the limits are $1,160,000 with a total phaseout at $2,890,000. For tax year 2024, the limits are $1,220,000 with a total purchase of $3,050,000

Taxpayers can choose to take a portion of Section 179 instead of the entire amount of the asset. For example, Solomon purchased a tractor for his farming business. The tractor cost $45,000, and Solomon decided to use 50% of the cost as Section 179. The remaining $22,500 would be used as a yearly depreciation deduction.

Section 179 is reported on Form 4562, part I.

Line 1 reports the maximum amount of Section 179.

Line 2 reports total cost of Section 179 that was placed in service in the current tax year.

Line 3 reports the maximum amount the taxpayer would elect to claim. The amount could be reduced based on taxpayer.

Line 4 reports the reduction limitation.

Line 5 reports the dollar limitation for the current tax year.

Bonus Depreciation

Bonus depreciation was designed to stimulate investment in business property that is not land or buildings. Accelerated depreciation is explained in IRC section 168(k). The IRS sometimes refers to bonus depreciation as a "special depreciation allowance." For tax year 2023, the allowable depreciation is 80% of qualified business property. The immediate deduction is eligible for property placed in service between September 27, 2017, and January 1, 2023. After January 1, 2023, the phaseout amounts are:

2023: 80%
2024: 60%
2025: 40%
2026: 20%
2027 and beyond: 0%

Property that qualifies for bonus depreciation must have a useful life of 20 years or less. The property must also be new for the taxpayer. If the taxpayer leased the equipment prior to purchase, the property is disqualified for bonus depreciation.

Part II reports Special Depreciation Allowance and other Depreciation, such as bonus depreciation.

The Beginning and End of Depreciation

Depreciation begins when the property is placed in service for use in the trade or business or for the production of income. Depreciation ends when the cost and added basis, if any, have been fully recovered or when the property is retired from service, whichever comes first.

Property is placed in service when it is ready and available for a specific use for a business activity, an income-producing activity, a tax-exempt activity, or a personal activity. Even if the property is not being used, it is still placed in service when it is ready, available, and capable of performing its specific use.

When a taxpayer places an improvement or addition in service after the original asset was placed in service, improvements or additions are treated as a separate asset. For example, Gabriela placed her rental in service and then made some major improvements. The improvements were more than the purchase price of the rental. The improvements will be a separate line item to be depreciated and could have a different class life. See §1.263(a)-3T(e)(3) or (e)(5) for more information.

Example 1: Joel purchased a copy machine in December of last year for his printing business. The machine was delivered in January but not installed. Joel had the machine installed and ready for use in February of the current tax year. The machine would be considered to have been placed in service in February of the current year, not December or January, because it wasn't until it was installed in February that the machine became ready to be placed in service.

If the property has been converted from personal to business use, the "placed in service" date is the date it was converted to business use or to an income-producing activity. In other words, depreciation begins when the property has been placed in service.

Example 2: Nicolas purchased a home as his primary residence in 2010, and on February 10, 2022, he converted it to a rental property. Therefore, depreciation begins the day it was placed into service as an income-producing property.

Property That Can Be Depreciated

Most types of tangible property can be depreciated. Examples of tangible property are:

➢ Building
➢ Vehicles
➢ Machinery
➢ Furniture
➢ Equipment
➢ Storage facilities

Some intangible items that can be depreciated include:

➢ Copyrights
➢ Patents
➢ Computer software (if the software life value is more than one year)

Property that can be depreciated must meet the following requirements:

- ➢ Must be the taxpayer's own property
- ➢ Must be used in the taxpayer's business or income-producing activity
- ➢ Property must have a determinable useful life
- ➢ The property is expected to last more than one year

Property Owned

To claim depreciation, one must be the owner of the property, even if the property has debt. Leased property can be claimed only if ownership of the property includes the following:

- ➢ The legal title to the property
- ➢ The legal obligation to pay for the property
- ➢ The responsibility to pay maintenance and operating expenses
- ➢ The duty to pay any taxes on the property
- ➢ The risk of loss if the property is destroyed, condemned, or diminished in value through obsolescence or exhaustion

Example: Amanda made a down payment on a rental property and took over Tom's mortgage payments. Amanda owns the property and can depreciate it.

If the property is held as a business or as an investment property as a life tenant, the taxpayer may depreciate the property.

Property Having a Determinable Useful Life

Property must have a determinable useful life to be depreciated. It must be something that wears out, decays, gets used up, becomes obsolete, or loses its value from natural causes.

Property Lasting More than One Year

To be able to depreciate property, the useful life should extend significantly beyond the year the property was placed in service.

Example: Ms. Wilson maintains a library for her tax business and purchases yearly technical journals for its use. The library would not be depreciated because the technical journals do not have a useful life of more than one year. The technical journals should be taken as a yearly business expense.

Property Used in Business or an Income-Producing Activity

To claim depreciation on property, the income-producing activity must be used in business. If the taxpayer uses the property to produce an investment use, then the income is taxable. Personal property cannot be depreciated.

If the property is used for business and personal use, the portion used as business may be depreciated. For instance, the individual cannot deduct depreciation on a car used only for commuting to and from work or for personal shopping trips and family vacations. A taxpayer must keep records showing business and personal use of their property.

Containers used for the products offered for sale are considered inventory and cannot be depreciated. Containers used to ship products can be depreciated if they have a life expectancy of more than one year and meet the following requirements:

> ➢ Qualify as property used in business
> ➢ Title to the containers does not pass to the buyer

To determine if the above requirements are met, the following things need to be considered:

> ➢ Does the sales contract, sales invoice, or some other type of order acknowledgment indicate whether the taxpayer has retained the title of the containers?
> ➢ Does the invoice treat the containers as a separate item?
> ➢ Do the taxpayer's records indicate the basis of the containers?

Auto Depreciation Limits

The maximum deprecation for passenger vehicles acquired after September 27, 2017, and placed in service in 2023, for which the taxpayer did not opt-in for special depreciation is:

First year	$19,200
Second year	$18,000
Third year	$10,800
Fourth year and later	$6,460

For sport utility vehicles (SUV) placed in service beginning 2022, the maximum deduction is $27,000. For passenger automobiles placed in service for 2022, it is $19,200, if special depreciation is allowed, or $11,200 if special depreciation is applied. For IRS purposes an SUV is different than a passenger automobile because the depreciation limits are based on the vehicle weight.

Property That Cannot Be Depreciated

Land does not wear out; therefore, it cannot be depreciated. The cost of land generally includes clearing, grading, planting, and landscaping. Although land is never depreciated, certain improvements to the land can be depreciated, such as landscaping and improvements to a building.

The following exceptions are property that cannot be depreciated even if the requirements are met:

> ➢ Property placed in service and disposed of in the same year
> ➢ Equipment used to build capital improvements
> ➢ Section 197 intangibles that must be amortized
> ➢ Certain term interests

Inventory is not depreciated. Inventory is any property held mainly for sale to customers in the ordinary course of business. If the taxpayer is in the rent-to-own business, certain property held for business may be considered as depreciable instead of inventory. See Publication 946.

Property Acquired by Like-kind Exchanges

Like-kind property is property of the same nature, character, or class. Quality or grade does not matter. For example, real property that is improved with a residential rental house is like-kind to vacant land. Most common like-kind exchanges are real property, or better known as a 1031 exchange.

A 1031 exchange gets its name from Section 1031 of the U.S. Internal Revenue Code, which allows a taxpayer to postpone paying capital gains taxes when they sell an investment property and reinvest the proceeds from the sale within certain time limits in a property or properties of like-kind and equal or greater value.

Like-kind exchanges completed after December 31, 2017, are limited to real property exchanges not held primarily for sale. See IRC Section 1.168(i)-6.

De minimis Safe Harbor Election

The taxpayer can elect to deduct small dollar amounts for expenditures for acquiring or manufacturing of property that generally needs to be capitalized under the general rules. The amount spent needs to be ordinary and necessary expenses to carry on the trade or business for the taxpayer. Costs include materials, supplies, repairs, and maintenance usually under $2,500. See IRC Section 1.263.

Depreciation Methods

Depreciation methods include modified accelerated cost recovery system (MACRS), along with straight-line and accelerated cost recovery system (ACRS). ACRS was used prior to 1987. The IRS now uses MACRS and straight-line.

Modified Accelerated Cost Recovery System (MACRS)

The Modified Accelerated Cost Recovery System (MACRS) is the current depreciation method used in the United States to calculate depreciable assets. MACRS should be used to depreciate property. MACRS is not used in the following circumstances:

- ➢ Property placed in service before 1987
- ➢ Property owned or used in 1986
- ➢ Intangible property
- ➢ Films, video tapes, and recordings
- ➢ Certain corporate or partnership property that was acquired in a nontaxable transfer
- ➢ Property that has been elected to be excluded from MACRS

Property Placed in Service Before 1987

If property was placed in service before 1987 (unless the taxpayer elected to use MACRS after July 31, 1986) it must use ACRS or Straight Line. See Publication 534.

MACRS is generally used to depreciate property that was acquired for personal use before 1987 but placed in service after 1986. Improvements made to the property placed in service before 1986 are depreciated as a separate entry using MACRS depreciation.

Certain property that was acquired and placed in service after 1986 may not qualify for MACRS. MACRS cannot be used in any of the following personal property situations:

➢ The taxpayer or someone related to the taxpayer owned or used the property in 1986
➢ The taxpayer acquired the property from a person who owned it in 1986, and, as a part of the transaction, the user of the property did not change
➢ The taxpayer leased the property to a person (or someone related to them) who owned or used the property in 1986
➢ The taxpayer acquired the property in a transaction in which the following took place:
  o The user of the property did not change
  o The property was not a MACRS property in the hands of the person from whom the taxpayer acquired it due to one of the reasons above

A taxpayer cannot depreciate Section 1250 property using MACRS in any of the following situations:

➢ The taxpayer or someone related to the taxpayer owned the property in 1986
➢ The taxpayer leased the property to a person who owned the property or to someone related to that person in 1986
➢ The taxpayer acquired the property in a like-kind exchange, involuntary conversion, or repossession of property that was owned by the taxpayer, or someone related to the taxpayer in 1986

MACRS only applies to the part of basis in the acquired property that represents cash paid or unlike property exchanged. It does not apply to the carried-over part of the basis.

Exceptions to the above include the following:

➢ Residential rental property or nonresidential real property
➢ Any property if, in the first tax year that it is placed in service, the deduction under Accelerated Cost Recovery System (ACRS) is more than the deduction under MACRS using the half year convention. See Publication 534

The following are related persons who cannot depreciate Section 1250 property:

➢ An individual and a member of their family, including only a spouse, child, parent, brother, sister, half-brother, half-sister, ancestor, and lineal descendant
➢ A corporation or an individual who directly or indirectly owns more than 10% of the value of the outstanding stock of that corporation
➢ Two corporations that are members of the same controlled group
➢ A trust fiduciary and a corporation if more than 10% of the value of the outstanding stock is directly or indirectly owned by or for the trust or grantor of the trust
➢ The grantor and fiduciary; and the fiduciary and beneficiary of any trust
➢ The fiduciaries of two different trusts and the fiduciaries and beneficiaries of two different trusts if the same person is the grantor of both trusts
➢ A tax-exempt educational or charitable organization and any person (or a member of that person's family) who directly or indirectly controls the organization
➢ Two S corporations, an S corporation and a regular corporation, if the same individual owns more than 10% of the value of the outstanding stock of each corporation
➢ A corporation and a partnership if the same persons own both of the following:
  o More than 10% of the value of the outstanding stock of the corporation
  o More than 10% of the interest gained from the capital or profits of the partnership
➢ The executor and beneficiary of any estate

> ➤ Two partnerships, if the same person directly or indirectly owns more than 10% of the capital or profits of each
> ➤ The related person and a person who is engaged in trades or businesses under common control. See IRC section 52(a) and 52(b)

The buyer should determine the nature of a relationship before the property is acquired.

Intangible Property

Intangible property is anything of value that can be owned that has no corresponding physical object (e.g., a patent, copyright, or partnership interests). These are generally depreciated using the straight-line method. The taxpayer may choose to depreciate intangible property by using the income forecast method, which is not covered in this course. See Publication 946.

Straight Line Method

The straight-line method of depreciation allows the taxpayer to deduct the same amount each year over the useful life of the property. To determine the deduction, first determine the adjusted basis, salvage value, and estimated useful life of the property. Subtract the salvage value, if any, from the adjusted basis. The balance is the depreciation that can be taken for the property. Divide the balance by the number of years in the useful life. This is the yearly depreciation deduction. To use the straight-line method, prorate the depreciation deduction by dividing the value proportionally based on a unit of time or number of months in use.

Example: Francisco purchased a patent in August for $5,100. Tax treatment of patents under the IRC is defined in Section 197. Francisco will depreciate the patent using the straight-line method. The useful life for a patent is 17 years with no salvage value. Francisco would divide the $5,100 basis by 17 years to get the yearly depreciation of $300. In the first year of business, Francisco only used the patent for 9 months so he would have to multiply the $300 x 9/12 to get his deduction of $225 for the first year. Over the next full year, Francisco would claim the $300 depreciation deduction.

Computer software is generally a Section 197 tangible and cannot be depreciated if the taxpayer acquired it in connection with the acquisition of assets constituting a business. However, when it meets the following tests, computer software that is not a Section 197 intangible can be depreciated even if it's acquired in a business acquisition:

> ➤ It is readily available for purchase by the general public
> ➤ It is subject to a nonexclusive license
> ➤ It has not been substantially modified

If the software meets the above test, it may also qualify for Section 179. If computer software can be depreciated, use the straight-line method over a useful life of 36 months.

Part 2 Review

To obtain the maximum benefit from each part go online now and watch the video.

Part 3 Depreciation Basis and Depreciation under MACRS

While depreciation and basis can seem overwhelming to the beginner tax professional, with an understanding of the basic depreciation and basis are not difficult to determine.

Basis of Depreciable Property

To calculate the depreciation deduction, you must know the basis of the property. To determine the basis of the property, you must know the cost of the property.

Cost Basis

The basis of property that has been purchased is the cost plus the amounts paid for certain items. The cost includes the amount paid in cash, debt obligations, other property, or services. Some items that might be added to basis are:

- ➢ Sales tax
- ➢ Freight charges
- ➢ Installation fees
- ➢ Testing fees
- ➢ Settlement costs such as:
  - ○ Legal and recording fees
  - ○ Abstract fees
  - ○ Survey charges
  - ○ Owner's title insurance
  - ○ Amounts the seller owes that the buyer agrees to pay, such as back taxes, interest, recording or mortgage fees, charges for improvements or repairs, and sales commissions.

Other Basis

Other basis refers to the way the owner of the property received the property. Was the property acquired by a like-kind exchange, as payment for services performed, as a gift, inheritance, or some other way? See Publication 551.

Adjusted Basis

Certain events can trigger an increase or decrease to the basis in property. These events occur between the time that the property was acquired and placed into service, and could include any of the following:

- ➢ Installing utility lines
- ➢ Paying legal fees for perfecting the title
- ➢ Setting zoning issues
- ➢ Receiving rebates
- ➢ Incurring a casualty or theft loss

Reduce the basis of property by the depreciation allowed or allowable, whichever is greater. "Depreciation allowed" is depreciation that the taxpayer was entitled to and has already deducted as a tax benefit. "Depreciation allowable" is depreciation that the taxpayer was entitled to but did not yet deduct. See Publication 551.

Figuring Depreciation Under MACRS

The Modified Accelerated Cost Recovery System (MACRS) is used to recover the basis of most business and investment property placed in service after 1986. MACRS consists of two depreciation systems: the General Depreciation System (GDS) and the Alternative Depreciation System (ADS). These two systems provide different methods and recovery periods to figure deductions. The most common method used is GDS unless the law requires the ADS method to be used, or the taxpayer has elected to use ADS.

If the taxpayer is required to use ADS to depreciate the property, no special depreciation allowance can be claimed on the property. Although the property may qualify for GDS, the taxpayer can elect to use ADS. The election must cover all property in the same property class that was placed in service during the same year.

GDS Property Classifications

There are nine property classifications under GDS. The classifications are divided by the length of the depreciation period and by the type of property being depreciated. Most of the classifications have the same recovery period as the title of the year. The following are some samples of the type of asset for each classification. See Publication 946.

Classification One, 3-year Property:

➢ Racehorses that were over two years old when placed in service
➢ Any other horses that were over 12 years old when placed in service
➢ Qualified rent-to-own property

Classification Two, 5-year Property:

➢ Automobiles, taxis, buses, and trucks
➢ Office machinery such as calculators, copiers, and computers
➢ Dairy cattle and breeding cattle
➢ Appliances, carpets, solar, and wind energy property

Classification Three, 7-year Property:

➢ Office furniture and fixtures such as desks, chairs, and a safe
➢ Railroad tracks
➢ Any property that does not have a class life and has not been designated by law as being in any other class
➢ Certain motorsports entertainment complex property

Classification Four, 10-year Property:

➢ Any tree or vine bearing fruit or nuts
➢ Any single-purpose agricultural or horticultural structure
➢ Vessels, barges, tugs, and similar water transportation equipment
➢ Qualified small electric meter and qualified grid systems placed in service on or after October 3, 2008

Classification Five, 15-year Property:

➢ Certain improvements made directly to land or added to land, such as shrubbery, fences, roads, sidewalks, and bridges
➢ Any municipal wastewater treatment plant
➢ The initial clearing and grading for land improvements for gas utilities

> ➢ Electric transmission section 1245 property, used in the transmission at 69 or more kilovolts of electricity placed in service after April 11, 2005

Classification Six, 20-year property:

> ➢ Farm buildings, other than single-purpose agricultural or horticultural structures
> ➢ Initial clearing and grading land improvements for electric utility transmission and distribution plants
> ➢ Municipal sewers not classified as 25-year-property

Classification Seven, 25-year Property:

> ➢ Property that is an integral part of the gathering, treatment, or commercial distribution of water; all other property regarding water would be 20-year property
> ➢ Municipal sewers other than property placed in service under a binding contract in effect at all times since June 9, 1996

Classification Eight, Residential Rental Property:

Residential rental property includes any building or structure available for dwelling and rented out for income, which includes single-family homes, townhouses, apartments, condominium units, duplexes, and mobile homes. Motels, hotels, and other similar establishments that use more than 50% of the rooms for transients are not included; for these, the property class-life is 27.5 years.

Classification Nine, Nonresidential Real Property:

This is Section 1250 property, such as an office building, store, or warehouse that is not a residential rental property or a property with a class life of less than 27.5 years. There are always exceptions to the rules. If this is the case, one must do research related to the particular situation. Any other GDS recovery periods not listed above can be found in Appendix B of Publication 946.

Which Convention Applies?

A convention method is established under MACRS to determine the portion of the year to depreciate property both in the year the property was placed in service and in the year of disposition. The convention used determines the number of months for which one can claim depreciation. The three methods are: Mid-month (MM), Mid-quarter (MQ), and Half-year (HY).

Mid-month convention is used for nonresidential real property, residential real property, and any railroad grading or tunnel bore. Under this convention, one-half month of depreciation is allowed for the month the property was placed in service or disposed of.

Example: Josue uses the calendar year accounting method and placed nonresidential real property in service in August. The property is in service for 4 months (September, October, November, and December). Josue's numerator is 4.5 (4 months plus 0.5). Josue would multiply the depreciation for a full year by 4.5/12, or 0.375.

If the taxpayer does not use the asset solely for business, then the asset must be multiplied by the business percentage for the year, and the result is multiplied by the fraction found in the MACRS depreciation tables.

Example: In February 2022, Jennifer purchased office furniture for $2,600. She used the office furniture for her business only 50% of the time. Furniture is a 7-year property. The depreciation percentage is taken from Table A-2 found in Publication 946. Since Jennifer purchased the furniture in the first quarter of the year, she would use the mid-quarter convention placed in service in the first quarter. The amount Jennifer could depreciate her first year would be the cost of the furniture ($2,600) times the percentage of its use for business (50%) times the percentage provided from the depreciation table (25%), which amounts to $325.00.

The Mid-quarter convention is used if the Mid-month convention does not apply, and the total depreciable basis of MACRS property placed in service is in the last three months of the tax year. If the Mid-quarter convention is used for a particular year, each item of depreciable personal property placed in service during that year must be depreciated using the Mid-quarter convention for its entire recovery period.

Nonresidential real property, residential rental property, railroad grading or tunnel bore property placed in service and disposed of in the same year, and property that is being depreciated under a method other than MACRS, are all excluded from using the Mid-quarter convention. Under this convention, treat all property placed in service or disposed during any quarter of the tax year as placed in service. This means that 1.5 months of depreciation is allowed for the quarter the property is placed in service or disposed.

The Half-year convention is used if neither the Mid-quarter nor the Mid-month convention applies. Under this convention, treat all property placed in service or disposed of during a tax year as placed in service or disposed of at the midpoint of the year. This means that one-half year of depreciation is allowed for the year the property is placed in service or disposed.

When the taxpayer elects to use the half-year convention, a half-year of depreciation is allowed in the first year their property is placed in service, regardless of when the property is placed in service during the tax year. For each of the remaining years of the recovery period, the taxpayer can claim a full year of depreciation. If the property is held for the entire recovery period, a half-year of depreciation is claimed for the year following the end of the recovery period. If the property is disposed before the recovery period ends, a half-year of depreciation is allowable for the year of disposition.

If the personal property has been placed into a farming business after 1988, and before 2018, the taxpayer must depreciate by using 150% of GDS. The exception to the rule is if the farmer must depreciate real property using the straight-line method. For 3-, 5-, 7-, or 10-year property placed in the farming business after 2017 no longer have to use the 150% declining balance.

Changing Accounting Methods

To change the accounting method used for depreciation, the taxpayer needs to file Form 3115, Application for Change in Accounting Method, to be approved by the IRS.

The following are examples of a change in the method of accounting used for depreciation:

➢ A change from an impermissible method of determining depreciation for property if it was used in two or more consecutively filed tax returns
➢ A change in the treatment of an asset from non-depreciable to depreciable, or vice versa
➢ A change in the depreciation method, period of recovery, or convention of a depreciable asset
➢ A change from not claiming to claiming the special depreciation allowance if the election was made to not claim the special allowance

➤ A change from claiming a 50% special depreciation allowance to claiming a 100% special depreciation allowance for qualified property acquired and placed in service after September 27, 2017, if the election was not made under IRC section 168(k)(10) to claim the 50% special allowable depreciation

Changes in depreciation that are not a change in method of accounting are as follows:

➤ An adjustment in the useful life of a depreciable asset for which depreciation is determined under Section 167
➤ A change in use of an asset in the hands of the same taxpayer
➤ Making a late depreciation election or revoking a timely valid depreciation election, including the election not to deduct the special depreciation allowance
➤ Any change in date of when a depreciable asset was placed in service

If the taxpayer does not qualify to use the automatic procedure by filing Form 3115, then they must use the advance consent request procedures. See Instructions Form 3115.

Idle Property

Depreciation can still be claimed on property that is placed in service, even if a property is temporarily idle and not being used. For instance, if Emilio owns a printing press but has not used it for six months of the current tax year because he has no jobs that require the machine, then he can continue claiming depreciation on his printing press.

Cost or Other Basis Fully Recovered

Property can no longer be depreciated once it has fully recovered its cost or other basis.

Retired from Service

When property has been retired from service, depreciation stops. Property is retired from service when it has been permanently withdrawn from use in trade or business; in production of income; or if the property has been sold or exchanged, converted to personal use, abandoned, transferred to a supply, or destroyed. Disposition of an asset includes the sale, exchange, retirement, physical abandonment, or destruction of an asset.

Understanding the Table of Class Lives and Recovery Periods

There are two sections in the *Table of Class Lives and Recovery Periods* for depreciation. Table B-1 is *Specific Depreciable Assets Used in All Business Activities, Except as Noted*; this table lists the assets used in all business activities. Some items included could be office furniture; information systems such as computers; and secondary equipment, like printers or computer screens.
Table B-2 is used for all other activities, such as those involving agriculture, horse racing, farm buildings, and single purpose agricultural or horticultural structures.

Use the tables in numerical order. Look on Table B-1 first; if you do not find the asset you are looking for, then check Table B-2. Once the asset has been located, use the recovery period shown in the table. However, if the activity is specifically listed in Table B-2 under the type of activity in which it is used, then use the recovery period for that activity in that table.

Each table gives the asset class, the class life, and the recovery period in years. Understanding these tables is vital for the new tax professional. A tax professional does not have to memorize the tables – just know where to find the information and how to use it correctly.

If the property is not listed in either table, check the end of Table B-2 to find *Certain Property for Which Recovery Periods Assigned.* Generally, non-listed property has a recovery period of 7 years GDS or 12 years ADS.

Example: Peter Martinez owns a retail clothing store. During the year, he purchased a desk and cash register for business use. Peter finds "office furniture" in Table B-1, under asset class 00.11. Cash register is not listed in Table B-1. Peter then looks in Table B-2 and finds the activity "retail store" under asset class 57.0, *Distributive Trades and Services*, which includes assets used in wholesale and retail trade. The asset class does not specifically list office furniture or a cash register. Peter uses asset class 00.11 for the desk. The desk has a 10-year class life and a 7-year recovery period for GDS. Peter elects to use ADS; the recovery period is 10 years. For the cash register, Peter uses asset class 57.0 because a cash register is not listed in Table B-1, but it is an asset used in the retail business. The cash register has a 9-year class life and a 5-year recovery period for GDS. If Peter elects to use the ADS method, the recovery period is 9 years.

Part 3 Review

To obtain the maximum benefit from each part go online now and watch the video.

Takeaways

Taxpayers are in the business of farming if they cultivate, operate, or manage a farm for profit, either as an owner or tenant. A farm includes livestock, dairy, poultry, fish, fruit, and truck farms. The farm can also include plantations, ranches, ranges, and orchards.

Depreciation is a complex concept that must be understood by the tax professional to prepare accurate business tax returns. Depreciation is used to benefit the taxpayer; the IRS has defined the convention and class type and has figured the percentage amount. All the tax professional needs to do is find the correct class type and percentage to calculate the correct depreciation for the taxpayer. A tax professional should not rely solely on software to do the calculation but should understand depreciation to verify that the software is calculating depreciation correctly.

TEST YOUR KNOWLEDGE!
Go online to take a practice quiz.

Chapter 12 Extensions and Amendments

Introduction

If taxpayers are unable to file their federal individual tax returns by the due date, they may be able to qualify for an automatic six-month extension of time to file. The taxpayer can either electronically file or mail Form 4868 to the IRS to file for the extension. If the taxpayer has filed a return and realizes that a mistake was made, they would file an amended return using Form 1040-X.

Objectives

At the end of this lesson, the student will:

➢ Understand when to use Form 4868
➢ Know when an amendment must be filed
➢ Be able to identify when the installment agreement should be used

Resources

Form 1040	Publication 17	Instructions Form 1040
Form 1040-X	Publication 54	Instructions Form 1040-X
Form 4868	Tax Topic 308	Instructions Form 4868
Form 9465		Instructions Form 9465
Form 13884		Instructions Form 13844

Part 1 Form 4868: Extension of Time to File

File Form 4868, Application for Automatic Extension, to file for an automatic six-month extension for filing a federal return. The extension is for filing the tax return only. If the taxpayer has a balance due, the payment must be paid by April 15 or the due date of the return. There are three ways to request an automatic extension:

➢ File Form 4868 electronically
➢ Pay all or part of the estimated income tax due using the Electronic Federal Tax Payment System (EFTPS) or a credit or debit card
➢ Mail Form 4868 to the IRS and enclose the tax payment

To qualify for the extension for extra time, taxpayers must estimate their tax liability as accurately as possible and enter it on Form 4868, line 4, before filing Form 4868 by the regular due date of the return. If the IRS does not accept the application for extension of time, the taxpayer will receive a letter of denial informing them of when they are required to file. If the application was accepted, the taxpayer can file any time prior to the extension's due date.

If the taxpayer is a U.S. citizen or resident who is out of the country, the extension is valid for four months. Part I of Form 4868 is used to identify the taxpayer. Part II is for information about how the tax return should be filed.

Late Payment Penalty

The taxpayer may be charged a late payment penalty of 1/2% (.005) of any tax (except estimated tax) not paid by the regular filing deadline. An additional monthly penalty with a maximum rate of 25% of the unpaid amount is charged on any unpaid tax. If the taxpayer can show reasonable cause for not paying on time, a statement should be attached to the return (not to Form 4868), and the late penalty payment will not be charged. Both of the following requirements must be met to be considered reasonable cause:

➤ At least 90% of the tax liability was paid before the regular due date of the return via withholding, estimated payments, or payments made with Form 4868
➤ The remaining balance is paid with tax return on the extended due date

If the taxpayer has a balance due, interest is accrued on the unpaid balance. The penalty is 5% of the amount due for each month or part of a month the return is late. If the return is more than 60 days late, the minimum penalty is $450 or the balance of the tax due on the return, whichever is smaller. The maximum penalty is 25%

Making Extension Payments

For extensions, payments can be made electronically by credit card, debit card, money order, the Electronic Federal Tax Payment System (EFTPS), a direct transfer from a bank account using Direct Pay, or an ACH from the taxpayer's checking or savings account. When making a payment with the extension, remember to include the payment amount on Form 1040, Schedule 3, Part 2, line 13z. EFTPS can also be paid via phone. The taxpayer must write down the confirmation number they received when making an electronic payment. If the electronic payment has been designated as an extension payment, then do not file Form 4868.

Señor 1040 Says: If the taxpayer and spouse filed separate Form 4868s with payments and then chose to file the tax return as married filing jointly, make sure to include both payment amounts on Form 4868, line 5.

When paying by check or cashier's check, Form 4868 should be included and mailed to the address on the form. Make sure the check or money order is made payable to United States Treasury. The taxpayer should include their SSN and write Form 4868 in the memo on the check. Do not send cash. Checks over $100 million or more are not accepted, so any payments exceeding that amount will have to be split into two or more payments. The $100 million limit does not apply to other payment methods (such as electronic payments). As with Form 1040, there are specific mailing addresses to mail extension payments. To find which mailing address should be used, see Instructions Form 4868, page 4. The address is determined by where the taxpayer lives.

Installment Agreement Request (Form 9465)

If a taxpayer owes the federal government more than they can pay at one time, they can file Form 9465, *Installment Agreement Request*, which asks permission to pay the taxes monthly. The IRS charges a late-payment penalty of 25% per month. If the return was not filed in a timely manner, the late payment penalty is 5% per month. The IRS usually notifies the taxpayer within 30 days of approval or denial of the proposed payment plan.

The user fee for new installment agreements is $225. The taxpayer can also set up a payroll deduction installment agreement, and that fee is $225. If the taxpayer uses an online payment portal, the user fee would be $31.00; if using credit card, check or money order, the payment set-up fee is $149.00. If the taxpayer's income is below a certain level (250% of the annual poverty level), the installment agreement may be reduced to $43. Form 13844 must be completed to qualify. Form 13844, *Application for Reduced User Fee For Installment Agreements.*

Taxpayers can apply for a short-term payment plan (up to 180 days) online, by phone, mail, or in-person with no set-up fees. (Only individuals can apply for this online. Businesses must use the other application methods.)

If the taxpayer elects to use the installment agreement, interest and a late-payment penalty will still apply on the unpaid amount by the due date. In agreeing to an installment payment, the taxpayer also agrees to meet all future tax liabilities. If the taxpayer does not have adequate withholding or make estimated payments so their tax liability will be paid in full on a timely filed return, the taxpayer will be considered in default of the agreement, and the IRS can take immediate action to collect for the entire amount. Form 9465 can be filed electronically with the taxpayer's tax return. Penalties and interest can be avoided if the tax bill is paid in full on the due date.

If the taxpayer can make the payment in full in 180 days, to avoid the installment agreement fee, the taxpayer can call the IRS or apply online and ask for a payment agreement. See Instructions Form 9465, *Installment Agreement Request.*

By completing Form 9465 the taxpayer agrees to the following terms. The terms of the installment agreement are:

> ➤ The Installment agreement will remain in effect until all liabilities (including penalties and interest) are paid in full
> ➤ The taxpayer will make each payment monthly by the due date that was chosen on Form 9465. If unable to make a monthly payment, the taxpayer will notify the IRS immediately.
> ➤ The agreement is based on current financial conditions. IRS may modify or terminate the agreement if the taxpayer's information changes. When requested, taxpayer will provide current financial information.
> ➤ The taxpayer must file all federal tax returns and pay on time any federal taxes owed
> ➤ The IRS will apply federal refunds or overpayments to the entire amount owed, including the shared responsibility payment under the ACA, until paid in full
> ➤ If the taxpayer defaults on the installment agreement, they will be charged an additional $89 fee to reinstate the agreement. The IRS has the authority to deduct this fee from the first payment after the agreement is reinstated. Starting January 1, 2019, the fee is $10 if the agreement was restructured through an online payment agreement (OPA).
> ➤ The IRS will apply all payments made on this agreement in the best interest of the United States. Generally, the IRS will apply the payment to the oldest collection period.

The IRS can terminate the installment agreement if the taxpayer does not make the monthly payment as agreed. If the agreement is terminated, the IRS could collect the entire amount owed, except the Individual Shared Responsibility Payment under the ACA, by levying the taxpayers' income, bank accounts, or other assets, and even seizing property. If the tax collection is in jeopardy, the IRS may terminate the agreement. The IRS may file a Notice of Federal Tax Lien, if one has not already been filed.

Part 1 Review

To obtain the maximum benefit from each part go online now and watch the video.

Part 2 Amended Returns

Form 1040-X can be e-filed as long as the original return was filed electronically. A tax professional should always double check the IRS website to verify the correct mailing address. This could affect the taxpayer's payment, tax return, or communication with the IRS. Remember, the correct address is determined by the taxpayer's address, not that of the tax professional.

Form 1040-X can be e-filed as long as the original return was filed electronically. A tax professional should always double check the IRS website to verify the correct mailing address. This could affect the taxpayer's payment, tax return, or communication with the IRS. Remember, the correct address is determined by the taxpayer's address, not that of the tax professional.

When corrections to an original return will alter the current tax calculations, the taxpayer must file an amended tax return. The taxpayer cannot file an amended return until the original return has been completed and filed. However, once the original return has been filed, the amended return becomes the new tax return for the taxpayer. The taxpayer uses the amended return to adjust items that were previously claimed and now need adjusting because they were originally over- or understated.

For example, if the taxpayer needs to report additional income from a W-2 that arrived after the taxpayer filed the original return or if the taxpayer needs to remove a dependent because they were not eligible to claim the dependent, the taxpayer will file an amended return. Taxpayers who wish to receive a refund from an amended return must file the amendment within three years (including extensions) of the date the original return was filed or within two years of the date the tax was paid, whichever was later.

Example: Isabella filed her original return on March 1 of the current tax year, and her return was due April 15 of the same year. Isabella is considered to have filed her return by April 15. However, if Isabella had filed for an extension until October 15 and filed her return on July 1, her return is considered to be filed on July 1.

Other reasons a taxpayer might need to file an amendment are:

> ➤ To add or remove dependents
> ➤ To report the proper filing status
> ➤ To report additional income from a W-2, Form 1099, or some other income statement
> ➤ To make changes in above-the-line deductions, standard deductions, or itemized deductions
> ➤ To add or remove tax credits
> ➤ To report bad debt or worthless security
> ➤ To report foreign tax credit or deduction

Taxpayers can check the status of an amended return using the IRS "Where's My Amended Return?" tool on the IRS website. The tool requires entry of the taxpayer's identification number (SSN, ITIN, etc.), date of birth, and zip code, and is generally not intended for use by tax preparers.

Do not file Form 1040-X in the following situations:

➢ The taxpayer is requesting a refund of penalties and interest or an addition to tax that has already been paid. Instead, use Form 843, *Claim for Refund and Request for Abatement*
➢ The taxpayer is requesting a refund for their share of a joint overpayment that was offset against a past-due obligation of the spouse. Instead, file Form 8379, *Injured Spouse Allocation*

Interest and penalties will also be charged from the due date of the return for failure to file, negligence, fraud, substantial valuation misstatements, substantial understatements of tax, and reportable transaction understatements.

Complete Form 1040-X

Most software will have the preparer add Form 1040-X, save the form to the return, and make changes to the form that was added or removed from the original return. For example, Jimmy received an additional W-2. The tax preparer would enter the W-2 as an additional form, and software will flow the information to Form 1040-X. Filing the form electronically helps since one does not need to mail the return and information.

To make changes that affect lines 1-31 of the original tax return, the taxpayer would use Part 1 of the 1040-X. Part II is where the taxpayer can choose to have $3 go to the Presidential Election Campaign Fund. This must be done within 20.5 months after the original due date of the return. Part III is for the explanation of changes. The IRS wants to know what was changed on the return and why the taxpayer is filing Form 1040-X.

The three columns on Form 1040-X are as follows:

➢ Column A: The original return amount
➢ Column B: The Net Change. Enter the change in amount for each line that is altered
➢ Column C: The correct amount. Add or subtract column B (if there is an entry) from column A and enter amount in column C.

Example: Robert reported $41,000 as his adjusted gross income on Form 1040 for the current year. He received another Form W-2 for $500 after he had already filed his return. He should complete line 1 of Form 1040-X as follows:

On Form 1040-X, input the income, deductions, and credits as originally reported on the return in Column A, input the changes being made in Column B, and place the difference or sum in Column C. Next, figure the tax on the corrected amount of taxable income and calculate the amount owed or to be refunded. If the taxpayer owes taxes, the taxpayer should pay the full amount with Form 1040-X. The tax owed will not be subtracted from any amount credited to estimated tax.

If the taxpayer cannot pay the full amount due on the amended return, the individual can ask to make monthly installment payments using Form 9465. If the taxpayer overpaid taxes, they would receive a refund. The overpayment refunded based on the amended return is different and separate from any refund gained from the original return.

When assembling an amended return to be mailed, make sure that the schedules and forms are behind Form 1040-X and that the taxpayer (and spouse if filing jointly) sign the 1040-X. If the amendment was prepared by a paid tax preparer, the tax preparer must sign as well.

Señor 1040 Says: Make sure to use the correct form for the year that is being amended. To find the forms you need, go to www.irs.gov, and choose the correct form(s) to amend the tax return.

Attach forms to the front of Form 1040-X that support changes made on the return. Attach to the back of Form 1040-X any Form 8805, *Foreign Partner's Information Statement of Section 1446 Withholding Tax*, that supports the changes made.

When sending a check or money order to the IRS for payments of taxes due, do not attach the check to the return. Instead, enclose it in the envelope and make sure the check is made out to "United States Treasury."

State Tax Liability

If a return is changed for any reason, it may affect the taxpayer's state income tax liability. This includes changes made as a result of an examination of the return by the IRS. The IRS will inform the taxpayer's state if adjustments are made on the federal tax return.

Part 2 Review

To obtain the maximum benefit from each part go online now and watch the video.

Takeaways

This chapter gives a brief understanding of extensions and amendments. The paid tax professional must understand who should file for an extension and when to file an amendment as these are two separate processes.

If more time is needed to file the tax return, the individual should file for an extension. However, an extension of time to file is not an extension of time to pay. Payment is still owed by the April 15 deadline or the taxpayer will pay late payment penalties. An extension of time to file does not change this. Although an extension of time to pay and various payment plans do exist, these should not be confused with extensions of time to file.

TEST YOUR KNOWLEDGE!
Go online to take a practice quiz.

Chapter 13 Electronic Filing

Introduction

Electronic filing (also referred to as e-file and e-filing) is the process of submitting tax returns over the internet via approved tax software. The e-file system has made tax preparation significantly easier, and the IRS notifies electronic filers within 24 to 48 hours if their tax return was accepted or rejected. E-filing is not available year-round. It begins in January and ends in October. The IRS determines when e-filing begins and ends each year, and states follow the IRS dates. An individual who originates electronic submission of a tax return is referred to as an electronic return originator (ERO). A tax preparation professional who files returns electronically on behalf of clients must be an Authorized IRS e-file provider.

Objectives

At the end of this lesson, the student will:

➢ Understand the different e-filing options
➢ Know which form(s) to use when the taxpayer opts-out of e-filing
➢ Identify which forms cannot be e-filed

Resources

Form 8453	Publication 17	Instructions Form 8453
Form 8878	Publication 1345	Instructions Form 8878
Form 8878-A	Publication 3112	Instructions Form 8878-A
Form 8879	Publication 4164	Instructions Form 8879
Form 9325	Publication 4557	Instructions Form 9325

Part 1 Electronic Return Originator (ERO)

An electronic return originator (ERO) is an authorized IRS e-file provider that originates submissions of returns they either prepare or collect from taxpayers who want to e-file their returns. An ERO originates the electronic submission of a return after the taxpayer authorizes e-filing. The ERO must have either prepared the return or collected it from a taxpayer. An ERO originates the electronic submission by one of the following methods:

➢ Electronically sending the return to a transmitter that will transmit the return to the IRS
➢ Directly transmitting the return to the IRS
➢ Providing the return to an intermediate service provider to transmit it to the IRS

Obtaining, Handling, and Processing Return Information from Taxpayers

If the return was prepared by a paid preparer, the ERO must always identify the paid preparer in the proper field of the electronic record and include the paid preparer's following information:

➢ Name
➢ Address
➢ EIN (if a member of a firm)

> PTIN

If while originating an electronic return they did not prepare and was not prepared by their firm an ERO discovers and corrects substantive errors, they become the tax preparer A non-substantive change is a correction limited to a transposition error, a misplaced entry, a spelling error, or an arithmetic correction. The IRS considers all other changes substantive, and the ERO becomes the tax preparer if such corrections are made.

e-File providers

An authorized IRS e-file provider is a business or organization authorized by the IRS to participate in their e-file program. A Provider may be an Electronic Return Originator (ERO), an Intermediate Service Provider, a Transmitter, a Software Developer, a Reporting Agent, or an Affordable Care Act (ACA) Provider. These different roles are not mutually exclusive, and one person or entity can have more than one. For example, a Provider may be an ERO while also being a Transmitter or a tax return preparer. Even though the activities and responsibilities for IRS e-file and return preparation are distinct and different from each other, one person can possess both titles, duties, and responsibilities at the same time.

A Transmitter is the person, entity, or software that literally sends the return data electronically directly to the IRS. A provider is one who has been authorized by the IRS to file tax returns electronically, typically through a third-party transmitter such as a tax software provider; filing a return is not the same thing as sending it.

Becoming an e-File provider

To become an e-file provider, an individual must submit an application to the IRS, a process that usually takes 45 days. To complete the application quickly, the individual should have the following information prepared:

> Know which provider options can be furnished to taxpayers
> Enter identification information for the company
> - Employer Identification Number
> - Name of the company
> - Enter the name, date of birth, Social Security number, current professional information, and citizenship status of the organization's Principal and Responsible Official. Indicate if either or both are an attorney, certified public accountant, enrolled agent, officer of a publicly traded corporation, or a bonded bank official.

Who are Principals and Responsible Officials?

Anyone who is a Principal or Responsible Official must:

1. Be a U.S. citizen or an alien who has permanent residence as covered in 8USC 110(a)(20)(1994)
2. Be at least 18 years old at the time of completing the application
3. Meet applicable state and local licensing and bonding requirements to be able to prepare and collect tax returns

The Principal is the individual who is ultimately responsible for anything and everything that occurs regarding e-filing at the firm. Although a firm can have more than one "Responsible Official," there can be only one Principal, and the information for the individual designated as the Principal must be on the application. Any of the following individuals that participate in the e-file operations of the company are eligible to be designated as the Principal:

➢ A sole proprietor of the business. For sole proprietorships, the sole proprietor must be the Principal.
➢ A partner who has at least 5% or more interest in the partnership
➢ The President, Vice-President, Secretary, or Treasurer of a corporation are all eligible to be a principal
➢ The Principal for an entity that is not any of the above needs to be an individual with the authority within the company to act on behalf of the entity in legal or tax matters

If any of the above individuals are not involved in the e-file operations of the company, then a large firm with multilayered management can substitute a "Key Person" who participates substantially in the firm's electronic filing operations as the principal for the e-file application.

Unlike the Principal, who is the single person responsible for e-file matters across the whole company, Responsible Officials are the people in charge of the day-to-day e-file operations at specific locations such as offices. They are the first point of contact with the IRS and have the authority to sign and revise IRS e-file applications. Responsible Officials must set the revenue procedures for e-filing and for all publications and notices thereof and ensure that employees follow them.

Responsible Officials can oversee the operations at more than one office, and though there can be more, each firm must have at least one Responsible Official, although it can always add more later; the Principal can also be the Responsible Official.

Step One: Accessing the Application

Before starting the e-file application process, the individual must create an account with IRS Secure Access. To do this, the individual will register using a two-factor authentication process at irs.gov. After this, they will be asked to provide the following information to create the account:

➢ Full legal name
➢ Home address
➢ Social Security number
➢ Date of birth
➢ Phone number
➢ Email address

Any other individuals that the firm wishes to appoint as either the Principal or as Responsible Officials must also create e-services accounts. Account creators must return to the e-Services site within 28 days of receiving the confirmation code to confirm the registration thus allowing the firm to continue the application process.

Step Two: Complete and Submit the Application

Once all relevant individuals have confirmed their e-Services accounts, the firm can apply to become an authorized IRS e-file provider. The next steps of the application process are:

1. Log in to e-Services to access the online application to become an IRS e-file provider
2. Select the e-file provider type (Transmitter, ERO, etc.)
3. Enter the identification information of the firm and services provided
4. Enter the name, home address, SSN, DOB, and citizenship status for each principal and responsible party for the firm
5. Enter the Principal and Responsible Official(s) current professional status (attorney, certified public accountant, enrolled agent, etc.) and any other requested information
6. Each Principal and Responsible Official must answer several personal questions and sign the Terms of Agreement (TOA) using the PIN they selected when creating their e-services accounts
7. Each Principal and Responsible Official must declare under penalty of perjury that all the personal information they entered is true

Submit the IRS e-file application and retain the tracking number provided after the successful submission of the application.

Any individuals appointed to become the Principal or a Responsible Official who are not an EA, CPA, or attorney must pass a background check before the application can continue. To do this, first request a fingerprint card from the IRS by calling their toll-free number (1-866-255-0654). Once the IRS has mailed the cards, take them to a trained professional at your local police department or to a company certified to provide fingerprinting services. They will fingerprint each Principal and Responsible Official, who must each sign the card that has their fingerprints.

Suitability Check

Once the IRS has received, processed, and reviewed the application, they will conduct a "suitability check" to determine if the firm qualifies to become an e-file provider. The "suitability check" consists of the following checks on the firm, and on each person listed as a principal or responsible official on the application and on all documents related to the application:

➢ A credit check
➢ A tax compliance check
➢ A criminal background check
➢ A check for prior noncompliance with IRS e-file requirements

If the firm passes the suitability check they will receive their acceptance letter from the IRS with the electronic filing identification number (EFIN), which should not be confused with the firm's EIN.

Denial to Participate in IRS e-File

If the firm, a Principal, or a Responsible Official fails the suitability check, the IRS will notify the applicant of denial to participate in the program, the date they may reapply, and if they may reapply sooner if the suitability issues are resolved.

Acceptance to Participate in IRS e-File

After an applicant passes the suitability check and the IRS completes the processing of the application, the IRS will notify the applicant of their acceptance or rejection to participate in the program. A provider does not have to reapply unless the IRS suspends the provider from participation in the program for a violation. If any of the information on the original application changes, the provider will have 30 days to update the information by resubmitting the application with the required changes.

If the professional status of a Principal or Responsible Official changes, the firm must update its e-file application and resubmit the individual's fingerprints for a new background check. If a Principal or a Responsible Official dies, the provider must remove or replace the deceased within 30 days by resubmitting the application. If this is not done, the IRS will independently remove the deceased individual(s) from the e-file application. This could lead to the rejection of returns due to the lack of coverage for one of the firm's offices. The IRS will also remove providers if they are unable to contact the provider or if mail is returned to the IRS as undeliverable because the provider failed to update their physical mailing address, in which case the IRS will reject all returns submitted by the provider until the provider updates their information

Monitoring

The IRS monitors providers by visiting the locations where IRS e-file activities are performed, and by reviewing the required e-file records. Monitoring may include, but is not limited to, the following:

- ➢ Reviewing the quality of e-file submissions for rejections and other defects
- ➢ Checking adherence to signature requirements on returns
- ➢ Scrutinizing advertising material
- ➢ Examining records
- ➢ Observing office procedures
- ➢ Conducting periodic suitability checks

The IRS monitors the regulations put in place by the providers to ensure they are in compliance with IRC §6695(g).

Revocation

The IRS will revoke participation from an authorized provider, Principal, or Responsible Official if so ordered by a federal court or a federal or state legal action. If the legal action expires or is reversed, the revoked Provider may reapply to participate in IRS e-file after the legal action expires or is reversed.

Sanctioning

IRS e-file violations may result in warning or sanctioning an authorized IRS e-file provider, a Principal, or a Responsible Official. Sanctioning may take the form of a written reprimand, suspension, or expulsion from the e-file program. In most circumstances, a sanction is effective 30 days after the date of the letter informing individuals of a sanction against them or the date that the reviewing officers or the Office of Appeals affirm the sanction, whichever is later. If a provider, Principal, or Responsible Official is suspended or expelled from participation in e-filing, every entity that listed the suspended or expelled Principal or Responsible Official on their e-file application may also be suspended or expelled. Although notice must be given eventually, the IRS has full authority to immediately suspend or expel anyone without a prior warning or notice.

Infractions

The IRS categorizes the seriousness of infractions in three different levels.

Level One Infractions are infringements of IRS e-file rules and requirements that have little-to-no harmful effect on the quality of the returns or on the IRS e-file program. This infraction could result in a written reprimand but may not lead to a suspension or expulsion. Level Two Infractions are violations of IRS e-file rules and requirements that have an unfavorable impact upon the quality of the returns or on the IRS e-file program. The continuing occurrence of Level One Infractions after the IRS has notified the person about a violation could cause an increase to Level Two Infraction. Depending on the nature of the infraction, the IRS may limit participation in IRS e-file or suspend the authorized IRS e-file provider from participation in IRS e-file for a period of one year.

Level Three Infractions are violations of IRS e-file rules and requirements that have a significant adverse impact on the quality of tax returns. Level Three Infractions include continued Level Two Infractions after the IRS has brought a Level Two Infraction to the attention of the provider. A Level Three Infraction may result in suspension from IRS e-file for two years or, depending on the severity of the infraction (such as fraud, identity theft, or criminal conduct), in removal without the opportunity for future participation. The IRS reserves the right to suspend or expel a provider prior to administrative review for Level Three Infractions. See Publication 3112.

Safeguarding Taxpayer Information

"Taxpayer information" is any piece of information that has been furnished for or by the taxpayer in any form or manner such as in person, over the phone, by mail, or by fax for the purpose of preparing the taxpayer's tax return. It includes, but is not limited to, the following information:

➢ Name
➢ Address
➢ Identification number
➢ Income
➢ Receipts
➢ Deductions
➢ Dependents
➢ Tax liability

Criminal and monetary penalties may be imposed on individuals preparing taxes or providing tax preparation services that knowingly or recklessly make unauthorized disclosures with the preparation of income tax returns. See Title 26 IRC §301.7216.1 and §6713. Some common safeguarding strategies are:

➢ Lock doors to restrict access to files
➢ Passwords to access computer files
➢ Encrypting electronically stored taxpayer data
➢ Keep a backup of electronic data for recovery purposes. Backup files regularly
➢ Shred taxpayer information

For more information about safeguarding personal information, go to the official website of the Federal Trade Commission at www.ftc.gov.

Nonstandard Document Awareness

The IRS has identified key indicators of potential abuse and fraud such as altered, forged, or fabricated Forms W-2, W-2G, and 1099-R, especially when prepared by hand. Information on reporting forms should never be altered. If the employer must make changes, the employer should provide the employee with a corrected document, and a corrected reporting form should be sent to the IRS and the SSA. Any time the tax professional has a questionable income document, they should report it to the IRS.

Verifying Taxpayer Identification Numbers (TINs)

To help safeguard taxpayers from fraud and abuse, the tax preparer should confirm the identity and identification number of taxpayers, spouses, and dependents listed on every tax return prepared. Taxpayer Identification These numbers include SSNs, EINs, adopted taxpayer identification numbers (ATINs), and individual taxpayer identification numbers (ITINs). To confirm identities, the paid preparer should request to see both a current government-issued photo ID and the taxpayer's original identification number.

If the identification card does not have the same address as the one on the tax return, the preparer should ask additional questions to verify the taxpayer's identity. Even though the addresses are not required to match, confirmation of the taxpayer's identity is a fundamental part of a tax professional's due diligence. Using an incorrect identification number, the same number on multiple returns, or an incorrect name with the wrong identification number are some of the most common causes for rejection of e-filed returns. To minimize rejections, the preparer should verify the taxpayer's name and identification number prior to submitting the tax return electronically to the IRS.

Client Protection

The IRS has created several basic security guidelines for tax preparers to follow while preparing returns, which will protect clients' data and their businesses:

- ➤ Learn to recognize phishing emails, especially those that look like they originated from the IRS. Never open an embedded link or attachment from an email that looks suspicious
- ➤ Create a data security plan using the guidelines found in Publication 4557, *Safeguarding Taxpayer Data*
- ➤ Review internal controls:
  - ○ Install anti-malware and anti-virus security software on all devices (laptops, desktops, routers, tablets, phones, etc.) and keep the software up to date
  - ○ Use strong passwords of eight or more characters with a mixture of upper and lowercase letters, numbers, and special symbols that do not start or end with a space or include common phrases or the names of loved ones or pets
  - ○ Encrypt all sensitive files and emails and use strong password protections
  - ○ Back up sensitive data to a safe and secure external source that is not always connected to a network
  - ○ Wipe, clean, or destroy old hard drives or printers containing sensitive data
  - ○ Limit access to taxpayer data exclusively to individuals who need to know
  - ○ Perform weekly checks on the number of returns filed with the company's EFIN through the eServices account and compare that number with the number of returns the firm has actually prepared to make sure no one is fraudulently using their EFIN to e-file returns without one's knowledge. Individuals can do the same thing via their PTIN account.

➢ Report any data theft or data loss to the appropriate IRS Stakeholder Liaison
➢ Sign up on the IRS website to receive email notices from e-News for Tax Professionals, Quick Alerts, and news from IRS social media channels

The Gramm-Leach-Bliley Act

Enacted by Congress in 1999, the Gramm-Leach-Bliley Act implemented a number of safeguard rules along with the financial privacy rule to protect taxpayers' private information. Safeguard rules require tax return preparers, data processors, transmitters (ERO), affiliates, service providers, and others to ensure the security and confidentiality of customer records and information. The financial privacy rule requires the following individuals and financial institutions to provide their customers with privacy notices that explain the financial their information collection and sharing practices:

➢ Tax return preparers
➢ Data processors
➢ Transmitters
➢ Affiliates
➢ Service providers
➢ Anyone significantly engaged in providing financial products or services that include the preparation or filing of tax returns

Reporting Security Incidents

Online providers of individual tax returns shall report any adverse event or threat of an event that could result in an unauthorized disclosure, misuse, modification, or destruction of information. These types of incidents can affect the confidentiality, integrity, and availability of taxpayer information or the ability for a taxpayer to prepare or file a return. Types of incidents include theft of information, loss of information, natural disasters (such as floods, earthquakes, or fires that destroy unrecoverable information), and computer system or network attacks using such tools as malicious code or denials of service. If the tax professional experiences a security incident or is hacked, they should report it to the IRS immediately.

Part 1 Review

To obtain the maximum benefit from each part go online now and watch the video.

Part 2 Transmitting Returns

The IRS introduced electronic filing in 1986. Opting for electronic filing and choosing to have refunds directly deposited into a bank account is not only the quickest but also the most environmentally friendly method for filing a return. If the taxpayer has a balance due, it could be withdrawn from their bank account as well. Electronic filing and refund processing is considerably faster than USPS mail.

Electronic filing is mandatory for tax preparers who file 11 or more Form 1040 returns during any calendar year. If the firm has more than one preparer, all individual returns prepared by the firm contribute to that number. For example, Javier is the owner of a tax preparation company and does not prepare returns. His employee, Rosemarie, prepares five tax returns that contain a Schedule C. Oscar prepares 10 returns, and Mario prepares 100 individual tax returns. Javier's company needs to file the returns electronically because the firm prepared more than 11 returns.

All authorized IRS e-file providers must ensure that returns are promptly processed on or before the due date of the return (including extensions). An ERO must ensure that stockpiling of returns does not occur at the company. "Stockpiling" is both collecting returns from taxpayers prior to official acceptance in the IRS e-file program and waiting more than three calendar days to submit a return to the IRS once the ERO has all the necessary information for an e-file submission. Tax professionals who are EROs must advise their clients that they cannot transmit returns to the IRS until the IRS begins accepting transmissions. Tax returns held prior to that date are not considered "stockpiled."

Filing the Completed Return

Once the return has been completed and signed by all the necessary parties (taxpayer, preparer, etc.), it is ready to file with the IRS. If the preparer is submitting the return by mail, it should be placed in an envelope with adequate postage and mailed to the address designated by the IRS. Make sure to use the correct address, which is based on the taxpayer's address not the preparer's address.

Submission of Paper Documents

As discussed throughout this course, there are a multitude of forms that may need to be completed and attached to a taxpayer's return for submission to the IRS. Some software companies allow forms to be attached as PDFs to the tax return prior to submission. If the software company does not support this feature, the documents need to be attached to Form 8453 (which does not need to be signed) and mailed to the IRS using the address on page 2 of Form 8453. The following is a list of the supporting documents that will need to be mailed with Form 8453 if the software does not allow PDF attachments to the return:

- Form 1098-C: Contributions of Motor Vehicles, Boats, and Airplanes
- Form 2848: Power of Attorney
- Form 3115: Application of Change in Accounting Method
- Form 3468: Investment Credit, Historical Structure Certificate
- Form 4136: Certificate for Biodiesel and Statement of Biodiesel Reseller
- Form 5713: International Boycott Report
- Form 8283: Noncash Charitable Contributions, Section B Appraisal Summary
- Form 8332: Release of Claim to Exemption for Children of Divorced or Separated Parents
- Form 8858: Information Return of U.S. Persons with Respect to Foreign Disregarded Entities
- Form 8885: Health Coverage Tax Credit
- Form 8864: Certificate for Biodiesel and Statement of Biodiesel Reseller
- Form 8949: Sales and Other Dispositions of Capital Assets, or a statement with the same information

Providing Information to the Taxpayer

The ERO must provide a complete copy of the return to the taxpayer. EROs may provide this copy in any medium—electronic or another form that is acceptable to both the taxpayer and the ERO. The copy does not need the Social Security number of the paid preparer, but the preparer's PTIN is required. A complete copy of a taxpayer's return includes, when applicable, Form 8453 and any other documents that the ERO cannot electronically transmit in addition to the electronic portion of the return.

The electronic portion of the return can be printed onto a copy of an official form or in some unofficial form. However, if the ERO uses an unofficial form, the data entries and relevant line numbers must match the descriptions found on the associated official forms. If the taxpayer provided a completed paper return for electronic filing, and the information on the electronic portion of the return is identical to the information provided by the taxpayer, the ERO does not have to provide a printout of the electronic portion of the return to the taxpayer. The ERO should advise the taxpayer to retain a complete copy of their return and all supporting material. The ERO should also advise taxpayers that amended returns beginning 2019 can be e-filed. All others prior to 2019 must be filed as paper returns and mailed to the IRS submission processing center.

Processing Return Information from Taxpayers

Before an ERO can originate the electronic submission of a return, they must first either prepare the return or collect the already completed return and its various documents from the person who prepared it. If the return was prepared by someone else, the ERO must always identify the paid preparer in the appropriate field. EROs may either transmit the return directly to the IRS or transmit it through another provider. An authorized IRS e-file provider may disclose tax return information to other providers for the purpose of preparing a tax return under Reg. 301.7216. For example, an ERO may pass on return information to an intermediate service provider or a transmitter for the purpose of having an electronic return formatted or transmitted to the IRS.

File Accurate Tax Return to Receive Timely Refund

An electronically filed tax return is the best way for the tax professional to file an accurate tax return. To ensure the tax return is processed quickly, the ERO should take the following steps:

➢ File electronically
➢ Submit an accurate, complete, error-free return
➢ Verify that the Social Security number(s) or Taxpayer Identification Number(s) are accurate for all individuals included on the tax return
➢ Enter the taxpayer's correct mailing address, which enables the IRS to mail a refund check
➢ Provide the correct bank account and routing number for a direct deposit

Resubmitting Rejected Tax Returns

If the taxpayer's tax return is rejected by the IRS, the ERO has 24 hours to explain to the taxpayer the reason for the rejection. If the return can be fixed and resubmitted, then the changes can be made and the return can be retransmitted. The taxpayer could decide to mail the tax return instead of retransmitting the return. If the taxpayer chooses to mail the return, they will need a paper copy to send to the IRS. If the taxpayer chooses not to have the electronic portion of the return corrected and transmitted to the IRS or if it cannot be accepted for processing by the IRS, the taxpayer must file a new paper return. This must be filed by the due date of the return or within 10 calendar days after the date the IRS gave notice of the return's rejection, whichever of the two is later. The paper return should include an explanation of why the return is being filed after the due date.

Electronic Postmark

When a tax return is e-filed, a transmitter will electronically postmark it to show when it was filed. The postmark is created at the time the tax return is submitted and includes the date and time of the transmitter's time zone. An e-filed tax return is a timely filed return if the electronic postmark is on or before the filing deadline.

Acknowledgment of Transmitted Returns

The IRS electronically acknowledges the receipt of all transmissions and will either accept or reject the transmitted returns for specific reasons. Accepted returns meet the processing criteria and are considered "filed" as soon as the return is signed electronically or by hand. Rejected returns fail to meet processing criteria and are considered "not filed." See Publication 1345, *Handbook for Authorized IRS e-File Providers of Individual Income Tax Returns*.

The acknowledgment record of accepted returns contains other useful information for originators, informing them if the IRS accepted a PIN, if the taxpayer's refund will be applied to a debt, if an elected electronic funds withdrawal was paid, and if the IRS approved a request for extension on Form 4868. EROs should check the acknowledgment records stored by their tax software regularly to identify returns that require follow-up action and should take reasonable steps to address the issues specified in those records. For example, if the IRS does not accept a PIN on an individual income tax return, the ERO must provide a completed and signed Form 8453 for the return.

Rejected returns can be corrected and retransmitted without new signatures or authorizations if changes do not differ from the amount in the electronic portion of the electronic return by more than $50 to "total income" or AGI, or more than $14 to "total tax," "federal income tax withheld," "refund," or "amount owed." The taxpayer must be given copies of the new electronic return data if changes are made. If the required changes result in differences greater than the amounts referenced above, new signatures will be required, and the taxpayer must be given copies of the updated forms with their new signatures.

Balance Due Returns

A taxpayer who owes additional tax must pay their balance due by the original due date of the return or be subject to interest and penalties. An extension of time to file may be filed electronically by the original due date of the return, but it is an extension of time to file the return, not an extension of time to pay a balance due. Tax professionals should inform taxpayers of their obligations and options for paying balances due. Taxpayers have several options when paying taxes owed on their returns and making estimated tax payments.

As discussed previously, tax returns with amounts due can still be filed electronically, and the payment can also be made directly to the IRS via ACH withdrawals. The taxpayer can schedule a payment on or before the tax payment deadline. If a return with a balance due was submitted after the due date, the payment date must be the same day the provider transmitted the return. Taxpayers can make payments by Electronic Fund Withdrawal for amounts due from the following forms:

> ➤ Current year Form 1040
> ➤ Form 1040-ES, *Estimated Tax for Individuals*. When filing the tax return, the taxpayer can select all four dates to electronically make the payment.
> ➤ Form 4868, *Application for Automatic Extension of Time to File U.S. Individual Income Tax Return*
> ➤ Form 2350, *Application for Extension of Time to File U.S. Income Tax Return for Citizens and Resident Aliens Abroad Who Expect to Qualify for Special Tax Treatment*

The tax professional needs to make sure the client's banking information is accurate and includes the routing transit number (RTN), the bank account number, the account type (checking or savings), the date the payment will be withdrawn (year, month, and day), and the amount of the payment. If the payment is made after the due date, it should include interest and penalties as well.

As discussed previously, there are other ways to pay the balance due, such as IRS Direct Pay, via credit or debit card (though some credit card companies may charge an additional fee called a "cash advance" to use this method), using the Electronic Federal Tax Payment System (EFTPS), by check or money order, or through an installment agreement.

Pay by Check

Taxpayers may still mail their payment due to the IRS, but the payment should be accompanied by Form 1040-V. The paid preparer must supply taxpayers with copies if they mail Form 1040-V with their check or money order. Taxpayers must mail the payment due by the April due date, even if the return was electronically filed earlier.

Form 1040-V is a statement that is sent with a check or money order for any balance due on the taxpayer's current tax year. If the taxpayer files electronically, the voucher and payment are sent together. Most tax preparation software will generate Form 1040-V automatically.

Electronic Funds Withdrawal

Taxpayers can authorize an electronic funds withdrawal (EFW) when they e-file their return if they have a balance due on the return. Taxpayers who choose this option must provide the tax professional with the account number and routing transit number for a savings or checking account. If the financial institution is unable to locate or match the numbers entered in a payment record with account information given on the tax return for the taxpayer, the institution will reject the direct debit request and return the money back to the sender.

Credit or Debit Card Payments

Taxpayers may also pay electronically using a credit or debit card. Taxpayers can make credit or debit card payments when e-filing, by telephone, or the Internet. A third-party provider may charge a service fee to process the payment.

Electronic Federal Tax Payment System (EFTPS)

Individual taxpayers who make more than one payment per year should enroll in EFTPS. After the taxpayer has been enrolled, they will receive two separate mailings. One is the confirmation or update form; the second is a letter that includes the taxpayer's enrollment trace number, PIN, and instructions on how to obtain an Internet password. Payments on EFTPS can be made 24 hours a day, 7 days a week; however, to make a timely payment, it must be submitted before 8:00 p.m. EST at least one calendar day prior to the tax due date. Taxpayers can schedule payments up to 365 days in advance.

Returns Not Eligible for IRS e-File

The following individual income tax returns and related return conditions cannot be processed using IRS e-file and must be paper filed:

  ➢ Tax returns with fiscal-year tax periods
  ➢ Amended tax returns prior to 2019
  ➢ Returns containing forms or schedules that cannot be processed by IRS e-file

Refund Delays

Before issuing a refund to a taxpayer, the IRS will verify that the taxpayer does not owe any past taxes or other debts such as child support, student loans, unemployment compensation, or any state income tax obligation. If the taxpayer or spouse owes any of these, a portion or all the refund will be applied to the amount owed before the refund is paid to the taxpayer. If the amount owed is greater than the amount of the refund, then the entire amount of that refund and any future refunds will be applied to offset the amount owed until it has been paid in full.

The following are other reasons a refund could be delayed:

➢ The return has errors, is incomplete, or needs further review
➢ The return includes a claim for refundable credits and was held until February 15
➢ The return is impacted by identity theft or fraud
➢ The tax return includes Form 8379, Injured Spouse Allocation, which can take up to 14 weeks to process and review
➢ Errors in the direct deposit information that cause the refund to be sent by check
➢ Financial institution's refusal of direct deposit, which will result in the refund being sent by check
➢ The estimated tax payments differ from the amounts reported on a tax return
➢ Bankruptcy
➢ Inappropriate claims for EITC
➢ Recertification to claim EITC

When the refund is delayed, the IRS will send a letter to the taxpayer explaining the issue(s) and how to resolve them. The letter or notice includes the telephone number and address the taxpayer can use for further assistance. If there is a delay, the taxpayer can learn more on the "Where's My Refund?" section of the IRS website (See *Where's My Refund?* below.)

Refund Offsets

When a taxpayer owes a prior-year balance, the IRS will offset their current-year refund to pay the balance due on the following items:

➢ Back taxes
➢ Child support
➢ Federal agency non-tax debts such as student loans
➢ State income tax obligations

If taxpayers owe any of these debts, their refund will be offset until the debt has been paid off or the refund has been spent, whichever occurs first.

Where's My Refund?

"Where's My Refund?" is a portal on the IRS website that provides status information on a taxpayer's refund. This system is updated every 24 hours (usually at night). The taxpayer can begin checking their refund within 24 hours after the IRS has acknowledged receipt of the tax return—not the date that the provider transmitted the tax return.

Taxpayers will need the following information to track their refund

 ➤ SSN
 ➤ Filing status
 ➤ The full refund amount

To receive assistance from the IRS or a Taxpayer Assistance Center (TAC) over the phone or in person, a return must have been filed electronically and also have a refund. Otherwise, they will not be able to help. IRS personnel can only research tax returns that were filed at least 21 days previously. If the return was mailed, the taxpayer must wait at least six weeks for the return to be processed.

The Protecting Americans from Tax Hikes Act, or PATH Act, of 2015 allowed Congress to hold refunds from tax returns with refundable credits until February 15 to give the IRS more time to process and check those returns, thereby reducing the potential for fraud. Any refunds from tax returns with refundable credits that were held are released after February 15 in the order that they were received and electronically approved. If the taxpayer is claiming a refundable credit, they should only call the IRS when the "Where's My Refund?" portal directs them to call.

Bank Products

Tax-related bank products are another way for a taxpayer to receive their refund and can be offered to clients to simplify payment of tax preparation fees. The most common types of bank products are as follows:

 ➤ Bank Cards: When the deposit is loaded on a bank card to be used like a debit card. Additional fees may apply to the taxpayer.
 ➤ Cashier's Check: A paper check that the taxpayer can either cash at a check cashing service or deposit into their personal checking or savings account
 ➤ Refund Advance Loans: A loan from the bank that is based on the taxpayer's refund or a flat amount

The advantage of using a third-party bank is that the tax preparer's fee can be deducted from the taxpayer's refund. While tax-related bank products are a convenient option for many taxpayers, there are additional fees associated with each bank product, which can vary from bank to bank.

If the tax professional marks a tax return for electronic filing when preparing a tax return using software, he or she will be prompted to choose how they would like to receive their refund. There are additional fees charged by the bank and the provider of the filing software for each type of bank product. The remaining balance will be distributed to the taxpayer by direct deposit, prepaid debit card, or check. Each bank offers different products, so determine which products are best for your clients. The downside to using a bank product is that if the taxpayer owes child support, back taxes, student loans, or other debts, these debts will be paid before the tax professional receives their preparation fees. This could result in additional charges to the taxpayer because the preparer might need to collect their fees directly.

E-File Guidelines for Fraud and Abuse

A "fraudulent return" is a return in which an individual is attempting to file using someone else's name or SSN, or in which the taxpayer is presenting documents or information that have no basis in fact. A potentially abusive return is a return that the taxpayer is required to file but which contains inaccurate information that may lead to an understatement of a liability or the overstatement of a credit that could result in a refund to which the taxpayer may not be entitled.

Providers must be on the lookout for fraud and abuse. EROs must be particularly diligent because they are the first point of contact with taxpayers' personal information, and they are the ones who compile their information to prepare and file the returns. An ERO must be diligent in recognizing fraud and abuse, reporting it to the IRS and preventing it whenever possible. Providers must cooperate with IRS investigations by making available to the IRS upon request information and documents related to returns with potential fraud or abuse. An ERO who is also the paid preparer should exercise due diligence in the preparation of all returns involving refundable tax credits, as those credits are a popular target for fraud and abuse. The Internal Revenue Code requires paid preparers to exercise due diligence in determining a taxpayer's eligibility for the credit.

Double Check the Taxpayer's Address

Tax professionals should inform taxpayers that the address on the first page of the return, once processed by the IRS, will be used to update the taxpayer's recorded address. The IRS will use the taxpayer's address of record for notices and refunds.

Avoiding Refund Delays

Tax professionals should make sure that all the information is current when they e-file a tax return to avoid refund delays. The tax professional should also inform clients how to avoid delays by ensuring their information is correct – encouraging them to double-check the info they provide. The tax preparer should be aware of the following to help avoid delays:

➢ Make sure to see the actual Social Security card and other forms of identification for all taxpayers and dependents
➢ Double-check the data entry of all information prior to submission for e-file
➢ Don't allow the taxpayer to insist upon filing erroneous tax returns (if the taxpayer does, return their documents and do not complete the return)
➢ If the client is new, ask if they filed electronically in the past
➢ Keep track of the issues that result in a client's refund delays, document the delays, and add the documentation to the client's files

Signing an Electronic Tax Return

As with an income tax return submitted to the IRS in paper form, an electronic income tax return is signed by both the taxpayer and the paid preparer. The taxpayer would sign electronically. The taxpayer must sign and date the "Declaration of Taxpayer" to authorize the origination of the electronic submission of the return to the IRS prior to its transmission. The taxpayer must sign a new declaration if the electronic return data on an individual's income tax return is changed after the taxpayer signed the Declaration of Taxpayer and if the amounts differ by more than $50 to "total income" (or AGI) or $14 to "total tax," "federal income tax withheld," "refund," or "amount owed."

Electronic Signature Methods

Individual income tax returns are signed using a PIN number generated in one of two ways: the taxpayers can pick it themselves, or the paid tax preparer can generate one for them. Both methods allow the taxpayer to use a personal identification number (PIN) to sign the various forms, although self-selecting a PIN requires the taxpayer to provide their prior year adjusted gross income (AGI) amount so the IRS can confirm the taxpayer's identity, link it with the taxpayer's previous returns, and detect any future returns fraudulently filed under the taxpayer's name. Signature documents are not required when the taxpayer signs using the self-select method and enters their PIN directly into the electronic return. This does not apply to the practitioner-generated PIN. In all instances, the taxpayer must sign Form 8879, Signature Authorization Form, even if a practitioner-generated PIN was used.

IRS e-File Signature Authorization

When taxpayers are unable to enter their PINs directly into the electronic return, taxpayers must authorize the ERO to enter their PINs by completing Form 8879, *IRS e-file Signature Authorization*.

The ERO may enter the taxpayer's PIN in the electronic return record before the taxpayer signs Form 8879 or 8878, but the taxpayer must sign and date the appropriate form before the ERO originates the electronic submission of the return. In most instances, the taxpayer must sign and date Form 8879 or Form 8878 after reviewing the return and ensuring that the information on the form matches the information on the return.

A taxpayer who provides a completed tax return to an ERO for electronic filing may complete the IRS e-file signature authorization without reviewing the return originated by the ERO. The line items from the paper return must be entered on the application Form 8879 or Form 8878 prior to the taxpayer's signing and dating of the form. The ERO may use pre-signed authorizations as authority to input the taxpayer's PIN only if the information on the electronic version of the tax return agrees with the entries from the paper return.

The taxpayer and the ERO must always complete and sign Forms 8879 or 8878 for the practitioner PIN method for electronic signatures. The taxpayer may use the practitioner PIN method to electronically sign Form 4868, *Application for Automatic Extension of Time to File U.S. Individual Income Tax Return* if a signature is required. A signature is only required for Form 4868 when an electronic funds withdrawal is also being requested. The ERO must retain Form 8879 and Form 8878 for 3 years from the return's due date or the date received by the IRS, whichever is later. EROs must not send Form 8879 and Form 8878 to the IRS unless the IRS requests that they do so.

Guidance for Electronic Signatures

If the tax professional's software allows electronic signatures for Forms 8878 and 8879, the taxpayer can choose to sign that way instead of using a PIN. Technology has created many different types of e-signatures. The IRS does not require a specific technology for e-signatures. There are a variety of methods approved by the IRS for capturing an acceptable signature:

- ➢ A handwritten signature that is inputted on an electronic signature pad
- ➢ A handwritten signature, mark, or command inputted on a display screen by means of a stylus device
- ➢ A digitized image of a handwritten signature that is attached to an electronic record
- ➢ A name typed in by the signer (for example, typed at the end of an electronic record or typed into a signature block on a website form)
- ➢ A digital signature
- ➢ A mark captured as a scalable graphic
- ➢ A secret code, password, or PIN used to sign the electronic record

The software must record the following data for the e-signature to be valid:

➢ Digital image of the signed form
➢ Date and time of the signature
➢ Taxpayer's computer IP address; used for remote transactions only
➢ Taxpayer's login identification (username); used for remote transactions only
➢ Method used to sign the record (typed name) or a system log or some other audit trail that reflects the completion of the electronic signature process by the signer
➢ Identity verification; taxpayer's knowledge-based authentication, past results for in-person transactions and confirmation that government photo identification has been verified

IRS e-File Security and Privacy Standards

The IRS has mandated security, privacy, and business standards to better serve taxpayers and protect the information collected, processed, and stored by Online Providers of individual income tax returns.

1. Extended validation of SSL Certificate and minimum encryption standards
2. Periodic external vulnerability scan
3. Protecting against bulk filing of fraudulent tax returns
4. The ability to isolate and investigate in a timely manner the potential of information being compromised

Part 2 Review

To obtain the maximum benefit from each part go online now and watch the video.

Takeaways

Electronic filing, often referred to as e-filing, is a method of submitting tax returns to the Internal Revenue Service (IRS) using electronic means rather than paper forms. It allows taxpayers and tax professionals to transmit tax returns directly to the IRS through authorized electronic filing providers. Here's how electronically filing for the IRS works:

Once the tax return is complete and verified for accuracy, taxpayers electronically sign the return using a Personal Identification Number (PIN) or other authentication method. The tax return is then transmitted securely to the IRS through the electronic filing system.

After successfully submitting the tax return, taxpayers receive from the IRS confirmation or acknowledgment of receipt of the return. This confirmation typically includes a unique tracking number for reference.

The IRS processes electronically filed tax returns much faster than paper returns, typically within a few weeks. If there are any errors or discrepancies, the IRS may contact the taxpayer for clarification or additional information.

If the taxpayer is owed a refund, the IRS issues the refund electronically, usually through direct deposit into the taxpayer's bank account. If the taxpayer owes taxes, they can choose to pay electronically using various payment options, such as electronic funds withdrawal or credit/debit card.

Overall, electronically filing tax returns with the IRS offers several benefits, including faster processing, increased accuracy, and the convenience of submitting tax returns from the comfort of home or office. It's also environmentally friendly, as it reduces paper usage associated with traditional filing methods. Electronic filing is one of the safest ways to file a tax return, and paid tax preparers are mandated to e-file federal tax returns if they prepare more than 11 returns. Title 26 can impose criminal and monetary penalties on any person who fraudulently engages in preparing or providing services in connection with the tax preparation business. A paid tax professional must guard their clients' information to avoid such penalties. The acceptance of e-filing has saved preparers time and resources. Although there are individuals who still prepare returns by hand, the vast majority use tax preparation and filing software and reap the benefits of all the advantages that come with automation and electronic filing.

TEST YOUR KNOWLEDGE!
Go online to take a practice quiz.

The Latino Tax Professionals Association (LTPA) is *the* premier professional educational organization dedicated to empowering tax practitioners serving the Latino community. Whether you are an individual practitioner, an accounting or bookkeeping service, an enrolled agent, a certified public accountant, or an immigration attorney, LTPA is your trusted partner for professional growth and success in serving the dynamic Latino market.

Our mission is to equip tax professionals with exceptional knowledge, professionalism, and a vibrant community of practice, enabling them to deliver exemplary services to Latino taxpayers. We are unwavering in our commitment to helping you expand your practice, boost profitability, and attract a growing Latino client base.

At LTPA, we leverage decades of collective experience and a deep understanding of the unique needs of the Latino community. Our innovative training methodologies, developed and refined by seasoned tax experts, and delivered on the powerful Prendo365 tax education platform, ensure that our members stay ahead of the curve, mastering the latest tax laws, regulations, and best practices.

Latino Tax Professionals Association, LLC
1588 Moffett Street, Suite A
Salinas, California 93905
866-936-2587
www.latinotaxpro.com

For support: edsupport@latinotaxpro.org

Made in the USA
Columbia, SC
11 July 2024

38433201R00176